KYOTO CSEAS SERIES ON ASIAN STUDIES 8
Center for Southeast Asian Studies, Kyoto University

STRONG SOLDIERS, FAILED REVOLUTION

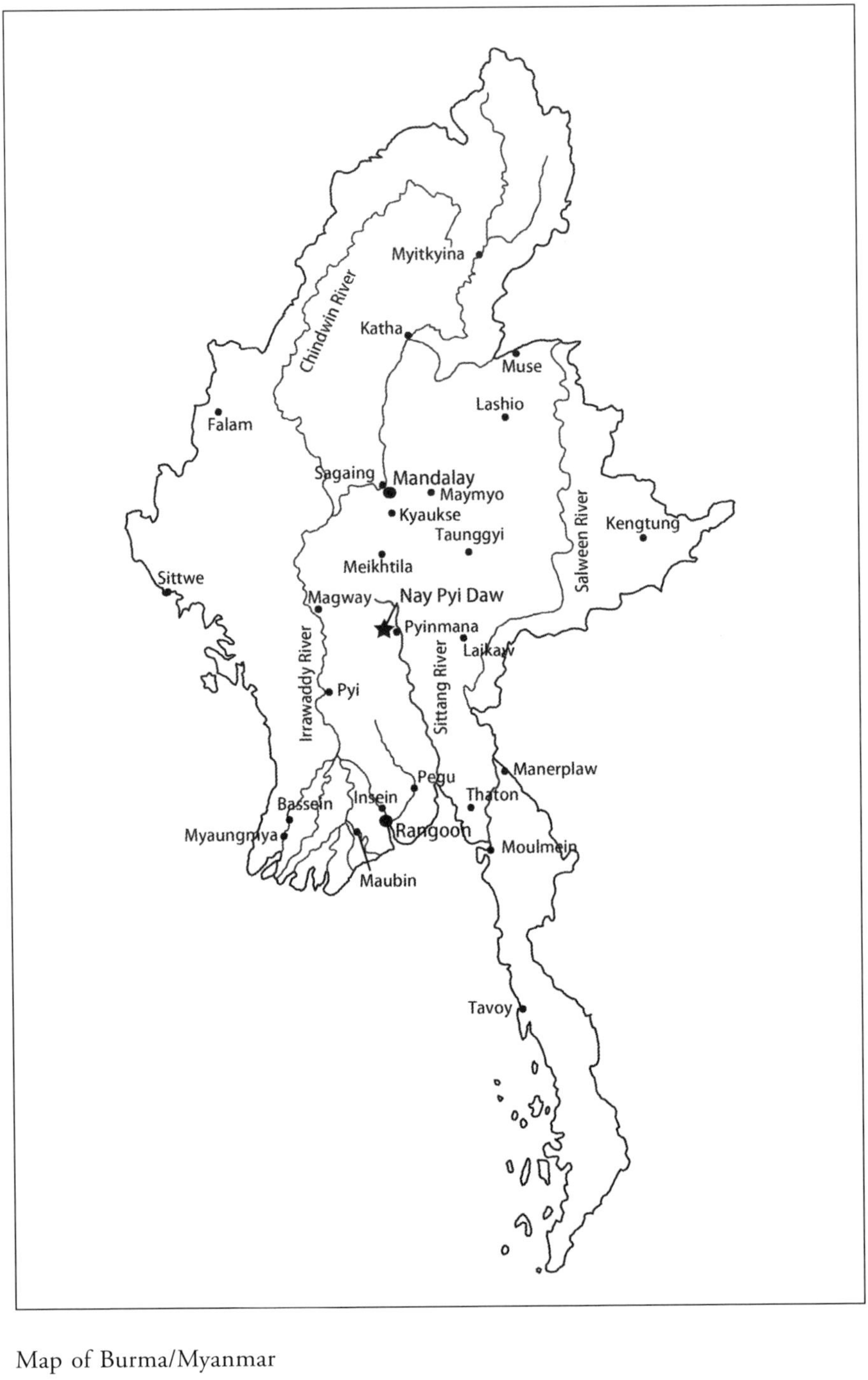

Map of Burma/Myanmar

KYOTO CSEAS SERIES ON ASIAN STUDIES 8
Center for Southeast Asian Studies, Kyoto University

STRONG SOLDIERS, FAILED REVOLUTION

The State and Military in Burma, 1962–88

Yoshihiro Nakanishi

NUS PRESS
Singapore
in association with
KYOTO UNIVERSITY PRESS
Japan

This publication was partially funded by the Japan Society for the Promotion of Sciences (JSPS) as Grant-in-Aid for publication of Scientific Research Result.

NUS Press
National University of Singapore
AS3-01-02, 3 Arts Link
Singapore 117569
www.nus.edu.sg/nuspress

ISBN 978-9971-69-702-0 (Paper)

Kyoto University Press
Yoshida-South Campus, Kyoto University
69 Yoshida-Konoe-Cho, Sakyo-ku
Kyoto 606-8315
Japan
www.kyoto-up.or.jp

ISBN 978-4-87698-357-5

National Library Board, Singapore Cataloguing-in-Publication Data

Nakanishi, Yoshihiro, 1977–
Strong soldiers, failed revolution: the state and military in Burma, 1962–88 / Yoshihiro Nakanishi. – Singapore: NUS Press in association with Kyoto University Press, 2013.
p. cm. – (Kyoto CSEAS series on Asian studies; 8)
ISBN: 978-9971-69-702-0

1. Military government – Burma. 2. Burma – Politics and government – 1962–1988. 3. Burma – History – 1962–1988. I. Title.

DS530.56
959.1052 — dc23 OCN820776649

Cover image: A Propaganda Statue in Mawlamyaing (Moulmein), Mon State (author's personal collection).

Printed by: Mainland Press Pte Ltd

CONTENTS

LIST OF TABLES

LIST OF FIGURES

LIST OF ILLUSTRATIONS

LIST OF ABBREVIATIONS

AFO	Anti-Fascist Organization
AFPFL	Anti-Fascist People's Freedom League
B.L.	Bachelor of Law
BCP	Burma Communist Party
BCS	Burma Civil Service
BDA	Burma Defence Army
BIA	Burma Independence Army
BMP	Burma Military Police
BNA	Burma Nationalist Army
BSM	British Services Mission
BSO	Bureau of Special Operations
BSPP	Burma Socialist Programme Party
BWP	Burma Workers Party
CC	Central Committee
CDC	Central Drafting Commission
CEC	Central Executive Committee
CIA	Central Intelligence Agency
COC	Central Organizing Committee
CPB	Communist Party of Burma
CS	Council of State
CIPS	Central Institute of Political Science
DIG	Deputy Inspector General
DMT	Directorate of Military Training
DPW	Directorate of Psychological Warfare
DSA	Defense Services Academy
DSMHRI	Defense Services Museum and Historical Research Institute
EAYL	East Asia Youth League
GCBA	General Council of Burmese Associations
GSO	General Staff Officer
HPP	higher party path
ICS	Indian Civil Service

KMT	Chinese Nationalist Party
KNDO	Karen National Defence Organization
KNU	Karen National Union
LLDC	Least less-development country
LPP	lower party path
MBSS	Bachelor of Medicine
MOD	Ministry of Defence
MP	military path
MPS	Military Planning Staff
NAH	National Archives Department
NIB	National Intelligence Bureau
NLD	National League for Democracy
NUF	National United Front
NUP	National Union Party
OTS	Officers Training School
PBF	Patriotic Burmese Forces
PC	People's Council
PP	People's Parliament
PRP	People's Revolution Party
PVO	People's Volunteer Organization
RC	Revolutionary Council
SEAC	South-East Asia Command
SLORC	State Law and Order Restoration Council
SP	Socialist Party
SPDC	State Peace and Development Council
SPDC	State Peace and Development Council
TMP	top military path
UMP	Union Military Police
USDP	Union Solidarity and Development Party
YMBA	Young Men's Buddhist Association

NOTES

1. *The Country Name*
The name "Burma" is used throughout this book except in the Epilogue, the main reason being that this name was commonly used in the world during the period that is the main focus of this book. Thus the usage of Burma in the body of the text has nothing to do with the controversy the junta caused when on 18 June 1989 it announced that the country's official name in English was being changed from "Union of Burma" to "Union of Myanmar."

2. *The Alphabetical Spelling of Burmese Words*
The alphabetical spelling of Burmese words (other than people's names) adopted in this book follows the Burmese spelling method designed by Ryuji Okudaira in the following source.

    The Burma Research Group, *Burma and Japan: Basic Studies on Their Cultural and Social Structure* (Tokyo: Burma Research Group, 1991).

3. *The Citation of Japanese and Burmese Names*
In this book, Japanese names are written in western-style order: given name first, family name second (Yoshihiro Nakanishi). Burmese names are written in full as most Burmese make no distinction between family and given names.

PREFACE

Every era has its share of "crooked" governments. Burma, a country at the western edge of Southeast Asia, is a perfect example of crooked government in our age. For half a century from 2 March 1962, when the *tatmadaw* (the Burma Armed Forces) seized power in a coup d'état, until 2011 and the establishment of a "civilian-led" (but military influenced) parliament form of government, Burma was ruled by a military junta that grew all the more anachronistic in the region as the decades passed. Even the massive anti-government movements that broke out all over the country in 1988 resulted not in democratization as occurred in neighbouring Thailand and nearby Indonesia, but in suppression, coup d'état and harsher authoritarian rule by the tatmadaw. The brutal aftermath of 1988 and subsequent military rule earned Burma pariah status in the international community, leading the U.S. and EU to impose economic sanctions against the country. The junta's ill treatment of Aung San Suu Kyi, the hugely popular and internationally acclaimed leader of Burma's democracy movement, the years of oppressive house arrest that she heroically endured, and the continual brutal suppression of her political followers reinforced that status for two long decades. To outside observers including me it seemed that Burma's relentlessly suppressive military regime was set to remain in power, robust and unchallengeable.

However, to the surprise of practically everyone who has been watching Burma, the situation in the country has begun to change rapidly. The 2010 general election, the first to be held in Burma in two decades, was followed by a shift to a new regime in March 2011. The new president, Thein Sein, who was the prime minister in the previous junta, has astonished people around the world with his announcement of reforms and reconciliation with the democratic forces in the society, contrary to expectations that the new government would simply aim to perpetuate the military's dominance in another disguise. The reforms and Aung San Suu Kyi's decision to participate in the new parliament have created a favourable international environment which led the U.S. to ease financial sanctions on Burma in April 2012 and lift its ban on imports from that country in September.

So far the reform since 2011 has been widely accepted both inside and outside of Burma. What is going to happen next? Will the reform really progress toward a full-fledged democracy? Or should we be ready for an eventual backlash from anti-reform forces in the ruling elite? This study seeks to find answers to these questions from a historical perspective by examining the causes of the durability of the socialist military regime created by General Ne Win, which lasted from 1962 to 1988 and left institutional legacies for the post-1988 junta. My argument is as follows. In order to build the socialist state in Burma, General Ne Win gave a small cadre of military officers an opportunity to dominate the pivotal posts of the government and the political party he created, which allowed him to retain an iron grip on power for a long period and at the same time created an incentive structure that maintained the cohesion of the ruling elite, namely the officer corps of the tatmadaw.

Although Ne Win's rule collapsed in 1988, the power structure and informal institutional legacy created by Ne Win has remained intact. I would go so far as to say that Ne Win's failed revolution made the strong military regime in Burma. Even though we are witnessing reforms toward a more democratic polity today, I believe that a historical analysis that seeks to explain the robustness of the previous military regime can provide great insights into exploring the consequences of the drastic changes currently taking place in Burma. By including theoretical analysis and comparative studies between Burma and other countries, I also seek to set forth some broader implications from the perspective of political science.

* * *

This book is based on the Japanese edition, titled *Gunsei Biruma no Kenryoku Kōzō: Ne Win Taisei ka no Kokka to Guntai* (*The Power Structure of the Military Regime in Burma — The State and Military under the Ne Win Regime*), published by Kyoto University Press in June 2009. In translating the book into English, I made some modifications to its structure and contents, and I slightly expanded my theoretical analysis; but basic argumentation and its factual verification have remained the same.

I started this project at Kyoto University, finalized the Japanese edition at the Institute of Developing Economies (IDE-JETRO), and revised the English manuscript for this book at the Paul H. Nitze School of Advanced International Studies (SAIS), Johns Hopkins University. All three institutions provided an excellent intellectual environment and different inspirations. The Southeast Asian Ministers of Education Organization, Center for History and Tradition (SEAMEO-CHAT) in Yangon, Burma, hosted me at a crucial time, allowing me to conduct field research from June 2003 to March 2005 in Yangon; for this, I am very grateful to U Tun Aung Chein, Daw Nyi Nyi Myint and Daw Saw Khin Gyi. For data collection and research interviews, I would like to thank Akio Takahashi, Toshihiro Kudo, Kazuo Ando, Nobuhiro Ohnishi, Saw Pyone Naing, Oung Ma Htwe, the late Maung Maung, Naw Sit Blut, Win Myat Aung, Col. Zaw Win, Maj. Cho Cho Win, Zaw Zaw, Aung Myoe, Aung Min Naing, Aung Win Naing, San Tun, Thein Thein Win, Yaza and anonymous used-book sellers at Pansodan Street in Yangon downtown. Although for obvious reasons I cannot mention the names of Burmese people whom I interviewed, I have been allowed to acknowledge two respectful ex-communists, Chit Hlaing and Thakin Tin Myat.

I cannot thank enough Yoshifumi Tamada and Takashi Shiraishi; they helped me very much with their wise mixture of encouragement and criticism when I faced difficulties in the process of thesis writing at Kyoto University. Three examiners for my dissertation, Yoko Hayami, Masaaki Okamoto and Kei Nemoto, provided valuable feedback toward making it into a book. Thanks to Karl Jackson, William Wise and Jacqueline Ganem, I was able to prepare the manuscript for publication in the wonderful environment of SAIS in Washington, D.C. I received excellent advice on improving the book manuscript itself from Khoo Boo Teik, Maung Aung Myoe, and Bo Bo Lanzin. I am greatly indebted to the Japan Society for the Promotion of Science for its financial support (a Grant-in-Aid for Publication of Scientific Research Results) in publishing this book.

While I would not have been able to accomplish this book project without responsible support from the administrative staff of IDE-JETRO and input from editors include Nana Izumi, Sanae Tomisaki, Noburu Yoshida, Chisato Ishii, Masahiro Morinaga, Tetsuya Suzuki, Itaru Saito, Paul Kratoska, Qua Lena, Ye Min Tun, Linn Zablotsky and Erklaren Inc. I owe a particular debt to William Swan for his patient dedication to translating and editing my manuscript.

Lastly I dedicate this work to my wife and my parents, Maiko, Yoshimi and Fumiko Nakanishi, who provided continuing emotional and material support, without which this book could not have come into existence.

Yoshihiro Nakanishi
October 2012

CHAPTER 1

Introduction: A Failed Revolution Made a Strong Military Regime

Sometimes in the course of an everyday conversation a casual comment can suddenly reveal something about a country's political uniqueness. Such moments in a variety of forms stimulate our thinking, and such stimuli produce new ideas that may ultimately grow into a thesis for a book. The impetus for this book on the relationship between the state and the military in Burma came from conversations like the following one that took place in Yangon in 2005 with a former military commander who had served as a cabinet minister in the 1980s.

> Author: "How did you feel when you were appointed a cabinet minister?"
>
> Former commander: "From long back I had not wanted to be in the military doing administrative or logistical work. I wanted to reach the top of the military working in military operations. To be honest, that's why I was disappointed when I was appointed a cabinet minister about a year after becoming a director general in the Defence Ministry."[1]

Another experience that similarly caught my attention occurred in August 2007 when I met with a local Burmese journalist in a middle-grade Chinese restaurant in Mandalay, Burma's second largest city. While carefully watching the restaurant staff and speaking discreetly so as not to be overheard, the journalist related the following story:

[1] An interview in 2005 with a former commander.

> One evening a military regional commander in Upper Burma gave a dinner party at his home. The commander's subordinates, his relatives and influential business people attended the dinner. In the middle of the dinner, the commander's cell phone rang. After the conversation, the commander locked himself in his room and refused to come out. Not knowing what to do, the guests all left. Why do you think the commander refused to come out of his room? Later it was discovered that during the phone call he received news that he would soon be made a cabinet minister.[2]

These stories did not interest me because they seemed incompatible with the norms of someone from a democratic country. It did not seem strange to me that a commander would become a cabinet minister without going through any democratic process because the country was under military rule at that time. I was most interested in the fact that both commanders were moved directly from the military into high ranking cabinet positions and both expressed disappointment about having to leave their military command. Here one could certainly criticize the routine placement of military commanders into civilian cabinet roles, and certainly those people who are working toward a democratic government would not look upon this process favorably. Yet most people in Burma would not find the attitudes of these commanders strange. And my studies of Burma, my ability to speak Burmese, although not fluently, and my conversations with Burmese friends had taught me to no longer find anything odd about stories of this kind. Since 1962, for 50 years, the country has known only authoritarian regimes controlled by low-profile dictators and a robust military. Therefore it stands to reason that greater value is placed upon reaching the top ranks in the military than becoming a cabinet minister.

This study will examine from a historical perspective the formal as well as informal institutions that have led Burma to this state of affairs. It also seeks to solve one of the riddles of Southeast Asian politics: How has Burma's military been able to maintain its political power for over 50 years? Addressing this question leads to a number of corollary questions such as: What has the military regime from 1962 to 2010 brought to the state and society in Burma? How durable is the military's political power? How long can it last?

---

[2] An interview in August 2007 with a journalist.

In this book, I reveal that the military regime has maintained itself through the informally institutionalized assignment of state as well as political party posts to the officer corps of the *tatmadaw* (the Burma Armed Forces). In order to demonstrate this, the book follows a political trajectory approach by exploring General Ne Win's military regime and tracing the formation of the informal institutionalization of assigning posts that took place through a series of state reforms carried out in the name of "revolution" (*tohlânyêi* or *khi'pyáun tohlânyêi*) after Ne Win took power in 1962. In the analysis I describe the "revolution" as an amalgam of the development of three formal and informal institutions: dictatorship, party-state, and defence-state. The relationships of these three institution-building processes will be illustrated as both mutually reinforcing and conflicting. Then I argue that Ne Win's failed revolution created an unusually durable military regime in Burma. Furthermore, these institutions created by Ne Win continue to support Burma's current political regime centered around the tatmadaw, although Ne Win's rule ceased to exist in 1988. It is an ironic lesson; a dictator put his own political dreams, i.e., "revolution," before the corporate interests of the military, the failure of which resulted in the creation of a state where the political role of the military has become greater than that found anywhere else in the world.

The Durable Military Regime and Political Development in Southeast Asia

Why study Burma's military regime when the world entered an era of democratization more than two decades ago? It is important for the following three reasons. First, although we are supposedly in an era of democratization, about half of the world population is still living under undemocratic political regimes.[3] In this regard, an examination of Burma as a case contributes to the literature on undemocratic political regimes. Since the publication of Samuel Huntington's classic study on democratization,[4] research on the subject has continued to expand, and over the past ten years it has led to further studies on the sustainability of authoritarian regimes. However, little attention has been paid to long-

[3] Beatriz Magaloni and Ruth Kricheli, "Political Order and One-Party Rule," *Annual Review of Political Science* 13 (2010): 125.

[4] Samuel Huntington, *The Third Wave: Democratization in the Late Twentieth Century*, (Norman: University of Oklahoma Press, 1993).

lasting military regimes. A long-lasting military regime such as Burma's can be considered an "outlying observation" in political science.

Eztow and Frantz suggest one of the reasons for the shortage of studies on long-lasting military regimes. Their survey on the average duration of three types of dictatorships: personal, single-party, and military dictatorships, showed ten, eight, and three years, respectively.[5] Further evidence of this may be found in a study of democratization carried out by Barbara Geddes. In this study, Geddes divided the period between 1945 and 1994 into five-year segments and calculated the mortality rate of authoritarian regimes. Her results showed that "the proportion of military regimes that fell during any particular five years between 1945 and 1994 was about 50 per cent higher than the proportion of personalist regimes and about four times the proportion of single-party regimes."[6] Thus military dictatorships generally do not last very long compared to other type of authoritarian regimes, and this rareness makes it difficult for us to detect factors associated with the durability of military rule.

The second reason for studying Burma's military regime is that a historical examination of that regime is helpful and provocative in understanding the political development of Southeast Asia. The political regimes of Southeast Asia are extremely diverse and include rapidly growing market oriented party-states (Vietnam and Laos), a internationally created quasi democracy (Cambodia), post-developmental dictatorship democracies (the Philippines and Indonesia), an unstable democracy with a political monarchy (Thailand), economically successful competitive authoritarian states (Singapore and Malaysia), and an economically stagnant military-led regime (Burma).[7] As a region characterized by a variety of

---

[5] Natasha Eztow and Erica Frantz, *Dictators and Dictatorships: Understanding Authoritarian Regimes and Their Leaders* (New York: The Continuum International Publishing Group, 2011), p. 87.

[6] Barbara Geddes, "What Do We Know About Democratization After Twenty Years," *Annual Review of Political Science* 2 (1999): 134. Eric Nordlinger also gives the average life span of a military regime as five years. See Eric A. Nordlinger, *Soldiers in Politics: Military Coups and Governments* (Englewood Cliffs, N.J.: Prentice-Hall, 1977), p. 132.

[7] Levitsky and Way define competitive authoritarian regime as "civilian regimes in which formal democratic institutions exist and are widely viewed as the primary means of gaining power, but in which incumbents' abuse of the state places them at a significant advantage vis-à-vis their opponents." For this definition, see Steve Levitsky and Lucan A. Way, *Competitive Authoritarianism: Hybrid Regimes After the Cold War* (Leiden: Cambridge University Press, 2010).

political outcomes within a similar geographical and international environment, Southeast Asia is highly suitable for natural experiments in macro-level comparison of political development and can provide us with meaningful insights in comparative politics.[8] But Burma remains a missing piece in our understanding of Southeast Asian politics simply because few empirical studies of the country have been undertaken so far. To further theoretical study as well as to enhance our understanding of Southeast Asian political development, it is necessary to examine the historical origins of and internal factors for the long duration of the military regime in Burma.

The third reason for studying Burma's military regime is that it provides us with a more accurate understanding of the changes now taking place in Burma and may help discuss the future course of the country. In 2010 Burma held a general election for the first time in 20 years, and on 30 March 2011 government authority was transferred from the State Peace and Development Council (SPDC) to the People's Assembly (the *Pyidaungsu Hluttaw*) under the ruling Union Solidarity and Development Party (USDP) and to a new civil administration under President Thein Sein, the former Army commander and prime minister. Many observers did not see this change as a genuine democratization, but merely a transition from direct military rule to a relatively institutionalized authoritarian regime, which is taking place for the second time in Burma's history. The first was in 1974 when a transfer of power from the Revolutionary Council to the new civilian people's parliament (*Pyithu Hluttaw*) took place. At that time most of the cabinet ministers were retired soldiers who had left the military only a short time earlier in order to run for elected office, as is the case today.

Lessons can be drawn from a comparison of the military regime under General Ne Win with those of General Than Shwe and the "civilian" government of President Thein Sein. While many have considered Burma's previous junta as a tyranny, even a tyranny in fact is also a type of political order. Without an understanding of how this order has worked to ease the tensions and conflicts that result from the shifting disparities of power among the state leadership, the tatmadaw and civilians, we cannot fully comprehend Burma's current situation or predict

---

8 See Eric Martinez Kuhonta, Dan Slater, and Tuong Vu, ed., *Southeast Asia in Political Science: Theory, Region, and Qualitative Analysis* (Stanford: Stanford University Press, 2008).

its future, which will complicate establishing effective relations between Burma and other countries. One can gain a greater understanding of Burma's enigmatic political regime, which could make the diplomatic efforts of the developed countries toward Burma more effective.

Concepts and the Puzzling Case of Burma

Concepts

Before examining the main questions of this book, several concepts related to political development need to be defined. The primary emphasis and concern of this study is the *state*. In this study, the state is defined as an organization that demands a monopoly on the legitimate use of physical force and strives to reproduce the rule of law over a society demarcated by geographical borders. This definition enables us to differentiate between the state as an organization and as an order; such a differentiation ensures that confusion over the dimension of the institutional aspect and its effect as they are related to the state is avoided. In this regard, as an actor that influences the social order, the state is extremely significant in modern politics; however, it does not completely control all activities in society. Therefore studies focusing on the state need to be prudent when examining its impact on society.[9]

As used here, the term *nation-state* means a set of two social phenomena: nation and state. The *nation* here may be defined as people who live within a state's territory and have a shared sense of community. The emergence of state preceded that of nation in Southeast Asia. While the modern state came about either directly or indirectly during the colonial period in the eighteenth and nineteenth centuries (with the important exception of Thailand), the nation emerged in the early twentieth century through the modern education, the mass media, the anti-colonial movements and so on. In the modern political systems it is hard for the state to assert the legitimacy of its existence without the approval of the nation based on the legal concept of sovereignty. In general, however, it is extremely hard to share a sense of community as a nation without the state

[9] Regarding the history of comparative politics related to the state, see Joel S. Migdal, "Researching the State," in *Comparative Politics: Rationality, Culture, and Structure*, ed. Mark Irving Lichbach and Alan S. Zuckerman (Cambridge: Cambridge University Press, 2009), pp. 162–92.

as a ruling system because the state is a principal driving force behind nation-building.[10] In this sense nation and state are interdependent.

Collectively, the formal or informal institutions that determine the essential functions of the state may be defined as a regime; one that is concerned with political decision-making is called a political regime. Among political regimes, a military regime is one in which the political role of the military is institutionally guaranteed and civilian control is fairly limited. A military regime is a type of authoritarian regime, but unlike communist one-party rule or theocratic Islamic states, military regimes often come about through coups d'état and the seizure and consolidation of power by high-ranking military officers.

The main focus of this study is the relationship between the military officer corps and the state under a military regime. As Weber argued, the monopoly on the legitimate use of physical force by the state is an important characteristic of a modern state.[11] In this regard, a modern state strives to disarm social forces and to continuously develop weapons, equipment, and capable personnel in order to defend against domestic anti-government movements and foreign invasions. A case in point is Western Europe at the beginning of the nineteenth century when old-order aristocrats and mercenaries who led armies on an ad hoc basis transformed themselves into professional military leaders functioning autonomously apart from society. This autonomous military officer corps, or "military caste," the term used by Michael Mann, was created through bureaucratization, professionalization, and democratization.[12] The members of this caste received a salary, and their ranks and job duties were defined by a functional hierarchy. In addition, the process of bureaucratization of the officer corps took place, which featured the adaption of objective qualifications upon entry and for promotion in or exit from the hierarchy.[13] At the same time, the military caste developed into a group of professionals with special skills related to military affairs. As

---

[10] See Benedict Anderson, *Imagined Communities: Reflections on the Origins and Spread of Nationalism* (London: Verso, 2006), Chapter 10.

[11] Rinehard Bendix, *Max Weber: An Intellectual Portrait* (London: Routledge, 1998), p. 413.

[12] Michael Mann, *The Sources of Social Power, Volume 2: The Rise of Classes and Nation-States, 1760–1914* (Cambridge: Cambridge University Press, 1993), pp. 419–38.

[13] J. Van Dorn, "The Officer Corps: A Fusion of Profession and Organization," *European Journal of Sociology* 6 (1965): 262–82.

weaponry, equipment and strategy/tactics became sophisticated, these professionals became increasingly more specialized.

Political Deadlock in Burma: Weak Governance, Strong Regime

Contrary to the popular perception that Burma's military regime took control over the people in a violent show of force, in fact it came to power relatively quietly with little display of force. In the early dawn of 2 March 1962, the tatmadaw, led by General Ne Win, the Chief of General Staff, carried out a coup d'état. The military arrested the prime minister and his cabinet as well as some members of the parliament and established a commanding organ for new rule, the Revolutionary Council (RC) (*tohlânyêi kaunsi*), where it concentrated all state powers. The RC was comprised of 17 senior tatmadaw officers and chaired by Ne Win. The people's reaction to the coup was subdued. No large-scale resistance movements broke out, although there were some anti-coup demonstrations by student activists of Yangon University. Many people were cautiously optimistic that the condition of the country might improve under Ne Win's rule because at the time it was widely recognized that Burma's economic and political situation was far removed from what had been expected when colonial rule ended on 4 January 1948.[14]

In the context of this discussion, it is important to highlight that when the tatmadaw came to power, Burma was facing a serious economic and political crisis. The devastation the country suffered during the Pacific War crippled the economy following the country's independence. In the agriculture sector, which was central to Burma's economy, it took about 10 years for rice production to recover to the pre-war (Fiscal Year 1936–37) level.[15] The post-colonial transition was also a difficult process. There was a lack of consensus concerning the type of political system for

[14] In the early 1960s, Burma faced problems with the political system, the ability to govern, and national unification; many other emerging countries that had experienced colonization also faced such problems. Parliamentary democracy was limited in its ability to deal with these problems because of factors such as military coups. Therefore, it was not unusual for authoritarian regimes to arise with authority concentrated in a small number of leaders. These failures of democracy in the emerging nations were examined in the classic study by Samuel Huntington, *Political Order in Changing Societies* (New Haven: Yale University Press, 1968).

[15] See Louis J. Walinsky, *Economic Development in Burma, 1951–1960* (New York: Twentieth Century Fund, 1962).

the new nation-state, who should be recognized as citizens of the state, and how much autonomy should be given to regions inhabited by ethnic minorities. In the midst of all the uncertainty, communists and some ethnic minority groups took up arms against the new government.[16] The establishment of the People's Republic of China in 1949 and the intensification of the Cold War in Asia added further complications. The U.S. government, mainly through its Central Intelligence Agency (CIA), began providing military assistance to the Chinese Nationalist Party (KMT) forces that had occupied some areas of northeast Burma.[17] Furthermore, in domestic politics intra-party conflicts and the break-up of the ruling party, the Anti-Fascist People's Freedom League (AFPFL), undermined the stability of the country's parliamentary democracy. These were the circumstances afflicting Burma when Ne Win's coup d'état took place. At the time, the tatmadaw's political intervention was not necessarily perceived as negative. Following the pacific war, the tatmadaw, founded by Aung San, the nation's martyred hero, enjoyed broad support among the people and was seen as the driving force behind national liberation.

After taking power, the RC issued a policy declaration, "The Burmese Way to Socialism" (*myanmàsosheli'lânzin)*, in which it announced the establishment of Burma's version of the socialist state. This declaration was soon followed by the onset of large-scale state reforms. The regime that came into being under the banner of "The Burmese Way to Socialism" was headed by Ne Win and will be referred to hereafter as the Ne Win regime. This regime led Burma through a period of reform that lasted from the 1962 coup until 1974 when the adoption of a new constitution completed the regime's institutionalization. The Ne Win regime remained in power until 1988 when it was rocked by massive anti-government movements, which led to another coup d'état by the tatmadaw on 18 September of that year.

What were the consequences of Ne Win's long-standing regime? A significant one was its extreme backwardness politically and economically compared to other contemporary regimes in Southeast Asia. In terms of political backwardness, the military's absolute control made it impossible for pluralistic politics to develop. For instance, Ne Win insisted on

---

[16] See Martin Smith, *Burma: Insurgency and the Politics of Ethnicity*, 2nd ed. (Dhaka: The University Press, 1999).

[17] Robert Taylor, *Foreign and Domestic Consequences of the KMT Intervention in Burma* (Ithaca: Cornell University, Department of Asian Studies, Southeast Asia Program, 1973).

holding on to his position as Burma's leader even when he was in his 70s. Moreover, most of his cabinet ministers were either top-ranking active or retired tatmadaw officers. Shortly after the coup in 1962, the regime targeted existing political parties, foreign capital, private industries, and landowners for "destruction" as they were seen as the cause for the failure of socialism to develop in Burma, and their activities were banned by the RC. In place of the multi-party system, the RC created the Burma Socialist Programme Party (BSPP) and initiated the depoliticization of the society through the control of labor unions and peasant organizations in order to achieve absolute one-party rule. Political rights such as freedom of assembly and expression were severely restricted in the name of "organizing" (*sîyôunyêi*) and "unity" (*sîlôunyêi*). For all practical purposes, the ethnic-minority states lost their autonomy under a strong centralized system of government.

In parallel with these political reforms, the RC adopted a planned economy. Complete state control over industries was launched with the nationalization of 24 private banks in February 1963. Most of the private businesses in manufacturing, shipbuilding, mining and the newspaper industry became state-owned enterprises.[18] Under the government's land reform policy, private land ownership was prohibited. On paper the state maintained ownership of the land, and farmers, including tenant farmers and agricultural labourers, were granted the right to cultivate the land. However, in reality this right was given only to those farmers who independently or as tenants had actually been cultivating the land. The reforms excluded agricultural labourers who comprised the low-income class in Burma's society.[19]

Although rice exports were expected to be the principle means to acquire foreign currency earnings, they increased only temporarily as a

---

[18] Nobuyoshi Nishizawa, *Myanma no Keizai Kaikaku to Kaiho Keizai: Gunsei 10 Nen no Sokatsu* [Economic reforms and liberation policy: Summarization of the ten years under military rule] (Tokyo: Keiso Shobo, 2000), pp. 19–20.

[19] Akio Takahashi, *Biruma Deruta no Beisakuson: "Syakaisyugi" Taisei ka no Noson Keizai* (Tokyo: Ajia Keizai Syuppankai, 1992), pp. 76–81. The percentage of non-farmers in farming villages was 41.7% in 1931, 46.5% in 1953–54, and between 42.0% and 44.5% in 1973, showing little change. This data was obtained from Koichi Fujita, "Josho: Myanma ni okeru Shijo Keizaika to Keizai Hatten Kozo," in *Myanma Iko Keizai no Henyo*, ed. Koichi Fujita (Chiba: Ajiakeizai Kenkyujo, 2005), p. 275. It should be noted, however, that "non-farmers" here include not only agricultural laborers but also tenant farmers and non-agricultural laborers.

result of the "green revolution". But even this increase was not as much as expected due to the decline in farmer incentive because of government controls and to the fall in the quality of rice. With the economy producing insufficient revenue, by the mid-1970s, repayment of the external debt became a major burden on the country's finances. From that time on, Burma continued to stagnate, in contrast to neighbouring Thailand, which experienced rapid economic growth in the 1970s and 1980s. In 1987, Burma's debt problem prompted an application to the United Nations to have it recognized on the "Least Developed Countries" list.

Although Ne Win's revolution ended in 1988, military-led rule continued. The new leaders, General Saw Maung and his successor, General Than Shwe, laid down the framework for authoritarian rule through the State Law and Order Restoration Council (SLORC) (1988–96) and the State Peace and Development Council (SPDC) (1997–2010). The SLORC abandoned the socialist cause and tried to establish its legitimacy by claiming that Burma was not ready for democracy; it needed a period of transition to build the foundation for democracy, and that could be realized only under the tatmadaw's guidance. This imposed, paternalistic provisional rule lasted for 22 long years. During that time the market economy gradually expanded encouraging private companies to take a larger role in the economy.[20] This economic growth, however, slowed down at the end of the 1990s and the rising cost of living and high unemployment adversely affected the population. Meanwhile, in the political arena, there was little progress in developing mechanisms through which the people could express their political dissent. Indeed, the government violently suppressed the opposition democratic forces, and until the political changes since 2011, this anti-democratic policy damaged relations with the Western international community.

Arguably, the most significant reason for Burma's retarded political and economic development is that state leaders have never accepted responsibility for their obvious mismanagement of the country's affairs and their persistence in remaining in leadership positions. As a result problems are continually being ignored. Of course, a change in leadership does not necessarily guarantee an improvement in the situation. However, as long as leaders continue to maintain their political power

[20] See Koichi Fujita, Fumiharu Mieno, and Ikuko Okamoto, *The Economic Transition in Burma After 1988: Market Economy versus State Control* (Singapore: NUS Press, 2009).

Table 1.1 "Government Effectiveness" in Eleven Countries in Southeast Asia

Country	*Percentile*	*Standard Error*
Singapore	99.5	0.15
Malaysia	80.4	0.15
Brunei	70.3	0.25
Thailand	66.0	0.15
Philippine	55.5	0.15
Vietnam	45.0	0.15
Indonesia	37.3	0.14
Cambodia	18.7	0.18
East Timor	14.8	0.22
Laos	12.0	0.19
Burma	2.4	0.18

Source: Kaufmann Daniel Aart Kraay and Massimo Mastruzzi 2005 "Governance Matters IV: Governance Indicators for 1996–2004" World Bank Policy Research Working Paper 3630 Washington DC

without acknowledging the mismanagement of the past, there can be little hope for improvement. While a lack of change in the political leadership may have brought some sense of stability, this stability has required the stifling of political development and has not led to an improvement in state governance.

Table 1.1 shows a comparison of government effectiveness in 11 Southeast Asian countries in 2005 according to the governance index provided by the World Bank.[21] Burma's score of 2.4 was by far the lowest percentile among the countries, suggesting that the government of Burma is unable to efficiently make and implement effective policy.[22] In this respect, it differs greatly from Vietnam (45.0) and Singapore (99.5), which also have authoritarian political regimes. Weak governance often results in political instability because incumbent leaders cannot effectively control

---

[21] The data here is presented as reference only, as that for the period of the Ne Win regime does not exist.

[22] In the words of the World Bank, "[G]government effectiveness captures perceptions of the quality of public services, the quality of the civil service and the degree of its independence from political pressures, the quality of policy formulation and implementation, and the credibility of the government's commitment to such policies." <http://info.worldbank.org/governance/wgi/pdf/ge.pdf> [accessed 27 Nov. 2012].

against secret manoeuvring by opponents to carry out political revolts. Indeed, weak civilian governments in the 1950s and 1960s were often overthrown by military coups and communist revolutions. But even a successful change of regime does not necessarily guarantee better outcomes for the country, because improvement in governance takes time to realize, certainly longer than the act of overthrowing the government itself. Moreover, following a regime change that has no legal sanction, the new government often lacks political legitimacy, which can easily lead to another regime change. However, contrary to this general expectation, in Burma the military regime has been robust although its governance remains low.[23]

Many observers see the tatmadaw as the cause of both the weak governance and the durability of authoritarian rule in Burma. They argue that because the tatmadaw is able to forcefully suppress popular discontent, any social unrest or expression of social dissatisfaction resulting from low governance does not present serious problems in political terms. As a consequence, low governance adversely affects the provision of public goods needed for economic growth resulting in stagnation, which effectively hinders improvement in state governance. Civil society and political competition remain so weak that there is no functioning of checks-and-balances against the political leaders. Consequently there can be little improvement in governance, and those in power are able to protect their vested interests and keep the political regime robust.

At first glance, this argument appears to provide a plausible explanation for the political situation in Burma, but in fact it has a serious flaw because it assumes that the military regime in Burma relies on a highly monolithic and strongly consolidated military dictatorship. However, it is not a simple matter for a dictator to direct the military to mobilize troops to suppress civil society because a potential conflict always exists between a dictator and the military and even among factions within the military. The dictator has to cope with the difficult problem of coordination among political elites. This difficulty is one reason that military regimes do not last long. Or, to put it the other way around, such difficulty also explains why a dictatorship never survives without the support of the military. Therefore an analysis of the relationship between the

---

[23] This situation contrasts with neighboring Thailand where a total of 16 coups have taken place since the end of the Pacific War, of which nine have succeeded and seven have failed.

dictator, the military, and the state is critical in understanding the durability of the military regime in Burma.

Burma Studies: Monopoly on Power

Table 1.2 presents the approaches, significant factors, and main arguments of previous studies in Burma Studies and Comparative Politics on the military regime. In Burma Studies literature three major approaches emerge. The first, the cultural approach, emphasizes fatalism; the state is viewed as all powerful and the Burmese people are submissive to the authoritarian state.[24] Maung Maung Gyi offers the following example of the cultural approach:

> The Burmese public, by and large, are not very worried because the government, no matter what form it takes, is in their view invariably extortive and arbitrary. As long as there is no widespread famine, which is highly unlikely in a normally grain-surplus nation, and a few necessities of life are made available to the masses, there will be no uprising of any magnitude. The built-in values of fatalism widespread in the society and the loyal support of the armed forces recruited mainly from among the peasants are primarily responsible for keeping Ne Win in power for so long.[25]

Although some scholars and many ordinary Burmese embrace this kind of argument, the cultural approach has two serious flaws. First, the approach is empirically weak. Contrary to its emphasis on the submission of the people, some studies of Burmese village communities, notably those by Ardeth Maung Thawnghmung and Akio Takahashi, have shown that while farmers appear to be obedient, in reality they employ a variety of strategies to avoid cooperating with the government.[26] Second, although

---

[24] Similarly, it is a commonly accepted idea in Burma that along with water (flood), fire, thieves, and despised persons, the king (or the government) is recognized by people as one of the "five major enemies (*yandumyô ngâbâ*)," and they avoid approaching the enemy, meaning in effect that people easily become indifferent to politics.

[25] Maung Maung Gyi, *Burmese Political Values: The Socio-Political Roots of Authoritarianism* (N.Y.: Praeger, 1983).

[26] See Ardeth Maung Thawnghmung, *Behind the Teak Curtain: Authoritarianism, Agricultural Policies and Political Legitimacy in Rural Burma/Myanmar* (London: K. Paul, 2004); Akio Takahashi, *Biruma Deruta no Beisakuson* [The economy of farm villages under the "socialist" regime in the Burmese delta]; James C. Scott, *Weapons of the Weak: Everyday Forms of Peasant Resistance* (New Haven: Yale University Press, 1985).

Table 1.2 Overview of Existing Explanations for the Durability of Burma's Military Regime

Field	*Approach*	*Significant Factors*	*Main Argument*
Burma Studies	Cultural Approach (e.g., Gyi)	political culture	obedient political culture accepts supressive military regime
	Economic Approach (e.g., Fujita, Kudo)	shared poverty, weak civil society	low price of basic needs mitigates political grievances
		rentier state	revenue from natural resources helps an authoritarian regime survive
	Military Approach (e.g., Than, Callahan)	military tradition	national liberation army takes political role
		military institution	strong military institution supports military regime durability
Comparative Politics	Civil-Military Relations (e.g., Hungtington, Stepan])	praetorian society, new professionalism	the weaker the institutionalization of society, the greater the military intervention
	Developmental Dictatorship (e.g., Suehiro, O'Donnel)	economic development	the better the economic performance, the more durable the military regime
	Democratization Theory (e.g., Casper, Boudreau)	military cohesion, weak opposition	the stronger the military cohesion and the weaker the opposition, the less the democratization
	Political Trajectories (e.g., Slater)	contentious politics, elite collective action	the type of counter-revolution decides the durability of the authoritarian regime

the argument may provide insight into the national character of Burma in terms of accepting authoritarian rule, it does not explain the reason that the regime had to be a military one and not a communist or some other type of authoritarian regime.

The second approach to Burma in the literature emphasizes the uniqueness of the country's economy and the impact of economic factors in explaining the people's obedience. As James Scott writes, "The test for the peasant is more likely to be 'What is left?' than 'How much is taken?',"[27] meaning that farmers generally do not resort to acts of violence against the state as long as their livelihoods are not threatened. Thus it stands to reason that the durability of Burma's military regime may be explained by the same economic argument. In fact, it is frequently said that Burma's abundant agricultural resources have been an underlying factor in the people's obedience.

A corollary factor in controlling social unrest, one that Koichi Fujita raises, has been the low prices of basic consumer goods, most importantly rice, that have remained stable under government price controls.[28] This argument, when taken together with the weakness of Burma's middle class, seems highly plausible. It should be noted that the collapse of democracy and shift to an authoritarian regime in 1962 occurred at a very early stage in the country's economic development (in 1962, Burma's annual per capita income was 312 USD).[29] At the time, the size of the middle class and the industrial sector were very small. Moreover, there was little change in the employment structure from 1964 to 1990. During Ne Win's rule, Burma remained largely an agricultural society with nearly 70 per cent of the population engaged in farming. The hypothesis that the expansion of the middle class leads to democratization may be overly simplistic; nevertheless, it is highly likely that increased social mobility, including the expansion of middle class, will accelerate political change. Therefore, the low prices of basic consumer goods in Burma along with the existence of a relatively small middle class may be

[27] James C. Scott, *The Moral Economy of the Peasant: Rebellion and Subsistence in Southeast Asia* (New Haven: Yale University Press, 1976), p. 7.
[28] Koichi Fujita, "Josho," p. 7. In fact, I often encountered people during his fieldwork who reminisced nostalgically about life under the Ne Win regime, remembering it as a peaceful time (*êichânthaya*) and mentioning the low cost of living at that time.
[29] Adam Przeworsky, *et al.*, *Democracy and Development: Political Institutions and Well-Being in the World, 1950–1990* (New York: Cambridge University Press, 2000), Table 2.6.

able to explain the lack of social unrest in the country. However, since the 1990s, the domestic price of rice has neared international levels and overall prices of basic consumer goods have risen, undermining the conditions for creating a compliant population. On the other hand, rising natural gas export revenue since the early 2000s has enabled the government to rule the society with less reliance on taxation and popular support. There can be no doubt that natural gas exports are helping to maintain a stable political regime in Burma.

Both the cultural and economic approaches appear to be grounded on the same fragile assumption that the military regime in Burma is durable only because the civil society does not resist this undemocratic and suppressive political regime. Such an argument may be true in the sense that democratization never happens without mounting social pressure for democracy. However, the argument would be too simplistic to sufficiently understand the complicated mechanism that makes Burma's authoritarian regime work, mainly because these two approaches treat the politics among the ruling elites as a black box.

A third approach seeks to explain the durability of the military regime from an organizational standpoint. The conventional view takes into account the importance of the tatmadaw's origin. This can be traced back to the 1930s and 1940s when nationalistic young people took up arms to fight against the British and the Japanese. In the words of Tin Maung Maung Than, "The first-generation military leadership who made their mark during the antifascist revolution against the Japanese had fashioned a military tradition extending beyond national defence requirements and bordering on the political."[30] And according to Dorothy Guyot, the behavioral pattern of the tatmadaw can be understood as "a political movement in military garb."[31] Without a doubt, up until the 1970s, many of the tatmadaw's top officers were not people who had chosen to be military officers as a professional career. Rather, many of them, at least in their youth, sought to liberate their country, a goal that greatly inspired them to become soldiers. However, this perspective is not enough to explain the involvement of the tatmadaw in subsequent

[30] Tin Maung Maung Than, "Burma: The 'New Professionalism' of the Tatmadaw," in *Military Professionalism in Asia; Conceptual and Empirical Perspectives,* ed. Muthiah Allagappa (Honolulu: East-West Center, 2001), p. 163.

[31] Dorothy Guyot, "The Burma Independence Army: A Political Movement in Military Garb," in *Southeast Asia in World War II: Four Essays*, ed. Josef Silverstein (New Haven: Yale University, Southeast Asia Studies, 1966), p. 51.

political events because the Japanese occupation lasted only about three years from 1942 to 1945. Even if the occupation period is critical in determining the origin of the tatmadaw's political orientation, we need another explanation of why and how it was firmly established as an institution.

Also, this emphasis on the tatmadaw's origin overlooks the possibility that the political orientation of a military can also undermine its organizational integrity, which can lead to the emergence of military cliques or violent internal conflicts. Indonesia's experience in the 1950s is a case in point. The Indonesian military, like its counterpart in Burma, grew out of a movement for national liberation. But after Indonesia's independence in 1949, its military was plagued by factionalism among its regional commands,[32] because it turns out that a military that continues to be an extension of a political movement cannot function successfully as a military organization.

Along with this deficiency, Mary Callahan critically points out that such an argument is also insufficient in explaining the durability of Burma's military regime. Callahan suggests that a more likely explanation can be found by examining the institutional development of the tatmadaw in the 1950s. In her *Making Enemies: War and State Building in Burma*, she closely examines state-building in Burma since the colonial period making reference to Charles Tilly's "war makes the state and the state makes war" model.[33] Then in contrast to conventional understanding, which regards 1948–62 as a period of "the displacement of the state,"[34] Callahan argues that during that time the tatmadaw developed institutionally through counter-insurgency operations and achieved political autonomy from civilian control, enabling it to successfully launch a coup on 2 March 1962. In shedding light on this overlooked aspect of the tatmadaw's institutionalization in the 1950s, Callahan claims to

---

[32] See Ruth McVey, "The Post Revolutionary Transformation of the Indonesian Army," Pts. 1 and 2, *Indonesia* 11 (1971) and *Indonesia* 12 (1972).

[33] Mary Callahan, *Making Enemies: War and State Building in Burma* (Ithaca: Cornell University Press, 2003).

[34] For a discussion of the Burmese state, see Robert Taylor, *The State in Myanmar* (London: Hurst & Company, 2009). Also, see the doctoral dissertation by Saw Rock Top, a study of the Burmese military in the 1950s that makes the same argument as Callahan. Saw Rock Top, "The Development and Role of Army in Burma (1941–1962)," PhD dissertation, Tokyo University, 1989.

address the issue of regime durability, but I would argue that she only accounts for the prerequisite of a successful military coup and subsequent lasting durable military regime. Again, maintaining a military regime for a long time is far more difficult than carrying out a coup. In Burma political intervention by the military has become unusually persistent. Not only have soldier dictators kept the conflicting interests among the elites under control and provided institutional stability, but they have also effectively prevented the emergence of capable, experienced, and reform-oriented politicians and bureaucrats. This case raises an empirical anomaly. As Dankwart Rustow has stated, "the ultimate success of a military regime depends on its skill in slowing or promoting the rise of effective civilian institutions that will render future military intervention superfluous".[35] How have military officers monopolized the political leadership over such a long period of time in Burma?[36] This question still remains unresolved.

Comparative Politics: Military Cohesion

During the 1960s and 1970s, civil-military relations in developing countries was a central topic in comparative politics. In discussing political intervention by the military, Samuel Finer writes: "The wonder, therefore, is not why it rebels against its civilian masters, but why it ever obeys them."[37] By "it," of course, he means the military since it is in an absolutely superior position in terms of its potential for violence to seize state power. Indeed, between the latter half of the 1950s and the first half of the 1980s, 10 to 25 coups d'état occurred each year in the Third World, almost all of them taking place in newly-independent states, highlighting

[35] Dankwart A. Rustow, "The Military in Middle Eastern Society and Politics," in *The Military in the Middle East*, ed. S.N. Fisher (Columbus: Ohio State University Press, 1963), pp. 3–20.

[36] For recent important studies on the organizational development of the *tatmadaw* and the modernization of its equipment, see Anthony Selth, *Burma's Armed Forces: Power Without Glory* (Norwalk, CT: East Bridge, 2002) and Maung Aung Myoe, *Building the Tatmadaw: Myanmar Armed Forces since 1948* (Singapore: Institute of Southeast Asian Studies, 2009). However, the examination of the relationship between the tatmadaw and the state is outside their interest.

[37] Samuel E. Finer, *The Man on Horseback: The Role of the Military in Politics*, 2nd ed., extended (Boulder: Westview Press, 1988), p. 5.

the fragile balance of power between governments and their militaries.[38] Thus, with intended exaggeration Finer asserts that it is only natural for the military to intervene in politics.

A number of studies have examined not only civilian control, but also political intervention by the military. Many have attempted to categorize political interventions by the military, with the coup d'état being the principal type, or to find the causes of political intervention. For instance, Samuel Huntington redefined the concept of "praetorian society" as a society in which military and social forces seek direct political participation, at times violently, because praetorian society lacks sufficient political institutions to mediate political conflicts in society.[39] Finer referred to the concept of "political culture" and argued that the political culture of a society affects the level of military intervention. His study divides political culture into four types: mature, developing, low, and minimal, and discusses how each one determines the degree of military intervention in politics (influence, threat, exclusion, and overturning of civilian government).[40]

Other studies of civil-military relations have examined the particular nature of the military as an interventionist actor. The focus of this literature varies widely, some analyzing the military organization in relation to social class, others seeing it as the promoter of modernization,[41] and

[38] Charles Tilly, *Coercion, Capital, and European States, AD 990–1990* (Cambridge: Basil Blackwell, 1990), pp. 214–6.

[39] Huntington, *Political Order in Changing Societies*, pp. 192–263.

[40] See Finer, *The Man on Horseback*, p. 78. Finer's terms "Low Political Culture" and "Minimal Political Culture" closely resemble the image of Huntington's "Praetorian Society," and they can explain the conditions conducive to military intervention into politics and the degree of that intervention in a Praetorian Society setting.

[41] Lucian Pye, a recognized advocate of modernization who has written on nation-building in Burma, argues that for the political and economic development of a country, it is better to have military intervention than to entrust the government to corrupt politicians, who lack the ability to coordinate politics (Lucian Pye, "Armies in the Process of Political Modernization," in *The Role of the Military in Underdeveloped Countries*, ed. John J. Johnson [N.J.: Princeton University Press, 1962b], pp. 68–89). Also see Moshe Lissak, *Military Roles in Modernization: Civil-Military Relations in Thailand and Burma* (Beverly Hills: Sage Publications, 1976) for a comparison of Burma and Thailand in the modernization and role of the military; and Chao-Tzang Yawnghwe, "The Politics of Authoritarianism: The State and Political Soldiers in Burma, Indonesia, and Thailand," PhD dissertation, The University of British Columbia 1997 for a comparison of Burma, Thailand, and Indonesia.

still others delving into the relationship between military professionalism and political intervention.[42] While most of these studies deal with coups, few of them focus on durable military regimes such as the one in Burma. The main reason for that may be due to a lack of case studies. Most soldiers-turned-state-leaders find themselves facing difficulties after their military overthrow of a government as they come to realize that they lack the ability to manage complex state functions, or if they fail to mobilize popular support from the people.[43] Even in studies that have quantitatively measured the duration of undemocratic regimes, in most cases the military steps in to restore order, then shortly after returns to the barracks. Therefore, the duration of a military regime, i.e., how long it lasts, is a question that has been rarely addressed.[44] As a result, direct military rule is usually temporary, and many military regimes, regardless of whether indeed they actually follow through, promise a future transition to civilian rule. Even when the military maintains control of the government for a long period of time, it cannot sustain its rule without demonstrating legitimacy through expressions of commitment to some political value such as nationalism, democracy, or revolution that transcends military interests. If the military does not fulfil its promises, there will inevitably be a backlash from the people. The military will then step down and transfer authority to a civilian government. Alternatively it will take steps to actively recruit technocrats and civilian politicians to compensate for its own lack of appropriate expertise, will rationalize policies (e.g., a policy change from import-substitute to export-oriented industrialization), will seek to develop the economy, to improve infrastructure, and will undertake social policies that produce visible results.

---

[42] Since Huntington defined the concept of professionalism as characterized by expertise, responsibility, and corporateness, this concept has been regarded as essential for explaining military behavior. Huntington himself in dealing primarily with America connected professionalism with the military's non-political nature. The accumulated research since then, presented in a wide variety of studies, has not supported this connection, and it is now commonly recognized that professionalism does not guarantee the non-political nature of a military; rather it structurally prescribes military behavior which includes both a political and non-political nature. See Samuel Huntington, *The Soldier and the State: The Theory and Politics of Civil-Military Relations* (Harvard: Harvard University Press, 1985).

[43] Finer, *The Man on Horseback*, pp. 12–9.

[44] Jennifer Gandhi, *Political Institutions under Dictatorship* (Cambridge: Cambridge University Press, 2008), p. 173.

The idea of the developmental dictatorship was raised as a framework to explain the compatibility of long-lasting authoritarian regimes and economic development in East and Southeast Asia. Akira Suehiro writes, "Without the systematization of developmental policy and the acceptance of growth ideology on the part of the general public, these so-called dictatorships of person or party would never have lasted as long as they did."[45] Later in the argumentation he emphasizes the primary importance of technocrats who institutionalize developmental policies. At the same time, this perspective sees military leaders as staying in the background of economic development while being in charge of the government, and the crucial factor sustaining their authoritarian rule is basically regarded as the trade-off between political rights and economic benefits within state-society relations.[46]

In comparative politics during the latter half of the 1980s a boom took place in the study of democratization which renewed interest in the study of civil-military relations. However, since the focus of research was on democratization, the question of concern was the sort of behavior of the military contributed to democratization. Countries such as Burma and China, where democratic rule had not been established despite popular democratization movements, tended to be taken up as cases for control experiments to strengthen the explanation of democratization. These studies then argued that a lack of any factors associated with democratic transition accounted for the durability of the authoritarian regimes in those countries. A study by Casper and Taylor, for example, dubbed the experience of Burma, where an authoritarian regime remained in power despite a large-scale pro-democracy movement, the "Extreme Conflict Path" to authoritarianism. The authors concluded that: "Actually,

---

[45] Akira Suehiro, *Catch-Up Industrialization: The Trajectory and Prospects of East Asian Economies* (Singapore: NUS Press, 2008), p. 111.

[46] Regarding developmental dictatorship or the developmental state, see Meredith Woo-Cumings, ed., *The Developmental State* (Ithaca: Cornell University Press, 1999). Another approach to the study of developmental dictatorship, one that focused primarily on Latin America, was bureaucratic authoritarianism which sought to explain the interrelationship between the world-wide prevalence of authoritarian (including military) regimes and the stage of economic development. As propounded by its advocate, Guillermo O'Donnell, bureaucratic authoritarian regimes were undemocratic political regimes formed by an alliance of military officers, bureaucrats and business faced with economic stagnation brought on by the failure of democracy, and these regimes sought to industrialize by introducing foreign capital through the internationalization of the domestic market.

neither the Defender nor the Challenger was willing to make concessions, so the regime choice process in Myanmar was characterized by the actors stating and restating demands. However, the Defender had the advantage of controlling the coercive apparatus of government."[47] They, in essence, attribute the failure of democratization to the absence of compromise between the regime's leadership and the pro-democracy forces.[48] Rather than this explanation, however, it was the ability of the tatmadaw to maintain its unity that thwarted the victory of the opposition forces, unlike the experiences in Indonesia and Thailand. So why did the tatmadaw maintain its cohesion?

This military cohesion riddle has not been solved even within the study of durable authoritarian regimes, which has been a highly productive field of research in recent years. A relevant study beneficial to this book is one by Dan Slater, which also employs a political trajectory approach. He explains the diversity of the state and political regimes in seven Southeast Asian countries (the Philippines, Indonesia, Singapore, Malaysia, Thailand, South Vietnam, Burma) through tracing the political trajectory formed by the influence of contentious politics on elite collective action. He sees the durability of an authoritarian regime as dependent on the stability of the coalition amongst the elites, and suggests that the casual mechanism that creates this elite coalition is the collective perception of threat arising from the country's many domestic conflicts. Slater's argument is unique and provides theoretical support for this study.[49] Among the different trajectories the Southeast Asian countries have experienced, he calls Burma's the trajectory of "militarization" and says, "The elite collective action necessary for authoritarian durability in Burma is not channelled through the sort of state and party institutions that order power in Malaysia and Singapore; but what sustains Burmese

---

[47] Gretchen Casper and Michelle M. Taylor, *Negotiating Democracy: Transitions from Authoritarian Rule* (Pittsburgh: University of Pittsburgh Press, 1996), p. 70.

[48] See, for example, Vince Boudreau, *Resisting Dictatorship: Repression and Protest in Southeast Asia* (New York: Cambridge University Press, 2004) and Yasuhiro Takeda, *Minshuka no Hikaku Seijigaku: Higashi Ajia Syokoku no Taisei Hendo Katei* (Kyoto: Mineruba Shobo).

[49] From the perspective of civil-military relations, his study reminds us of the one by Amos Perlmutter, who tried to link the civil-military relations and comparative political history. See Amos Perlmutter, *The Military and Politics in Modern Times: On Professionals, Praetorian, and Revolutionary Soldiers* (New Haven: Yale University Press, 1977), pp. 9–17.

military rule is elite collective action — originally forged in response to specific types of contentious politics — nonetheless."[50] Unfortunately, while Slater presents a detailed examination of Burma's contentious politics, he does not seem to adequately discuss how it influenced the elite collective action. Thus we are little closer to solving the riddle of Burma's military cohesion.

The Research Questions, Strategy, and Argument

In theory, political monopoly and military cohesion could be inconsistent with each other. That is because the military, a specialized profession, tends to avoid politicization, which may trigger an organizational break-up. Military officers are always sensitive about their corporate interests being violated and losing their organizational cohesion. The military usually retreats to the barracks upon an election or after the amending of a constitution in the aftermath of a coup. Or a political cleavage between military and state leaders can appear as the duration of a military regime lengthens.

The interesting thing in the case of Burma is that although the tatmadaw has intervened in politics to the extent that it can be said to hold a political monopoly, over the past 50 years it has remained cohesive enough to be able to continue its political participation. Clearly this military cohesion has contributed to the formation and maintenance of the strong regime. At the same time, this peculiar coexistence of long-term political monopoly along with retained military cohesion has caused political deadlock and weak governance. Thus, the questions for this study are: Why is Burma's military able to maintain its cohesion despite its deep intervention into politics? And, how is it that Burma's dictators have kept control over the military and been successful at controlling an authoritarian political regime?

This study will focus mainly on the period of the Ne Win regime (1962–88). Ne Win fundamentally altered the political development of Burma, and the foundations of the present political regime were laid down during that time. Through its analysis of the Ne Win regime, this study sets forth two revisions to the study of Burmese political history. Firstly, I argue that the durability of the military regime has been made

---

[50] Dan Slater, *Ordering Power: Contentious Politics and Authoritarian Leviathan in Southeast Asia* (Cambridge: Cambridge University Press, 2010), p. 26.

possible by the large and systematic distribution of official positions to military officers. This study highlights the relationship between the officer corps of the tatmadaw and other institutions of the state, these latter being: ideology, the one-party system, the civilian bureaucracy, the political elite, and the dictatorship. What will be revealed in each relationship is the process by which the officer corps has come to embed itself into the state by filling important positions in other sectors. This process was the development of the tatmadaw as a bureaucracy as well as the institutionalization of the pattern of interest distribution which contributed importantly to Ne Win's dictatorship and his regime's survival. It is not unusual in itself for military officers to be given government or party posts under a military regime. What is important here is the legitimacy these postings have, the way they are distributed, and how they become institutionalized.

In addition, this study reconsiders the significance of Ne Win's revolution and contends that his revolution was a failure in terms of achieving socialism, but a success in creating an institutional basis for a robust military regime. The literature of Burma Studies has not adequately grasped this significance. It basically assumes that the abandonment of socialism following the military coup of 18 September 1988 brought about the realization that Ne Win's political project was over. This may have been true for one-party rule and the planned economy, but the influence of the military's political power over the state and society remained intact. This means that we have not yet understood the continuity and discontinuity between the Ne Win regime period and that of post-1988. This study will show that the revolution became a catalyst for the officer corps to turn the elite coalition in Burma into an oligopoly of the officer corps. However, this is not to say that the revolution was in name only. Ne Win had believed in the revolution and had not used socialism as a guise to legitimize military rule. This study will suggest that the failure of Ne Win's revolution led to the success of the military regime as an unintended outcome.

Resources and Structure

Researchers of Burma studies have found it difficult to understand the country's "mysterious" politics due above all to insufficient resources, which often makes it hard to confirm if information about a political event is fact or not. So the first requirement in the research process for this study was to collect data and information through archival research and interviews conducted in Burma. My fieldwork was carried out during a two-year research stint in Yangon between June 2003 and March 2005 and continued thereafter with twice-yearly visits to the country. The resulting data presented in this study is based to the greatest possible extent on the facts and hard evidence that I gleaned from in-country research and investigation, the intent being to avoid unfounded conjecture and groundless analysis.

The source materials were unique and original. Though researching in restrictive circumstances, I had access to primary materials at the National Archives Department (NAD) and at the Defence Services Museum and Historical Research Institute (DSMHRI);[51] I was also able to find primary sources in used bookshops in Yangon. Also available were newspapers and magazines kept at local libraries. Especially valuable were the two databases compiled from primary materials: the profiles of the BSPP central committee candidates and parliament members, and the records of tatmadaw personnel from 1972 to 1987. Through analysis of the data, I could explore the power structure of the Ne Win regime and describe the incentive structure of the officer corps.[52]

The composition of this book is as follows. After this introductory chapter, Chapter 2 examines the historical background to the Ne Win regime period to see how the modern Burmese state, nation, and military developed and what political traditions were formed, the purposes being to elucidate the preconditions that gave birth to the Ne Win regime and to point out the historical characteristics of the state and people of Burma. While presenting by and large what is already known about this background period, the chapter also argues the importance of Burma's location on the periphery of two empires: the British Indian Empire and the Empire of Japan.

Chapter 3 examines the creation of the Ne Win regime from the aspect of its ideology. Chit Hlaing, a former Communist who became a

---

[51] The latter is the archives of the Burma Armed Forces.

[52] In the study of civil-military relations, the institutional placement of military personnel has been examined primarily from the perspective of civilian control under democracy. It has more or less emphasized the sanction of deviant behavior and has not paid much attention to the incentives that motivate the behavior of the officer corps. In this study I am not concerned with developing a theory; however, for an interesting effort to reconsider civil-military relations using agency theory, see Peter D. Feaver, *Armed Servants: Agency, Oversight, and Civil-Military Relations* (Cambridge, Mass: Harvard University Press, 2003).

civilian official working for the military, drafted the regime's state ideology. Through an examination of his personal history, it is possible to trace the formation of this state ideology, thereby revealing how the creation and enactment of the ideology underpinning Ne Win regime was influenced by the internal politics of the tatmadaw and national security policy.

Chapter 4 examines the one-party rule of the Burma Socialist Programme Party (BSPP) that was introduced after the abolition of the parliamentary democracy that had lasted since Burma's independence in 1948. This chapter will trace Ne Win's attempt to build a party-state and show how the attempt failed. Refuting the conventional understanding of the role of the BSPP, this chapter presents a hypothesis that Ne Win had the intention of shifting his political base from the tatmadaw to the BSPP. This hypothesis will be verified through an analysis of the informal rules for appointing senior executives of the BSPP.

Chapter 5 deals with administrative reform and examines its impact on the officer corps. It will be shown that the new administrative system introduced in 1972 and the enactment of a new constitution in 1974 fundamentally undermined the authority of civilian bureaucrats. These officials were substantially replaced by military officers who were assigned through informal personnel rules to posts in the government bureaucracy. This process made the Ne Win regime different from the developmental dictatorships of other Southeast Asian countries.

Chapter 6 presents a profile analysis of the political elite focusing on the "winner-take-all" political culture in Burma. A characteristic that has been pointed out in Burmese political history is that whenever a regime change takes place, there is a wholesale replacement of the political elite. To see if it holds true for the Ne Win regime, this chapter examines the social profiles of the Burmese political elite under the regime, specifically the members of the People's Parliament, the members of the BSPP Central Committee, and the senior officers of the tatmadaw, in order to see how they constituted the regime as a whole.

Chapter 7 addresses the way that Ne Win controlled the tatmadaw, focusing on the institutional framework and personnel composition of that dictatorship. Using a dataset of promotions within the officer corps, this chapter closely examines the triangular relationship between the dictator, the officer corps, and the state. It then argues that Ne Win successfully controlled the officer corps through a mixture of formal and informal institutions.

Chapter 8 examines the collapse of the Ne Win regime in 1988, re-interpreting the political crisis and coup d'état in that year as an internal reform or generational change of military leadership. There is a historical irony here. In the late 1980s, Burma was facing problems caused by the old dictator and his inner circle in politics and a growing economic stagnation in society. The people's dissent with politics and the economy erupted into a massive anti-government demonstration, leading to Ne Win's resignation as chairman of the BSPP. At the same time, however, it also created an opportunity for a new generation within the tatmadaw to take over and renew the regime.

The closing epilogue briefly explores post-1988 Burmese politics from the perspective of civil-military relations. While few people anticipated the recent political and economic reforms in Burma, these changes are not opaque, and can be best understood by looking at the historical context because the relationship between the tatmadaw and the state in post-1988 Burma still plays a crucial role in politics today. Hopefully this epilogue along with the analysis presented in this book will help readers understand the possible future courses of Burmese politics.

CHAPTER 2

Nation-State Building and the Coercive Apparatus in Modern Burma

The modern state was introduced to Burma in the nineteenth century when it was colonized by the British. As John S. Furnivall precisely describes, state building in Burma proved to be a difficult and unstable process because the economic motives that drove colonial state-building and the principles of the rule of law were completely different from Burma's traditional political order.[1] This chapter will discuss the history of the nation-state and the coercive apparatus in Burma from the colonial era to the establishment of the Ne Win regime in 1962.

This chapter will also lay the foundation for an analytical framework for the chapters that follow. The central argument I propose in this chapter centres on two fundamental structural factors that determined post-colonial civil-military relations. First, the construction of a modern state in Burma was a process by which Britain, starting in the 1820s, effectively ended the rule of the Konbaung Dynasty and incorporated the territory of Burma into the periphery of its Indian Empire. From this point until 1942, when the Japanese army invaded Burma, major policies were decided in London and New Delhi as much as in Rangoon. For imperial officers, Burma was simply a frontier region of the empire, and it did not draw serious enough attention to drive policymaking that fits the local indigenous situation in Burma. The application of colonial policies existing in India greatly weakened the social order of colonial Burma,

[1] Regarding the construction of periphery states, see John S. Furnivall, *The Fashioning of the Leviathan: The Beginnings of British Rule in Burma* (Canberra: Department of Anthropology, Research School of Pacific Studies, The Australian National University, 1991); Patricio N. Abinales, *Making Mindanao: Cotabato and Davao in the Formation of the Philippine Nation-State* (Quezon City: Ateneo de Manila University Press, 2000).

and the region became infamous for having the highest crime rate in the Indian Empire. At the same time there was the stirring of a national awakening and a rise in political movements. Second, because the Japanese occupation from 1942 to 1945 brought in a different geopolitical significance, Burma in the Pacific War was turned into a frontline state. The Japanese Empire proceeded to restructure the state and society through a variety of means, including mobilizing the native population, especially young nationalists, thereby gaining popular support and preparing a defence against Britain's counterattack.

The point here is that the building of the colonial state in Burma should be understood as the consequences of the colonial policies of two empires. In short, state building on the frontier of the Indian Empire and state rebuilding on the frontline of the Japanese Empire laid down the fundamental characteristics of the post-colonial state in Burma.[2] The state's coercive apparatus was also formed under these two empires. In the modern state, the military as a group of professionals generally accepts limits to its involvement in politics. During the British colonial era, especially after the Indian Rebellion in 1857, the coercive apparatus in Burma was kept under the strict control of the British Indian Army headquarters and the British Indian government, and no military officer imagined taking advantage of military authority for political ends. However, with the arrival of the Japanese Empire, the situation changed dramatically. Unlike the British, the Japanese created a native military of young Burmese nationalists for political purposes. It was Japan's occupation policy to provide nominal independence to native people and to defend the frontline of the empire at the same time. However, the Japanese occupation produced the unintended outcome of providing an opportunity for nationalist leaders to organize a "nation," an opportunity that the British were careful never to allow.

The Colonial Era

The End of the Burmese Empire

In the middle of the eighteenth century, Britain and France were engaged in intense competition for territorial acquisitions in the Indo-China

---

[2] Regarding nation building within an empire and the possibility for independence, see Philip G. Roeder, *Where Nation-States Come From: Institutional Change in the Age of Nationalism* (Princeton & Oxford: Princeton University Press, 2007).

region. One of these territories was Burma, then under the rule of the Kongbaung Dynasty, which gradually came under Britain's imperial control as a result of a dispute with the British East India Company over Arakanese refugees fleeing from Burma into Chittagong in the company's territory of Bengal. The dispute continued into the First Anglo-Burmese War, which began in 1824 and ended when British East India Company forces occupied Pagan in Burma's central plain. Under the Treaty of Yandabo, signed in February 1826, the regions of Arakan (Rakhine) and the southern part of Tenasserim (Tanintharyi) were ceded to the British East India Company. Arakan was incorporated into Bengal Province, and a commissioner from Penang, part of the Strait Settlements, was sent by the company to administer Tenasserim.

Twenty-six years later, in 1852, the Second Anglo-Burmese War occurred, and following Burma's defeat in that war, the British East India Company acquired Martaban and Pegu, meaning it occupied what was known as lower Burma. As a result, the dynasty lost the revenues from the economic and trade resources of the Irrawaddy delta. In particular, the gain of Rangoon at the mouth of the Irrawaddy River gave the company strategic control of the Kingdom's river lifeline. In 1858, with the passage of the Government of India Act in that year, the territories of the British East India Company were put under the control of the British government, taking away the company's authority to rule. After the Second Anglo-Burmese War, the commissioner of Tenasserim was given authority over Martaban, and a commissioner was assigned to Pegu, but the administration of the four regions of Arakan, Tenasserim, Martaban, and Pegu by separately appointed commissioners was widely regarded as inefficient. Consequently, in 1862, the administration of these regions was consolidated under the office of a chief commissioner located in Rangoon. Lieutenant Colonel Arthur P. Phayre, the former commissioner of Pegu, was the first to hold the position.

Meanwhile, the British made increasing economic and political demands on the Konbaung king in Mandalay, whose control had been relegated to the upper half of Burma. As tensions mounted, the new king, Mindon Min, attempted to modernize the state and reconstruct government finances.[3] However, the reforms were not successful. For instance,

[3] Regarding the relationship of the fall of the Konbaung Dynasty and modern Burma, see Thant Myint-U, *The Making of Modern Burma* (Cambridge: Cambridge University Press, 2001).

while the king sought to obtain additional revenue from timber concessions to foreign companies, this move negatively impacted the dynasty. Foreign concessionaires and the government of British India put pressure on the king to reduce timber prices. Meanwhile, the King's domestic opponents accused his ministers of selling Burma's properties to foreign enemies.

Then, in 1885, a serious dispute broke out between King Thibaw, who had succeeded Mindon Min following his death in 1878, and the Bombay Burmah Trading Corporation over the export of teak. At the same time, the British had growing concerns about French contact with the Burmese dynasty as the French expanded their interest elsewhere in the Indo-China region. The British demanded that all Burmese diplomatic relationships, especially with France, be approved by the government of India. However, as a monarch of an independent state, the king refused to accept such demands. The British then took military action, and, following a few skirmishes, easily took possession of Upper Burma. King Thibaw was exiled to Bombay, and the Konbaung Dynasty fell. The British now ruled all of Burma directly, and in 1886 it became one of the provinces of the Indian Empire.

Characteristics of the Modern State in Burma

A driving force of colonial rule was rationalization. Rationalization here refers to the process by which the political and administrative instruments for ruling the people are restructured to function more efficiently for the specific purposes of the colonizers. For the kings and aristocrats of traditional dynasties, state rule was embedded in religious and social life. By contrast, for colonial rulers, the state was considered separate from society and the people were ruled in a secular manner.[4] This did not mean that the British colonial policy was the same in all of its colonies across the world. Indeed, each colony had to be ruled by means and for purposes that depended upon the colony's institutional and policy traditions, as well as its socio-economic conditions, its natural environment, and its geopolitical location. The modern state in Burma was formed on the periphery of the Indian Empire. Within the rationalization framework of colonialism, the modern state in Burma developed five main characteristics.

---

[4] Robert Taylor, *The State in Burma* (London: Hurst, 2009), p. 67.

Table 2.1 The Number of Officers in the Indian Civil Services (1892–1914)

	Bengal	*Bombay*	*Burma Province*	*Central Province*	*Madras*	*Panjab Province*	*United Province*	*Total*
Administrative Services	184 26.0%	88 12.0%	81 11.0%	54 8.0%	91 13.0%	82 12.0%	130 18.0%	710
Judicial Services	76 30.4%	35 14.0%	21 8.0%	14 5.6%	31 12.4%	33 13.2%	40 16.0%	250
Political Services	11 24.0%	4 9.0%	0 0.0%	2 4.0%	2 4.0%	21 46.0%	6 13.0%	46
Specialist	6 12.2%	9 18.3%	3 6.1%	5 10.2%	10 20.5%	6 12.2%	10 20.5%	49
Proportion of Total	26.3%	12.9%	10.0%	7.1%	12.7%	13.5%	17.6%	100%

Source: Takehiko Honda. *Indo Shokuminchi Kanryo — Daieiteikoku no Cho Eriitotachi* (Indian Colonial Bureaucrats — The Super-elites in the British Empire), (Tokyo: Kodansha Selected Library Metier, 2001), 70

The first characteristic was that officials in London and New Delhi directed the building and management of the modern state in Burma. Until 1936 Burma was a province of the British Empire under the judicial, legislative, and administrative authority of the governor-general of India. In response to growing nationalist movements at the beginning of the twentieth century, Britain began gradually moving toward granting power to legislative bodies comprised of native people. This meant changing the system of rule to allow for greater self-government by local people while continuing to appoint civilian bureaucrats from Britain and India to major administrative posts. Indian Civil Service (ICS) officers had absolute authority over local administration. Table 2.1 shows the assignment of senior ICS officers by province between 1892 and 1914. In 1921 the total population of all the provinces of India was about 200 million people, of which about 13 million were in the province of Burma, or about 7 per cent of the total. Although the table only goes up to 1914, we can see that on average about 10 per cent of the total number of senior ICS officers were assigned to the province of Burma, indicating that the number of bureaucrats was assigned based approximately on the size of the population. After the Burma Act of 1937 took effect, the British government's newly established Ministry of Burma became responsible for governing Burma through the governor-general of Burma who was appointed directly by the king. The governor-general was accountable to the state minister in Britain in charge of India, who in turn reported to the British Parliament.

The second characteristic was that the central area (Burma Proper where the majority of population was Bahman) and the frontier areas (Shan, Kachin, Chin, and most of the other non-Bahman ethnic group regions) of Burma were ruled under different systems. When the British occupied Upper Burma after the Third Anglo-Burmese War, it sought to bring under its control several Shan states that had submitted to the rule of the Konbaung Dynasty. Some of the *sawbwa* (Shan chiefs) were hostile to the British until a British-appointed superintendent guaranteed their legal status and established a system of de facto indirect rule over these states. With the enactment of the Shan States Act in 1888 and the demarcation of the border between the Shan States and Siam in 1892, British indirect rule was formally established. Indirect rule was introduced in other ethnic minority frontier areas as well. In 1893 and 1895, a superintendent was posted to the Kachin and Chin states.[5] Thus, two methods of rule were in effect during the British colonial period in Burma: the central part of Burma, or Burma Proper, was ruled directly, while the Frontier Area was controlled through indirect rule. This system of dual rule was a significant factor leading to post-colonial ethnic conflict in Burma.

The third characteristic of the modern state in Burma was the introduction of a modern administration, which differed greatly from the dynastic method for controlling the state that had previously been in place. In geographic terms, the country was divided into an orderly top-to-bottom framework of administrative units controlled from the Province capital of Rangoon, with the largest administrative unit being divisions followed by districts, townships, wards, and village tracts, which consist of several natural villages. In the early period of colonial rule, a circle (*tai'*), a traditional administrative unit, existed between townships and village tracts. A township consisted of several circles; within each circle, there were local persons of authority known as *taik thugyi* (*tai' dagyî*) and *gaung* (*gâun*) who were in charge of tax collecting and policing. The post of *taik thugyi* was hereditary and guaranteed a certain degree of autonomy. Soon after Upper Burma was consolidated with Burma

[5] John F. Cady, *A History of Modern Burma* (Ithaca, N.Y.: Cornell University Press, 1958), pp. 132–7.

Province in 1886, Charles Crosthwaite, who took office as governor of the province, issued the Village Act, which abolished the post of taik thugyi. Consequently the village tract became the basic unit, and a village tract resident was appointed as *ywa thugyi* (*ywa dagyî*), the village headman. More natural villages were consolidated into village tracts, which resulted in a significant decrease in the number of village headmen. For instance, during the ten-year period starting in 1909, the number of village headmen fell from 17,980 to 15,661.[6] In this way, a new administrative authority paid by the colonial state replaced the traditional authority. In addition, the administrative unit became a rational entity for the purposes of security and taxation in the colonial territory.

According to John S. Furnivall, Crosthwaite's Village Act was based on the assumptions of the strict social order that existed in Indian villages, which was fundamentally incompatible with Burma's traditional social order with its position of taik thugyi at the top, with whom the traditional dynasty maintained a hierarchical, but not necessarily strict authoritative relationship.[7] Yet, based on his experience in India, Crosthwaite viewed the relatively lax authority in Burmese villages as ineffective. Thus, the laws that were enacted in Burma under Crosthwaite's direction changed the village social order and introduced a new element of instability. As a result, the peace and order of the Burma province rapidly deteriorated as evident, for example, from the number of prison sentences, which grew to three to four times higher than that of other provinces of India.[8]

The fourth main characteristic of the modern state in Burma was its socio-economic integration into the international capitalistic economic system within Britain's policy of economic liberalism. In the context of this discussion, it is important to highlight that Burma was one of the world's major rice producers in the mid-nineteenth century. Beginning in 1850, the cultivation of rice paddies rapidly increased in Lower Burma. Rice paddies increased from 1.8 million acres in the 1870s to 10 million acres in the 1930s, and total rice exports reached 3 million tons in the 1930s, up from 440 thousand tons in 1870.[9] In addition,

---

[6] John S. Furnivall, *Colonial Policy and Practice: A Comparative Study of Burma and Netherlands India* (New York: New York University Press, 1956), p. 75.

[7] Ibid., p. 74.

[8] Ibid., p. 138.

[9] Akio Takahashi, "Myanma: Konnan-na shijou-keizai e no ikou" [Myanmar: The difficult transition to a market economy], in *Ajia Keizai-ron* [Asian Economic Studies], ed. Yonosuke Hara (Tokyo: NTT Press), pp. 296–97.

the cultivation of frontier land in Lower Burma, primarily by migrants from Upper Burma and Southern India, significantly increased production and exports.[10]

However, the development of land for rice production changed as the frontier disappeared in the early 1920s. Many independent farmers who had borrowed money to cultivate land defaulted on their loans and lost their property, and most of the land that had been pledged as collateral was taken over by money lenders and landowners. In the 1930s the share of independent farmers decreased to less than 25 per cent, and the number of non-cultivating landowners, the majority of whom were foreigners, mostly from other parts of British India, gradually increased.[11] Meanwhile, European, Indian, and Chinese businesses and merchants had come to dominate the distribution business by the end of the nineteenth century, and it was difficult for Burmese merchants to compete with them, except in some areas of rice milling. Moreover, in the cities, businesses that had come in from India made little effort to hire inexperienced Burmese workers, as it was relatively easier to bring in workers from India. For instance, during the latter half of the 1920s, about 400,000 people a year entered the country through Burmese ports. As a result, a plural society emerged, consisting of numerous Indian and Chinese immigrants and a variety of other ethnic groups, all of whom lived separately while engaging in economic activities within a framework where the foreigners were in an economically superior position to the Burmese.[12]

The fifth main characteristic of the modern state in Burma was the gradual shift of British colonial policy from economic liberalism to one that paid increasing attention to the social welfare of the indigenous people. Around the turn of the century, a variety of social welfare policies, motivated by the doctrine of the "White Man's Burden," were introduced. The idea was a product of the self-justifying colonial power's desire to see its role in colonial rule as that of bringing civilization to

---

[10] There was an important influx of migrant workers, particularly immigrant laborers from India, due to high wages and easy access to transportation. See Teruko Saito, "Biruma nioketu bei-yushutsu keizai no hatten" [Development of a rice exporting economy in Burma], in *Koza Tonan Ajia-shi 6: shokuminshichi no hanei to chouraku* [Lectures in Southeast Asian History 6: The Prosperity and Decay of the Colonial Economy], ed. Teruko Saito (Tokyo: Iwanami, 2001), p. 155.

[11] Ibid., p. 159.

[12] Furnivall, *Colonial Policy and Practice*, p. 304.

native people. In accordance with this paradigm change, welfare policies such as public health and education were carried out, and ambitious public works, including railroads, telegraphic communications, road construction, and shipping, were also launched.[13] These undertakings were the subject of debate within the British and colonial government offices, and were also used as countermeasures in response to the growing sense of nationalism amongst the native people.

Here, the ramifications of Burma's location on the periphery of the larger empire can also be seen. A good example of this is the way that education was handled in Burma. Initially, colonial policy left education up to the private sector, with the colonial government playing a supporting role. Until the end of the nineteenth century, Christian (mainly American Baptist and French Roman Catholic) missionaries and Buddhist monasteries provided education to Burma's indigenous people. By 1880, only eight Burmese students had been admitted to Calcutta University, which was the top institution of higher education in British India at the time.[14] Until 1923, studying in India was the only way for a Burmese to become a physician or engineer, and, until that same year, there was no agricultural school in the Province of Burma even though agriculture was its main industry.[15] With the founding of Rangoon University in 1920, institutions of higher education began to provide more opportunities for Burmese to move up in society, which contributed to the formation of a middle class. In 1900 there were 115 students attending college or university; by 1940 the number had increased to 2,365.[16] A significant number of the young elite, who still represented less than 1 per cent of

---

[13] For instance, total railway distance expanded nearly fivefold from 327 miles in 1886 to 1,552 miles in 1914. See Teruko Saito and Lee King Kinong, *Statistics on the Burmese Economy: The 19th and 20th Centuries* (Singapore: Institute of Southeast Asian Studies, 1999), p. 167.

[14] Burma was not the only state where the education of the indigenous population was not a priority. A comparison of Southeastern Asian states between 1936 and 1939 revealed that the number of students attending government-recognized educational institutions was 10.75% of the total population in the Philippines, 9.69% in Thailand, 6.02% in Malay, 3.92% in Burma, 3.35% in the Dutch Indies, and 2.06% in French Indochina. See John S. Furnivall, *Education Progress in Southeast Asia* (New York: International Secretariat of the Institute of Pacific Relations, 1943), p. 111.

[15] Furnivall, *Colonial Policy and Practice*, p. 130.

[16] Robert Taylor, *The State in Burma* (Honolulu: University of Hawaii Press, 1987a), p. 114.

the total population, attended university and later went on to become figures who would significantly change Burmese politics and society.

Our Burma

In the early 1900s, when there was much popular discussion in Britain of the "White Man's Burden," the colonial regime turned its attention to the welfare of the indigenous people. At the same time, an important change was taking place in Burmese society. The first stirrings of Burmese nationalism appeared in the form of the Young Men's Buddhist Association (YMBA), a movement formed by Burmese youth (*lunge*) who had grown up under colonialism. Organized in Rangoon in 1906, the YMBA was modeled on the Young Men's Christian Association. Its members were Burmese middle-class intellectuals, government employees, and monks, who sought to bring about a "revival of Buddhism."

In 1920 some members of the YMBA, in the hopes of starting a movement more political in nature, formed the General Council of Burmese Associations (GCBA). The GCBA carried out consumer boycotts and strikes, refused to pay taxes, and launched a nationwide campaign aimed at gaining autonomy from Britain. The GCBA also participated in politics upon the establishment of the Legislative Council in 1923 and in the following diarchy system. It sent members to the two-chambered Parliament established under the Government of Burma Act of 1935, which took effect in 1937. In spite of its efforts, however, due to conflicts within the party, the GCBA failed to achieve its lofty goal of becoming a political organization with the power to unify the people nationwide.

Beginning in the 1920s, the rise of nationalism and the expansion of self-rule in Burma spurred the development of political expression with the Legislative Council serving as the main vehicle. However, deliberations and decisions in the council were still influenced by the colonial administration, and the authority of the British governor-general remained strong. This situation was not acceptable to some young radical nationalists. In 1930 one of these nationalists, Thakin Ba Taung, a translation assistant in the English Department at Rangoon University, helped found the Do Bama Asiayon (Our Burma Association), which later became known as the Thakin Party. The Do Bama Asiayon was led by young radical nationalists who disagreed with the GCBA's decision to accept the British proposal of limited autonomy. They called those who cooperated with colonial rule "Their Burma" (*thudò bàma*), as opposed to "Our Burma" (*dò bàma*), and regarded them as enemies to be defeated along with colonial rule.[17] The Thakin Party's agenda remained consistent as it aimed to expand the anti-British struggle throughout Burmese society and mobilize popular support. Many of Burma's later government leaders of the 1940s and 1950s, such as Aung San, U Nu, and Thakin Soe, belonged to the Thakin Party which gave them their first experience in politics.

Dr. Ba Maw, who took office as the first prime minister in 1937 before resigning in 1939 and forming the Freedom Block in cooperation with the Thakin Party, had the following recollection of the Thakins:

> They also called themselves *thakins* (masters) in defiance of the colonialists who called themselves by that name when dealing with the Burmese; they read, when they did so, such Sinn Fein publications as Dam Bren's *I Fight for Freedom*, Sun Yat-sen's writings, Fabian books, and an assortment of contemporary political tracts; they sang everywhere they went a rousing racial song, the *Do Bama* song, which has now become the Burmese national anthem; they wove around that song and its simple nostalgic phrases a pure form of racialism; they used the current political techniques, demonstrations, slogans, and salutes, to capture the masses; they caught, by lashing out at the British and almost everyone and everything with Feinian ferocity, the mood of those among the youth and workers who had begun to be seized by the fever of the times in which they lived; and so they forged ahead."[18]

Although Ba Maw wrote that the Thakins "forged ahead," that was not necessarily the case. By the middle of the 1930s, a political split appeared within the Thakin Party between the Ba Sein faction and the Headquarters faction, making it difficult to consolidate leadership. Furthermore, colonial authorities initiated a sustained crackdown on the Freedom Block (made up of the Thakin Party, the Sinyetha Wunthanu, and the All-Burma Federation of Student Unions). Approximately 2,000 people affiliated with the party were arrested,[19] and an arrest warrant was issued for Aung San as well. It seemed that although the Thakin Party was expanding, it was proving extremely difficult to carry out a

---

[17] Kei Nemoto, "The Concepts of *Dobama* (Our Burma) and *Thudo-bama* (Their Burma) in Burmese Nationalism: 1930–1948," *The Journal of Burma Studies* 5 (2000).

[18] Ba Maw, *Breakthrough in Burma: Memoirs of a Revolution, 1939–1946* (New Haven: Yale University Press, 1968), p. 54.

[19] Kei Nemoto, *Aung San: Fuin sareta dokuritsu Biruma no yume* [Aung San: The sealed up dream of Burmese independence] (Tokyo: Iwanami, 1996), p. 91.

movement of social mobilization that openly criticized the authorities in an environment of restricted political freedom.

Unable to move forward with their strategy of social mobilization, there seemed to be only two options. The first was to participate in politics like the GCBA in the limited political arena allowed by the colonial ruler. The second option was to forcefully overthrow colonial rule through revolutionary means. Under Aung San's leadership, the Thakins chose the second option. They tried to find a way to obtain weapons and military training from the Chinese Nationalist Party (KMT), the Communist Party of China, and the National Congress in India. But all three foreign political forces declined their request.

It was at that moment, when it seemed that the Thakins could find no outside support for their violent opposition to the colonial ruler, that the Japanese Army approached the Thakin Party. The Japanese wanted to cut the Burma Road running from Upper Burma to Yunnan, China, because it was one of the main routes for supplying aid from the Allied Powers to Chiang Kai-shek's army. They saw the Thakin Party as a potentially helpful collaborator in undermining British influence in Burma. Without doubt, the encounter between the Japanese Army and the Thakins fundamentally changed the trajectory of Burma's political development.

Colonial Rule and Coercive Apparatus

The Thakins' conspiracy to revolt against the colonial order was, in fact, a reckless plan because the colonial ruler had effectively disarmed Burmese society. Disarmament and the monopolistic use of legitimate physical violence is a characteristic of the modern state, as we saw earlier in Weber's definition. The question of how the colonial ruler maintained order in Burma through the management of violence will be examined in this section, as we focus on the formation of the coercion apparatus of the state. This examination is necessary in order to understand the impact that the transition from a colonial to a post-colonial period had on the coercive apparatus of Burma.

The colonial coercive apparatus had two characteristics. First, security in colonial Burma was to be maintained cheaply. As noted earlier, Burma was not very important strategically or economically to the British, and the colonial ruler had to maintain internal security on limited resources. One strategy was the deployment of troops from India to Burma. Because Burma was a province integrated into British India, this was a logical and cost-effective measure as opposed to creating a new, separate military force. After the British abolished the Konbaung Dynasty in the Third Anglo-Burmese War, they had to contend with rebellions by the nobility and peasantry.[20] To reduce the burden on the Madras Army, which had been sent from India to keep order in the newly occupied area, three Burma Infantry battalions and the Burma Military Police (BMP) were formed.[21] Despite the name of "Burma," most of the soldiers in the troops were Punjabis recruited from Northwest India, and British officers of the Indian Army took the initiative in organizing the new troops. As a result, Burma's position as a province on the periphery of British India led to Indian officers and soldiers having important positions, and it was extremely rare for a native Bahman soldier to attain a leadership position in the army, especially before the 1920s. A facility for training military officers was never established in the Province of Burma.

The second characteristic of the coercive state apparatus in Burma was that it was set up in line with that created in India, which had developed two institutional traditions: "martial race" and "divide and rule." Many of the soldiers in the British Indian Army were recruited from the Punjab, the Northwest Frontier region, and Nepal. These regions were relatively less developed socio-economically compared to other regions in India, and the colonial ruler believed that men from these were in racial terms brave and physically robust. Thus, they were described as belonging to the "martial races."[22] In 1914 about three-quarters of the infantrymen

---

[20] Regarding rebellions against colonization, see James C. Scott, *The Moral Economy of the Peasant: Rebellion and Subsistence in Southeast Asia* (New Haven: Yale University Press, 1976); Michael Adas, *The Burma Delta: Economic Development and Social Change on An Asian Rice Frontier, 1852–1941* (Madison: University of Wisconsin Press, 1974); Toshikatsu Ito, "Biruma nomin no ishiki henka [Burmese farmers' change in awareness]," in *Kawaru Tonan Ajia shijou* [Changing image of Southeast Asian history], ed. Setsuho Ikehata (Tokyo: Yamakawa Press, 1994); Kenji Ino, "Myanma kokugun no seiji kainyu no ronri: 'Kokumin seiji' gainen wo chushin toshite [The logic of Myanmar army's intervention in politics: the concept of 'people's politics' being central]," *Tonan Ajia: rekishi to bunka* [Southeast Asia: history and culture] 29 (2000).

[21] The following description is mainly taken from Furnivall, *Colonial Policy and Practice*, pp. 178–84.

[22] Shigeru Akita, "Teikoku to guntai: Igirisu no shokuminchi shihai to Indo gun [Empire and army: British colonial rule and the indian army]," in *Chiiki no sekai-shi 11: Shihai no chiiki-shi* [A regional history of the world 11: the regional history of dominance], ed. Takeshi Hamashita and Minoru Kawakita (Tokyo: Yamakawa Press, 2000), p. 184.

in the British Indian Army's 552 infantry companies and 138 infantry battalions consisted of men from the "martial races."[23] In Burma, the Kachin and Chin people, the hill people, were seen as belonging to the "martial races."

Employing men of the "martial races" was also consistent with the principle of "divide and rule," which meant governing the majority race with the minority race(s). This "divide and rule" policy was adopted in Burma where the "martial races" were from the minority ethnic groups, notably the Karen, Kachin, and Chin, with the Karen being the most important. Far more officers and soldier in Burma were recruited from these ethnic groups. In 1941, after Burma's separation from British India in 1937, 4,782 Karen soldiers accounted for 17.1 per cent of the 27,981 soldiers serving in the British Burma Army, commonly known as, the Regular Army, and the National Border Defence Force, making it the largest ethnic group in the colonial military forces. Indeed, they accounted for 28.3 per cent of the soldiers in the Regular Army alone. By comparison there were 3,742 Bahman soldiers in Burma's colonial forces (13.4 per cent), 1,893 of them serving in the Regular Army, far fewer than the Karen. At that time, the Bahman population in the Province of Burma made up 65.7 per cent of the total population, meaning that there was a great disparity in the ethnic composition of the military. Following the Karen and the Bahman in the colonial forces were the Chin (2,607/9.3 per cent), the Kachin (2,125/7.6 per cent), and the Shan (1,080/3.9 per cent).[24]

The coercive state apparatus in Burma changed over the course of the colonial period. Immediately following the First Anglo-Burmese War in 1823–24, the British East India Company formed the Arakan Light Infantry. The force was ethnically composed of Arakanese, Chin, and Manipurese. A Talaing Corps, made up of Mon and Malays, was the next to be formed. These units were part of the local corps that the army of the British East India Company stationed around its territories, and their organization, training and uniforms were modelled on those of Indian regiments; their officers came from military units in Bengal and Madras. The Arakan Light Infantry took part in the Second Anglo-Burmese War in 1855, but following the Indian Rebellion in 1857, the British

[23] Ibid., p.182.

[24] These figures are from Robert Taylor, *The State in Burma* (Honolulu: University of Hawaii Press, 1987), p. 17.

reformed the military structure. The local corps system was abolished, and a portion of the corps was integrated into the police.

During the Third Anglo-Burmese War, Karen units were organized with the support of American missionaries. Until then the Madras Army was the only one deployed against the army of the Konbaung Dynasty. After the war, to reduce the burden on the Madras Army, three Burma infantry battalions (later known as the Burma Rifles) and the BMP were established. Although they bore the name "Burma," the composition of the units was not native at all. British officers from Indian regiments were sent to organize the units and initially they recruited soldiers from the "martial race" of the Punjab region. The first unit made up of natives was a battalion of Karen military police. Starting with this unit, the British Indian Army introduced class companies, a system it had employed in India, to Burma. The purpose of the class company system was to avoid confrontations between soldiers of different castes within the same company. The British had implemented this system out of concern for communal customs in India. Men were assigned to companies according to their place of origin and ethnic group or caste. In Burma, when the system was introduced, such class companies were comprised of hill people recruited primarily from Bhamo in the Kachin area. The only unit organized specifically for Bahman was a combat company made up of engineers and sappers, which was established in 1887.

During World War I, the Burma Rifles increased to four battalions, with commissioned and non-commissioned officers coming from the British Indian Army and the BMP. The battalions were formed based on the class company system and were made up of Burma-born soldiers, with the Karen forming the largest contingent followed by Bahman, Arakanese, Kachin, Chin, Shan, and Gurkhas. After the war, the Burma Rifles decreased to three battalions, and the recruitment of Bahman stopped in 1925. The three surviving battalions included two Karen companies, a Kachin company, and a Chin company. Meanwhile, the company of Bahman engineers and sappers was disbanded in 1927. Thereafter, the only way a Bahman could participate in the coercive apparatus in colonial Burma was to join the BMP, which originally had one battalion deployed in each district. Then, the number of battalions was reduced by half; in 1918 it decreased to 13, and later to 10 battalions. Clearly the colonial ruler was reluctant to mobilize Bahman for its coercive apparatus.

When the Province of Burma was separated from India in 1937, the Burma Rifles were also separated from the 20th Regiment of the British

Indian Army and again increased from three to four battalions. The company system was maintained within the battalions, and soldiers' affiliation in the army remained linked to their ethnic origins. The recruitment of Bahman resumed at this time. These new Bahman soldiers inevitably held lower ranks compared to other ethnic groups as rankings in the military depended on seniority and experience. Regarding the military police, which at the time was made up of nine battalions, three of these were stationed in Burma Proper (two in Rangoon and one in Mandalay), with the remaining six battalions incorporated into the Frontier Force.

As of 1939, the total strength of the defence forces consisted of roughly 12,000 men in the Frontier Force and the BMP and 5,000 in the Regular Army. The Regular Army was made up of the four battalions of the Burma Rifles and two British infantry battalions. In 1939, when Britain went to war against Germany, nine more battalions were added to the Burma Rifles for a total of 13. This expansion necessitated the recruiting of more native soldiers. As a result, the ethnic composition of the forces was no longer limited to mostly Gurkhas, Indians, Sikhs, Punjabis and Karens; many were now newly recruited Bahman and Shan.

Another Empire, a Returned Empire, and Independence

In East Asia, Japan's expanding war in China following the Marco Polo Bridge Incident in 1937 turned into a quagmire. In 1939 Germany invaded Poland, and World War II broke out in Europe. With Europe at war, thus weakening its countries' ability to rule their colonies in Southeast Asia, Japan set its sights on the region, primarily as a way of securing a supply of natural resources. In September 1940, the Japanese Army marched into northern French Indochina, the first step in its southward advance. In January 1942 it invaded Burma, and by June of that year it had gained control of nearly the entire territory. As was the case in Indonesia and the Philippines, the colonial order was swept away by Japanese military rule, and, after a short period of turmoil, a completely new order emerged.[25] In both political and economic terms, Burma faced

[25] See Benedict R.O.G. Anderson, *Java in a Time of Revolution: Occupation and Resistance, 1944–1946* (Ithaca: Cornell University Press, 1972); Alfred W. McCoy, ed., *Southeast Asia under Japanese Occupation* (New Haven: Yale University, Southeast Asia Program, 1980); Paul H. Kratoska, *The Japanese Occupation of Malaya: A Social and Economic History* (London: Hurst, 1998).

a tumultuous period from the time of the Japanese invasion until the 1950s. The discussion in this section centres on three main aspects of this period. The first concerns the impact of the Japanese occupation on the political development of Burma. The second highlights the institutional transformation of the coercive apparatus, with an emphasis on the return of the British to Burma. And the third examines civil-military relations after 1948.

The Japanese Occupation

The Japanese occupation of Burma brought about three fundamental changes to the nation, the state and its coercive apparatus. The first was the partial dismantling of the British system of colonial rule. The colonial army almost completely disappeared from the territory of Burma, and the self-government that ethnic minorities had enjoyed since British colonization was abolished. The Japanese Army also disallowed and quickly disbanded the provisional administrative organizations that the Thakin party members had set up throughout the country in the wake of the invasion. The Japanese then appointed Dr. Ba Maw, who had been imprisoned by the British, as prime minister, and, under him they set up an occupation government that kept in place the colonial administrative structure and personnel. Thus while the system for administering colonial rule remained, it was now under the control of the Japanese Army. However, the Japanese did not retain the colonial Legislature, and GCBA-affiliated politicians in that body lost their significance and purpose, which was the authority to legislate. Sidelined during the war, most of these pre-war politicians played no significant role in the political process following the Japanese occupation. Instead, Dr. Ba Maw began cooperating with Thakin activists who had rejected the pragmatic strategy pursued by the GCBA of participating in the colonial legislature.

The second main structural change to the nation, the state and its coercive apparatus resulting from the Japanese occupation was social mobilization. In contrast to the British who actively sought to avoid social mobilization, the Japanese Army actively engaged in it. The Thakins had stayed out of colonial parliamentary politics, and instead focused efforts on mobilizing the masses and expanding their social base because their political goal was independence for Burma and the end of colonial rule. They did not believe it possible to achieve their goal of creating a completely independent nation-state by working through a legislature controlled by a colonial power. However, given their lack of resources and an environment conducive to mobilizing the population, their strategy of social mobilization was faltering. Accepting the Japanese army's offer of help in 1941 was something of a last resort for Aung San and his Thakin compatriots.[26] Against expectations, this last-ditch effort proved successful, leading to the formation of the Miniami Kikan (南機関), an espionage unit targeting Burma under the command of Colonel Keiji Suzuki sent from Imperial General Headquarters. The major members of the Thakin Party (later known as the "Thirty Comrades") received training at a Japanese naval base on Hainan Island. From there they proceeded to Bangkok where they formed the Burma Independence Army (BIA) led by the Japanese. In 1942, the BIA together with the 2nd Division of the Japanese 15th Army began to invade Burma.

Although the BIA was nominally an army, in fact, it was actually the military wing of the Thakin Party. Building on popular support, the BIA took steps to expand its organization rapidly and organized provisional administration committees in areas it moved into after dismantling the colonial administration. However, the Japanese Army, intent on setting up it own military rule, kept a vigilant eye on the BIA's actions and quickly shut down the provisional administration committees. Yet within two months of the Japanese invasion, the BIA grew to over 10,000 men, making it difficult for the Japanese to maintain full control over the organization. As the BIA's dissatisfaction with the existing order and social conditions grew, clashes broke out between Bahmans and Indians, and Bahmans and Karens in Rangoon and parts of the delta.[27] Consequently, in an effort to control the young nationalists, the Japanese reorganized the BIA into the smaller and more institutionalized Burma Defence Army (BDA).

---

[26] In August 1940, Aung San, then Secretary-General of the Thakin Party, escaped to Amoy in Japanese-occupied China after learning that a warrant had been issued for his arrest. See Kei Nemoto, "Biruma no Dokuritsu: Nihon Senryoki kara U Nu Jidai made [The Independence of Burma: From the Japanese Occupation to U Nu Era]," in *Iwanami Koza Tonan Ajia shi dai 8 kan: Kokumin Kokka Keisei no Jizai* [Iwanami course on the history of Southeast Asia, vol. 8, The era of nation-state building]," ed. Kanichi Goto (Tokyo: Iwanami, 2002), p. 176.

[27] On ethnic conflict, see Ba Maw, *Breakthrough in Burma: Memoirs of a Revolution, 1939–1946* (New Haven: Yale University Press, 1968), pp. 194–222; Kazuto Ikeda, "Nippon senryo-ki Biruma niokeru Myangmya jiken to Karen: Shwe Tun Kya wo meguru minzoku-teki keiken ni-tuite [The Myaungmya incident and the Karens under Japanese occupation in Burma: the Karen's experience through that of Shwe Tun Kya]," *Tonan Aji: rekishi to bunka* [*Southeast Asia – History and Culture*], p. 34 (2005).

If the Japanese Army's goal was to curtail the influence of young nationalists, it should have restricted social mobilization by the various political forces in Burmese society rather than intervene directly in the BIA's organization. However, instead of taking steps to guard against social mobilization, the Japanese actively formed mass-mobilization organizations such as the Do Bama Sinyetha Association, the East Asia Youth League (EAYL), and *Keibotai* (civil defense units).[28] Thus, despite the efforts of the Japanese Army to reorganize and bring greater control over the native military forces, Aung San and his Thakin followers were able to gather support through mass-mobilization organizations formed by the Japanese, and their influence on society kept growing.[29] For Aung San and the Thakins, it was not the BIA's military capability that was important for their political purpose, but rather its ability to gather popular support. In concrete terms, the BIA derived its strength from the number of Burmese who knew Aung San's name, listened to his speeches, and passed his message onto others. As long as social mobilization continued and Aung San was seen by more and more people as a national hero, the Japanese Army would not be able to maintain control.

The third fundamental change that the Japanese occupation brought to the nation, the state and its coercive apparatus was the rise of the politics of mobilization. Aung San's strategy of mobilization proved successful because it took place during the power vacuum between the transition from British colonial rule to Japanese military occupation. Nationalistic youths joined the BIA and the Thakin Party and took up arms in a struggle for independence or national liberation. More than simply participating in an army or a political party, they were contributing to the greater cause of revolution first against colonial rule and then against the Japanese. Thus the reorganization of the BIA did not resulting in weakening Aung San's political power despite its organizational downsizing.

BDA was established in August 1942 as the army of the state under the command of the Japanese Army with Aung San as its commander

---

[28] Guyot, Dorothy, "The Political Impact of the Japanese Occupation of Burma," PhD dissertation, Yale University, 1966, p. 275.

[29] On the relationship of the Thakin Party with mass mobilization organizations like the East Asia Youth Federation, see Takeshima Yoshinari, *Nippon senryo to Biruma no minzoku undo: Thakin seiryoku no seji-teki josho* [Japan's occupation and people's movements in Burma: the Political rise of Thakin power] (Tokyo: Ryukei Shosha, 2003).

along with 3,000 former BIA members. Unlike the BIA, however, this military force was organized under a specific law, the "Order for Organization of the Burma Defence Army (ビルマ防衛軍組織令)" (issued on 9 August 1942). It also had organizational regulations, an officer training school, and a salary system based on rank. Consequently, although Aung San was not allowed to mobilize people as he did when he led the BIA, the organizational reform consolidated his political power *vis-à-vis* the Japanese Army because a formal law stipulated his authority as commander (and later as Defence Minister in Ba Maw's administration). On the other hand, his collaboration with the Japanese was also risky as his position made him vulnerable to criticism. One of the principal critics of Aung San's "pro-Japanese stance" was the Burma Communist Party (BCP), which at the time was actively striving to expand its membership.

Under the circumstances, Aung San maintained his influence as a coordinator among competing political forces. In this regard, one of his most important achievements was uniting two major competing political groups, the BCP and the People's Revolution Party (PRP). In August 1944, under Aung San's leadership, the two groups came together with the BDA to form the Anti-Fascist Organization (AFO), a united front that later became known as the Anti-Fascist People's Freedom League (AFPFL). On 27 March 1945, with the invasion of the Allied Powers from India pushing deeper into Burma, the AFO launched its anti-Japanese struggle.

The Return of the British

In May 1945 the Allied Powers captured Rangoon, and in August of that year the Empire of Japan accepted the Potsdam Declaration which called for its unconditional surrender. In October of that year, Reginald Dorman-Smith was appointed governor-general of Burma, and British rule returned to Burma. As British and nationalist leaders bargained over Burma as a post-war state, the transition period between the time of the British return until independence in 1948 marked an important turning point in political developments in Burma. One of the most significant developments during this transition period was the creation of a new Burmese military.

On 6 and 7 August 1945, shortly before Japan's surrender, Admiral Louis Mountbatten from South-East Asia Command (SEAC), British army commanders, and Aung San and other Patriotic Burmese Forces (PBF) leaders held talks in Kandy, Ceylon, to discuss forming a new military for post-war Burma.[30] The talks became known as the Kandy Conference, and, under the resulting Kandy Agreement, the Allied Powers and Aung San agreed on a plan to integrate the Regular Army, whose forces had retreated with the British to India, and the PBF. The plan involved the formation of a new army, the tatmadaw, of 12,000 officers and soldiers; as part of the agreement, a minimum of 200 officers and 5,000 soldiers were to be from the PBF.[31]

This reorganization meant the integration of two potentially clashing organizations: the colonial army and the anti-colonial army. In order to avoid conflicts within the tatmadaw, the colonial army's class company system was scaled up to form class battalions. Under the class battalion system, the new army was basically comprised of ethnically segregated infantry battalions. As the Regular Army was primarily made up of ethnic minorities while the PBF was comprised of mostly Bahman, the adoption of the class battalion system meant that units of the Regular Army and those of the PBF would be assigned to different units of the new army. Thus this institutional arrangement was the result of a compromise between the British and Aung San. The British wanted to integrate the officers and soldiers of both militaries into the new army, while Aung San's aim was to continue consolidating the PBF by keeping its original units intact within the new army.

Louis Mountbatten of SEAC advocated inclusion of the PBF into the new army based on his perception that growing Burmese nationalism was irreversible. In order to re-establish stability in Burma, Mountbatten considered it essential to co-opt Aung San, the PBF, and the AFPFL into the British-run government. Therefore, he offered Aung San the position of Deputy Inspector General (DIG), which was next in rank to the British Inspector General who would direct the new military. As Aung San and the PBF were the leader and the central organization of the AFPFL, respectively, appointing Aung San the DIG and incorporating the PBF into the new army would make it possible for the British to capitalize on their popularity, while at the same time maintaining British control. The move can be seen as a first step by the British to restrain nationalist

---

30 In March 1945 the BDA renamed itself the Burma Nationalist Army (BNA), which then became the Patriotic Burma Force (PBF) in June 1945.

31 For additional information on the Kandy Agreement, see Mary Callahan, *Making Enemies: War and State Building in Burma* (Ithaca: Cornell University Press, 2003), Chapter 4.

social mobilization and disarm the society. But Aung San turned down the British offer to be DIG and decided to focus on his role as chairman of the AFPFL. He then was able to create a political foundation for national unity in his own way, rather than the way that the British intended.

In London Aung San led negotiations with the governor of British Burma, Major General Hubert Rance (who had replaced Dorman-Smith in 1946), and secured consent for Burma's independence through the Aung San-Atlee Agreement on 27 January 1947. After returning home, he held discussions with leaders of ethnic groups and assured them that Burma Proper and the Frontier Area would jointly become an independent state under federalism (as stipulated by the Panron Agreement). In the election for the Constituent Assembly on 9 April 1947, the AFPFL recorded an overwhelming victory, winning 176 of the total 182 seats. Just three months later, the momentum of this victory was cut short when Aung San and six members of the executive council were assassinated during a cabinet meeting on 19 July 1947. Aung San's position was taken over by U Nu, Deputy Chairman of the AFPFL.

Though irreplaceable, Aung San's leadership had relied mainly on his ability to coordinate interests among the elite, which was not sufficient to rebuild the post-war state and bring about a stable social order. The dissolution of the PBF is a case in point. According to the Kandy Agreement, the PBF was to be dissolved, but only a portion of its officers and soldiers would be selected for the tatmadaw. For discharged PBF members and for dissolving the PBF smoothly, Aung San set up a support organization called the People's Volunteer Organization (PVO). However, the new organization failed to disarm former PBF members, and the PVO soon turned into an armed organization.[32] Meanwhile, a faction of the Burma Communist Party rose up in rebellion after the party was expelled from the AFPFL in 1946, and, in 1947, the rest of the party boycotted the elections for the Constituent Assembly. These groups did not accept the new official political institutions and continued to mobilize for social revolution. Compounding the already unstable situation was the fact that a consensus on federalism could not be worked out with the Karen, the most powerful ethnic minority group.

---

[32] It seems that Aung San intended to arm and organize the PVO. It is not clear, however, whether this was his aim from the beginning or if it was his back-up plan after he realized how difficult it would be to disarm its members.

Independence: Euphoria and then Instability

On 4 January 1948 the Union Jack was taken down from government buildings and a new national flag was raised. The new flag had a large white star surrounded by five small stars in a blue square in the top left-hand corner against a red background. The large star signified the nine divisions where the majority of the population was Bahman, and the five stars represented the four states and one special division where the majority of the population were non-Bahman ethnic groups. With the raising of this new flag, the Union of Burma became independent. The 1947 Constitution provided for a republic and a bicameral union Parliament comprised of the Chamber of Nationalities and the Chamber of Deputies. As a nation-state based on federalism, state councils were set up in the Parliament for the Shan State, the Kachin State, the Karen State, the Karenni State, and the Chin Special Division, which consisted of parliament members from the constituencies of each state. The discussion that follows will examine the course that Burma's nation-state and coercive apparatus took from independence until 1962 in dealing with the many contentious forces the country confronted.

When Burma became independent, less than three years after the Pacific War, it was clear that the state lacked sufficient strength to cope with the many conflicts in its society. Immediately after independence, it was pushed to the brink of breakup. In the Parliament, the AFPFL occupied an overwhelming majority of the seats, which made decision-making easier for state leaders. But outside the Parliament, there were many people who refused to recognize the 1947 Constitution; these included the Red- and White-Flag communist parties that were seeking a social revolution, the Mujahids, who were attempting to establish an Islamic state in west of Arakan, the PVO, and the Karen National Union (KNU).

In March of 1946 a faction calling itself the Red-Flag Communist Party led by Thakin Soe split from the BCP went underground to start an armed struggle. The remaining Communist Party members (who later formed the White-Flag Communist Party) led by Thakin Than Tun went underground in March of 1948, and on 2 April, only three months after independence, started an uprising in Pegu District. These communists saw Burma as a quasi-colonial and quasi-feudalistic society, and their objective was to carry out a revolution through rural guerrilla warfare.[33]

---

[33] Bertil Lintner, *The Rise and Fall of the Communist Party of Burma (CPB)* (Ithaca, N.Y.: Southeast Asia Program, Cornell University, 1990), p. 14.

With a force of 15,000 fighters, they took up arms under the name of the "People's Liberation Army of Burma." The uprising later spread to areas of the delta cities such as Myingyan and Bassein. On 28 July the PVO revolted, and its clashes with the Karen in the delta region led to other conflicts between the Karen and Bahman in that region. Tensions reached a boiling point when the Karen National Defence Organization (KNDO), the military wing of the KNU, attacked an armoury in Insein and a government financial depository in Maubin. In response, the tatmadaw burned an American Baptist mission school. The KNDO was outlawed in January 1949.[34]

The outbreak of civil war was a blow to the domestic economy, making it even more difficult for the government to collect tax revenues. The rate of land tax collection by the government gradually decreased from 30 per cent in 1945 to 25 per cent in 1948 and to 13 per cent in 1949.[35] The year following independence, government workers' salaries were cut. In response to this measure, in February 1949, the All Burma Government Workers Union carried out a nationwide strike. Not only was the state losing control of society, but the state system itself was no longer functioning efficiently. Later that year, the KNDO occupied Insein, a suburb of Rangoon city, and it was feared that they would take over the capital.[36]

The crisis also destabilized the tatmadaw, causing internal cracks to resurface. Among former PBF officers in the army, the cracks were evident between Socialist Party (SP) supporters and those of the BCP. After the Red- and White-Flag communists rebelled, the BCP supporters in the army were compelled to demonstrate violently which flag they followed. The 6th Burma Rifles Battalion stationed in Pegu revolted on 24 June 1948, and many soldiers of the battalion joined the BCP. Then the 3rd Burma Rifles Battalion attempted a coup, but failed, and together with the 1st Burma Rifles Battalion, joined the rebellions of the BCP and the PVO.[37] Some of the federal military police, many of whom were from the PBF, also joined the rebellions.

---

[34] Hugh Tinker, *The Union of Burma: a Study of the First Years of Independence*, 2nd ed. (London: Oxford University Press, 1959), Chapter 2.

[35] Callahan, *Making Enemies*, p. 117.

[36] U Nu, *Saturday's Sun* (New Haven: Yale University Press, 1975), pp. 185–7.

[37] For details about the attempted coup and rebellion by the 3rd Burma Rifles Battalion, see the interview with then-Colonel Chit Myaing that appeared in *Burma Debate* <http://www.burmadebate.org/archives/julaug97bttm. html#Colonel> [accessed 20 March 2009].

Ethnic conflicts also spread within the army. The army included a number of minority groups like the Karen, Kachin, and Chin. Among the Karen were many former officers of the Regular Army who were given key posts by the British Services Mission (BSM), which was advising the new military in accordance with the Britain-Burma Defence Agreement that was ended after the Aung San-Atlee Agreement. One of the most prominent Karen officers was General Smith Dun, the first Chief of General Staff of the tatmadaw. Dun was a member of the first graduating class of the Indian Military Academy, which started native officer training in October 1932 in Dehradun, India. Following graduation, he spent most of his career in the BMP.[38] Because officers like Dun were trained as professional military officers who spent their careers in the BMP or the Regular Army, there was little doubt that they were far more professional than the former PBF officers who joined the army for the purpose of attaining national liberation. Moreover, many of the former PBF officers were younger, so it was not unusual for them to hold lower level positions in the tatmadaw where promotions were closely linked to seniority.

Regarding the professionalism of the military, in his biography Dun writes, "When Burma gained her independence in 1948, the Karens were well placed in the defence services and in their own right, not through any political pressure or string[s]." And after describing examples of outstanding Karen officers, he goes on to say, "With the exception of one or two who were wartime officers," most officers "had services ranging from fifteen to twenty-five years." Hence, Dun "claims it to be the Karen's own right to be in that position on Burma gaining Independence."[39] This citation indicates the difference of perception between former officers of the colonial army and those of the PBF. For Dun, the rightness of the Karen officers' position in the tatmadaw was based on seniority and experience, which were basic criteria for promotion in a modern bureaucratic military. But this reasoning did not convince the former PBF officers because to them the right criteria for promotion were more political. Unlike Karen officers, former PBF officers, having born the

[38] Regarding Dun, see Smith Dun, *Memoirs of the Four-Foot Colonel* (Ithaca: Southeast Asia Program, Department of Asian Studies, Cornell University, 1980).
[39] Dun, *Memoirs of the Four-Foot Colonel*, p. 115.

brunt of the battle for independence, were proud and confident of their wartime experience.[40]

Soon this intra-military disagreement became connected with social conflicts. To counter the threat of a Karen-led rebellion, Prime Minister U Nu ordered the disarmament of all Karens, including those in the tatmadaw. On 1 February 1949 most Karens in the army, officers and soldiers alike, were stripped of their ranks, temporarily held in a detention camp, then expelled from the tatmadaw. General Smith Dun, the Chief of General Staff, and Saw Kya Doe, the ex-Vice Chief of General Staff (Army), along with other former colonial military officers, left the tatmadaw and were replaced by officers from the PBF. The office of the Chief of General Staff was taken over by the Vice Chief of General Staff (Army), General Ne Win. This shift in military leadership was crucial for future political developments in Burma because Ne Win went on to lead the tatmadaw for 25 years.

A brief examination of Ne Win's life and career until his promotion to the highest position of the tatmadaw helps illustrate his character as a political leader. Ne Win was born the son of Boe Hka, a tax inspector, in present day Prome District, Pegu Division on 14 May 1911. His original name was Shu Maung, and he grew up in Paungdale in Prome District. Following his graduation from high school, he went on to study at Rangoon University in June 1929 with the aim of becoming a medical doctor. However, he was forced to drop out because he failed a biology exam at the end of his sophomore year. In 1930, during the time he was enrolled in college, the Saya San Rebellion broke out, which mainly affected Lower Burma, and student-organized nationalistic movements also developed on campuses. While a student, Shu Maung did not take an interest in political movements, but after dropping out of college and working for the postal service, he gradually became involved in politics, which led him to join the Thakin Party where he aligned himself with the Ba Sein faction. He was not particularly important in the party, and it is highly likely that people who knew him during that time never

[40] Exacerbating the friction between the two sides was a perception among the former PBF officers and some politicians in the parliament that the unequal treatment between the two groups represented a conflict between imperialists or rightists (Karen officers) and anti-imperialists or leftists (former PBF officers). See Callahan, *Making Enemies*, pp. 130–5.

imagined that one day Shu Maung would become the top leader of the state.

A series of events altered the course of Shu Maung's life and that of the nation. He was one of the Burmese nationalists selected by the Japanese for military training who became known as the "Thirty Comrades." In 1941, as a member of this group, he secretly left for Japan and then went on to Hainan Island where he received training at the Japanese military's naval base in San-a on the southern coast of the island. While training on Hainan, Shu Maung began using the Japanese name, Shin Takasugi (高杉晋). In Japanese "Takasugi" means "Tall Cedar Tree," and the name referred to his height (Shu Maung was the tallest in the group) and recalled the name of the famous samurai Shinsaku Takasugi (高杉晋作).[41] Later when the BIA was organizing in Bangkok in December 1941, all of the Thirty Comrades were given new names to protect their identity after the invasion of Burma. Thus, Shu Maung became Bo Ne Win ("Bo" being "military officer" and "Ne Win" meaning "Radiant Sun"). As a lieutenant colonel assigned to a detachment whose mission was to conduct guerrilla operations behind enemy lines, he entered Burma on 24 January 1942, just days after the Japanese invasion began.[42] After the Japanese Army had occupied Burma, it reduced the size of the BIA and reorganized it into the BDA in which Ne Win served as the commander (lieutenant colonel) of the 1st Battalion. When the Burmese army turned against the Japanese in March 1945, Ne Win served as the commander (colonel) of the Second Administrative Division, which covered Hanthawaddy, Pyapon, and Maubin districts.

Following the war, Ne Win became the commander of the 4th Burma Rifles Battalion of Burma's new army. Soon after that he was promoted to commander of the Northern Military Region where he celebrated the independence of the Union of Burma on 4 January 1948. On 1 August of that year, he assumed the post of Vice Chief of General Staff (Army) (Brigadier General). Then in January 1949, he became Chief of General Staff of the tatmadaw following the dismissal of Smith Dun.

---

[41] Maung Maung, *Burma and General Ne Win* (New York: Asia Publishing House, 1969), p. 87.

[42] Ohno Toru, "Biruma Kokugunshi (Sono 1) [History of the Burmese Army (1)]," *Tonan Ajia Kenkyu* 8, no. 2 (1970): 247.

At the time, Ne Win was only 37 years old, and his assumption of the highest position in the tatmadaw made clear where leadership resided within military politics.[43]

As Burma's new military organization grappled with internal ethnic and political conflicts, an external threat to the state arose. In January 1949 a Chinese Nationalist Party (Kuomintang: KMT) army entered from Yunnan Province occupying Kengtung, Kokang, and the eastern part of Shan State known as Wa. From an initial force of 200 men, the KMT army expanded to 12,000 by 1952. In 1953 the Burmese army undertook a large-scale campaign called "Victory Dragon" (*nàgâ nâin*) to suppress the KMT forces but was defeated within a few weeks. This campaign would come to be known as "Loser Dragon" (*nàgâ shôun*).[44] The tatmadaw's poor showing resulted in moves by the military leaders and politicians to modernize it. The aim of this military modernization was to restrain intra-military politics and develop the tatmadaw as an autonomous, centralized bureaucratic organization. As will be detailed in the next chapter, starting in the mid-1950s, the tatmadaw would undergo reform starting with the expansion of the General Staff Office.

But in 1949 and 1950, when the threat from the KMT army was still incipient, the young state of Burma was struggling to survive, with government authority over the country reduced to the point where for a time it was referred to as the "Rangoon Government." The area under the government's control gradually expanded, and, in June 1951, Burma successfully held its first general election, and the AFPFL became the ruling party with an overwhelming victory. The AFPFL held onto its ruling-party status in the second general election in April 1956, while the National United Front (NUF), the largest opposition party alliance, increased its number of seats in parliament. Following these two elections, it appeared outwardly that parliamentary democracy had been

---

[43] The summary dismissal of Karen officers weakened the tatmadaw as a combat force, because the military lost 10,885 officers and soldiers only a year after independence. Consequently, it was a particularly severe blow to Burma's military. See Callahan, *Making Enemies*, p. 138.

[44] The KMT army was receiving aid from the American CIA. There is still little known about American espionage operations in Burma. One study on the topic is Kumada Toru, "Myanma no minshuka to kokumin togo mondai niokeru gaisei yoin: Beikoku koshiki kiroku ni miru shijitsu wo chushin toshite [Democratization in Myanmar and exogenous factors affecting integration of the people: based on historical facts recorded in the official records of the U.S.]," *Ajia Kenkyu* (*Asian Studies*) 47, no. 3 (2001): 1–27.

established in Burma.[45] In fact, however, it had reached a stalemate for several reasons.

First, the AFPFL's long hold on power did not lead to stable leadership and party organization building; on the contrary, the country experienced significant instability caused by rivalry and division among the AFPFL leaders. After Aung San's assassination, the AFPFL was guided by four leaders: U Nu, Ba Swe, Kyaw Nyein, and Thakin Tin, all of whom had been involved in the AFPFL since the struggle for independence. In the beginning, they adopted a collective leadership system with U Nu as prime minister, a position he held from July 1947 until June 1956, and Ba Swe as leader of the SP, the largest group within the AFPFL. However, over the course of his long premiership, U Nu's actions grew increasingly autocratic, leading to increased conflict with Ba Swe and Kyaw Nyein.[46] Following U Nu's speech criticizing Marxism at the AFPFL convention in January 1958, the AFPFL split into two factions, one calling itself the Clean AFPFL (led by U Nu and Thakin Tin) and the other, the Stable AFPFL (under Ba Swe and Kyaw Nyein).

The Stable faction consisted of the Socialist Party under Ba Swe and had more Parliament members than the Clean faction. In order to regain the prime minister's office (which he did in March 1957), U Nu entered into a cooperative relationship with the NUF, the largest opposition party. The NUF was ideologically close to the BCP, and U Nu's action stimulated anti-communist sentiment in the military. This became one of the major factors that led to the military's intervention and organization of a caretaker government headed by General Ne Win between September 1958 and March 1960.

The second reason for the dysfunction of democracy in Burma was that the 1947 Constitution created an institutional obstacle to a pluralistic democracy based on federalism. Burma adopted a limited federalism to compensate for the numerical disadvantage of the minority ethnic groups. Instead of local legislative organs, State Councils for Shan State, Kachin State, Karen State, Karenni State and Chin Special Division were

---

[45] In the second general election, the AFPFL took 173 out of the total of 250 seats, while the NUF won 47 seats.

[46] There have been some good studies on U Nu and AFPFL politics of the 1950s. See for example Hugh Tinker, *The Union of Burma: a Study of the First Years of Independence*, 2nd ed. (London: Oxford University Press, 1959); John S. Furnivall, *The Governance of Modern Burma*, 2nd ed. (New York: Institute of Pacific Relations, 1960); Richard Butwell, *U Nu of Burma* (Stanford: Stanford University Press, 1969).

made up of Parliament members from the states, and the minister in charge of each state was appointed from within the union (i.e., national) parliament. Legislative and administrative authority related to the ethnic minority states was granted to these councils (Chapter 4 of the 1947 Constitution). Since this situation actually limited the autonomy of the states, ethnic minority politicians increased their efforts to obtain greater autonomy for their own states. The Constitution itself provided for the right of secession to some ethnic minority states after ten years following its enforcement. Article 202 stated: "The right of secession shall not be exercised within ten years from the date on which this Constitution comes into operation." Citing this article, in 1958, Shan State and Karenni State representatives were able to negotiate for broader self-government. In Shan State in particular, whose former *sawbwas* (traditional rulers among the Shan) were politically influential in parliament, there was growing demand for greater autonomy.

The third reason for the dysfunction of democracy was that electoral politics aroused social unrest mainly due to U Nu's electoral strategy. As mentioned earlier, following the Clean-Stable split within the AFPFL, U Nu and his faction entered into a cooperative relationship with the NUF and other leftists, which heightened the tatmadaw's concern. Even during the caretaker government led by Ne Win (28 October 1958 to 4 April 1960), U Nu did not adjust his position, although he did desperately attempt to expand the base of his popular support in the election campaign for the third general election to take place in 1960. He not only criticized the tatmadaw's political intervention in the name of caretaker government, but also openly advocated making Buddhism the state's official religion in his next administration.[47] Furthermore he called for the establishment of states for Arakan and Mon people, who had not gained their own state in the 1947 Constitution. While U Nu's favoring of a particular religion and ethnic minorities drew the support of some groups, his brand of populism was enough to make some people, the tatmadaw leaders particularly, nervous about his potential for promoting social instability and undermining national unity. Seemingly oblivious to the danger that it was creating, U Nu pursued his populist strategy, which proved effective, as his Union Party (the renamed Clean AFPFL faction) emerged victorious in the February 1960 election.

---

[47] Butwell, *U Nu of Burma*, Chapter 7.

Conclusion

The state of Burma was formed on the periphery of Britain's Indian Empire. British colonial rule in Burma sought to maintain order through the introduction of a modern, rational administration and by limiting indigenous autonomy. Burma's geopolitical position was crucial to state formation, because given its location on the periphery of the empire; the British did not require a strong state. Instead they sought to maintain their colonial rule in as cheap a way as possible. To achieve this end, the administrative practices applied to Burma were those employed in India despite the social differences between the two. In accordance with these practices, bureaucrats of the British Indian Empire held authoritarian sway over most areas of Burma. In addition, the separate system of ruling Burma proper from that of the frontier areas and favouring the use of ethnic minorities in the coercive apparatus based on the principles of "martial race" and "divide and rule" to control the majority Bahman had implications for future ethnic conflict. All of these factors affected state formation in Burma.

Colonial rule also introduced new political ideas which produced modern politics in Burma. During the colonial era, the British kept a close watch on social movements that grew out of nationalism, communism, and anarchism. By contrast, the Japanese Empire unintentionally allowed these movements to flourish. Thakin party members who had been trained by the Japanese Army took the initiative in the national liberation struggle against the British Empire and the Japanese Empire and largely replaced the conventional politicians of the colonial era. In essence, the British Indian Empire built a modern state and helped the national awakening in Burma while the Japanese Empire, during its occupation, undermined the state's functions and at the same time provided an opportunity for young Burmese nationalists to mobilize popular support for their political purpose: independence from colonial rule. Burma's independence was a result of Aung San's charisma and ability to coordinate different interests among elites. However, such an ability was not in itself sufficient to resolve the social conflicts that the war generated.

The tatmadaw was a product of two empires. While its modern bureaucratic organization derived from the state building of the British Indian Empire, its leadership and legitimacy were created by the social mobilization of the Japanese Empire. General Ne Win developed its organization, discipline, and political orientation in the 1950s in the wake of the intra-military conflict between the former Regular Army officers (mainly Karen) and the former PBF officers (mainly Bahman).

Burma's parliament democracy did not work well. The split in the AFPFL in 1958 was a critical moment. It pushed U Nu to ally with leftist groups in the Parliament and to adopt populist strategies in the election. Unstable party politics created distrust of democracy within the tatmadaw, while the demand for autonomy by ethnic minorities was mounting. To many in Burma, it seemed that the parliamentary democracy was no longer the optimal way to solve the intractable conflicts inflicting the country. The coup d'état of 1962 led by Ne Win was in response to this seeming failure of parliament democracy and crisis of national unity.

CHAPTER 3

The Origin of "the Burmese Way to Socialism:" Formation of State Ideology and Military Politics

One of the peculiarities of the Ne Win regime is that it was a leftist military regime, which stood in marked contrast to the right-wing military-led governments in power in Southeast Asia at the time. The Sarit-Thanom regime in Thailand, whose rule began in 1957, and that of General Suharto in Indonesia were both staunch right-wing military regimes that adopted suppressive policies against communists and other leftist groups, as most military governments do. By contrast, Burma's military regime led by Ne Win was markedly different. Although it saw communist insurgents as the main enemies to national security, the Ne Win regime adopted policies that were clearly leftist. These were expressed through a Burmese type of socialism, which was outlined in the policy declaration, *The Burmese Way to Socialism*, issued on 30 April 1962. This chapter will focus on the formation of the state's ideology under the Ne Win regime, seeking to answer why and how Ne Win chose to establish a leftist military government.

The two main documents ideologically underpinned the Ne Win regime: (i) the Revolutionary Council's policy declaration: *The Burmese Way to Socialism* (*myanmà hsosheli' lânzin*) (hereafter called *The Way*) and (ii) the Burma Socialist Programme Party's official ideology: *The System of Correlation between Man and His Environment* (*lu hnin' pa'wânkyindò ì innyà minnyà dabôthàyâ*) (hereafter called *The System)*. The literature on these two documents regards them as products of Burmese nationalism with ideological roots that go back to the Thakin Party of the 1930s. Robert Taylor, for example, finds in *The Way* and *The System* a similar rhetoric to that of the Thakin Party,[1] and David Steinberg emphasizes that both documents "clearly were in the Burmese tradition, appealing to and melding the three central concepts in modern Burman life — nationalism, socialism, and Buddhism."[2] These studies assume that the ideological foundation of Ne Win's regime followed a linear path of ideological development in Burmese nationalism since the early twentieth century. Indeed, many top military officers, including Ne Win, were former Thakin party members, and so it is hardly surprising that the policy declarations issued after the tatmadaw's takeover of the state were in a discourse which was familiar to them. Yet, the relationship between nationalism, socialism, and Buddhism in the political discourse of Burma was far more complex than the literature suggests.

One example of this complex relationship concerns the frequently used Buddhist terminology in *The System*. In 1963, the year after the Ne Win regime took power, Dr. Ba Maw, a conservative nationalist since pre-independence days, commented in *The Guardian* newspaper as follows:

> Basically, the [Revolutionary] Council has done the right thing. But what, as I see it, is wrong about this is that a common error has been repeated of confusing race with religion and religion with society, and so turning religio-metaphysical speculations into social truths and laws. In this way, a social philosophy based upon laws and conditions

---

[1] Robert Taylor, *The State in Burma* (Honolulu: University of Hawaii Press, 1987a), pp. 296–7.

[2] David I. Steinberg, *Burma: A Socialist Nation of Southeast Asia* (Boulder: Westview Press, 1982), p. 76. For further information, see John W. Wiant, "Ideology and Organization in Revolutionary Burma" (final draft), an unpublished PhD dissertation, Cornell University, 1982; Ryuji Okudaira, "Kokumin Togo no Seiji Shiso: Biruma-teki Shakaishugi-ron [Political thought of national integration: Burmese way to socialism]," in *Koza Tonan Ajia-gaku Dai-rokkan Tonan Ajia no Shiso* [Southeast Asian studies, vol. 6, the ideas of Southeast Asia], ed. Tsuchiya Kenji (Tokyo: Kobundo, 1990); Akio Takahashi, "Biruma: gun ni yoru kaihatsu no teitai [Burma: the military as the cause of economic stagnation]," in *Iwanami Koza Tonan Ajia-shi 9: "Kaihatsu" no Jidai to "Mosaku" no Jidai* [History of Southeast Asia 9: the age of development and the age of uncertain searching], ed. Akira Suehiro (Tokyo: Iwanami, 2002), pp. 210–20; Teruko Saito, "Nashonaruizumu to keizai shiso: Biruma no kokumin keizai koso o megutte [Nationalism and economic thought: on Burma's national economic plan]," in *Tonan Ajia ni totte nijusseiki towa nani-ka: nashonarizumu o meguru shiso jokyo* [What was the 20th century for Southeast Asia?: the study on nationalism], ed. Takashi Nomoto (Tokyo: Tokyo University of Foreign Studies Research Institute for Languages and Cultures of Asia and Africa, 2004).

> which are continually changing has been kept tied to religious dogmas which claim to be absolute and unchanging and go centuries back to an age immeasurably different from today.[3]

For Dr. Ba Maw, the use of Buddhist terminology in *The System* was not suitable for developing a state ideology, even if it seemed appropriate in terms of morality, because it might cause the government to employ dogmatic solutions to social issues. Yet the Ne Win regime did make use of this seemingly unsuitable terminology in its ideology, which suggests that the literature so far has not focused on why and how Ne Win adopted the two texts as the official ideology of his political regime.

The man who drafted the two documents was Chit Hlaing, a former communist who became a civilian official working in the Ministry of Defence and a closer look at the development of his political thought in the context of Burma's military politics in the late 1950s and early 1960s may help to clarify Ne Win's decision to adopt these two texts. We shall begin with an analysis of Chit Hlaing's political discourse, focusing on the relationship between this discourse and his position in military politics. This will be followed by a review of the organizational reform undertaken by Brigadier General Aung Gyi and Colonel Maung Maung, the two men who effectively held the reins of leadership within the tatmadaw in the 1950s and will show that the aim of their reform was to modernize the tatmadaw's organization and to establish its non-political character while preserving the 1947 Constitution and maintaining its anti-communist stance. The next section provides a comprehensive examination of the journal articles that Chit Hlaing wrote while he was engaged in anti-communist propagandizing conducted by the military. This leads into a detailed investigation of how and why he searched for a Burmese style of socialism. Finally, I will offer a reconsideration of Burma's military politics between 1958 and 1962 and provide an explanation of how Chit Hlaing's anti-communist propaganda articles were transformed to become the state ideology of the Ne Win regime.

Chit Hlaing

Chit Hlaing was born in Katha District, Sagaing Division in Upper Burma on 15 March 1926 when Burma was a province of the Indian

[3] *The Guardian*, 23 January 1963.

Empire.[4] When the Japanese army began its invasion of Burma in January 1942, Chit Hlaing, who was still a high school student, joined the Burma Independence Army (BIA) to fight against colonial rule. When the BIA was reorganized into the Burma Defence Army (BDA), he received six months of training from Japanese army officers as a cadet in the second class of the newly established officer training school, thereby becoming an officer of the BDA.[5]

Chit Hlaing was interested in politics and sympathetic to communism since his early teens. He was also influenced by Thakin Soe's work, titled *Socialism* (*hsosheli'wadà*), published in 1939, which was a key factor in his participation in the communist movement in Burma. Chit Hlaing joined the Burma Communist Party (BCP), which had been established in 1939, while still an officer of the BDA.[6] Shortly after joining the party, he started to study under Thakin Soe, the leader of the BCP. During 1942 and 1943, under Thakin Soe's tutelage, Chit Hlaing developed his understanding of Marxism-Leninism and other leftist theories, and worked to expand party cells in the BDA.

During this time, he met with Aung San, who had a significant impact on his life. He was deeply impressed with Aung San's personality and ideas. Recalled in an article the experience of meeting Aung San, Chit Hlaing wrote:

> As I made my way to the military unit in Sanchaung from the house of U Naung Cho (Aung San's *nom de guerre*), my misunderstanding about him had completely disappeared. I had thought he was a fanatic

[4] Ethnically Chit Hlaing was a Shan Burmese. The information on his life is largely based on this author's four interviews with him and on his magazine articles written under the pennames of Shwe Moe and Koe Koe Maung. In 2011, after the Japanese version of this book was published, Chit Hlaing's autobiography came out.

[5] Through his activities in the BDA and his underground work in the anti-Japanese struggle, he established a network of contacts with the leaders of the nationalist movement such as Thakin Soe, Aung San, and Ne Win, as well as with leading postwar politicians and military leaders and communist party members who later rose up in rebellion.

[6] Regarding the Burma Communist Party, see Bertil Lintner, *The Rise and Fall of the Communist Party of Burma (CPB)* (Ithaca: Southeast Asia Program, Cornell University, 1990). The communist party was late to organize in Burma partly because an earlier version organized by the overseas Chinese was not successful. In addition, the period of Japanese military rule after 1942 was one of social instability, and the BCP at that time was such a fragile organization that it could be seen as a loose network of people who called themselves communist party members rather than a political party.

> militarist. Now I could believe he was a democrat. I had thought he was an enemy of Marxism. Now I respected him as a bona fide and true socialist.[7]

Although Chit Hlaing's comment suggests that at the time, the BCP was hostile to Aung San because he was trying to build a cooperative relationship with the Japanese military government, it also shows a young man who was drawn to the charismatic Aung San. It was during this time that Chit Hlaing established personal connections with the "Thirty Comrades" and other future political party leaders and senior military officers. Like many of his contemporaries, the period of Japanese military rule would change the course of his life.

At the end of the war, Chit Hlaing left the army. When the Red-Flag Communist Party, led by his mentor Thakin Soe, went underground in March 1946 to turn to armed struggle, Chit Hlaing did not follow him because of doubts concerning Thakin Soe's hostile attitude toward the Anti-Fascist People's Freedom League (AFPFL). Instead, he decided to collaborate with the Socialist Party (SP) under the AFPFL. Although his ideological sympathies were still with Marx, Lenin, and Mao Tse-tung, he worked as an independent ideologue supporting the SP, which aimed at state socialism rather than radical revolution. One of his activities was translating influential leftist books. He established the People's Literature Company (*pyithù sapei thai'*) together with Ba Swe, Thakin Cho Sein, and Dagon Hla Pe. Under the pen name Maung Chit Gyi (*maun ci' gyî*), Chit Hlaing translated and published commentaries on Marxism-Leninism and the ideas of Mao Tse-tung.

In August 1951, as a representative of the AFPFL, Chit Hlaing attended an international youth convention held in East Berlin under the auspices of the Soviet Union.[8] This became another turning point of his life. At the time, he was hoping to study abroad in the Soviet Union and planned to make arrangements for that during his visit to East Berlin. Although he contacted a representative of the Communist Party of the Soviet Union, he was unable to obtain permission from the Soviet government for his studies. He realized that the obstacle was the opposition of Htun Shein, the representative of the BCP who was also

---

[7] Shwe Moe, "kywunno thì thô u naun cho [The U Naung Cho that I know]," *myàwàdi* 4, no. 9 (1956): 8.

[8] Along with Chit Hlaing as representative was Bo Thein Hlaing, a member of the National Assembly.

attending the convention.[9] He then decided not to pursue the idea of studying in the Soviet Union and instead went from East Berlin to France on a study tour. Through the Burmese ambassador to France, U Myat Sein, Chit Hlaing was able to prolong his stay in the country, so he settled in Paris.

His stay in Paris lasted for about four years until 1955 when he returned to Burma. From April 1955 to the beginning of 1957, he wrote a regular column about his experience abroad titled "Staying in Paris" ("*pari twin thauntin hkè singà*") in the monthly magazine *Myawaddy* (*myàwàdi*). According to the "Staying in Paris" articles, Chit Hlaing's life in that city seemed far from politically active.[10] He was an overseas student attending the Alliance Française to learn French.[11] There appear to be two simple reasons for Chit Hlaing's lack of active contact with the communist party or other leftist political groups in France, despite his interest in communism. First, there were very few Burmese in Paris, and he did not have enough language skill or interest to become politically involved with French people. Second, Chit Hlaing was cautious about letting it be known that he was a communist party member as he hoped to enter a French university.

Nevertheless, Chit Hlaing underwent a certain ideological conversion during his stay in Paris. It was prompted by a letter he received at the end of October 1951 shortly after he started his life in France. The sender was Thein Hlaing, who had travelled with Chit Hlaing from East Berlin on the study tour. After they parted, Thein Hlaing went to England and then visited Yugoslavia. In his letter, Thein Hlaing wrote that Yugoslavia was harshly criticizing the Stalinism of the Soviet Union. Yugoslavia was also searching for its own foreign policy after relations with the Soviet Union and other Eastern European countries worsened following the country's expulsion from the Cominform in 1948. After

[9] Interview with Chit Hlaing, 20 December 2004.

[10] This was unlike a contemporary communist from Southeast Asia, the Cambodian Saloth Sar (later Pol Pot), who was in Paris around the same time. It is known that he participated in discussion meetings on Marxism centering on the Cambodian people led by the famous Cambodian intellectual, Keng Van Suk. About Saloth Sar in Paris, see David Chandler, *Brother Number One: A Political Biography of Pol Pot* (Boulder, Colo.: Westview Press, 1999).

[11] Ko Ko Maung, "pari twin thauntin hkè singà [Staying in Paris]," *myàwàdi* 4, no. 3 (1956): 50–9.

reading Thein Hlaing's account of the situation in Yugoslavia, Chit Hlaing was struck by the second half of the letter where Thein Hlaing listed the following five problems concerning the Soviet Union:

> (1) The Cominform problem is nothing more than a manifestation of the confrontation between developed countries and under-developed countries;
> (2) Russia has created a new type of colonial policy;
> (3) The Soviet Union has: (i) an enormous bureaucracy within the country so it tends toward state capitalism, and (ii) has built bureaucratic relations with its fellow socialist states. The first is military influence; the second is economic exploitation;
> (4) It is wrong not to have broken up the large state-run corporations;
> (5) It is wrong for Russia to monopolize the interpretation of Marxism.[12]

Thein Hlaing's letter was short and did not go into details. However, Chit Hlaing wrote that he was so moved by the letter that "it set in motion a serious change in my political thought." He explained the change as follows:

> I was going to stay in the Soviet Union for one or two years. As for me, I was eager to stay in the Soviet Union, study Russian hard, make a proper study of Russian history as well as Marxism-Leninism, and the ideology for building socialism and so on. That's what I had hoped. Things had not gone as I had hoped, and I was disappointed. When I read the letter from Thein Hlaing, my depressed spirit became excited again.[13]

Undoubtedly Chit Hlaing was disappointed that his goal of studying in the Soviet Union was not realized. This was not necessarily the fault of the Soviet government. But, somehow the disappointment over that missed trip resulted in his becoming disillusioned with the Soviet government itself. This was his mood when he received Thein Hlaing's letter telling him about Yugoslavia's criticism of the Soviet Union. Chit Hlaing wondered if there might be a type of socialism in Yugoslavia that was different from the Soviet version.

---

[12] Ko Ko Maung, "pari twin thauntin hkè singà [Staying in Paris]," *myàwàdi* 3, no. 10 (1955): 66–7.

[13] Ibid., p. 68.

He began reading literature in English dealing with Yugoslavia, notably Marshal Tito's *Workers Manage Factories in Yugoslavia*, Edvard Kardelj's *On People's Democracy in Yugoslavia*, and Milovan Djilas's *Lenin on Relations between Socialist States* and *On New Roads of Socialism*. He also undertook his own study project, focusing on critiques of Stalinism.[14] At the time, Chit Hlaing said in regard to the Yugoslav leaders' criticism that he "could not judge how correct it was." But on the other hand, his own idea about Marxism, his will to realize a socialist society, and his worldview were changing.[15]

A visit to Yugoslavia pushed the ideological conversion further. In June 1952 Chit Hlaing was summoned to take part in a study mission of about one month to Yugoslavia led by Kyaw Nyein, Burma's Minister of Industry. The mission arrived in Beograd on 24 June, visited ministries and agencies, and observed the activities of the League of Commu-

[14] Chit Hlaing summarized his self-taught knowledge in the following five points. "(1) Following the death of its leader Lenin, the Soviet Communist Party, which seized power in the October Revolution, revised Lenin's program of constructing a democratic socialist state due to the betrayal by Stalin and other people who established the rule of a dictatorial bureaucratic class made up of the members of a privileged political party that rested on the military and the secret police. They created state capitalism (too). (2) While pretending to advocate world revolution, the Soviet Union had changed communist parties all over the world into fifth columns that followed the foreign policy of the Soviet Union (only Yugoslavia and China did not become fifth columns of the Soviet Union). (3) In such ways the Soviet Union influenced labor movements around the world, cunningly disguising its competition in dividing up the world as the tactics or strategy of communism (as for example, the secret agreement between Stalin and Churchill during World War II to divide Yugoslavia in two). (4) It is contrary to the disposition of the soviet that the workers who do the real producing do not own their factories in the Soviet Union. Therefore, the building of socialism has frequently confronted difficulties caused by the dictatorial rule of the privileged bureaucrats (e.g., murders, power struggles within the government, non-attainment of goals of the five-year plans, concentration camps, the difficulties of the communist parties in East European countries). (5) Making the Soviet experience the model would be a revisionist dogmatism. The realization of socialism cannot always happen in the same way. It will emerge in various forms in response to times, locations, influence and environments. Therefore, the way that the Soviet Union is pulling strings at the center and giving out orders saying that only the Soviet Union is orthodox could lead to nothing but the destruction of socialism. Socialists and communists in every country will be able to make progress toward a socialist society only by following their own ways." This quotation is from Ko Ko Maung, "*pari twin thauntin hkè singà* [*Staying in Paris*]," *myàwàdi* 4, no. 2 (1955): 251–2.

[15] Ibid., p. 253.

nists of Yugoslavia, labor unions, and youth organizations. It also held discussions with party leaders. Chit Hlaing later wrote the following about the mission:

> I had studied the thoughts on Marxism of the leaders of the League of Communists of Yugoslavia before I visited Yugoslavia. After discussions with Milovan Djilas and other thinkers, I really became strongly attracted to the Marxist thought worked out by the Yugoslavian communists themselves and I liked it.[16]

There was no mention in the essay of what he discussed with Djilas, but in an interview, Chit Hlaing told me that he had been impressed with Djilas's idea of a "new class."[17] The "new class" became a key aspect in the criticism of communist parties (mainly the Communist Party of the Soviet Union) that Djilas wrote about following his dismissal as vice president in 1954. Briefly summarized, he argues that the socialist state could not solve the problem of class conflict because party bureaucrats would inevitably replace the ruling class as a "new class" even if the bourgeoisie was removed.[18] Although the visit to Yugoslavia was for less than a month, it was an experience that brought about a decisive change in Chit Hlaing's political thought, particularly his view of Marxism.

At that time, he did not have any specific ideas about what Burma's unique type of socialism should be.[19] In fact, he seems to have been little interested in Yugoslavia's system of worker self-management, although ownership of the means of production and the planned economy are the main pillars of socialism. What he learned from Yugoslavia was simply rhetoric for criticizing Marxism-Leninism and the Soviet Union. However, even if it was only rhetoric, criticizing the communist party while maintaining socialism as a principle was convenient for the tatmadaw in its fight against the BCP rebels as socialism was one of the sources of

---

[16] Ibid., p. 259.

[17] Interview with Chit Hlaing, 20 Dec. 2004. Milovan Djilas together with Tito organized the Yugoslav partisan war against the Nazis. He became the vice president of Yugoslavia in 1953, but was dismissed the following year.

[18] Milovan Djilas, *The New Class: An Analysis of the Communist System* (New York: F.A. Praeger, 1957).

[19] While the basic tenor of Yugoslavia's diplomacy was anti-Soviet, the uniqueness of the country's socialism was still seen in workers' self-management, a point that Chit Hlaing, perhaps strangely, never addressed in his essays.

Chit Hlaing. (Personal collection of the author)

Burma's political legitimacy at the time. In 1955, Chit Hlaing left Paris and returned to Burma at the request of Colonel Aung Gyi in the War Office.[20]

Military Reform in the 1950s

Following his returned to Burma in 1955, Chit Hlaing worked as a member of the election staff for the AFPFL in the second general election in 1956; then in August of that year he began working as a civilian employee attached to the Directorate of Psychological Warfare (DPW) of the General Staff Office (called War Office until 1956) along with Saw Oo who was an editor by profession and former BCP member. They were called up to help strengthen psychological warfare program, which at the time was going thorough a large-scale organizational reform of the tatmadaw.

[20] Apparently, Chit Hlaing returned to Burma somewhat reluctantly as he had hoped to stay in France long enough to acquire a degree.

As mentioned in Chapter 2, the tatmadaw had its roots in the Regular Army of the colonial government and the Patriotic Burmese Forces (PBF), the final permutation of the Burma Independence Army. Both were integrated on 7 September 1945 under the Kandy Agreement concluded between Admiral Mountbatten, then Supreme Allied Commander, Southeast Asia, and Aung San following Britain's return to Burma. The Regular Army was made up of mostly ethnic minorities such as the Karen, Kachin, and Chin, while the PBF was made up largely of majority-group Bahman. Added to this ethnic cleavage was one that divided the former PBF officers between those who were communist or socialist supporters. In that sense the tatmadaw was an organization rife with political and ethnic conflict.

The Red-Flag faction of the BCP was the first to go underground in 1946 followed by the White-Flag faction, the People's Volunteer Organisation (PVO), and some ethnic minority insurgents. In coordination with these revolts, the 1st and 3rd Burma Rifles battalions of the tatmadaw began working underground in support of the rebellions. Then in response to the revolt of the Karen National Union (KNU), its military wing, the Karen National Defence Organisation (KNDO) and two of the three Karen Rifles battalions, which were class battalions made up solely of Karen soldiers, joined the rebellion. Although the Karen officers in the tatmadaw did not necessarily share the interests of the Karen insurgents seeking independence of Karen State, Prime Minister U Nu dismissed most of the Karen officers and soldiers in the tatmadaw on 1 February 1949.

Thus, the Karen officers inherited from the colonial Regular Army were mostly eliminated from the tatmadaw, resulting in less ethnic tension within the tatmadaw. However, BCP sympathizers remained in the tatmadaw and were a destabilizing factor. As it struggled with its internal conflicts, the tatmadaw also had to deal with the task of suppressing anti-government rebellions and with the Chinese Nationalist Army (Kuomintang: KMT) troops that had moved in from China and occupied parts of Shan State. Given the weak state of its troop strength, weaponry, and organization, the tatmadaw was not up to the task, which increased the urgency for its reform.

In 1951, following instructions from Ne Win, the Military Planning Staff (MPS) was established. Headed by Colonel Aung Gyi, the aim of this committee was to reform the tatmadaw. Although the military reforms of the 1950s led by Aung Gyi and Maung Maung were wide ranging, central to the initiative was the reorganization and expansion of the General Staff Office to provide a more consolidated base for the weakly centralized chain-of-command structure. Aung Gyi, with the assistance of Maung Maung, forged the reform. In 1953, when Aung Gyi was promoted to Vice Chief of General Staff (Army), number two in the tatmadaw, Maung Maung replaced Aung Gyi as head of MPS and then played the role of coordinator of the reforms.[21]

A first major step in the reform was dealing with the shortage of human resources in the War Office, the predecessor of the General Staff Office.[22] This shortage was clearly evident in a report presented to the Tatmadaw Conference in 1950, which pointed out that, "There are 3,000 senior officers in the British General Staff Office who manage 700,000 men, while in Burma a military force of 100,000 men is managed by 80 high-ranking officers (in the War Office), and that number has been decreased still more by the Karen problem."[23] With the reforms implemented by the MPS, the Ministry of Defence Organization Chart 100/2/56, that took effect on 1 January 1956, set the number at over 160 officers.[24] On that same date, the reorganized War Office was renamed the Ministry of Defence. Under the Ministry of Defence was the General Staff Office. The General Staff Office's leadership was comprised of the

---

[21] Maung Maung was appointed as Director of DPW from 1954 and then as Director of the Directorate of Military Training (DMT) from 1956. For the military careers of Aung Gyi and Maung Maung, see Myat Win, *ta'madaw gâunzâun myâ thàmaîn akyînkyou' 1941 khùhni' hmà 1990 pyìhni' ahtì* [The Outline of the history of the military leaders from 1941 to 1990] (yangon: pyankyàyê wankyîhtanà, 1991); their careers are listed on pp. 22 and 34–5 respectively. For a detailed examination of the military reforms they oversaw, see Mary Callahan, *Making Enemies: War and State Building in Burma* (Ithaca: Cornell University Press, 2003), Chapters 6 and 7.

[22] The War Office was staffed by only forty-five officers as prescribed by War Office Organization Chart BA/100/1/48 that took effect on 14 April 1948.

[23] Quoted from si'thàmâin pyàdai' hnìn ta'màdo mogûndai'hmûyôun [Defense Services Museum and Historical Research Institute], *ta'madothamâin sàtou'htàtwè 1948–1962* [The History of the military, 1948–1962] 4 (1996): 160. However, the forces on the front lines suffered the same shortages of manpower and equipment, so putting priority on restructuring the War Office likely had a negative impact on relations between the War Office staff and the troops on the front lines.

[24] These figures estimated from Appendix 1, *kagweyêi ûsîgyou' (kyî) thàmâin akyîn 1948–84* [The history of the General Staff Office (Army) 1948–84], DR-8482, DSMHRI. However, BA/100/1/48 does not include the number of officers in the Navy and Air Force General Staff offices, and 100/2/56 does not include that of the Navy, Air Force and the Directorate of Education and Psychological Warfare.

Vice Chief of General Staff (Army), the Vice Chief of General Staff (Navy), and the Vice Chief of General Staff (Air Force).

As part of this reorganization, operations for psychological warfare were expanded. Psychological warfare by the army had its roots in 1949, soon after independence, with radio broadcasts of tatmadaw victories directed at the rebel forces.[25] During "Operation Liberation" (*lu'myau'yêi si'hsinhmù*), which was conducted in Kyaukse in January 1952, a psychological warfare unit was temporarily organized, which together with the Army's 6th Infantry Brigade carried out propaganda operations for over two months during which the unit disseminated more than 75,900 propaganda leaflets.[26] From then on, psychological warfare gradually became an established part of the tatmadaw's counter-insurgency operations. In November of 1952, a Psychological Warfare Section was set up in the War Office; then in 1954 it became the Psychological Warfare Office, and then the Directorate of Psychological Warfare on 1 August 1956. In 1960 it was merged with the Directorate of Education to become the Directorate of Education and Psychological Warfare. It was in the midst of the reorganization and expansion of the General Staff Office and the organizing of psychological warfare operations on a permanent basis that Chit Hlaing was recalled in 1955 by Aung Gyi to work for the tatmadaw.[27]

Among the roles that psychological warfare operations fulfilled in the tatmadaw at that time, two major tasks were the drafting of military doctrine and conducting anti-communist propaganda operations.

A concerted effort by the tatmadaw to formulate a doctrine began with the Tatmadaw Conference in 1956.[28] But it could contribute little

---

[25] si'thàmâin pyàdai' hnìn ta'màdo mogûndai'hmûyôun [Defense Services Museum and Historical Research Institute], *ta'madothamâin sàtou'htàtwè 1948–1962* [The history of the military, 1948–1962] 4 (1996): 164.

[26] Ibid., pp. 164–6.

[27] It is not clear why Chit Hlaing was selected. Perhaps it was because he had been in the BIA and was personally acquainted with Aung Gyi and other army officers and civilian politicians. Another possible reason may have had to do with his being a former communist party member and that he was knowledgeable about communism, although he had distanced himself from the party. These reasons were mentioned by Saw Oo who belonged to the Directorate of Psychological Warfare along with Chit Hlaing.

[28] See Maung Aung Myoe, "Military Doctrine and Strategy in Myanmar: A Historical Perspective" (Strategic and Defence Studies Centre, Australian National University No. 339, 1999).

to the formation of military doctrine while a formal doctrine stipulating the relationship between politics and the tatmadaw was being developed. This period almost overlapped with the time when the Indonesian military modified its doctrine from "territorial operations" to one of "two functions" that would legitimize its participation in politics.[29] In Burma, the direction was almost the opposite; the effort was to formulate a doctrine that created a norm making the military separate from politics. The result of efforts to formulate the doctrine was a document titled "The National Ideology and Our Military" which was adopted at the Tatmadaw Conference in 1958. The Ministry of Defence published this document the following year under the revised title *The National Ideology and the Role of the Defence Services* (hereafter the *National Ideology*).

Along with providing a historical overview of the tatmadaw's ideological development, the *National Ideology* laid out the national ideology (*naingando wadà*) that the tatmadaw was expected to defend. There were three points in the ideology that were to be defended: (1) the rule of society by peaceful and lawful means (*ya'ywa êichânyêi hnìn tàyâ ùbàdei ou'sôeyêi*), (2) the development of democracy (*dimoekàreisi htûnkâyêi*), and (3) the establishment of a socialist economic system (*hsousheli' sîpwâyêisa ni'htuhtaunyêi*).[30]

The *National Ideology* did not contain anything particularly new in terms of ideology. The "rule of society by peaceful and lawful means" was an affirmation of the reason that the tatmadaw was fighting against communists and ethnic insurgents in many parts of the country. The "development of democracy" and "establishment of a socialist economic system" were a reaffirmation of the political and economic principles set down in the 1947 Constitution. The preamble of the Constitution quoted at the beginning of the *National Ideology* clearly suggested this point. More important than what the *National Ideology* contained, however, were the political intentions and the military politics behind the formulation of this doctrine.

The DPW was responsible for drawing up the doctrine, which was drafted by Chit Hlaing under Maung Maung's leadership. In a retrospective, Chit Hlaing commented that when drafting the doctrine, Maung

---

[29] Jun Honna, *Military Politics and Democratization in Indonesia* (New York: Routledge Curzon, 2003), Chapter 2.

[30] pyidaunsù myanmanainngando asôya kagweyê wangyîhtanà [Government of the Union of Burma, Ministry of Defense], *nainngando wadà hnìn ta'mado lou'ngânzin* [*The National Ideology and the role of the defence services*] (1959), p. 18.

Maung's constitutionalism strongly affected his work. This constitutionalism was reflected in Maung Maung's book titled *The Basics of Military Doctrine* (*si'àcheihkan dàbomyâ*), which included a note that its content was the "author's personal opinion." In that book, Maung Maung highlighted 87 provisions from the 1947 Constitution that the personnel of the tatmadaw were always expected to respect.[31] Chit Hlaing also referred to the 1947 Constitution itself, Burma's Declaration of Independence, and the speech by Sao Shwe Thaik, Burma's first president, to the First Union Parliament when he drafted the *National Ideology*.[32]

In scholarly literature, the *National Ideology* has been regarded as evidence that the tatmadaw was becoming increasingly interested in political intervention. This interpretation would be correct only if the tatmadaw were a professional military and its officers shared the normative ideal in a separation between the role of politics and that of the military. But considering that the tatmadaw leadership was composed of people who had been key players in the country's liberation, and who were concerned with building a stable and unified country, this assumption arguably is false. For contemporary military leaders, the 1947 Constitution stood as proof of their victory, won at the risk of their own lives, as Maung Maung's constitutionalism shows. It would not have been easy for tatmadaw leadership to deny the values contained in their Constitution. Indeed, there are few if any indications to show that civilian politicians perceived any threat of political intervention by the tatmadaw when the *National Ideology* was published. It would be more logical to think that it was natural at the time for the tatmadaw to hold up the Constitution as its behavioral principle, as was done in the *National Ideology*.

Perhaps more important for Maung Maung was the weakness of the tatmadaw as a modern military. It was still threatened by internal divisions, particularly by the BCP, which was in revolt against the state. Within the ranks of the tatmadaw were officers and soldiers sympathetic

---

[31] Bohmûgyî Maung Maung, *si'àcheikhandabomyâ* [The basics of military doctrine] (si'pinnya àthîn, 1959), pp. 1–6. According to the preface, Colonel Maung Maung had been reviewing the content of the booklet since 1954.

[32] Chit Hlaing, *myanmà hsousheli' lânzin hnin' lânzin pati ì twêkho myomyinpoun dabôtayâ pyi' polapoun akyîn khyou' hma' tân* [The Burmese way to socialism and a record summarizing the process in formulating the ideology of the Programme Party] (held in the Yangon University Historical Research Center) (HRC: X/15 AP/1992), p. 4; Interview with Chit Hlaing on 20 December 2004.

to and willing to work with the communists, as exemplified by the case of Brigadier General Kyaw Zaw, commander of the Northern Military Region, who was dismissed in 1956 because he was suspected of secretly communicating with the BCP. The tatmadaw also remained threatened internally by continuing ethnic conflict. Although many of the Karen had been removed in 1949, there were still soldiers from the Chin, Kachin, and other minority ethnic groups who backed movements calling for autonomy.

Maung Maung's aim in drawing up the *National Ideology* was to counter this sort of conduct against military cohesion. Rather than being a document providing a motive for future political intervention by the military, it would be more accurate to see the *National Ideology* as part of the effort of the General Staff Office to bring about a loyal, unified, and centralized tatmadaw in itself by reaffirming the significance of the 1947 Constitution eight years after independence. The reform of the tatmadaw under the guidance of Aung Gyi and Maung Maung, which aimed at establishing a unified chain-of-command structure from the center to the field commands, was also meant to counter intra-military divisions by establishing overall control by a reorganized and expanded General Staff Office. When drawing up the *National Ideology*, neither Chit Hlaing nor Maung Maung had in mind the use of the document to legitimize future political intervention by the tatmadaw.[33]

Anti-Communist Propaganda

Another important part of Chit Hlaing's work in the DPW was disseminating anti-communist propaganda. The principal vehicle for this was the magazine *Myawaddy* owned by the tatmadaw and started in 1952. In 1956 the magazine printed 18,000 copies and its issues were filled with novels, poems, essays, and political articles, making it one of the

33 The author wonders how effective the military reform was in modernizing the organization, because the biggest complaints of local commanders were concrete problems at the frontline such as the troops, weapons, insufficient equipment, and delayed salary payments, and budgetary measures would have been the most effective way of dealing with these issues; they were not the sort of problems that would be resolved by a plan of action in words only. So it is possible that the moves by Aung Gyi and Maung Maung to focus on drawing up the *National Ideology* and reorganizing the General Staff office led to the front lines being slighted and growing discontent among local commanders.

most influential magazines in Burma at the time.[34] Chit Hlaing began writing for the *Myawaddy* before formally taking up work with the military under the pen name Shwe Moe (*shwei môu*) and wrote an article published in 1955 titled "The Contradiction of Before and After," which offered a commentary critical of the Soviet Union.[35]

Table 3.1 lists the anti-communist articles that Chit Hlaing, as Shwe Moe, wrote for *Myawaddy*. From 1954 to 1959, the articles can be divided by content into four chronologically divided groups. The first group contains a series of criticisms of Stalinism written between April and July 1955. During this first period, Chit Hlaing used in his anti-communism propaganda the same techniques of criticizing Stalinism that Yugoslavian leaders like Milovan Djilas were using. This period began with the publication of "The Contradiction of Before and After." In this article Chit Hlaing was critical of a Soviet official statement that, "Burma's independence is not the real thing; it is nothing but a sham. Burma has not yet been freed from the hand of the British Empire."[36] Despite this comment, however, in the February 1955 issue of the *Cominform Journal*, another Soviet official remarks, "Together with India, Indonesia and Burma also escaped from the yoke of colonial rule." Chit Hlaing criticized this major change in the Soviet view of Burma, concluding that it was because "The Soviet Union is not the great socialist country that many people consider it to be. It is a fascist state under bureaucratic, colonialist rule like that in Britain and the U.S."[37]

---

[34] In an interview with Callahan, Aung Gyi stated that he published *Myawaddy* to provide a counter balance to the popular magazine *Shumawa* (*shùmàwà*), which carried articles critical of the government. See Callahan, *Making Enemies*, p. 183. However, this author could not find any articles that criticized the government directly when he searched the back issues of *Shumawa* from the first issue. When enquiring of people who were active as writers, it seems that *Shumawa* and *Myawaddy* were both strongly perceived as literary magazines and not as publications for political discussions.

[35] Besides the political articles he wrote for his work in the Psychological Warfare Directorate, Chit Hlaing also wrote love stories and essays such as "Staying in Paris" under the name Ko Ko Maung (*koe koe maun*). The six years from April 1955 to April 1961 was his most prolific period, during which he published 72 political articles and essays in *Myawaddy* along with writing anti-communist articles for *Current Affairs* (*khi' yê*), a magazine issued inside the tatmadaw; he published several novels as well.

[36] Chit Hlaing does not state in his original text when and where the Soviet Union made this comment on Burma.

[37] Shwe Moe, "chènau' ma ni thô [The contradiction of before and after]," *myàwàdi* 3, no. 6 (1955): 54–5.

Table 3.1 Shwe Moe's Articles in *Myawaddy*

Vol.	*No.*	*Year*	*Month*	*Article Title*	
3	6	1955	Apr	The Contradiction of Before and After	The First Period
3	7	1955	May	Fascist Bureaucratic Colonialism of the Soviet Union	
3	8	1955	June	Criticizing the Bureaucratism of the Soviet Union	
3	9	1955	July	A Big Mistake by Traitors Tito and Stalin	
3	12	1955	Oct	World Peace and the Burma Communist Party	The Second Period
4	9	1956	July	The U Naung Cho That I Know	
4	12	1956	Oct	Stalin and Khrushchev	
5	3	1957	Jan	Oh, Thakin Soe, Thakin Soe	
5	5	1957	Mar	If I Were Thakin Than Tun	
5	8	1957	June	Abandon Factionalism	
5	9	1957	July	The Solidarism of U Naung Cho	
5	12	1957	Oct	Burma and Democratic Socialism	The Third Period
6	1	1957	Nov	Democratic Socialism and Namarupa wada	
6	2	1957	Dec	Namarupa wada and the Formation of Human Society	
6	3	1958	Jan	Namarupa wada and the Formation of Human Society	
6	4	1958	Feb	Namarupa wada and Human History	
6	5	1958	Mar	Monopolistic Capitalism	The Fourth Period
6	6	1958	Apr	Bureaucratic Capitalism under the Dictatorship of the Soviet Union	
6	7	1958	May	The Conflict Between Yugoslavia and the Soviet Union	
6	8	1958	June	Marxism and Communism	
6	9	1958	July	Marxism	
6	10	1958	Aug	Marx's Materialistic Interpretation of History	
6	11	1958	Sep	Lenin, Stalin and Mao Zedong	
6	12	1958	Oct	Facts About Marx and Revolution	
7	1	1958	Nov	The New Class of the Communist Party	
7	2	1958	Dec	The Absolute Rule of Communism	
7	3	1959	Jan	The Communist State	
7	5	1959	Mar	Democracy and Communism	
7	6	1959	Apr	Democracy and the Socialist Economy	

Source: *Myawaddy*.

The theme of the second group of articles, printed between late 1956 and mid-1957, was criticism of the Burma Communist Party (BCP). The main targets were Thakin Soe, leader of the Red Flag Communist Party, and Thakin Than Tun, who led the White Flag Communist Party. Chit Hlaing's argument was much the same as his previous criticism of Stalinism. An example was his article "Oh, Thakin Soe, Thakin Soe" in which Chit Hlaing wrote that the problem with "my teacher" Thakin Soe was his ignorance, the ignorance of not understanding that socialism can easily fall under the rule of bureaucratism, which was the case in the Soviet Union.

With this move from criticizing the Soviet Union to targeting the BCP, Chit Hlaing finally began to develop his own form of socialist thought, and this was the theme of his writing from late 1957 until early 1958. The five published commentaries during this period dealt with Chit Hlaing's ideology of *namarupa wada* (*namà rupà wadà*), which is important for the purposes of this study and will be summarized here.

Each of the commentaries was a short article; altogether they totaled 33 pages and were published in five consecutive monthly issues of *Myawaddy*. Chit Hlaing's commentary begins with the history of socialist thought and socialist states, starting with the rise of capitalism 200 years earlier. He discusses how socialism arose as an opposing concept developing first from utopian socialism then scientific socialism, one of its outcomes being the Russian Revolution in 1917 and the establishment of the Soviet Union. He then describes how the Soviet-style communism of "bureaucratic dictatorship" came to predominate, and how socialism (i.e., democratic socialism) lost its influence. In his commentary he also discusses how the Soviet Union since Stalin's dictatorship sought to expand its influence through the communist parties in other countries and how Yugoslavia opposed it.[38] Up to this point, Chit Hlaing is making the same argument as he does in his anti-communist propaganda.

Then in a section dealing with Burma, Chit Hlaing argues that the country was facing a crisis of disunity as a nation-state and that it would be colonized again if it could not achieve unity. What was needed to restore such unity was an ideology (*wadàdàbôtàyâ*), and that ideology had to be "Socialism based on Democracy" (*dimokàresi achehkantô hsosheli'wadà*). However, although this ideology would be socialist, it

[38] Shwe Moe, "myanmanainngan hnin' dimokàresi hsousheli' wada [Myanmar and Democratic Socialist thought]," *myàwàdi* 5, no. 12 (1957): 13–7.

could not be based on Marxism-Leninism, nor could it be a western-style democratic socialism, which represents the middle class. In Chit Hlaing's words, it would have to be "a socialism based on the democratic ideology and socialistic economic institutions as prescribed in the Constitution of the Union of Burma."[39] In this sense, the institution for ideology was already in place. However, according to Chit Hlaing, Burma had not yet been able to pursue the goal of creating the socialism prescribed in the Constitution because there were elements in Burma attempting to destroy the Constitution. What is needed now, Chit Hlaing argues in this article, is a philosophical foundation for a socialist state based on democracy, and that philosophical foundation was what he termed *namarupa wada*.

Namarupa is a compound word composed of two Pali words, *nama* (*namà*) and *rupa* (*rupà*).[40] Although *nama* means psychological elements, and *rupa* means physical elements in *Buddha Abhidhamma* (*àbìdanma*), one of the three collections of the teachings of Buddha (*Tipitaka*), Chit Hlaing did not used the precise dictionary definitions of the two words when utilizing the compound. Instead, he defined *nama* as "mind" and *rupa* as "material." He argues that the world is composed of *nama* and *rupa*, meaning the two principles of mind and material, and combining these two principles in the word *namarupa* conveyed the interaction between the two principles.

Chit Hlaing then proceeds to explain the three characteristics of *namarupa wada*. First, the world is composed of three worlds: the world of material (*thèmê you' lôkà*), the world of living things (*thèshì lôkà*), and the world of phenomena (*hpyi'phe'pyùpyin lôkà*); only humans are involved in all three worlds. Second, humans consist of a principle of the mind and a principle of the body, and the three actions — the action of the body (*kayàkan*), the action of the mouth (*wàsikan*), and the action of will (*mànôkan*) — are controlled by the mind through the body. Third, a person's mind and body are constantly changing, and both support each other through providing mutual benefits (*àpyanàhlan kyêzûpyù di*).[41]

---

39 Shwe Moe, "dimokàresi sousheli' sàni' hnin' namàrupa wada [The Democratic Socialist system and namarupa wada]," *myàwàdi* 6, no. 1 (1957): 286.

40 For *nama* and *rupa*, see Dr. Mhan Tin Mon, *The Essence of Buddha Abhidhamma* (Yangon: Mya Mon Yadanar Publication, 1995), pp. 17–8.

41 Ibid., pp. 289–92.

In the next section of the article, Chit Hlaing presents a review of human history from the perspective of *namarupa wada*. Interestingly, however, most of his review is based on the Marxist materialistic view of world history and not on his concept of *namarupa wada*. For instance, he writes:

> Who possesses the means of production and the capital for production in economic activity? Which class possesses them? What sort of relationship exists between those who possess the means of production and those who don't possess them? The answers to such questions represent the economic systems of each age.[42]

Chit Hlaing then continues his summary of world history up until World War II, dividing it into periods of feudalism, capitalism, and imperialism.

In creating his concept of *namarupa wada*, Chit Hlaing intended for it to be the philosophical foundation of the state in Burma. In his writing, Chit Hlaing reduces Marxism-Leninism to only materialism, and then contraposes it to idealism, and defines human beings as the embodiment of both materialism and idealism at the same time. His attempt to combine materialism and idealism, or Marxism-Leninism and Buddhism, made sense in the political discourse of Burma,which had long discussed the anti-religious aspect of Marxism.[43] This discussion took place even among Burmese communists. In an effort to bring an end this long-running controversy, Ba Swe, the leader of the ruling AFPFL party, made an important speech in 1952:

> Marxist philosophy rejects the theory of creation; but it does not oppose religion. In point of fact, Marxist theory is not antagonistic to Buddhist philosophy. The two are, frankly speaking, not merely similar. In fact, they are the same in concept. But if we want to have the two distinguished from each other, we can safely assume that Marxist theory occupies the lower plane, while Buddhist philosophy occupies

[42] Shwe Moe, "namàrupà wada hnin' lu' lôkà hpyi'sin [Namarupa wada and the formation of human society]," *myàwàdi* 6, no. 2 (1957): 81–2.

[43] Kei Nemoto, "1930 nendai Biruma nashonarizum inokeru shakai-shugi juyou no tokushitsu: Takin-to no shisou-keisei wo chushin ni [The characteristics making Socialism acceptable to 1930s Burmese nationalism: focusing on the formation of Thakin Party thought]," *Tonan Ajia Kenkyu* (*Southeast Asian Studies*) 27, no. 4 (1990): 445.

> the higher. Marxist theory deals with mundane affairs and seeks to satisfy material needs in life. Buddhist philosophy, however, deals with the solution of spiritual matters with a view to seek spiritual satisfaction in life and liberation from this mundane world.[44]

Chit Hlaing's motive was similar to Ba Swe's. Chit Hlaing invented *namarupa wada* as a potential national ideology to put an end to controversy by choosing a middle way between materialism and idealism. He did this by proposing an original socialism that was anti-communist, nationalistic, and acceptable to Buddhists.

At the same time, Chit Hlaing was proposing his ideology as a philosophical foundation for a socialism based on democratic ideology and socialistic economic institutions as prescribed in the Constitution of the Union of Burma. His argument was that the country's deviation from the Constitution had caused the crisis that Burma was facing at that time. In this respect, *namarupa wada* was basically a discourse on constitutionalism that was also anti-communist. Chit Hlaing clearly intended to critically reexamine conventional historical materialism. However, as an idea, *namarupa wada* was so abstract that readers were left with the impression of an empty philosophy filled with a jargon of difficult and ambiguous Pali words. And although his commentaries were carried in the then well-known magazine *Myawaddy*, Chit Hlaing's idea of *namarupa wada* provoked little response from readers or the upper echelon of the tatmadaw as well.[45] Indeed, neither readers nor military leaders, nor Chit Hlaing himself, ever imagined that a series of magazine articles would one day become the basis for the state ideology. At the time, they were seen as anti-communist propaganda articles by the government.

Chit Hlaing continued to develop his ideas in his work at the Ministry of Defence. In December 1957, he began teaching political thought as an instructor of the tatmadaw's first Psychological Warfare training course. In the class he discussed world communism and the ideology of the BCP. The textbook used in the course was an 18-page booklet written by Chit Hlaing himself titled *Ideology Critical for the Development of Human Nature and Democracy* (*lù thàbawà tayâ*

---

[44] Donald Eugene Smith, *Religion and Politics in Burma* (Princeton, N.J.: Princeton University Press, 1965), pp. 128–9.

[45] Interview with Chit Hlaing, 25 January 2005.

hnin'dimokàresi ì wehpan ta'thô tôte'yê dabôtayâ) (hereafter *Critical Ideology*), and the content was based on his *namarupa wada* articles.[46]

Briefly stated, the first half of *Critical Ideology* describes in largely the same terms as the articles the worldview of *namarupa wada*: the world made up of three worlds — the world of material (*the'mê you' lôkà*), the world of living things (*the'shì lôkà*), and the world of phenomena (*hpyi'phe'pyùpyin lôkà*) — the interaction of *nama* (mind) and *rupa* (material) and the impermanent relationship between them. The second half of the text is not concerned with *namarupa wada* and can be summarized essentially as follows. In the human mind, there exists what the textbook terms "immorality," examples of which are greed (*lôbà*), anger (*dôthà*), and ignorance (*môhà*). People cannot overcome this "immorality" by material satisfaction alone. That is because an egoistic mind and an altruistic mind always coexist together in human nature. The realization of human happiness starts only with learning this aspect of human nature in a critical way and then mastering that knowledge. Marxism-Leninism, by giving priority to material satisfaction alone, does not understand this principle. For Chit Hlaing, it is a vicious ideology that ignores human nature.

The new content that Chit Hlaing added in the latter half of *Critical Ideology* did not alter in any significant way his arguments that had already been published in *Myawaddy*. His criticism of Marxism-Leninism was consistent with previous anti-communist propaganda in two ways.

---

[46] Chit Hlaing, *myanmà hsousheli' lânzin hnin' lânzin pati ì twêkho myomyinpoun dabôtayâ pyi' polapoun akyîn khyou' hma' tân* [The Burmese way to Socialism and a record summarizing the process in formulating the ideology of the Programme Party] (held in the Yangon University Historical Research Center) (HRC: X/15 AP/1992), pp. 2–3; Chit Hlaing, *lù thàbawà tayâ hnin' dimokàresi ì wehpan ta'thô tôte'yê dabôtayâ* [Critical ideology for the development of human nature and democracy]," (1959; privately held by Chit Hlaing). This author accepted a copy of the textbook directly from Chit Hlaing. He had submitted the booklet via Colonel Ba Than, then head of the Directorate of Psychological Warfare to Aung Gyi and to Maung Maung, the director of the Directorate of Military Training. While getting Aung Gyi's approval that the booklet be used as teaching material for officer use only, Maung Maung reviewed it in detail and sent his comments to Chit Hlaing. With the general election in 1960 and the end of the caretaker government under Ne Win, Chit Hlaing's lectures were discontinued, but they were restarted in November 1961 for young officers in the Psychological Warfare Directorate. He worked as an instructor of political education directed at implementing anti-communism propaganda and for training personnel in charge of the anti-communism political education of military officers.

First, he pointed out that Marxism-Leninism is wrong because it lacks the human mind (*rupà* or *sei'*). Second, he made frequent use of Pali words from the Theravada Buddhist thought set forth in the *Abhidhamma* in order to counter the modern thought of the West with Burma's own Buddhist thought. By doing so, Chit Hlaing was attempting to create a dichotomous framework of mind/material = Buddhist thought/Western thought = friend/enemy. However, he never went into a more detailed invocation of the *Abhidhamma*. Rather, the emphasis of his argument was a criticism of Marxist-Leninist thought. In this way, Chit Hlaing's political discourse, while making its way into a textbook used in a course aimed at tatmadaw officers, never moved beyond a series of anti-communist propaganda articles. Only a small number of the military officers ever knew about the texts.

The Moderates Versus the Hardliners

Why and how did Chit Hlaing's anti-communist propaganda and his discourse on *namarupa wada* ultimately turn into the state ideology? The backdrop to this development was a transformation in Burma's political situation at the end of the 1950s and the beginning of the 1960s. During these years, the hardline faction in the tatmadaw came to the fore, and the moderates in the General Staff Office such as Aung Gyi and Maung Maung, who had been politically powerful inside the tatmadaw during the middle of the 1950s, were gradually marginalized. This section will examine the process of this marginalization with a comparison of two coups d'état, first in 1958 and then in 1962.

The political turmoil in 1958 had its origin in a split in the AFPFL the previous year. The AFPFL was an alliance of political parties centered on the Socialist Party and led by U Nu together with Ba Swe, Kyaw Nyein, and Thakin Tin, the three heads of the SP. Differences among the four men over party personnel and other party affairs led to a split on 29 April 1957 that created a Nu-Tin faction and a Swe-Nyein faction. This divide finally led to an organizational split in the AFPFL itself on 13 June of that year.[47] Table 3.2 shows the voting results of the

[47] Regarding the split in the AFPFL, see Sein Win, *The Split Story; An Account of Recent Political Upheaval in Burma, with Emphasis on AFPFL* (Rangoon: The Guardian, 1959); John S. Furnivall, *The Governance of Modern Burma*, 2nd ed., extended (New York: Institute of Pacific Relations, 1960), Chapter 5; Butwell, *U Nu of Burma*, Chapter 16.

Table 3.2 Results of the No-Confidence Vote on 4 June 1957

	Approval (Swe-Nyein Faction)	*Disapproval (Nu-Tin Faction)*
AFPFL	97	51
NUF	1	44
ANUO[1]	0	6
Shan State	9	16
Kachin State	4	3
Chin State	3	3
Kayah State	0	3
Karen State	5	2
Total	119	128

Note: [1] ANUO: Arakan National United Organization

Source: Toru Yano, *Study of the Contemporary Political History of Thailand and Burma* (Kyoto: Center for Southeast Asian Studies, Kyoto University, 1968): Table 3.

no-confidence motion brought against the Nu cabinet. The motion was submitted by the Swe-Nyein faction to the Union Parliament on 4 June 1957 shortly before the AFPFL split. It shows that within the AFPFL, the Nu-Tin faction (later known as the Clean AFPFL) had fewer assembly members than the Swe-Nyein faction (later known as the Stable AFPFL). U Nu countered this move by bringing the National United Front (NUF), the opposition party coalition and a leftist force, over to his side, and in the end the no-confidence motion was voted down. Thereafter U Nu continuously tried to broaden his support from leftist forces. For instance, in August 1958 he proclaimed an amnesty for insurgent groups including the Red Flag and White Flag Communist Parties, which was followed by legalization of the People's Volunteer Organisation Party.

The split of the AFPFL and U Nu's subsequent closer relations with leftist forces caused a stir within the tatmadaw. The most radical expression of this unease took place at the Northern Military Region command. In 1958, Brigadier General Aung Shwe, the commander of the region, began planning a coup together with Lieutenant-Colonel Chit Khain, the General Staff Officer (1), and Colonel Kyi Win, the brother-in-law of Ba Swe of the Stable AFPFL faction.[48] The Home Minister, Bo Min Gaung (a supporter of the Clean faction), having been informed of the planned coup, deployed Union Military Police (UMP) units of an army brigade under his command to protect the capital, Yangon.[49] This move deepened the division between the tatmadaw and both AFPFL factions, and tensions quickly escalated, leading the northern regional command group to propose to Aung Gyi that a coup d'état be carried out. Although Aung Gyi rejected the proposal, this did not deter the group from planning a coup. Indeed, they intended to execute it on 27 September.[50]

Meanwhile Maung Maung focused on undermining the northern regional command group and other hardliners in the tatmadaw. He also conferred with Aung Gyi and Colonel Khin Nyoe on 22 September over concerns of a split within the tatmadaw. It was clear that the General Staff Office by itself did not have the strength to put down the northern regional command group. But they knew that Brigadier General Ba Lay, head of the Southern Military Region, opposed the coup plan and agreed to follow the decision of the General Staff Office.[51] This meant that, given the situation, a coup d'état by the northern regional command group was certain to lead to a clash with the UMP, and could even cause a split in the tatmadaw. To prevent this, Aung Gyi and Maung Maung planned a "counter-coup" to prevent the northern regional command group's coup,[52] and Colonel Kyi Maung, Commander of the Rangoon Military Region, was ordered to deploy his 106th Infantry Battalion around the capital.

---

[48] It is frequently claimed that a large majority of the personnel affiliated with the tatmadaw became supporters of the Stable AFPFL because of U Nu's approaches to the leftists. However, as Makoto Igarashi points out, a look at the voting of military-affiliated personnel in the February 1960 general election shows that the number of Nu-Tin faction supporters in the tatmadaw was competitive with that supporting the Swe-Nyein faction. Makoto Igarashi, "Biruma niokeru kokumin togo to minshu-shugi: kokugun no minshu-shigikan no hensen katei kara [National Unity and Democracy in Burma: [as seen] from the Transformation in the Military's Perception of Democracy]," Master's thesis, Hitotsubashi University Graduate School of Social Sciences, 2001, Chapter 3.

[49] Callahan, *Making Enemies*, p. 186.

[50] Dr. Daw Myint Kyi and Dr. Naw In Gya Lin, *1958–1962 myanmà nainganyê dùtìyàtwê* [Myanmar politics 1958–1962] (Yangon: te'kàtomyâpounhnei'tai', 1991), p. 107.

[51] Ibid., pp. 109–10.

[52] Callahan, *Making Enemies*, p. 187.

Following these moves, Aung Gyi and Maung Maung met with Prime Minister U Nu on 23 and 24 September to find a possible compromise, the two officers' advantage in the negotiations being the threat of a coup. The outcome was a scenario whereby state authority would be legally transferred to General Ne Win, the Chief of General Staff of the tatmadaw, to avoid violent clashes. Consequently, on 26 September, Prime Minister U Nu, Deputy Prime Minister Thakin Tin, Home Minister Bo Min Gaung, and Minister of Public Works and Housing Tin Maung met with Aung Gyi, Maung Maung, and Brigadier General Tin Pe, the tatmadaw Quarter Master General, and during their meeting, a formal letter was exchanged concerning Ne Win's appointment as prime minister and the transfer of power back to a civilian administration after the third general election to be held in 1960. Then on 28 October 1958, the president nominated Ne Win as prime minister based on Clause 1, Article 56 of the Constitution.[53]

When looking at this series of events in the context of military politics, what stands out the most are the maneuvers by Aung Gyi and Maung Maung aimed at working out a deal among the civilian politicians and the hardliners in the tatmadaw. In this regard, they managed to avoid a split in the tatmadaw, which would have pitted the Northern Regional Command that was ready to bring down of government in a violent coup against the Clean AFPFL faction that was only vaguely aware of the threat against it; at the same time, they were also able to maintain the institutional legitimacy of the 1947 Constitution. Within the legal framework of the Constitution, they managed to achieve a compromise with the Clean AFPFL faction by showing the possibility of a coup while at the same time halting the moves of the northern regional command group by making Ne Win prime minister.

My argument here is that the political crisis and the creation of a caretaker government in September 1958 were the result of the mutual concessions between hard-liners in the tatmadaw who wanted to challenge the civilian politicians, in particular the Clean faction, and U Nu who did not grasp the threat posed by the tatmadaw; and the achievement of this compromise was due to the coordinated efforts of Aung Gyi and

---

[53] Dr. Daw Myint Kyi and Dr. Naw In Gya Lin, *myanmà nainganyê dùtìyàtwê* [Myanmar politics 1958–1962], pp. 111–23.

Maung Maung in the General Staff Office.[54] As a result, following his accession to the prime minister's post, Ne Win expressed on several occasions to those both inside and outside the tatmadaw his commitment to the principle of non-intervention in politics by the military. In addition, he also called for adherence to the Constitution, both actions offering further evidence that Aung Gyi and Maung Maung maintained their hold on leadership in the tatmadaw. On 31 October 1958, Ne Win, the Chief of General Staff and now also the prime minister, made the following remarks in a speech to the Union Parliament:

> I would like all of you in this assembly to earnestly believe in the Constitution and democracy as I myself believe in them. I would like all of you to protect the Constitution and democracy as I protect them. As a citizen, as Prime Minister, as a soldier, in any situation, it is my duty to protect the Constitution and democracy even at the sacrifice of my life, and I would like all of you in this assembly to also fulfill the same duty in whatever situation you find yourselves.[55]

Thereafter, following the third general election in February 1960 and in accordance with his own words, Ne Win handed back authority to the Union Party led by U Nu which had won the election, an action of such special mention in the world of that time that he was nominated for the Ramon Magsaysay Award.[56] Seen at the time as keeping himself aloof from either the moderates or the hardliners in the tatmadaw, Ne Win would gradually begin to distance himself from the former.

The 2 March 1962 Coup d'état

Aung Gyi maintained a largely negative view toward political intervention by the tatmadaw. Had his attitude and that of Ne Win's remained

---

[54] In his autobiography, U Nu wrote that the legal handover of power had been a result of his efforts; however, in reality, it was rather that he realized that a failure to make such a compromise would have resulted in a coup d'état. U Nu, *Saturday's Son* (New Haven: Yale University Press, 1975), pp. 325–9.

[55] *khi' yê* 1, no. 9 (1958): 24.

[56] According to the official site of the Ramon Magsaysay Award, it "is given to persons — regardless of race, nationality, creed or gender — who address issues of human development in Asia with courage and creativity, and in doing so have made contributions which have transformed their societies for the better." <http://www.rmaf.org.ph/?id=2&page=history> [accessed 5 July 2011].

aligned, the tatmadaw would likely have refrained from intervening in politics. However, the 2 March 1962 coup d'état was carried out under Ne Win's lead. Exactly how the Ne Win-led coup of 1962 was planned has yet to be revealed, and although more research will be required for us to understand this historical event, the analysis presented here suggests that in 1958 the leaders in the General Staff Office were united in their intention to put down the northern regional command group, whereas in 1962 the general staff office was united in its intent to intervene actively in politics via a coup d'état.

Very likely one important factor for this change was Maung Maung's departure from the tatmadaw. On 1 February 1961, 11 top military officers were dismissed; the reason given for their dismissal was their interference in the general election in February of the previous year. Among those dismissed were one officer in the general staff office, nine brigade commanders, and one regional commander. The dismissed officer in the General Staff Office was Maung Maung. He was forced to retire from the tatmadaw and was appointed ambassador to Israel on 22 March of the year. The formal reason given for Maung Maung's dismissal was his alleged relationship with the U.S. Central Intelligence Agency rather than his interference in the general election, but whether this claim was true or not remains unknown to this day.[57] Regardless of the reason, it was a heavy blow for Aung Gyi, because the one officer who had formed the moderate faction with him in the General Staff Office was gone.[58]

[57] An example is the story of Maung Maung's alledged cooperation with the CIA in the construction of espionage-related facilities in the border area with China, which the Chinese government is said to have learned about. According to the story, when the Chinese passed this information on to Prime Minister U Nu, Maung Maung was dismissed. It has also been suggested that Colonel Bo Lwin, head of the Directorate of Defence Services Intelligence, had a confrontation with Maung Maung, and in order to oust him, Bo Lwin sent a report to Ne Win that included the allegation concerning Maung Maung's close association with the CIA.

[58] However, the dismissals themselves targeted mainly local commanders. Among those included were Brigadier General Aung Shwe, the central figure in the 1958 coup threat (and commander of the Southern Military Region since 25 February 1959) and Colonel Kyi Win, commander of the 7th Regiment (the brother-in-law of Ba Swe and a ringleader in the 1958 coup threat). It is not known to what extent they intervened in the elections to actively support the Stable AFPFL faction. Another reason given for these dismissals was that influential local commanders were said to have been in consultation in order to continue military rule; concerning this conjecture, see Callahan, *Making Enemies*, pp. 200–1.

Before dawn on 2 March 1962, the tatmadaw carried out a coup d'état, detaining the president, prime minister, cabinet ministers, attorney general, and the politicians elected from Shan and Kayah states who were attending a Union Seminar that had begun on 24 February. A version of the coup as it was related to this author in an interview had four people as the masterminds: Ne Win, Tin Pe, Colonel Than Sein, the Colonel General Staff, and Colonel Kyaw Soe, the Military Appointment General. In that version, Aung Gyi was not involved and is said to have known nothing at all specific about the planning of the coup, although he was still Vice Chief of General Staff (Army) at the time.[59] A Revolutionary Council (RC) was established, and all powers of the state were concentrated in the council. The tatmadaw had now seized power. Aung Gyi would later write the following describing the reins of power after the coup:

> General Tin Pe, Colonel Than Sein, U Ba Nyein, Colonel Tin Soe, and Colonel Tan Yu Hsain formed a small government within the government, created a small council within the [Revolutionary] Council; and after secret meetings, they brought [their decisions] to the government and the Council. I think they imported the practice of forming a faction into the realm of the Council, government and military.[60]

Apart from whether this was "the practice of forming a faction," Aung Gyi's comment indicates that he was outside the decision-making process of the RC. The next citation shows that he no longer had any hold on leadership even in the Army.

> I was responsible for everything concerning the Army. However, they sent as many Army officers as they wanted to other ministries, drafted as many as soldiers as they wanted, transferred as many people as they wanted and chose as many as they wanted; they did all these things without ever informing me, the Vice Chief of General Staff (Army). It was in the Ministry of Home Affairs, which was the second government in fact, where these [personnel-related decisions] were implemented.[61]

---

[59] Interview with a former BSPP cadre member, 8 February 2006.

[60] Aung Gyi, *(màsàlà) bàhoe kawmiti thòe pê sa* [A letter to the (Burma Socialist Programme Party) Central Committee] (1976), p. 4.

[61] Ibid., p. 15.

The reason that decisions on Army personnel matters were taking place in the Ministry of Home Affairs was likely because Colonel Kyaw Soe, one of the coup masterminds, was appointed the minister of Home Affairs and controlled personnel matters in the new government. This meant that Aung Gyi had lost his influence within the tatmadaw to the point where he, even as the Vice Chief of General Staff (Army), no longer had control over the personnel of the Army.

This also meant that the guidelines for military conduct, which Aung Gyi together with Maung Maung had drawn up, were being discarded. At the same time, the institutional framework of the 1947 Constitution, held up as the pillar supporting the unity of the tatmadaw, collapsed with the suspension of the Union Parliament (RC Proclamation No. 4) and the abolition of the State Councils that had administered the states under the federal government (RC Proclamation No. 6 through No. 11). Under the new government all state authority was vested in the military controlled RC. Clearly, the tatmadaw was departing from the institutional framework of the 1947 Constitution and changing course toward long-term political intervention.

The Birth of the State Ideology

Although Ne Win and the tatmadaw leadership had led a coup d'état and set a course for long-term political intervention, they did not have any clear idea of a political ideology for their new regime. What they did have was the realization that they needed something that would give legitimacy to the new regime, and they had a vague idea that it would be Burma's own type of socialism, one different from the type that existed at the time. The speech Ne Win made at the first Tatmadaw Conference after the coup clearly illustrates this realization. At that time he told the commanders that they needed an "ism" (*wadà*) for their new government. In his address he said the following.

> Ideologically speaking, since before independence we have believed in a socialist system, a socialist state. This was also the goal toward which the [1947] Constitution was written. Therefore, it is this [ideology of] socialism that we will execute [in administering the government]. So I would liked to explain to you Comrades that it will not be the sort of socialism that others have put into practice. We must not depart from this principle. It will not be any imitation. It will be a socialism

> adapted to our Burma, suitable to our Burmese way of thinking, and appropriate to Burma's natural conditions and situation.[62]

To formulate an ideology of socialism specific to Burma, Ne Win turned to Chit Hlaing because Ne Win never allowed people outside of the tatmadaw to be involved in top decision making, and he knew as well that Chit Hlaing was one of the few people in the tatmadaw knowledgeable about political thought.

There were two occasions when Ne Win issued instructions to Chit Hlaing about formulating ideology for the new regime. The first was four days after the coup d'état when Ne Win ordered the drafting of a policy declaration for the RC. This was announced on 30 April 1962 as *The Burmese Way to Socialism* that became the basic ideology of the Ne Win regime advocating the construction of a Burmese socialist economic system. The second was in November 1962 when Ne Win assigned Chit Hlaing to draft the official ideology of the Burma Socialist Programme Party (BSPP), the future sole legal political party of the state. The course of events from the time of the coup until the announcement of this ideology (*The System of Correlation between Man and His Environment*), as later described by Chit Hlaing, can be summarized as follows.

Soon after the coup, with the aim of unifying all the existing parties, the RC held a meeting with the leaders of the three major political parties: the Union Party, the AFPFL (the former Stable faction), and the NUF. Shortly after the negotiations broke down with no agreement over adopting a one-party system, the RC took steps to create its own political party by organizing the BSPP, which was officially established on 4 July. On 7 November, four months after establishing the party, Ne Win directed Chit Hlaing to draft the ideology that was to be the guideline for the party. At the end of 1962, he submitted the draft document to an informal meeting of the RC. According to him, this document was essentially a revision of his ideas set forth in his aforementioned textbook *Critical Ideology*. The draft was then approved at an RC meeting on 17

---

62 "*1962 khùhni' ta'màdaw nilahkan kagweyê ûsîgyou' ì mèingûn myâ hnìn tâin si' htanàgyou' athîdî hmà hsêinwêiche' myâ* [The 1962 Tatmadaw Conference: Chief of General Staff Speech and Discussion from Each Region Commander]," CD-878(1), DSMHRI, pp. 4–5.

January 1963, and the official ideology of the BSPP was issued the same day as *The System of Correlation between Man and His Environment*.[63]

As set forth in Chit Hlaing's original commentaries on *namarupa wada* and then repeated in his textbook, *The System* described nature as composed of three worlds, that of material (*the'mè you' lôkà*), of living things (*the'shì lôkà*) and of phenomena (*hpyi'pye'pyùpyin lôkà*) in Chapter 1, "The Three Worlds" (*lôkàgyî thôunbâ*). In Chapter 2, "Man and His Society" (*lu hin' lùlôkà*), it is argued that in the world of living things, human society is the most important; therefore, humans have to be the basis of analysis in order to understand the three worlds and solve the problems of human society. The chapter then listed six points to conclude the ideology: (a) man is concerned with all the three worlds, of which he is an image. (b) The flux of man's mind (*sei'da'*) depends on his aggregate of material (*you' hkanda*); man's mind cannot exist without this aggregate of material on which it must continually depend. (c) While man's mind is dependent on his aggregate of material, it leads all his bodily, verbal, and mental actions (*kayà kan*, *wàsi kan* and *mànô kan*) in his social life. (d) Material and mind in man are inseparably linked on the ever-turning wheel of change. (e) The process develops through insignificant and imperceptible degrees into significant and striking strides. (f) Man has both a selfish nature (*a'tàhîtà*) of pursuing self-interest and an altruistic nature (*pàràhìtà*) of looking after the interest of society.[64] In Chapter 3, "The Laws of Process of the History of the Human Society" (*lùbaunthàmain ì pyâunlêyêitàyâ*), Chit Hlaing sought the fusion of the world view set forth in the first two chapters with the historical view of dialectical materialism wherein the interaction of the mind and material of humans working on the environment sets the mode of production; the change in the mode of production is the development of history, and

---

[63] Chit Hlaing, *myanmà hsousheli' lânzin hnin' lânzin pati ì twêkho myomyinpoun dabôtayâ pyi' polapoun akyîn khyou' hma' tân* [The Burmese way to Socialism and a record summarizing the process in formulating the ideology of the Programme Party] (held in the Yangon University Historical Research Center) (HRC: X/15 AP/1992), p. 17.

[64] Chit Hlaing came to use the more common *sei'da'* (mind) and *you'hkanda* (material) instead of the terms *nama* and *rupa*. According to him, there was no particular meaning in this change other than making the terms easier to understand by using the common words. Interview with Chit Hlaing, 6 January 2005.

revolution as one form of this development arises from the confrontation between the forces trying to prevent development and the forces trying to promote development.[65]

There are two points of note revealed in the above discussion. First, neither Ne Win nor any of the other coup leaders had a clear idea about an ideology for the new regime, and Chit Hlaing was simply directed to draw up an ideology. Given the task at hand, Chit Hlaing fell back on his own ideological thought of *namarupa wada* that he had developed some five years earlier and had set forth in his textbook *Critical Ideology*. These sources became the basis for the new regime's ideology. Second, no significant modification of Chit Hlaing's draft was made in the RC meetings, meaning that the process of formulating the official ideology was a product resulting from the interaction of Ne Win's directive and Chit Hlaing's response. In effect, the essence of the draft was the same as that of the textbook written and used in his class for psychological warfare officers. It was a repeat of the arguments he had developed in his anti-communist propagandizing in the late 1950s. However, by 1962 the political environment had altered significantly, and now Chit Hlaing's personal ideological musings and a small textbook based on constitutionalism and anti-communism suddenly and with the leadership's uncritical acceptance turned into the regime's official ideology of socialism that denied the 1947 Constitution.

Although Aung Gyi resisted the radical economic socialism that the RC began pursuing, his opinions no longer gained Ne Win's support and he lost hope of regaining political influence in the regime. In February 1963 he stepped down from all of his official positions, which included his seat on RC and his post as Vice Chief of General Staff (Army), and also resigned from the tatmadaw. In contrast to Aung Gyi, Chit Hlaing assumed the position of vice-principal of the Central Institute of Political Science (*bàhou nainganyêi thei'pan kyâun*), the leadership training school of the BSPP, on 1 June 1963 and engaged in the training of party cadre until he retired in 1971 because of political infighting in the school. As vice-principle his position was fairly important in party activities, but he was less influential as an ideologue of the state. Indeed, he never was

[65] Chapter 4 of *The System* entitled "The Determining Role of the Working People", explains the essence of human beings, and Chapter 5, "Our Attitude to Our Own Ideology" stresses the point that the arguments in "the System" are not absolute but modifiable depending on the time and situation.

directly involved in the policy process after his formulation of the state and party ideology.

Conclusion

During the mid-1950s, the prevailing mood in the tatmadaw leadership was constitutionalism and avoidance of political intervention, which was one of the central goals of the military reform under Aung Gyi and Maung Maung. However, in the early 1960s, as Ne Win distanced himself from the moderates, he formed an alliance with the hardline officers that led to a coup in March 1962. The new regime was built in an extremely haphazard way under Ne Win's strong leadership.[66] They were not interested in cooperating with forces outside the tatmadaw, and after the coup most decisions were made only by the tatmadaw leadership. At the time, Chit Hlaing was one of the few people in the tatmadaw that the leadership could turn to who was knowledgeable about political thought. Thus, to a great extent, circumstances dictated that Chit Hlaing would play a key role in the new regime as he was called upon to draft the new ideology, which was based on writings he had published earlier. In the late 1950s, he wrote a draft of the military doctrine and a number of anti-communism articles under the wing of Aung Gyi and Maung Maung. His works were directed at strengthening the unity of the tatmadaw and establishing the principle of its political neutrality by protecting the 1947 Constitution and promoting anti-communism. These objectives were not those of Ne Win nor the hardline officers who staged the 1962 coup d'état. Ironically, however, the same text written in the context of protecting the Constitution and promoting anti-communism

[66] In his opening speech at the Tatmadaw Conference in 1962 held soon after the coup d'état, Ne Win explained that he had overheard "extremist" (*pyìnpyìnhtanhtan*) talk at a Union seminar on 24 February of that year and thought that the National Assembly members from Shan State were going to attempt some sort of rebellion connected with the movement toward federation, so he had no choice (*màlou' màpyi'*) but to carry out a coup to suppress these moves beforehand. See "1962 khùhni' ta'màdaw nilahkan kagweyê ûsîgyou' ì mèingûn myâ hnìn tâin si' htanàgyou' athìdî hmà hsêinwêiche' myâ" [The 1962 Tatmadaw Conference: tatmadaw Chief of General Staff Speech and Discussion from Each Military Region Command], CD-878(1), DSMHRI, p. 1. However, that particular Union seminar did not focus on the exercise of a state's right to secede. The talk there had been about the more moderate expansion of autonomy; there was no crisis and the breakup of the state was not imminent.

became the very document that would legitimize the Ne Win regime's break from the institutional framework of the 1947 Constitution and the construction of one-party rule.

Ne Win appeared to quite opportunistically adopt the text for the new state ideology after the coup. However, likely one of the most important functions of the state ideology for Ne Win was to contain ideological contention over the multifaceted and disputatious concept of socialism; in which case, the establishment of a state ideology was more significant than its content, because thereafter the state could deny other possible interpretations of socialism through the control of free speech. Following the distribution of *The System*, discussions about socialism and democracy were expelled from the formal realm of public speech. What remained was only official rhetoric aimed at eliminating national security threats posed by radical political thoughts.

General Ne Win. (© AP/Aflo)

CHAPTER 4

Party-State *Manqué*: Ne Win's Revolution and the Burma Socialist Programme Party

This chapter will examine the party-state that Ne Win sought to build and its ultimate failure. As defined here, the party-state means a political system having a single ruling party that leads and controls the state. The regime Ne Win built after the coup of 2 March 1962 began in a haphazard way, but he did have existing models to follow in the party-states that had been previously created predominately in communist countries. The Burma Socialist Programme Party (BSPP) (*myanmà hsosheli' lânzin pati*), which later became the sole legal political party allowed in Burma, was formed in July 1962, and one-party rule became formalized with the enactment of the new constitution in 1974. What exactly was one-party rule by the BSPP? Why did Ne Win need it? Did he believe in socialist revolution? Or did he just want to put a civilian face on military rule? While it is questionable whether the Ne Win regime was a party-centered political system like that in communist countries, it is equally questionable whether the BSPP was a political organization created solely to disguise military rule. I intend to reveal in this chapter that the Ne Win of the 1970s, at least, was shifting his power base from the tatmadaw to the BSPP. In order to analyze the process of this power-base shift, this chapter will focus on the three-way relationship among Ne Win, the tatmadaw, and the BSPP, discussing the formation and development of the Ne Win regime during the 1960s and 1970s, and examining the shift to a party-state and its consequences.

Among the varied aspects of the BSPP, the focus will be on party personnel. Analyzing the party's policy-making process and its factions is also needed; however, investigating such aspects is still not easy to do in Burma, and at present it is more realistic and effective to make inferences about the party workings from relatively accessible information like data on personnel. Also, personnel changes take place on a short-term basis, which makes possible a more dynamic analysis when compared with analyzing the party in terms of organization or ideology. Most importantly, it is possible to make inferences about the organizational autonomy of the BSPP from changes in the rules for its personnel. The party must be autonomous from the state apparatus in order for it to guide the state. By the 1974 Constitution the BSPP's autonomy was institutionally guaranteed; however, we still lack any solid verification of whether this was actually the situation, and the predominant view among Burma scholars is that the tatmadaw maintained its influence over the BSPP. In order to better understand what the actual situation was, this chapter will examine the informal rules of personnel management of the BSPP and the changes in these rules, which offer a method for gauging the party's autonomy, and from this seek to determine the extent that the Ne Win regime created a party-state.

The remainder of this chapter proceeds as follows. It will begin with an analysis of the personnel that made up the state leadership from 1962 through 1970 when Burma was in the formative stage of its development as a party-state, and will also examine the process of organizing the BSPP. The chapter will then examine the transformation of the political regime that started in 1971 using the data available. This will suggest that although Ne Win himself intended to build a party-state, the Third Party Congress in February 1977 and the political crisis he subsequent confronted clearly indicate that this attempt ended in failure.

Dictatorship and Military

Following its coup d'état and seizing of power in 1962, the Revolutionary Council (RC) turned to socialism as its model for reorganizing the state.[1] One reason for this choice was to justify the coup. It also provided a prescription for the crisis of unity and economic stagnation that Burma

[1] This book separates politics from economy in analyzing the regime and focuses on the former. Although there is the argument in socialism that both are closely intertwined and cannot be separated, in Burma the military rather than the communist party seized power with the aim of building socialism. Not being or having its own political party, the military had to build a party from scratch, which created a time lag between the socialization of the political system and that of the economy.

was confronting. The choice would bring profound changes to the country's economic and political systems. The RC began moving ahead with socialization of the economy relatively soon after taking power. A succession of private enterprises in petroleum, banking, cigarette manufacturing, gem mining, and other lesser industries were nationalized, and the existing policy for nationalizing agricultural land was enforced. Change in the political system, however, did not move ahead so easily. This was because Burma's revolution began with a coup, and the RC had to create a wholly new revolutionary party around which to build Burma's socialist system.

In *The Burmese Way to Socialism* policy declaration, the RC rejected parliamentary democracy as ineffective for Burma, and called instead for a democracy that would promote the development of socialism and the stability of the state. In line with this view, Ne Win, the RC chairman, initially aimed at setting up a united front of the existing political parties, and on 7 May 1962 he undertook separate talks with the representatives of the Union Party, the Anti-Fascist People's Freedom League, and National United Front. However, the negotiations broke down due to objections from the political parties. Ne Win's next move was to set up a wholly new revolutionary party, and this was the BSPP, which was officially inaugurated on 4 July 1962. This was in line with Article 2 of the party's constitution, which stated that, "The revolution should be led by a revolutionary party." In 1963 the BSPP set up party regional offices in Rangoon and the Northwest, Southwest, East, Southeast, and Central regions corresponding to the six military regional commands, and 15 party division offices largely corresponding to the country's division and state administrative units. The party also set up a leadership training school named the Central Institute of Political Science (CIPS) (later renamed the Central University of Political Science), and the funding of party operations was to be financed by the national treasury as stipulated in Revolutionary Council Ordinance No. 47. On 28 March 1964 the Law to Protect National Solidarity took effect prohibiting the activities of all political parties and bodies except the BSPP.

With this series of steps, one-party rule was set legally in place. However, it took another seven years and the First Party Congress in June 1971 before the BSPP actually started to function as a revolutionary party. It had spent the preceding years building up its basic party organization, and, during that time, the Central Organizing Committee (COC), the BSPP's top executive organization, did not perform any important political function.[2] An analysis of the BSPP after 1971 and a closer look at the members of the RC and the government cabinet, the personnel central to the state, will help to clarify the power structure during the formative years of the BSPP.

Revolutionary Council and Cabinet

The 1962 coup succeeded without destabilizing military politics, except the marginalization of General Aung Gyi, because it was staged by Ne Win, the Chief of General Staff, and the members of the RC were from the top military leadership and totalled 17 officers: four from the General Staff Office: the Chief of General Staff of tatmadaw and the Vice Chief of General Staff of the Army, Navy and Air Force; six officers holding important posts in the Ministry of Defence which included the Quartermaster General and Adjutant General; the five army regional commanders; one officer involved in administering the border areas; and the Deputy Commissioner General of the People's Police (Table 4.1).

The composition of the RC reflected the power relationship within the tatmadaw. It demonstrated the overwhelming predominance of the Army. This has been a characteristic of the tatmadaw since its establishment, and in 1962 when Ne Win took power, the size of the Army was about 120,000 men compared to the Navy and Air Force with about 3,000 and 2,500 men, respectively.[3] Therefore most of the important positions on the RC were held by Army officers, and the Navy and Air Force were represented only by their vice chiefs of General Staff. The composition also reflected a power balance in the relationship between the General Staff Office and the regional commanders. The split between the central command and regional commanders had been a longstanding problem for the tatmadaw, and it seems that all five regional commanders were made RC members because Ne Win intended to stabilize the center-region relationship within the tatmadaw. In addition to the RC, Ne Win appointed new cabinet ministers. It was composed of eight members. All but one of them held multiple ministry portfolios; all except one

[2] Many members of the Party Organizing Central Committee are not known, but Article 3(c) of the party constitution stipulated that a member was to be "appointed only from among the Revolutionary Council members." It is also known that Ne Win served as chairman and San Yu as deputy chairman of the RC.

[3] *Tonan Ajia Yoran* [Southeast Asia Directory], 1962, p. 223.

Table 4.1 Members of the First Revolutionary Council

Post	*Name*	*Rank*	*Post in the Military*
Chairman	Ne Win	GN (A)	CGS
Member	Aung Gyi	BG (A)	V-CGS (A)
Member	Than Pe	BG (N)	V-CGS (N)
Member	T. Criff	BG (AF)	V-CGS (AF)
Member	Tin Pe	BG (A)	QMG
Member	Than Sein	CL (A)	CGS
Member	Kyaw Soe	CL (A)	MAG
Member	Chit Myaing	CL (A)	VQG
Member	Khin Nyo	CL (A)	DDMT
Member	Hla Han	CL (A)	DDMS
Member	San Yu	BG (A)	CNMR
Member	Sein Win	BG (A)	CCMR
Member	Thaung Kyi	CL (A)	CSEMR
Member	Kyi Maung	CL (A)	CSWMR
Member	Maung Shwe	CL (A)	CEMR
Member	Saw Mint	CL (A)	ABA
Member	Than Yu Saing	CL (A)	VCGPP

Note: A: Army, N: Navy, AF: Air Force, GN: General, BG: Brigadier General, CL: Colonel, CGS: the Chief of General Staff, V-CGS(A): Vice-Chief of General Staff (Navy), V-CGS(A): Vice-Chief of General Staff (Navy), V-CGS(AF): Vice-Chief of General Staff (Air Force), QG: Quartermaster General, CGS: Colonel General Staff, MAG: Military Appointment General, VQG: Vice-Quartermaster General, DDMT: Director General of Directorate of Military Training, DDMS: Director General of Directorate of Medical Services, CNMC: Commander of Northern Military Command, CCMR: Commander of Central Military Region, CSEMR: Commander of Southeast Military Region, CSWMR: Commander of Southwest Military Region, CEMR: Commander of Eastern Military Region, DBA: Administrator of Border Regions, VCGPP: Vice-Commissioner of General of People's Police

Source: U Mya Han [*et al.* 1993: 3]

were active military officers, and all of these officers worked in the headquarters of regional commands.[4]

An examination of the changes that took place among the membership of the tatmadaw command, the RC and the cabinet between 1962 and the first BSPP congress in 1971 reveals two prominent characteristics of the leadership power structure. One is the continued predominance

[4] The following information on the personnel of the RC and cabinet members is mainly from *Tonan Ajia Yoran* [Southeast Asia Directory]; and *Ajia Doko Nenpo* [Asian Trends Annual Report].

of tatmadaw (particularly Army) officers. A total of 33 people had been appointed as RC and cabinet members by June 1971, but only three, Thi Han (who served as Foreign Minister and National Planning Minister among other posts), Nyi Nyi (Deputy Minister of Education), and Ba Nyein (Deputy Minister of Cooperatives) were not active officers. However, Thi Han was a retired officer who had headed the Quartermaster General Office, while Nyi Nyi and Ba Nyein were not appointed to the cabinet until 1970. This meant in effect that for nearly the entire period from 1962 to 1971, virtually all of the members of the RC and cabinet were active tatmadaw officers; moreover they all were Army officers except for the vice chiefs of General Staff of the Navy and Air Force and the Deputy Commissioner General (later Commissioner General) of the People's Police. One very important reason for the overwhelming presence of military officers in the leadership was Ne Win's very great reliance on trusted followers to run the government (which will be pointed out below), all of whom were tatmadaw officers, a factor that in itself led to the RC and cabinet being composed almost entirely of active tatmadaw (especially Army) officers.

The other characteristic was the rise of a two-tiered differentiation of power in the regime's leadership structure, meaning that two types of officers came to exist within the RC. The first type on the upper tier of power was made up of officers who had Ne Win's confidence and were entrusted to run the government as his aides. Brigadier General San Yu, Brigadier General Tin Pe, Brigadier General Sein Win, Colonel Kyaw Soe, Colonel Hla Han and Colonel Than Sein were in this group; and among these officers, those from the General Staff Office worked both as staff officers and as cabinet members, while those who were Army regional commanders became cabinet members after completing their tours as commanders. Together with Ne Win, these men were central to the operations of the government.[5]

The second type of officer at the lower tier of power was the group that became cabinet ministers or deputy ministers after completing their tour of duty as regional commanders. There were cases where officers of the first type who were regional commanders, e.g., San Yu, went on to become cabinet members; however, for second-tier regional commanders,

[5] There continue to be many unclear and unknown points regarding the power relationships within the RC, so it is not possible to draw a clear line separating the two tiers of power.

the transfer from commander to cabinet minister was essentially automatic and was not necessarily connected with being a Ne Win aide. The first such transfers took place in 1964 when Colonel Sein Win, ex-commander of the Central Military Region, was appointed Minister of Housing and Public Works; Colonel Thaung Kyi, ex-commander of South-eastern Military Region, was made Minister of Agriculture and Forestry as well as Minister of Land Nationalization; and Colonel Maung Shwe, ex-commander of Eastern Military Region, became Minister of Industry.

The second transfers were in 1969, but by that time no cabinet minister positions were left for new ex-regional commanders. So deputy minister posts were newly created to be filled by four ex-regional commanders. From this time on it became an informal rule for Army officers who completed their tours of duty as regional commanders to be appointed directly to cabinet positions. Through this process a two-tiered power structure came to exist within the RC, one tier made up of Ne Win's aides who together with him held the reins of power in the government, and a second tier made up of former regional commanders who became cabinet members after completing their time as commanders. The question that arises here is why this two-tiered differentiation occurred.

Ne Win held all power of the state in his hands, and two requirements were essential for maintaining his stable grip on power. One was to keep people he could trust close to him to consolidate his power. This group of close, trusted aides came to form the upper tier of officers in the RC. And he purged his potential enemies, notably Aung Gyi, second only to Ne Win in the tatmadaw at the time of the coup, who was compelled to resign from the RC on 9 February 1963.[6]

---

[6] There have been some explanations for Aung Gyi's resignation, that it was caused by a conflict of views between Aung Gyi the realist and Ne Win the idealist; that it was the result of a factional confrontation in the tatmadaw in which an officer in Brigadier General Tin Pe's faction told Ne Win disreputable things about Aung Gyi leading to his dismissal; or that Aung Gyi was dismissed because of repeated instances of unauthorized political statements that Ne Win was no longer able to tolerate, not so much due to their content as to the willfulness of Aung Gyi's behavior. Regarding this issue, see Hirayoshi Sakuma, *Biruma (Myanma) Gendai Seiji-shi Zoho-ban* [Burma (Myanmar) Modern Political History Enlarged Edition] (Tokyo: Keiso Shobo, 1993), pp. 70–1; Colonel Chit Myaing, "In His Own Words," Burma Debate 4(3) <http://www.soros.org/burma/burmadebate/Bdjulaug97.html> (1997); Kyaw Yin Hlaing, "The Politics of State-Business Relations in Post-Colonial Burma," PhD dissertation, Cornell University, 2001, pp. 144–5.

Ne Win's hold on power was based in the RC, but the way he used the officers who made up the RC had the potential to cause trouble within the tatmadaw. Only a portion of the officers held cabinet posts, which provided power and benefits, and these officers were largely concentrated in the General Staff Office. Meanwhile the regional commanders were the officers whose time was wholly spent fighting anti-government rebels, so it was understandable that they were displeased about the benefits going to those in the General Staff Office. Having been at the top of the tatmadaw since its establishment and the chief of general staff until 1972, Ne Win understood his commanders' feelings, and from this emerged his second requirement for maintaining his grip on power: distributing benefits among the tatmadaw leadership to maintain the institutional stability of the military. By providing cabinet positions to officers who had completed their tours of duty as military region commanders, Ne Win tempered their dissatisfaction as well as that of the incumbent regional commanders. At the same time he sought to stabilize the tatmadaw as a bureaucratic organization by having commanders replaced periodically. This appears to be how the second level of the two-tiered power structure in the RC came about. This two-tiered organization of the council reflected its dual nature. It was both a body that allowed Ne Win to maintain his power and one that distributed benefits to tatmadaw leaders and moved them out of the military into government positions.

Until 1970 the functioning of the state was characterized by the coexistence of dictatorship and military rule. Although the regime advocated socialism, this was not due to any influence of its revolutionary party, the BSPP. That situation would begin to change in 1971. Until then, from 1962 to 1970, the party remained under construction. However, this eight-year stage of building would have an important impact after 1971.

The Human Resources of the BSPP

The RC termed the period from the establishment of the BSPP until the First Party Congress in 1971 as the time of the "cadre party," and strove to develop and expand it for an eventual transition to a "people's party." *The System of Correlation between Man and His Environment*, published in January 1963 and the *Characteristics of the Burma Socialist Programme Party* that came out the following year, along with other sources mentioned in Chapter 3, indicate that the BSPP acquired an elaborate ideology at a comparatively early stage. Party organization was led by a COC set up in BSPP central headquarters. Under its direction central offices were established; these were a Peasants Affairs Bureau, Workers Affairs Bureau, Mass Organization Affairs Bureau, Education Affairs Bureau and Administrative Affairs Bureau. Regional inspection committees were placed in the six party regions and division inspection committees in the 15 party divisions; below these were party units organized at the township level. Party units were also set up in the CIPS and inside the tatmadaw. A figure published in 1967 indicated that as of 1966, the BSPP had organized 334 units all over the country.[7] Under each township party unit were local party cells spread out amongst the village tracts, wards, factories, and other such places. There were only 20 formal party members, and, from 1963, when acceptance of applications for entry to the party started, until 1970, most of the people affiliated with the BSPP were provisional members. They numbered slightly less than 100,000 in 1965, over 180,000 in 1966, and were reported to have reached 250,000 by 1970. Party expenditures also steadily rose in parallel with organizational expansion and growth in provisional party membership. Although progress was indeed slow, the BSPP gradually expanded in organization, party membership, and the size of its expenditures,[8] and over the course of this building process, party seminars were held in 1965, 1966, 1968, and 1969 to discuss issues concerning the party.[9]

There is little contemporary material to draw on when analyzing the human resources of the BSPP. It is hard to know the source of these resources or how they change over the course of the party's expansion. Therefore, this section examines the profiles of the candidates for the party's first Central Committee (CC) in 1971 to show what kind of people became party executives.[10]

---

[7] *Tonan Ajia Yoran 1967 nenban* [Southeast Asia Directory 1967], p. 559.

[8] Regarding the BSPP's expansion process, see Robert Taylor, *The State in Burma* (Honolulu: University of Hawaii Press, 1987), pp. 300–26.

[9] For example, the Third Party Seminar in 1968 dealt with the theme of "quality over quantity," and discussions took place on the need for organizational reforms within the party, relations with administrative organizations, the transition to a people's party, and drafting a constitution.

[10] As used here, party executives refer to the following positions: At the party center were: the Affairs Committee members of the Party Organizing Central Committee, and the assistant bureau chiefs, directors, deputy directors, section chiefs, and subsection chiefs of each bureau (Peasant Affairs Bureau, Workers Affairs Bureau, Mass Organization Affairs Bureau, Education Affairs Bureau, Administrative Affairs Bureau) in the party headquarters. (The chiefs of each bureau were RC members, so they were

Table 4.2 First CC Member Candidates from Party Headquarters

<table>
<tr><th colspan="2">Party Position</th><th>Rank</th><th>No. Persons</th></tr>
<tr><td colspan="2" rowspan="6">Member of Affairs Committees</td><td>CL(A)</td><td>2</td></tr>
<tr><td>LC(A)</td><td>6</td></tr>
<tr><td>LC(AF)</td><td>1</td></tr>
<tr><td>CP(A)</td><td>2</td></tr>
<tr><td>MA(N)</td><td>1</td></tr>
<tr><td>Civilian</td><td>11</td></tr>
<tr><td rowspan="11">HQ officer</td><td rowspan="2">Assistant Director General</td><td>LC(A)</td><td>3</td></tr>
<tr><td>CL(AF)</td><td>1</td></tr>
<tr><td rowspan="2">Director</td><td>CL(A)</td><td>1</td></tr>
<tr><td>LC(A)</td><td>2</td></tr>
<tr><td>Deputy Director</td><td>MA(A)</td><td>1</td></tr>
<tr><td rowspan="4">Section Chief</td><td>MA(N)</td><td>2</td></tr>
<tr><td>MA(AF)</td><td>4</td></tr>
<tr><td>CO(A)</td><td>3</td></tr>
<tr><td>Civilian</td><td>2</td></tr>
<tr><td rowspan="2">Subsection Chief</td><td>MA(A)</td><td>2</td></tr>
<tr><td>CP(A)</td><td>1</td></tr>
<tr><td colspan="2">Total</td><td>43</td><td></td></tr>
</table>

Source: [bahoukomiti winlâunmyâ î kôuyêi hma'tân acînjou' 1971?]

Table 4.2 presents the number of military and civilian members that made up the party headquarters executives, and the number by rank that were also tatmadaw officers. Most of the executives were officers, both within the headquarters staff, who primarily did clerical work, and within the Affairs Committee, whose work was more political. These officers did not retire but were seconded from the tatmadaw to the BSPP and other state organizations where they moved from one position to

excluded from this analysis.) At the local level were the chairmen of the party regional inspection committees; deputy chairmen and chief secretaries of the party division inspection committees; the heads, chief secretaries and executive committee members of the party units; and the chief secretaries and assistant secretaries of the party class.

another.[11] Their status in the party tended to be related to their ranking in the military.

All twelve officers serving on the Affairs Committee held some concurrent position in a state organization while none of the officers making up the headquarters staff had any concurrent post. Affairs Committee members transferred out of the tatmadaw to the BSPP or other administrative bodies by age 65, and thereafter the number of concurrent positions they served in increased along with their promotions. This meant for officers that membership on the party's Affairs Committee translated into an enjoyable position in which power and benefits increased hand in hand with promotions, while being a member of the party headquarters staff was an entry position for middle-grade officers seconded from the tatmadaw and where they began following the path of promotions that led up through the BSPP and other administrative organizations.[12]

It is evident that decisions over matters of BSPP central personnel were in the hands of the tatmadaw and that the party had little autonomy in this area. This brings into question the function of the CIPS, which was designed to be a leadership training organization.[13] Close to

---

[11] Therefore, officers serving as executives in party headquarters could move back and forth between the tatmadaw and the BSPP. An example was the career of Lieutenant Colonel Maung Aye, assistant chief of the Mass Organization Affairs Bureau of the Party Organizing Central Committee, who was attached to a logistics unit in the Northern Military Region from 1962 to 1963, then worked as subsection chief in the Education Bureau before moving on to serve as the commander of the First Shan Rifle Battalion. From 1966 he took over as assistant chief of the Mass Organization Affairs Bureau in the party headquarters.

[12] However, the posting of personnel in BSPP headquarters was not determined solely by circumstances within the tatmadaw, which is evident from the civilian members of the Affairs Committee. Among them were learned individuals such as university professors and Supreme Court justices; they also included former members of political parties. Among the latter, for example, were four people who had belonged to the Communist Party and two who were from the National United Front, a union of leftist parties. They worked in the party headquarters as special officials from the time the BSPP was established and continued to work there until 1971, their duty apparently being to guide the organizing of the party. Although they were few in number, the way these civilian personnel were managed was different from the way positions were allocated to officers in party headquarters.

[13] The institute offered a one-year four-month course on ideology and methods of party organization. Between 1963 and 1971, it offered twenty-two kinds of courses that were taught a total of 156 times and were attended by a total of nearly thirty thousand people.

thirty thousand people had attended courses at the institute by 1971,[14] but almost none of the executives in the party headquarters were among these. This was because most of the graduates became local party executives. Among the 177 such executives who were included as candidates for the CC in 1971, at least 101 of them had attended some sort of course at the CIPS.[15]

Some course attendees were from the tatmadaw. Table 4.3, which gives the number of students at the CIPS by profession, shows that 1,156 military personnel attended courses and only made up about 4 per cent of the total student body. However, courses focused on training the party's local senior executives (courses for training special executives, deputy committee chairmen and secretary's general, division inspection executives, and re-education courses for division inspection executives) were offered only once to an attendee who had to be a member of the tatmadaw. The bias toward military personnel was evident among the local party executives who became candidates for the CC in 1971. These candidates were executives of the party regional and division inspection committees, and all but one were military officers (see Table 4.4). At the party unit level, the military was less dominant with 61 of the 139 party unit executives coming from the tatmadaw; the remaining 78 were civilians. However, it is clear that despite the existence of an independent educational organization for training local BSPP executives (i.e., the CIPS), military personnel, few of whom attended the institute, had priority in the operations of the party. As a result, higher ranking positions in the BSPP, from those of office chiefs of division inspection committees and above came to be filled overwhelmingly by tatmadaw officers. The composition of the local party executives came to reflect the hierarchy

---

14 pati sîyôunyê bahoukomiti.[Party Organizing Central Committee], *pàhtámà acein patinyilahkan pati bahoukomiti ou'katàgyî ì mèingônmyâ hhnìn pati sîyôunyê bahoukomiti î nàinnganyêi àsiyinhkansa* [The First Party Congress, Central Committee Chairman's Speech and Party Organizing Central Committee Political Report] (1971), Table 10.

15 These are the figures calculated from Burma, anonymous, 1971. *bahoukomiti winlâunmyâ î kôuyêi hma'tân acînjou'* [Profiles of the Candidates of the Central Committee]. The amount of information in the descriptions depended on the candidate, and it seems that some of them were not described even though they had attended a course at the institute. Therefore, the expression "at least" was used here. The breakdown of the candidates by the numbers who had attended courses was: 0 for party regional inspection committee executives, 13 out of 26 party division inspection committee executives, 86 out of 139 party unit executives, two out of four party class people, and none of the three people from party cells.

Table 4.3 Courses and Occupations of Students in the Central University of Political Science (1963–71) Unit: Person

	Course	*Number of Class*	*Occupation of Students*							*Total*
			Farmer	*Labor*		*Party Staff*	*Party Friend*	*Military*	
				Public Service	*Non Public Service*				
1	Special Cadre Course	1						24	24
2	Deputy Chairman, Secretary General	1						21	21
3	Division Inspection Cadre	1						117	117
4	Division Inspection Cadre Retraining	1						41	41
5	Higher Course	1				16		4	20
6	Instructor Course	6		41	1	109	6	70	227
7	Party Organization Course	7				408		189	597
8	Basic Political Science Course	23	51	2,185	101	446	328	445	3,556
9	Party Organization and Administration Reeducation Course	6				315		181	496
10	Basic Political Science and Administration Course	8	19	504	31	212	55	26	847
11	Party Organization/Basic Military Training Course	3				237			237
12	Ethnic Minority Cadre Course	3	14	25	6		50		95
13	Worker Affairs Course	30		8,976	1,763	252	172		11,163
14	Peasant Affairs Course	18	5,921	444	479	81	171		7,096
15	People's Peasants' Council Organization Course	1		4		111			115
16	People's Workers' Council Organization Course	2		56	5	112	8	38	219
17	Agricultural Mechanization Assistant Course	1	37	4					41
18	People's Workers' Council Administration Course	13		1,023	120	179	59		1,381
19	People's Peasants' Council Course	6	105	134	42	99	59		439
20	Township People's Peasants' Council Activity Course	3				558			558
21	People's Affairs Course	2	5	53	3	6	33		100
22	Party Office Officers Administration Course	19				1,751			1,751
Total		156	6,152	13,449	2,551	4,892	941	1,156	29,141

Source: [bahoukomiti winlâunmyâ î kôuyêi hma'tân acînjou' 1971: Table 10]

Table 4.4 First CC Member Candidates from the Tatmadaw in the Local Party Organization

Party Organization	*Post*	*Rank*	*No. Persons*
Regional Supervision Committee	Chairman	CL(A)	5
Division Supervision Committee	Deputy-Chairman	LC(A)	10
		LC(N)	2
		MA(A)	1
	Chief Secretary	MA(A)	4
		MA(N)	2
		MA(AF)	1
		CP(A)	4
	Office Manager	CA(A)	1
		Civilian	1
Party Unit	Chairman	MA(A)	1
		MA(AF)	1
		CP(A)	57
		LT(A)	1
		Civilian	58
	Chief Secretary	CP(A)	1
		Civilian	15
	Executive Committee Member	Civilian	5
Party Class	Leader	CL(A)	1
		Civilian	2
	Deputy-Leader	Civilian	1
Party Cell	Chief Secretary	Civilian	3
Total			177

Note: A: Army, N: Navy, AF: Air Force, CL: Colonel, LC: Lieutenant Colonel, MA: Major, CP: Captain, LT: Lieutenant

Source: [bahoukomiti winlâunmyâ î kôuyêi hma'tân acînjou' 1971?]

within the tatmadaw with a chairman of a party regional inspection committee approximately equalling the rank of a colonel, a deputy chairman of a party division inspection committee ranked like that of a lieutenant colonel, a chief secretary ranked as a major, and a party unit executive corresponding to the rank of a captain.

In sum, the growing demand for human resources as the BSPP expanded was supplied by officers seconded from the tatmadaw. Civilian party executives were consistently placed in subordinate roles with the highest office that a civilian could assume in accordance with the party's promotion system being the chief of a party unit. Thus the BSPP was far from being an autonomous party organization. It was an adjunct of the military with tatmadaw officers forming the human framework of the party.

Transition to a Party-State and Its Failure

After the prolonged process of building the BSPP, Ne Win sought to use it to transform the state in Burma into a party-state, and how this process began with an organizational reform of the party. Ne Win would ultimately fail in this effort, and, following a review of the party reform, we will look at how a change that took place in party personnel led to this failure.

Ne Win first publicly revealed his intention to "transition to civilian rule" in a speech at the BSPP's First Party Seminar in 1965. The "transition to civilian rule" would require a constitution, a national assembly, and a ruling political party, but moves in this direction began only after the party-building process had been completed. The first step was the creation of a constitution drafting committee, which was set up in 1971, and in June of that year the First Party Congress of the BSPP took place. These moves signalled the start of a large-scale organizational reform to change the party from its existing status as a "cadre party" to that of a "people's party." The drafting committee published the first draft of the constitution on 16 March 1972, and subsequently most government officials, including Ne Win, retired from the tatmadaw to become "civilians." Throughout 1973, as the review of the draft Constitution progressed, preparations began for a national referendum on the constitution and the establishment of a People's Parliament. In July of that year, the Second Party Congress took place, and the third draft of the Constitution was adopted as the final document. A national referendum was held in December with 90.19 per cent of the voters approving the new Constitution, which then went into effect on 3 January 1974. This was followed by elections for the People's Parliament, as called for by the new Constitution. These were held throughout the country during January and February. In accordance with Article 11, which stated, "The state adopts a one-party system. The Burma Socialist Programme Party is the only political party, and it is the leader of the state," all candidates were members of the BSPP. Following the elections, the first People's Parliament opened on 2 March 1974, which completed Burma's "transition to civilian rule."[16]

The Central Executive Committee

Along with reforming the organization of the state, Ne Win also changed his informal rules for controlling the personnel who made up the leadership of the state. His first step was taken in 1969 when he stopped the appointment of active military region commanders to the RC. Then in 1971, with the First Party Congress, he reorganized the BSPP, establishing a Central Executive Committee (CEC), which in practice became the supreme decision-making body of the state. Table 4.5 shows the members of the first CEC. Thirteen people out of 15 doubled as RC members, while the remaining two people served as RC members only until they became CEC members. In essence, there were no significant personnel changes per se. However, there would be changes thereafter in new appointments and in positions held concurrently.

Two of the three people who were newly appointed CEC members at the Second Party Congress were close to Ne Win, one of these was Colonel Kyaw Htin, a candidate for the tatmadaw Chief of General Staff position that Ne Win had vacated. His was not the per forma appointment of a military region commander who had completed his tour of duty. On 20 April 1972 many officers retired from the tatmadaw, leaving only three active officers among the CEC members; they were General San Yu, Vice Chief of General Staff (Army); Brigadier General Thaung Tin, Vice Chief of General Staff (Navy); and Brigadier General Thaung Dan, Vice Chief of General Staff (Air Force). Among the second round of appointees to the CEC, the only active officers were Brigadier General Thaung Tin, Brigadier General Thaung Dan, Brigadier General Tin Oo, who was Vice Chief of General Staff (Army), and Colonel Kyaw Htin, who would become Vice Chief of General Staff (Army) in 1974. Following the commencement of the First People's Parliament in March 1974, most of the CEC members gave up their concurrent ministerial posts, and the only positions held concurrently thereafter were those of deputy prime minister, National Planning and Finance Minister, Home

[16] Minoru Kiryu, "Biruma shakaishugi to sono henyou katei [Burmese Socialism and Its Transformation]," in *Biruma sono shakai to kachikan* [Burma: its society and sense of values], ed. Toru Ono, Minoru Kiryu, and Teruko Saito (Tokyo: Gendai Ajia Shuppan-kai, 1975), pp. 221–6.

Table 4.5 First Central Executive Committee in 1971

Rank	*Name*	*Age*	*Position*	*Position in RC*	*Other Positions*
GN(A)	Ne Win	61	Chairman	Chairman	Prime Minister, Defence Minister, Chief of General Staff
BG(A)	San Yu	54	General Secretary	Member	Deputy Prime Minister, Finance Minister, National Planning Minister, Vice Chief of General Staff (Army)
CL(A)	Thaung Kyi	49	Member	Member	Agriculture & Forestry Minister, Land Nationalization Minister
CL(A)	Kyaw Soe	53	Member	Member	Industry Minister, Labor Minister
CL(A)	Hla Han	53	Member	Member	Home Affairs Minister, Justice Minister, Local Administration Democratization Minister, Religion Minister, Irrigation-National Registration/Census Minister
CL(A)	Maung Shwe	51	Member	Member	Foreign Affairs Minister, Education Minister, Health Minister
BG(AF)	Tin Oo	48	Member	Member	Information Minister, Culture Minister, Rehabilitation/ Resettlement/Ethnic Consolidation Minister, Social Welfare Mnister, Vice-Chief of General Staff (AF)
CL(A)	Maung Lwin	47	Member	Member	Trade Minister, Cooperative Minister
CL(A)	Maung Lwin	53	Member	Member	National Planning Deputy Minister
CL(A)	Sein Mya	49	Member	Member	Home Affairs Deputy Mnister, Commander of Kachin Operations Command
Civilian	Ba Nyein	55	Member	Member	Cooperative Deputy Minister
CL(A)	Tin Oo	44	Candidate	Member	Commander of the Central Military Region
BG(N)	Thaung Tin	49	Candidate	Member	Mine Minister, Vice-Chief of General Staff (N)
CL(A)	Maung Maung Kha	52	Candidate	Former Member	Industry Deputy Minister
CL(A)	Aung Pe	46	Candidate	Former Member	Mine Deputy Minister

Note: A: Army, N: Navy, AF: Air Force, GN: General, BG: Brigadier General

Source: [bahoukomiti winlâunmyâ î kôuyêi hma'tân acînjou' 1971?] [*Tonan Ajia Yoran* 1972]

Affairs and Religion Minister, and Industry Minister. Ne Win was keeping his trusted aides close to himself as he elevated the CEC to the supreme executive body of the state and progressively separated it from the tatmadaw and the administrative machinery of the state.

Ne Win's reforms had an impact on the position of deputy minister. As previously noted, this position had previously been reserved for military region commanders who had completed tours of duty. There were four deputy minister posts as of 1969, but the number gradually increased, and reached 18 with the large-scale administrative reforms in 1972. Table 4.6 shows the previous and subsequent positions held by deputy ministers appointed in 1972. The newly appointed deputy ministers included military region deputy commanders and officers seconded to administrative bodies indicating that the distribution of deputy minister positions had begun going to a broader range of officers. Many of these officers became ministers following the transition to civilian rule in 1974, and most ministers became members of the State Council, a body chaired by the President of Burma that among other duties was responsible for convening the People's Parliament and interpreting the Constitution; its members were selected from among People's Parliament members.

Thereafter, every year in March when the People's Parliament made appointments, deputy ministers were frequently replaced. Tables 4.7 and 4.8, respectively, show the previous and subsequent positions held by deputy ministers appointed in 1974 and 1975. The tables show that the appointment of active officers as deputy ministers, as well as those retired and seconded to the BSPP and administrative bodies, was becoming an established procedure. The tables also show that promotions from deputy minister to minister decreased in 1975 compared to 1974, and that promotions were limited almost entirely to officers who had risen to the top of the tatmadaw, most of whom were military region commanders. This created a situation where ministers changed rather infrequently while deputy ministers were frequently replaced. In some cases after ministers stepped down from their positions, they left public office altogether or were transferred to honorary posts as State Council members or ambassadors.[17]

[17] For instance, Nyi Nyi, who stepped down as Minister of Mining in March 1975, was appointed ambassador to Australia, and Than Sein, Transportation and Communication Minister until resigning in 1975, became ambassador to the U.K. Among those transferred to the State Council upon retirement in 1976 were Prime Minister Sein Win and Lwin, who had been Deputy Prime Minister and concurrently the National Planning and Finance Minister.

Table 4.6 Newly Appointed Deputy Ministers in 1972

Rank	*Name*	*Age*	*Ministry*	*Previous Post*	*Succeeding Post*
RET(A)	Htun Tin	49	Co-operatives	Director of Military Training (MOD)	Co-operatives Min
BG(A)	Tin Oo	44	Defence	Commander of the Central Regional Command	Defence Min
RET(A)	Ban Ku	46	Social Welfare	Deputy Commander of Southeast Military Region	Social Welfare Min
LC(A)	Maung Cho	40	Mines	Director of Ordnance Services (MOD)	Industry Min
RET(A)	Htin Kyaw	51	Construction	Administrative deputy-minister (Construction)	Construction Min
RET(A)	Ye Gaung	50	Agriculture and Forestry	Administrative deputy minister (Agriculture and Forest)	Agriculture and Forestry Min
RET(A)	Tha Kyaw	50	Transportation and Communication	Administrative deputy-minister (Tranportation and Communication)	Transportation and Communications Min
RET(AF)	Chit Khin	52	Home Affairs and Religion	Director of Defence Services Intelligence	Information Min
RET(A)	Aye Maung	50	Culture	Deputy Chairman of People's Peasants' Council	Culture Min
Civilian	Aung Hmi	58	Labor	Deputy Chairman of People's Workers' Council	resign in 1974
Civlian	Chit Maung	45	Planning and Finance	Administrative deputy minister (Finance)	resign in 1975

Note: A: Army, N: Navy, AF: Air Force, RET: Retired, BG: Brigadier General, LC: Lieutenant Colonel

Source: [bahoukomiti winlâunmyâ î kôuyêi hma'tân acînjou' 1971?], [*Tonan Ajia Yoran* 1973]

Table 4.7 Newly Appointed Deputy Ministers in 1974

Rank	*Name*	*Age*	*Ministry*	*Previous Position*	*Succeeding Post*
CL(A)	Tint Swe	49	Defence	Commander of Southeast MR	the Industry (1) Minister
RET(A)	Oung Kyaw	47	Home Affairs & Religion	Deputy Commander of 77th LID	Social Welfare/Labor Minister
RET(A)	Myo Myint	49	Planning & Finance	Director General of Agriculture and Forestry Ministry	resign in 1978
RET(A)	Thein Nyunt	50	Trade	Chairman of Magway Division SAC	resign in 1977
RET(A)	Min Aung	50	Transporation & Communications	Assistant General Secretary of Party HQ	resign in 1980
RET(A)	Thein Htu	51	Co-operatives	Chairman of Chin State SAC	resign in 1977
RET(A)	Khin Nyein	47	Health	Deputy Chairman of Tanintharhy Division PSC	resign in 1980
RET(A)	Aung Tun	51	Education	President of DSA, Chairman of Pegu Division PSC	resign in 1975
RET(A)	Kyaw Khain	45	Labor	Deputy Commander of Southernwest MR, Chairman of Kayah State PSC	resign in 1975
RET(A)	Hla Tin	49	Construction	Director General of Party HQ	resign in 1975
RET(A)	Khin Maung Ti	47	Home Affairs & Religion	Chairman of Karen State PSC	resign in 1981
RET(A)	Win	53	Foreign Affairs	Administrative Secretary General of Foreign Affairs Ministry	resign in 1977
LC(A)	Tin Maung	51	Information	Chairman of Sagaing Division SAC	resign in 1977
RET(A)	Tin Oo	53	Industry	Chairman of Kayah State PSC	resign in 1975
Civilian	Thein Han	50	Agriculture & Forestry	Deputy Chairman of People's Peasants' Council	resign in 1977

Note: MR: Military Region, LID: Light Infantry Division, SAC: Security and Administration Committee, PSC: Party Supervision Committee

Source: [bahoukomiti winlâunmyâ î kôuyêi hma'tân acînjou' 1971?], [*Tonan Ajia Yoran* 1973]

Table 4.8 Newly Appointed Deputy Ministers in 1975

Rank	*Name*	*Age*	*Ministry*	*Previous Position*	*Succeeding Post*
BG(A)	Kyaw Htin	50	Defence	Vice-Chief of General Staff (A)	Defence Minister
CL(A)	Tint Swe	49	Prime Minister's Office	Defence Deputy Minister	Industry (1) Minister
CL(A)	Khin Oung	52	Transportation & Communications	Commander of Yangon MR	Transportation & Communications Minister
CL(A)	Than Tin	47	Mines	Commander of Southernwest MR	Mines Minister
CL(A)	Myat Maung	50	Information	Director General of Education (Party HQ)	Information & Culture Minister
CL(A)	Hla Maung	54	Industry (1)	administrative deputy minister (Home Affairs), administrative deputy minister (Justice)	State Council member
RET(A)	Aung Bwin	51	Trade	Deputy Commander of Southernwest MR, Chairman of Irrawaddy PSC	resign in 1977
Civilian	Bo Lay	41	Agriculture & Forestry	Lecturer at Yangon University, Secretary-General of Party Finance and Planning Committee	resign in 1980

Note: A: Army, BG: Brigadier General, CL: Colonel, RET: Retired, MR: Military Region, PSC: Party Supervision Committee

Source: [bahoukomiti winlâunmyâ î kôuyêi hma'tân acînjou' 1971?], [*Tonan Ajia Yoran* 1973]

It seems that Ne Win during this period intended to do away with the existing situation where his aides, active officers, and cabinet members were in effect melded into one, and instead create a new approach for maintaining power and running the government. This intention can also be discerned in his moves to made the CEC independent and to strengthen it by appointing his close aides and the top tatmadaw leaders (the Chief of General Staff and the Vice Chiefs of General Staff of the Army, Navy and Air Force) to the committee in order to solidify his own power base, while at the same time expanding the allocation of minister and deputy minister posts as well as membership on the State Council to active and retired military officers. Through these moves Ne Win was attempting to achieve three objectives simultaneously: maintain his dictatorship, build up the BSPP as an autonomous ruling party, and take control over the tatmadaw. His principal method for achieving these objectives was to restrict CEC members from concurrently serving as cabinet ministers and increasing the number of positions for tatmadaw officers which led to a low level of turnover within the CEC membership itself.

In order for Ne Win to create a regime with the BSPP as the leader of the state, the CEC had to be independent from other bodies of the state and also function as the highest executive organization of the party. Personnel-wise this meant that people doing party work needed to be elected to the CEC based on their performance in the party. But as noted previously, until 1971 the higher the positions became in the BSPP, the greater the number of tatmadaw officers filling them. This poses the question of whether the BSPP had become institutionalized as an autonomous organization by the time of "transition to civilian rule" in 1974. This question will be taken up in the next section with an analysis of the CC from which CEC members were elected.

The Party Central Committee

The First Party Congress of the BSPP opened on 28 June 1971. It adopted a new party constitution based on the "goal of changing from a cadre party to a people's party based on democratic centralism," and undertook a wholesale reorganization of the party.[18] Its organizational structure after this change is shown in Figure 4.1.

[18] *Working People's Daily*, 29 June 1971.

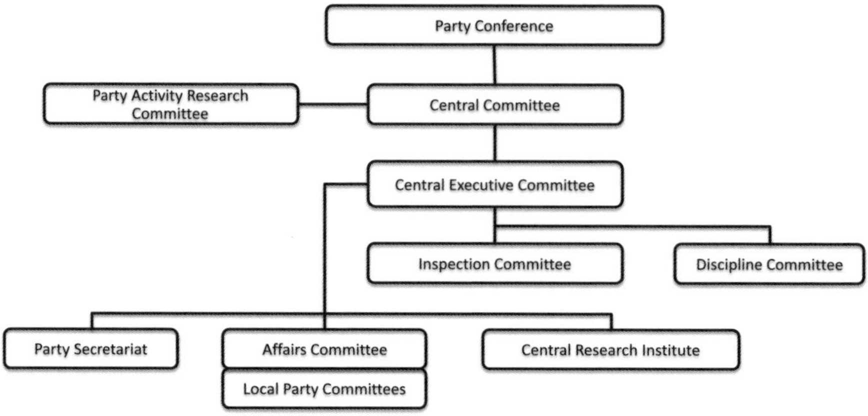

Source: Burma Socialist Programme Party Constitution

Figure 4.1 Organizational Structure of the BSPP

One of the most important points of the reorganization was the creation of the CEC and CC. The CEC became virtually the supreme decision-making body of the state. It was composed of about 15 members who were elected from among the CC members. The CC was responsible for putting into effect the plans and rules approved by the party congress which in principle met once every four years, and the committee was the highest decision-making authority of the party when the party congress was not in session (Party Constitution Article 79). The remainder of this section will examine how the first and second CCs became institutionalized by analyzing the composition of the candidates who ran for the CC, the CC members who won seats on the committee, and the CC candidate members.[19]

The members of the first CC were elected on 5 July 1971, the eighth day of the First Party Congress. The ballot of candidates was distributed in advance, and a total of 825 party congress members representing each party division, the party headquarters, and the tatmadaw

[19] CC candidates refer to candidates who ran in the election for the CC, whereas CC candidate members refer to candidates who were elected to the CC together with the CC members and had a seat on the committee, but who had no voting rights.

cast secret ballots at a total of eight separate booths.[20] A total of 300 candidates stood for the election made up of representatives from 15 of the party divisions and the COC, as well as the representatives at the party congress for the CIPS and the tatmadaw. From this total, 150 CC members and 50 candidate members were elected. However, it is not known how fair the election was.[21]

Table 4.9 shows the number of candidates in the election by the home organization they represented and the number elected as CC members and candidate members. It shows that among the candidates representing BSPP-related organizations who won election to the CC, those from organizations connected to the party headquarters (local branches of the HQ, the Central Political Academy, the COC) won the predominant number of seats. Although the 150 candidates from the party divisions, where they had been elected in district party congresses, accounted for 50 per cent of the candidates, only 21 (14 per cent) succeeded in getting elected to the CC. Meanwhile, 89 of the 100 candidates (89 per cent) representing organizations connected to the party HQ were elected. Thus, in the center-region relationship within the BSPP, the centre was overwhelmingly dominant. In the civilian-military relationship, the tatmadaw dominated the ballot; out of 300 candidates overall, 194 (65 per cent) were military officers. The tatmadaw was represented by 50 candidates at the party congress seeking election to the CC; 40 (80 per cent) of them won seats.

---

[20] *Working People's Daily*, 6 July 1971. More important than the election process, however, was how and by whom the ballot of candidates was created, and this is not known. While people did not simply stand as candidates, it is also highly unlikely that all 300 candidates were personally chosen by Ne Win. The party constitution stipulated that internal party elections "must be drawn up by the different committees and subcommittees based on the principle of democratic centralization and in consultations with groups of representatives" [Article 69 (a)]. This stipulation, however, is too abstract. Instead, it was the Party Congress Convening Commission, formed prior to the party congress in 1971, that actually prepared the ballot of candidates, and the names of six members of the Convening Commission can be found on that list. All of them were staff or standing members of the party headquarters.

[21] According to Kyaw Yin Hlaing who interviewed a former party executive, the election was actually carried out as a vote of confidence for the 200 people whom the party headquarters had already selected to be CC members and candidate members. See Kyaw Yin Hlaing, "The Politics of State-Business Relations in Post-Colonial Burma," p. 136.

Table 4.9 First BSPP Central Committee Election

Party Organization	*Nominated*	*CC Members*	*CC Candidates*	*Not Selected*
Party Divisional Committee Representatives (a)	150 (65)	21 (7)	30 (9)	99 (4)
Region No. 1 (Mandalay Division)	10 (6)	0 (0)	1 (0)	9 (6)
Region No. 2 (Magway Division)	10 (5)	1 (0)	0 (0)	9 (5)
Region No. 3 (Chin Special Division)	6 (3)	1 (1)	1 (0)	4 (2)
Region No. 4 (Sagain Division)	6 (1)	1 (0)	0 (0)	5 (1)
Region No. 5 (Kachin State)	7 (3)	2 (0)	2 (1)	3 (2)
Region No. 6 (Northan Shan State)	7 (3)	2 (0)	3 (2)	2 (1)
Region No. 7 (Eastern Shan State)	3 (1)	0 (0)	2 (1)	1 (0)
Region No. 8 (Southern Shan State)	8 (1)	1 (0)	4 (1)	3 (0)
Region No. 9 (Kayah State)	3 (1)	1 (0)	1 (0)	1 (1)
Region No. 10 (Kawthoolei State)	4 (0)	0 (0)	2 (0)	2 (0)
Region No. 11 (Tenasserim Division)	10 (5)	0 (0)	2 (0)	8 (5)
Region No. 12 (Irrawaddy Division)	9 (4)	1 (1)	2 (0)	6 (3)
Region No. 13 (Arakan Division)	9 (4)	0 (0)	3 (2)	6 (2)
Region No. 14 (Pegu Division)	24 (8)	3 (1)	1 (0)	20 (7)
Region No. 15 (Rangoon Division)	43 (20)	8 (4)	6 (2)	20 (14)
Party HQ Representatives (b)	100 (79)	89 (72)	10 (6)	1 (1)
HQ Party Units	2 (1)	1 (1)	1 (0)	0 (0)
The Central School of Political Science	2 (2)	2 (2)	0 (0)	0 (0)
The Central Committee of Party Organization	96 (76)	86 (69)	9 (6)	1 (1)
tatmadaw Party Conference Representatives (c)	50 (50)	40 (40)	10 (10)	0 (0)
Total (a + b + c)	300 (194)	150 (119)	50 (25)	100 (50)

Note: *Number in parenthesis indicates active military officers.

Source: [bahoukomiti winlâunmyâ î kôuyêi hma'tân acînjou' 1971?]

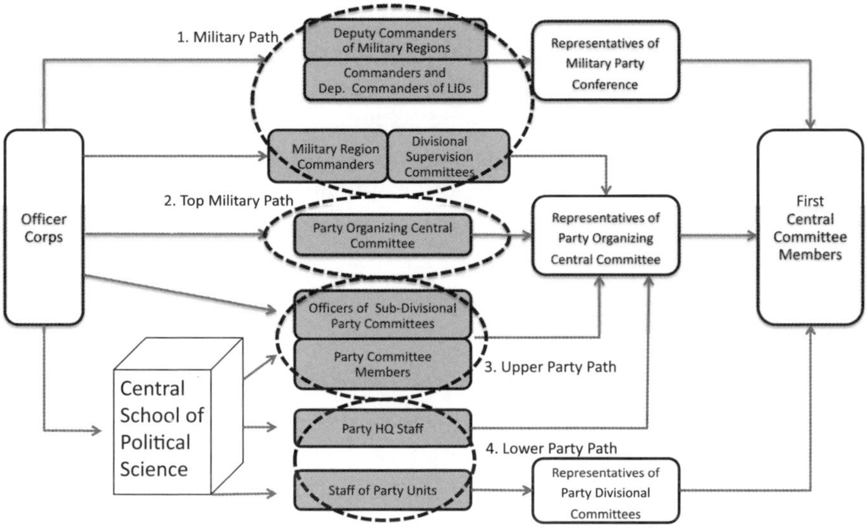

Source: bahoukomiti winlâunmyâ î kôuyêi hma'tân acînjou' (1971?)

Figure 4.2 Career Paths of Military Officers on the First Central Committee

The COC, with 96 candidates, had the most representatives standing for election, 76 of them were tatmadaw officers, and 90 per cent of them were elected to the CC. It seems that the number of tatmadaw officers increased as one moved closer to the centre of the party. Moreover, the tatmadaw was allowed to send candidates directly to the party congress as representatives of the military, so it had 119 officers among the 150 CC members. However, there were different categories of officers represented. They will be analyzed below by career path to show the relationship between the categories and the results of the election for the first CC.

Figure 4.2 illustrates the career paths of the officers who were candidates for the CC. They can be categorized into four groups: those on the military path (MP), those on the top military path (TMP), those on the higher party path (HPP), and those on the lower party path (LPP).

Military Path (MP) group

Most of the officers in the Military Path group had come up through the tatmadaw and this group can be considered the most successful in the military. The lowest position that any of them served in was regimental commander, and all of them were members of the military education committee, except for four who were military region commanders that worked for the BSPP as chairmen of party division inspection committees. They rose up through the tatmadaw without any real involvement in politics or administration, and were assigned pro forma to party posts based on their positions in the tatmadaw. In the election for the CC, the military region commanders were CC candidates as representatives of the COC, while the others were candidates as tatmadaw representatives to the party congress.

Top Military Path (TMP) group

The Top Military Path group was composed of the top military leaders and former military region commanders, most of whom were already engaged in political affairs as ministers or deputy ministers. Ne Win and San Yu were part of this group. They were members of the COC where they worked at furthering the party organization, but their own career advancement followed a course within the tatmadaw and differed from that of people in the "higher party" and "lower party" path groups described below. They became candidates for the CC as representatives of the COC.

Higher Party Path (HPP) group

The Higher Party Path group was comprised of executives of party division inspection committees and members of the party headquarters Affairs Committee. They were tatmadaw officers whose status in the party was relatively high among the officers who had been seconded from the tatmadaw to the BSPP and administrative bodies after 1962 and where they had built up their careers. Some of them had transferred directly into conducting high-level duties of party affairs; others had been promoted from the "lower party path" group described below. In either case, career advancement for these officers no longer lay in the tatmadaw but in the BSPP where they served as party executives. They became candidates for the CC as representatives of the COC, branches of the party headquarters, or the CIPS.

Lower Party Path (LPP) group

The officers making up the Lower Party Path group worked as staff in the BSPP headquarters and as party unit executives. Those working in the party headquarters became CC candidates as representatives of the

Table 4.10 Military Officers on the Central Committee Candidates, Members, Candidate Members

	Rank	*Nominated*	*Members*	*Can. Mem.*
Army	GN	1	1	0
	BG	1	1	0
	CL	41	41	0
	LC	44	36	8
	MA	19	17	1
	CP	67	5	13
	1L	1	0	1
Navy	BG	1	1	0
	LC	4	3	1
	MA	4	3	1
Armed Forces	BG	1	1	0
	CL	1	1	0
	LC	3	3	0
	MA	6	6	0
Total		194	119	25

Note: GN: General, BG: Brigadier General, CL: Colonel, LC: Lieutenant Colonel, MA: Major, CP: Captain, 1L: First Lieutenant

Source: [bahoukomiti winlâunmyâ î kôuyêi hma'tân acînjou' 1971?]

COC, while those who were party unit executives were candidates as representatives of their respective party divisions. These officers had also been seconded from the tatmadaw to work in party affairs, but they did not have very high status. They were different from the HPP group in that most of them had attended the CIPS and their training as executives had come via the party system.

A look at the above four categories shows that other than a few exceptions, there was a correlation of group with military rank, the TMP group correlating to generals and colonels, the MP group to colonels, the HPP group to lieutenant colonels, and the LPP group to captains. From this we can presume a power relationship where TMP > MP > HPP > LPP. Where the tatmadaw had penetrated deeply into the party, those officers who had succeeded better within the military, i.e., TMP and MP, had higher status than those who handled the work of the BSPP, HPP, and LPP groups.

The influence of the military's hierarchy based on rank inevitably affected the election of CC members. As shown in Table 4.10, candidates who won seats on the CC were overwhelmingly field-grade officers and above. Therefore, CC members and candidate member were made up of officers from the TMP, MP, and the HPP groups while most of the candidates from the LPP group were not elected. Moreover, all of the officers of the TMP were elected to the CEC at the first CC meeting held immediately after the election for the CC members.

Thus, the members elected to the first CC were mainly tatmadaw officers, but they were separated into three types, TMP, MP, and HPP, depending on the career path they followed. Previous studies by and large have looked upon the BSPP as a cover for military rule based only on the fact that many active and retired military officers made up the membership of the CC. However, that is not the whole story. Researchers such as Alfred Stepan, who have examined the relationship between politics and the military in Latin American countries, show that the latter is not monolithic; many cracks occur in the officer corps under military rule.[22] What is most important is the functional differentiation between the political role and the military role.[23] Such differentiation was clearly seen in Burma. The political function was in the TMP and HPP groups, while the military function was in the MP groups.

However, up to the time of the First Party Congress, officers in charge of political and party affairs were still assigned to the BSPP as temporary transfers from the tatmadaw; therefore the extent of functional differentiation was low. This became clearer after 1972 as the BSPP developed into a more autonomous political party. Civilians did not play an important role in the party, so the construction of the party-state in Burma was never a true transition to civilian rule; nevertheless, a sufficiently big change occurred within the tatmadaw between the separation of political and military functions.[24] By focusing on this functional

---

[22] For research on the occurrence of subgroups in the military, see Kazuo Ogushi, *Gun to kakumei – Peru gunji seiken no kenkyu* [The Army and Revolution: A Study of the Peruvian Military Regime] (Tokyo: Tokyo Daigaku Shuppan-kai, 1993), p. 8.

[23] Alfred Stepan, *Rethinking Military Politics: Brazil and the Southern Cone* (Princeton, N.J.: Princeton University Press, 1988), pp. 30–54.

[24] Yasuhiro Takeda examined the configuration of political and military functions within the military during the Ne Win regime and indicated that it was a "fusion type," meaning a state in which "politics and the military are highly unified." See Yasuhiro Takeda, *Minshuka no hikaku seiji: higashi-ajia shokoku no taisei hendo katei* [Comparative Politics of Democratization: The Process of Regime Transition in East Asian Countries] (Tokyo: Mineruva Shobo, 2002), pp. 88–91.

differentiation within the military, it is possible to see the institutional transformation of the tatmadaw, which cannot be discerned simply through the usual soldier/civilian dichotomy.

The CC's transition toward a more autonomous organization began in 1972 when many officers retired from the TMP, HPP, and LPP groups. Nearly all of them retired from the tatmadaw, but these retired officers were no longer seconded to the BSPP. Few officers in the MP group retired. This development did much to clarify the functional differentiation. This was followed by the election for the second CC, which took place on 17 October 1973. Only seven of the 35 newly appointed members were active officers.

Table 4.11 shows the ethnic groups and posts held as of 1971 for 22 of the first CC candidates who in 1973 became newly appointed CC members. It shows that 16 of them were party unit executives; moreover, they were of diverse ethnic backgrounds. This is a big change from the first CC where 120 of the members were Bahman. The reason for the large number of Bahman on the first CC was due to the many Bahmans among the tatmadaw officers.[25] As the BSPP established party units across the country, civilians from different regions began working as party unit executives; and because Burma is multi-ethnic state, an increasing number of people of different ethnic groups were promoted to the CC from party units which naturally led to diversification of the CC membership's ethnic composition.[26] The increased ethnicity of the newly-appointed members to the second CC indicates that the BSPP was gaining organizational autonomy as a political party. However, a great majority of CC members were still active or retired officers of the MP and HPP groups. Also as noted previously, there was no big change in the members of the CEC elected from the CC. In this partial state of "transition to civilian rule," with more civilians working in the party but tatmadaw officers still dominant, the People's Parliament convened in 1974 to give the BSPP legal status as the country's ruling party.

The above-discussed developments within the BSPP increased the party's autonomy, but they marked only the start of a transition to civilian rule. Meanwhile the party itself was still a work in progress, but by 1974 the Ne Win regime was confronting crisis. The biggest reason was

---

[25] See Chapter 8 for details.

[26] The Burmese government presently recognizes 135 ethnic groups.

Table 4.11 Ethnicity and Position of New 2nd CC Members Elected from First CC Candidate Members

Rank	*Name*	*Ethnicity*	*Position in 1971*
CL(A)	Yan Naung Soe	Bahman	Deputy Commander of 77th LID
CL(A)	Soe Thein	Bahman	Deputy Commander of Eastern MR
CL(A)	Hla Pe	Bahman	GSO(1) of Yangon MR
RET(A)	Thein Nyunt	Bahman	Officer of Northernwest MR
RET(A)	Kyin Tin	Bahman	Commander of a warship
RET(A)	Tun Mya	Bahman	Office Manager of PSC
RET(A)	Hla Maung	Bahman	Chairman of a party unit
RET(A)	Sai Mong	Shan	Chairman of a party unit
RET(A)	Peter La Hsan Gaung	Kachin	Chairman of a party unit
RET(A)	Cho Maung	Rakhine	Chairman of a party unit
Civilian	Lazum Htang	Kachin	Chairman of a party unit
Civilian	Saw Ye	Kayah	Executive Committee Member of a party unit
Civilian	Sai San Tun	Shan	Chairman of a party unit
Civilian	Sao Nyunt Aung	Danu	Chairman of a party unit
Civilian	Ba Phyu	Pao	Chairman of a party unit
Civilian	Saw Shwe Lay	Bahman	Chairman of a party unit
Civilian	Maung Maung Aye	Bahman	Secretary-General of a party cell
Civilian	Thet Tun	Paraung	Chairman of a party unit
Civilian	Saw Han Thein	Po Karen	Chairman of a party unit
Civilian	Kya Kyi	Mon	Chairman of a party unit
Civilian	Khin Maung	Mon	Chairman of a party unit
Civilian	Kyaw Yin	Rakhine	Chairman of a party unit

Note: A: Army, CL: Colonel, RET: Retired, LID: Light Infantry Division, MR: Military Region, GSO(1): General Staff Officer (1), PSC: Party Supervision Committee

Source: [bahoukomiti winlâunmyâ î kôuyêi hma'tân acînjou' 1971?]

the years of economic stagnation. Under the regime's economic policy, the state handled all exports of agricultural products, notably rice and teak, to acquire foreign currency for promoting industrialization of the domestic economy. However, rice production did not keep up with population growth, so exports actually declined. Without foreign currency revenues, production at state-run enterprises stagnated, and the country's industrialization stalled. A serious shortage of goods developed in the country; black marketing and smuggling grew widespread, and inflation climbed. The oil crisis in 1973 added another blow to the country's impoverished economy.[27] Deteriorating economic conditions created anxiety in the society, and in March and April of 1974, workers at state-run enterprises went on strike demanding an increase in wages and rice rations. Then in December, students and monks led anti-government demonstrations sparked by the funeral of the former United Nations Secretary General, U Thant. There is also evidence of heightened tension at this time within the leadership of the regime as indicated by the dismissal of Defence Minister Tin Oo (Chief of General Staff of the tatmadaw) in March 1976, and the uncovering of a coup plot by young dissatisfied officers.[28]

On the 29th and 30th of October 1976, Ne Win held an extraordinary party congress to respond to the critical economic and political situation. The conference concluded that the Third Party Congress had to be convened as soon as possible to deal with the country's critical state. It also decided to shorten the terms of the second CC members.[29] Following this, the Third Party Congress opened on 21 February 1977.

Political Crisis in 1977

Looking at the Ne Win regime as a process of party-state construction, 1977 was a pivotal year starting with the Third Party Congress in February. A new procedure was adopted for electing CC members, which incorporated into the party constitution the following provision that had been approved at an extraordinary party congress back in October 1974: "When compiling a list of candidates for the CC and for the Party Inspection Committee, 45 per cent of all candidates must be former members of both committees and the remaining 55 per cent must be

[27] Akio Takahashi, "Biruma: Gun ni yoru 'kaihatsu' no teitai" [Burma: the military and the stagnation of development]; Akira Suehiro, ed., *Iwanami Koza Tonan Ajia-shi 9 "Kaihatsu" no Jidai to "Mosaku" no Jidai* [Iwanami lectures: History of Southeast Asia 9: the age of development and the age of uncertain searching] (Tokyo: Iwanami Shoten, 2002), pp. 210–20.

[28] *Working People's Daily*, 6 October 1976. The reason for Tin Oo's dismissal is not known, and various opinions have been given, including that he criticized the government's request to raise the salaries of soldiers on the front lines, and that his calls for economic liberation lost out to San Yu's hardline stance of state control. See *Tonan Ajia Yoran 1977* [Southeast Asia Directory 1977], pp. 9–23.

[29] *Working People's Daily*, 30 October 1976.

new candidates elected from Party Congress representatives."[30] San Yu, Party Secretary General, explained at a CC meeting the reason for the amendment, saying that were the CC members not replaced, party elections would become dysfunctional because of personality cults, influential individuals, and corruption; elections in effect would become non-elections. This was a move against the party's previous principle of democratic centralism and was disruptive to the leadership of the party.[31] The wholesale replacement of the CC members at the Third Party Congress was institutionally guaranteed by the newly adopted provision.[32] Ne Win's intention was to increase the independence and leadership of the BSPP so as to stabilize the party and the political system.

What was the outcome? First and foremost, Ne Win's efforts to amend the candidate selection process failed to greatly change the CC membership. Although 190 out of the 360 candidates were new, a rate of 52.8 per cent, which approached the 55 per cent of the new provision, the percentage of new CC members and candidate members following the election was only 28 per cent (69 of 239 people). Having stipulated that 55 per cent of the people were to be newly-selected candidates, then failing to achieve a CC where 55 per cent of the members, or a percentage approaching that, were new made the newly adopted provision effectively meaningless. Meanwhile the number of CC members and candidate members had increased from the previous 200 to 239, which should have made it even more possible to increase the ratio of newly-elected people. However, following the election for the new CC, less than 30 per cent of the resulting membership was new. Clearly the 55 per cent

[30] With this change, Party Constitution 88(h), the previous provision, was deleted. This had read: "In the case of a candidate who runs three terms in succession for election at the CC level, that candidate will be elected only upon receiving 75% of the votes of Party Congress representatives qualified to vote" (*Working People's Daily*, 19 February 1977).

[31] *Working People's Daily*, 19 February 1977.

[32] At the same time that the level for newly-appointed candidates was set at 55%, the number of candidates was increased from the previous 300 to 360, while that for the CC was raised from 150 to 180. However, of these 360 people, only 162 (45%) could become candidates, and even after becoming candidates, they had to get through the election. At the Third Party Congress, 41 of the incumbent 203 members (including candidates) had to be excluded from the ballot of candidates, so Secretary General San Yu presented the criteria determining the 41 people at the 18th CC meeting of the second CC immediately before the party congress (*Working People's Daily*, 19 February 1977).

framework failed to function as Ne Win had intended. Moreover, many active and retired officers from the TMP and MP groups were among the new CC members. There were also officers and party civilians from the HPP and LPP groups, but their ethnic diversity was less than what it had been among the new members elected to the Second Party Congress. This outcome shows that the congress had not in fact strengthened the BSPP's organizational autonomy, nor had it furthered Ne Win's plans for establishing a ruling party. Ne Win himself admitted this failure in his closing speech to the congress.[33]

While Ne Win was stumbling in his effort to create a more autonomous BSPP, the independence of the CEC after 1971 had continued to grow. As shown in Table 4.12, seven people, including Lwin, Thaung Dan, Thaung Tin and Ko Ko, were ousted from the second CEC and replaced by eight new members. The only active officers among the new members were two vice chiefs of general staff; the other six people were retired officers who worked only in party affairs. Five of these people, Tin Win Nyo, Zaw Win, San Shein, Htun Lin and Kyaw Zaw, were retired officers of the HPP group who had been seconded from the tatmadaw to work in party affairs. Htun Lin and Kyaw Zaw took over ministerial posts in a Council of Ministers reshuffle that took place in March 1977, the former becoming the Transportation and Communication Minister, the latter Mining Minister as well as Labor Minister. These personnel changes broke with the established practice that no one without experience as a director general in the tatmadaw headquarters or as a military region commander could join the highest decision-making body of the state. These changes were a form of exceptional promotions for now officers in the HPP group who had not previously been in leadership positions in the tatmadaw were seconded from the military to high-ranking positions in the party where they could be elected to the CEC. The centre of political decision-making was starting to shift to the BSPP even though CEC membership was still limited to retired officers.

As shown above, the Third Party Congress was both a negative and a positive for the construction of the party-state. The negative aspect was the failure to get a greater number of new members elected to the CC. The positive was the exceptional promotions of officers in the HPP group to membership on the CEC. If the stipulation to make 55 per cent of the CC new members was nothing more than a show, the only

---

[33] *Working People's Daily*, 2 March 1977.

Table 4.12 Career Paths of New Third Central Executive Committe Members (February 1977)

Rank	*Name*	*Age*	*Career Path*	*Category*
RET(A)	Than Sein	48	Colonel General Staff (A) → Minister of Transportation and Communications → Member of State Council	TMP
BG(A)	Aye Koe	56	Commander of MR → Vice-Chief of General Staff (A)	MP
BG(AF)	Saw Pru	49	Colonel General Staff (AF) → Vice-Chief of General Staff (AF)	MP
RET(A)	Zaw Win	48	Deputy Commander of MR → Executive of the Ministry of Transportation and Communications → General Secretary of Party Discipline Committee	MP
RET(A)	Tin Win Nyoe	51	GS1 of MR → Chairman of Magwe Party Regional Committee → Member of CC	UPP
RET(A)	San Shein	47	Commander of an infantry battalion → Vice-Chairman of Mandalay Regional Party Committee → Chairman of Mandalay Regional Committee → member of CC	UPP
RET(A)	Tun Lin	55	Commander of an infantry battalion → Vice-Chairman of Party Inspection Committee → First Secretary of Party Secretariat	UPP
RET(AF)	Kyaw Zaw	54	Air Force base commander → Vice-Chairman of Party Inspection Committee → Member of the Party Secretariat	UPP

Note: A: Army, AF: Air Force, RET: Retired, BG: Brigadier General, MR: Military Region, TMP: Top Military Path, MP: Military Path, UPP: Upper Party Path

Source: [bahoukomiti winlâunmyâ î kôuyêi hma'tân acînjou' 1971?], [sàdou'tà acein patinyilahkan bahoukomiti winlâunmyâ î kôuyêi hma'tân acînjou' 1981]

people who might have benefited would have been Ne Win himself and the tatmadaw, and there would have been no need to elect officers from the HPP group to the CEC. It would have been more convenient to have simply appointed active or retired military leaders. Therefore, it seems evident that Ne Win did intend to proceed with the building of the party-state. Thus, the question is why this contradictory outcome occurred at the Third Party Congress. It is impossible to know the truth, but informed conjecture is possible.

The evidence comes from the extraordinary party congress held in November 1977. In a speech to the congress, San Yu said it was convened because of problems with the election for CC members held at the Third Party Congress. He said that a certain group had tried to manipulate the vote causing factions in the party and divisions within the leadership. Therefore, this extraordinary congress had to conduct a re-election of CC members "in order to recover the unity and solidarity of the party as quickly as possible."[34]

The vote manipulation that San Yu spoke of was, according to Kyaw Yin Hlaing, a manoeuvre to remove Ne Win from the CC. The masterminds behind the plot were Kyaw Zaw (HPP), Than Sein (TMP), and Htun Lin (HPP), all of whom had won seats in the CEC in the Third Party Congress. They had been deeply involved in preparing the ballot of candidates for the election of the third CC and had tried to persuade some of the members and candidate members of the second CC, who thought they would be eliminated as candidates by the 55 per cent provision, to cast non-confidence votes against Ne Win and support San Yu instead.[35] However, their machinations had failed, and Ne Win had been re-elected BSPP chairman. When the episode was brought to light, 113 representatives of the party congress, some of whom were CC members, were expelled from the party.[36] The purge reached into the CEC as well where four members of the HPP group, with the exception of Zaw Win, were removed from the party.

A former BSPP executive told this author in an interview that the number of votes for Ne Win fell in the February 1977 election for the third CC, and this likely led to the ouster of the 113 party congress

---

[34] *Working People's Daily*, 15 November 1977.

[35] Kyaw Yin Hlaing, "The Politics of State-Business Relations in Post-Colonial Burma," pp. 139–40.

[36] *Tonan Ajia Yoran 1978* (*Southeast Asia Directory 1978*), pp. 9–26.

representatives at the November 1977 extraordinary party congress. The former executive's narration of events between the two congresses differs slightly from that of Kyaw Yin Hlaing's interviews. Although the differences are small, and it is difficult to determine what actually happened so many years ago, these small differences are important. Therefore we need to look at the course of events as told by the former party executive.

The events began with the CC election at the Third Party Congress where, according to the former executive, Ne Win came in third behind San Yu and Kyaw Soe. Ne Win was extremely angry, went back to his house on Ayedi Street and locked himself in.[37] The only person allowed in was General Tin Oo, chief of the National Intelligence Bureau (not the same person as Chief of General Staff Tin Oo), whom Ne Win greatly trusted. Tin Oo persuaded Ne Win to let General Kyaw Htin, the Chief of General Staff of tatmadaw, pay him a visit; then Htun Lin, a CEC member, visited Ne Win accompanied by Tin Oo. According to what Htun Lin told the former party executive, Ne Win confided his intention to resign as BSPP chairman, saying words to the effect that, "I have followed my conscience (*sedàna*). If there is dissatisfaction about that, I'll have to resign." Tin Oo, of course, talked Ne Win out of doing this and proposed purging the party instead. He would make a list of problematic CC members; then an extraordinary party congress should be convened to hold a new election for the CC and thereby rid the BSPP of problematic party executives.[38]

Several days later, Tin Oo gave Ne Win a list of about 100 names. Deliberations also began within the party about holding an extraordinary party congress. Tin Oo was doing these things solely on his own; and the

[37] When asked about the drop in votes for Ne Win, some party executives testified that they had been involved in vote rigging, but they did not all name the same people as members of the group behind the rigging. In another interview, a former CC member told this author of testimonies about two Ne Wins being among candidates. Also the candidates were listed on the ballot in Burmese alphabetical order, and people might have mistakenly not voted for President Ne Win but for Ne Win, chairman of the People's Council of Kayah State whose name came further down after the president's (interview with a former party CC member, 27 June 2003). The ballot listing the candidates for election to the CC in 1981 had the names of Ne Win and a few other party executives placed at the top of the list, so it is conceivable that mistaken voting did take place. Moreover, to get Ne Win removed from the 180 members elected to the CC required a considerably large-scale plot, which rationally seems much too risky an undertaking.

[38] Interview with a former party CC member, 20 December 2004.

people on the list were not necessarily those who were involved in vote rigging at the Third Party Congress. No serious internal inquiry even looked into why Ne Win had lost votes in the Third Party Congress. Therefore, the list reflected personal animosities that existed in the government. Prominent on the list were the names of party executives and retired officers who had antagonized Tin Oo. There was resistance in the party. The former executive who related these events was part of that resistance. According to him, many people of the HPP group, including Htun Lin, opposed what Tin Oo was doing, arguing that it would destroy party unity. However, Ne Win did nothing to stop Tin Oo. An extraordinary party congress would be convened resulting in a large-scale purge of the BSPP. Although some party executives attempted to alter the list, adding the names of people in Tin Oo's faction, there was no possibility of ousting Tin Oo himself from the CC. In the end 113 people, many of them from the HPP group, were stripped of their party membership.[39]

What can we learn from the above events about the two phenomena that occurred at the Third Party Congress: the promotion of HPP officers to the CEC paired with the failure to elect an increased number of new CC members? Ne Win succeeded in the former likely because he was able to exert more of his influence on getting retired HPP officers elected to the smaller CEC. In the latter case, Ne Win did not greatly intervene in candidate selection, perhaps because of the large number involved: 360 candidates were on the CC election ballot; or perhaps because he trusted the electoral system. Either way, the key player was the party secretariat staffed by HPP group people who drew up the list of candidates. At the time of the election, the secretariat distorted the 55 per cent framework intended to make the party autonomous, leading to election results contrary to Ne Win's intention. It is also possible that part of the HPP group had attempted to bring Ne Win down, although it is not known why their discontent with Ne Win had grown. Perhaps they were fed up with his years of misrule and his dictatorial political style; or they may have wanted to protect their party posts and the associated vested interests that tatmadaw officers enjoyed. Whatever the case, right when Ne Win tried to move the BSPP toward being an autonomous ruling party, his efforts were sabotaged by the HPP group, the very people responsible for implementing his plans.

[39] Interview with a former party CC member, 20 December 2004.

Tin Oo, an intelligence officer, took advantage of the situation, but no matter how deeply trusted by Ne Win, this would not have enabled him to eliminate party executives from the state leadership. He had no support base other than the intelligence organization. Therefore, it seems there was support from tatmadaw leaders behind the move to oust party executives, that people in the MP group were unhappy about officers in the HPP group, who were clearly lower in rank, becoming CEC members and even ministers.

In an unedited tape recording of an oral history by Sein Lwin, who served as commander of the Northwest Military Region until 1974, he expressed his fears that, from his reading of the terminology and ideology in documents published by the BSPP, the party had been gradually moving toward communism.[40] Other regional commanders expressed similar views, and strong criticism seems to have existed against people who were former Communist Party members (notably Thakin Tin Myat and Saw Oo) and three party secretaries (Kyaw Zaw, Tin Win Nyo and Than Sein), all of whom were in the HPP group. What follows is a summary understanding of the political situation described above.

The important political forces in the government in 1977 were Ne Win along with the TMP group at the top, composed of the HPP group, the MP group and the intelligence office leadership. Over time the HPP group grew more important in Ne Win's work of building the party-state, and he began appointing some of the officers in this group as cabinet ministers. This created resentment within MP group and intelligence office leadership. They sensed a threat to their vested interests, and some in the tatmadaw saw a communist threat in the rise of HPP group to positions of leadership in the party and the state. However, they had no immediate influence over Ne Win's leadership, so the two groups had to acquiesce in the preferential promotions of officers in the HPP group. This situation changed following Ne Win's loss of votes in the Third Party Congress and his angry retreat to his residence. It is not certain if his drop in votes was due to the machinations of the HPP-controlled party secretariat; nevertheless, thereafter Ne Win developed a distrust of

[40] For certain reasons it is not possible to reveal neither where and when this tape was recorded nor where it is kept. Normally, it is not appropriate to use this kind of source material as it cannot be verified by others; however, I have chosen to base my argument on this material after deciding that its content, even without citing its source, is very significant for the study of Burma. I gained permission from the person possessing the tape regarding the release of its content.

the HPP group. Tin Oo, as a leader in the intelligence office, and the military region commanders at the top of the MP group most likely took advantage of the situation to purge the HPP group.

The above narration of events is open to question because of insufficient evidence. Nevertheless, what is certain is that the outcome of the Third Party Congress produced a decisive change in Ne Win and his regime. He replaced many of the CC members at the extraordinary party congress in November 1977. The 55 per cent provision was dropped in the CC re-election, and the membership of the fourth CC was expanded to 250 people. This all happened only nine months after the election for the third CC.[41] The media reported that an election had taken place,[42] but in all likelihood every one of the candidates was elected without following the stipulated procedures for election.[43] Five people from the MP and TMP groups were elected as new members to the CEC (see Table 4.13) while the committee members from the HPP group disappeared. This effectively marked the end of Ne Win's attempt to create a ruling party that was autonomous from the tatmadaw and the leader of the state.

Conclusion

Ne Win's approach to the BSPP clearly changed after 1978 as can be seen from Tables 4.14 and 4.15. These respectively show the careers of the new members to the fifth CEC (elected at the Fourth Party Congress in August 1981) and those to the sixth CEC (elected in the Fifth Party Congress in August 1985). All of the people, excluding Tin Oo in intelligence, had experience as light infantry division or military region commanders. The fifth CEC was made up of officers mainly from the MP group and the sixth was largely from the TMP group. This observation is interesting in itself, but the important point here is that no one from the HPP group was elected to the CEC. Although the CEC was institutionally an organization within the BSPP because its members were elected from the CC members, an officer involved in party affairs was never able to move up from the CC to the CEC. Even among tatmadaw

[41] The position of CC candidate member was discontinued along with the increase in the number of CC members.

[42] *Working People's Daily*, 17 November 1977.

[43] All of the candidates on the ballot for election to the CC at the 1977 extraordinary party congress and at the Fourth Party Congress in 1981 were elected to the committee.

Table 4.13 Career Paths of New Fourth Central Executive Committee Members (November 1977)

Name	*Rank*	*Age*	*Career Paths*	*Category*
BG(N)	Chit Hlaing	53	Naval Base Commander → Vice-Chief of General Staff (Navy)	MP
CL(A)	Sein Htun	50	GSO(1) of Department of Military Training → Ambassador → Director of Armour and Artillery	MP
CL(A)	Sein Lwin	53	Commander of MR → Minister of Cooperatives → Minister of Transportation and Communications → Minister of Home Affairs and Religion	TMP
RET(A)	Tun Tin	54	Director of Military Training → Deputy Minister of Cooperatives → Minister of Labor → Minister of Cooperatives	TMP
RET(A)	Ye Gaung	56	Military → Administrative Vice-Minister of Agriculture and Forestry → Deputy Minister of Agriculture and Forestry → Minister of Agriculture and Forestry	TMP

Note: N: Navy, A: Army, RET: Retired, BG: Brigadier General, GSO(1): General Staff Officer (1), MR: Military Region, TMP: Top Military Path, MP: Military Path

Source: [bahoukomiti winlâunmyâ î kôuyêi hma'tân acînjou' 1971?], [sàdou'tà acein patinyilahkan bahoukomiti winlâunmyâ î kôuyêi hma'tân acînjou' 1981]

Table 4.14 Career Paths of New Fifth Central Executive Committee Members (1981)

Rank	*Name*	*Age*	*Career Path*	*Category*
RET(A)	Than Sein	48	Colonel General Staff (A) → Minister of Transportation and Communications	TMP
BG(A)	Tin Oo	53	Director of Military Intelligence → Director of National Intelligence Bureau → Military Adviser to the President	MP
LG(A)	Htun Yi	55	Commander of a Light Infantry Division → Commander of Bureau of Special Operation (1) → Vice-Chief of General Staff (Army)	MP
LG(A)	Min Gaung	55	Commander of a Light Infantry Division → Commander of West MR → Adjutant General (MOD)	MP

Note: A: Army, BG: Brigadier General, LG: Lieutenant General, MR: Military Region, TMP: Top Military Path, MP: Military Path

Source: [sàdou'tà acein patinyilahkan bahoukomiti winlâunmyâ î kôuyêi hma'tân acînjou' 1981]

Table 4.15 Career Paths of New Sixth Central Executive Committee Members (1985)

Name	*Rank*	*Age*	*Career Path*	*Category*
LG(A)	Saw Maung	57	Commander of Light Infantry Division → Commander of MR → Adjutant General → Vice Chief of General Staff (Army)	MP
RET(A)	Tin Swe	59	Commander of Light Infantry Division → Commander of MR → Deputy Minister of Defence → Deputy Minister of Defence → Minister of Industry (1)	TMP
RET(A)	Hla Htun	56	Commander of Light Infantry Diivision → Commander of MR → Quartermaster General → Minister of Construction	TMP
RET(A)	Than Tin	58	Commander of Light Infantry Division → Commander of MR → Deputy Minister of Mine → Minister of Mines	TMP

Note: LG: Lieutenant General, RET: Retired, A: Army, MR: Military Region, MP: Military Path, TMP: Top Military Path

Source: [sàdou'tà acein patinyilahkan bahoukomiti winlâunmyâ î kôuyêi hma'tân acînjou' 1985]

officers who were military region commanders and above, only those whom Ne Win selected become CEC members. In effect, control over personnel at the top of the BSPP had returned to compatibility with dictatorship and military rule.

The proportion of new members elected to the CC remained low, that for the fourth, fifth and sixth CCs being only 22.4 per cent, 23.1 per cent and 33.9 per cent, respectively.[44] At the same time, the appointment of tatmadaw officers was becoming institutionalized. Almost all officers who were directors in tatmadaw headquarters, or who were deputy military region commanders or above, or deputy light infantry division commanders or above received seats on the CC. Those who were further promoted continued to hold concurrently a tatmadaw and a BSPP post, while those who lost out in the competition for promotion retired from the tatmadaw and became full-time party executives, some of them becoming ministers or deputy ministers. In effect, a "golden parachute" type of practice arose with tatmadaw leaders (particularly from the Army) moving over to positions in the BSPP and the government administration.

Thus, Ne Win's construction of a party state failed. But it was not a deliberately contrived failure to camouflage dictatorship and military rule. Ne Win intended to create a party autonomous from the military in order to spread his political power base. He planned to create a regime built on the shared power of the dictator, the tatmadaw, and the party. However, his steps to make the BSPP autonomous created political instability amongst the party elite and finally led to moves by party executives to bring him down. Left with no other option, Ne Win virtually suspended the political function of the party. Together with a number of close aides, he took control of political decision making and turned the BSPP into an organization for distributing benefits to the tatmadaw. No political party to lead the state ever came into existence. There was only a partly finished party-state and a party organization that the dictator used as fodder to feed benefits to the military. Arguably this outcome was to a large degree fated to happen given that the original framework of the BSPP was made up of tatmadaw officers who had been seconded to the party.

---

[44] The one-party system was abolished in 1988, and the sixth Central Executive Committee and CC were the last for both.

CHAPTER 5

Destroy the Bureaucracy!: Transformation of the Civilian Bureaucracy in the Name of Revolution

During the 1960s and 1970s, the same period as Ne Win's revolution, a number of developmental dictatorships appeared in East and Southeast Asia: the administrations of Park Chung-Hee and Chun Doo-Hwan in South Korea, those of Chiang Kai-shek and Chiang Ching-kuo in Taiwan, the Ferdinand Marcos regime in the Philippines, Suharto's New Order regime in Indonesia, Lee Kuan Yew's administration in Singapore, the Mahathir bin Mohamad administration in Malaysia, and the Sarit regime followed by that of the Thanom-Praphat duo in Thailand. All of these were far from democratic, but each country achieved surprising economic development.

This regime type, where undemocratic politics and high economic performance coexist, has been termed a developmental dictatorship. It can be described as a regime that restricts citizens' participation in politics to prevent the destabilization of society arising from mobilization and ideological struggle while justifying its authoritarian rule by the results of its active, state-led economic development.[1] Characteristics of such regimes are: strong political leadership, de-politicization of the society, establishment of an organization responsible for drawing up economic policies supporting development and for comprehensively coordinating

[1] See Akira Suehiro, *Catch-Up Industrialization: The Trajectory and Prospects of East Asian Economies* (Singapore: NUS Press, 2008); John Martinussen, *Society, State and Market: A Guide to Competing Theories of Development* (London & New Jersey: Zed Books Ltd, 1995).

these policies, and a focus on the training and recruitment of technocrats who operate the economic system.[2]

Ne Win came to power in a coup d'état as the Thai and Indonesian developmental dictatorships did; however, the aim of his regime was not development but revolution. The bureaucracy of his regime was modelled after those of socialist countries, thus its subsequent transformation differed from those of countries with developmental dictatorships. This chapter focuses on the civilian bureaucracy and will show that Burma's civil service rapidly lost influence over the political process under Ne Win's rule, in contrast to the increasingly important role of the civil service in Southeast Asian developmental dictatorships during the same period. The decreased influence of the civil service in Burma was inextricably linked with the increased influence of the military officers. This development was contrary to the point made in Chapter 1 that military regimes, whether of long or short duration, are usually a coalition of soldiers and civil servants;[3] and, while it is not unusual for a bureaucracy to develop by making itself autonomous from party politics, it is rare for the military to intervene in the administrative operations of the government as has happened in Burma.

Table 5.1 shows the distribution of the former occupations for cabinet ministers in Thailand and Burma from the middle of the 1970s to the end of the 1980s. In Thailand the civilian bureaucracy became a significant source for politicians, so much so that the country has been called a "bureaucratic polity."[4] In the late 1970s more than half of the Thai cabinet ministers had previously worked as public officials. As the country's economy expanded in the 1970s, business people also began to exert a greater influence on the government. This contrasts with Burma under its military regime where during the same decade and a half, 94 per cent of cabinet ministers were active or retired military officers. This

[2] For a discussion of whether Burma is a developmental dictatorship, see Akio Takahashi, "Biruma: Gun ni yoru kaihatsu no teitai [Burma: the military in the stagnation of development]," in *Iwanami Koza: Tonan Ajiashi 9 "Kaihatsu" no jidai to "Mosaku" no jidai* [Iwanami lectures: History of Southeast Asia 9: the age of development and the age of uncertain searching], ed. Akira Suehiro (Tokyo: Iwanami Shoten, 2002).

[3] Amos Perlmutter, *The Military and Politics in Modern Times: On Professionals, Praetorians, and Revolutionary Soldiers* (New Haven: Yale University Press, 1977), p. 97.

[4] Fred W. Riggs, *Thailand: the Modernization of a Bureaucratic Polity* (Honolulu: East-West Center Press, 1966).

Table 5.1 Occupations of Ministers in Thailand and Burma (1974–88)

	Burma		*Thailand (1976–88)*			
	1974–88		*1976–79 Military Regime*		*1979–88年 Military & Political Party*	
Military/Police	47	94.0 (%)	13	25.5 (%)	72	23.1 (%)
Army	44	88.0	8	15.7	38	12.2
Navy	2	4.0	3	5.9	13	4.2
Air Force	1	2.0	2	3.9	18	5.8
Police	0	0.0	0	0.0	3	1.0
Public Officer	3	6.0	29	56.9	60	19.2
Business	0	0.0	6	11.8	124	39.7
Others	0	0.0	3	5.9	56	17.9
Total	50	100.0	51	100.0	312	100.0

Source: Akira Suehiro. "Tai no Gunbu to Minshuka Undo: 73 nen '10 Gatsu Seihen' kara 92 nen '5 Gatsu Ryuketsu Jiken' he," *Shakai Kagaku Kenkyu* 44, no. 5 (1993): 71. And *pyihtaunzu hsousheli'thammada myanmanainngando patamaacein pyidu thou yweichetinhmyau'hchin hkanyatho pyidu hlwu'to kozahlemya i koyeihma'tan akyinjou'* (1974), (1978), and (1981)

high percentage of military officers in the cabinet has remained unchanged to this day.

The next section will examine the process through which the civilian bureaucracy in Burma lost its political influence in the course of Ne Win's revolution by analyzing the organizational reform and personnel of the bureaucracy as indices. Briefly summarizing this process, the institutional basis of the bureaucracy formed under British colonial rule was dismantled as Ne Win restructured the administration after 1962. As a result while the country's civilian bureaucracy, which should have been responsible for developing and implementing policies, remained undeveloped, tatmadaw officers were transferred into the administrative bureaucracy. We will first briefly look at the history of the bureaucracy in Burma, then look closely at the military intervention into the administration of the country's domestic affairs after the 1962 coup, and finally review Ne Win's plans for administrative reform, which were in full swing by the close of the 1960s. Following this, we will look at the careers of the people who held important positions in the central and local administrations to see what resulted from the administrative reforms implemented in the mid-1970s.

Modern State Transplantation and Post-Colonial Bureaucracy

When the Konbaung Dynasty collapsed after the three Anglo-Burmese Wars in the nineteenth century, Burma in its entirety was integrated into

Britain's Indian Empire. In 1862, the first Chief Commissioner for British Burma took office under the Governor of India with headquarters set up in Rangoon, a port town in Lower Burma. Thereafter the government administration for the Province of Burma was set in place. Below the Chief Commissioner, levels of local government were set up from division, district, township, on down to the village tract, and these were headed respectively by a division commissioner, a deputy commissioner or district officer, a sub-division or township officer, and a village headman. As John S. Furnivall pointed out in his study of Burma's political economy during the colonial period, colonization brought a different principle of order into traditional Burmese society, creating social resistance to and unrest against rapid change while at the same time building a new governing system operated by a new colonial ruling elite.[5]

The colonial ruling elite in the Indian Empire centered on the Indian Civil Service (ICS). The ICS was composed of a small elite group that occupied the majority of the positions of authority in the civil service, which together with the military services maintained Britain's rule over India. The characteristics of the ICS were "open entry based on academic achievement; elaborate training arrangements; permanency of tenure; responsible, generalist posts at central, provincial, and district levels reserved for members of the elite cadre alone; a regular, graduated scale of pay with pension and other benefits; and a system of promotion and frequent transfers based predominantly on seniority and partly on merit."[6] At its start, the ICS was composed mainly of upper-middle class Englishmen who had graduated from Oxford or Cambridge universities. The modern, centralized, hierarchical bureaucracy built up around the ICS was dubbed the "steel frame."

In governing Burma as well, British ICS officials held the important posts in the colonial government, but increasing demand for "native" recruitment by the ICS moved ahead following the Montague-Chelmsford reform in 1920, and Htin Htut became the first Burmese ICS official in 1921; by the early 1940s, a total of 43 Burmese ICS officials had been appointed (by which time the service had been renamed the Burma Civil

---

[5] John S. Furnivall, *Colonial Policy and Practice: a Comparative Study of Burma and Netherlands India* (New York: New York University Press, 1956).

[6] David C. Potter, "Bureaucratic Change in India," in *Asian Bureaucratic Systems Emergent from the British Imperial Tradition*, ed. Ralph Braibanti (Durham, N.C: Duke University Press, 1966), p. 142.

Service (BCS) in accordance with the Government of Burma Act that had taken effect in 1937).[7]

Within the ICS (BCS), bureaucrats in the administrative sector were trained solely as generalists, and they gained occupational experience as they moved between duties at local township and district offices and as administrative officers in ministries of the colonial government. They spent much of their time involved in local administration and were the mainstay of colonial rule. They were eventually promoted to the post of district officer, the position of highest authority in a district for maintaining law and order and collecting taxes.[8] After that point, they were separated into officials who continued as district officers moving from one district to another, and officials who worked in the colonial government headquarters and engaged in policy-making. Over time a career path for high-level bureaucrats was institutionalized in the colonial government whereby administrative officers moved between the ministries with some eventually rising to secretaries heading ministries.

Following the Japanese invasion and the imposition of military rule in 1942, some top Burmese bureaucrats escaped to India with the British staff of the colonial government, but for the most part, the colonial administrative machinery remained in place during the war both institutionally and in human resources.[9] After Britain's return to Burma, it was found that of the 145 BCS officials (Class I) from before the war, 93 (all Burmese) had remained at their duties. As Burma moved toward independence and the introduction of parliamentary democracy, expectations within the civil service were that politicians would likely interfere in the administrative bureaucracy, and a spoils system would arise affecting the selection of civil servants. Measures to prevent this were proposed, notably the establishment of a Union Public Services Commission as

---

[7] Kei Nemoto, "Biruma no toshi eriito to Nihon senryo-ki: GCBA, takinto, shokuminchi koto bunkan wo chus hin ni [The urban elite in Burma and the Japanese Occupation period: focusing on the GCBA, Thakin Party and Colonial Civil Service]," in *Tonan Ajia-shi no naka no Nihon senryo* [The Japanese Occupation in the history of Southeast Asia], ed. Kurasawa Aiko (Tokyo: Waseda Daigaku Shuppanbu, 1997), p. 47.

[8] Takehiko Honda, *Indo shokuminchi kanryo: Daiei-teikoku no cho eriito-tachi* [Indian Colonial Bureaucrats: The Super-elites in the British Empire] (Tokyo: Kodansha Sensho Mechie, 2001), p. 75.

[9] James F. Guyot, "Bureaucratic Transformation in Burma," in *Asian Bureaucratic Systems Emergent from the British Imperial Tradition*, ed. Ralph Braibanti (Durham, NC: Duke University Press, 1966), p. 386.

prescribed in Article 221 of the 1947 Constitution for the fair selection of public servants. This and other measures were intended to preserve the bureaucracy of the colonial period.[10] After independence in 1948, there was a gradual increase in the number of specialist bureaucrats appointed as secretaries (*àtwînwûn*) in ministries who were responsible for such matters as accounting, tax-related duties, and land surveying, but they remained few overall. So for a generalist bureaucrat, the path of promotion to important positions of responsibility remained as before independence.[11]

The career of a civil servant named Se Maung, who published an autobiography, *kyàno ì pyidùwandânbàwà-tàyâyêkandà hnìn ou'chou'yê kandà-* (*My Life as a Public Servant in Legal Affairs and Administration*), offers a typical example of a generalist bureaucrat's rise up the ranks of the BCS.[12] He was born in Pyinmana, Mandalay Division, in central Burma on 20 April 1929. He attended a school offering English education in Pyinmana but had to suspend his studies because of the Pacific War. He graduated from high school in 1947 and entered Rangoon University receiving a B.A. after completed a three-year college course. He then began a two-year Bachelor of Law course while working for an accounting firm. During his second year in the law program, he learned that the Junior Branch of the Public Service Commission was recruiting; he applied for a position and was hired. At that time his hometown of Pyinmana had been occupied until recently by Communist Party forces. This situation had caused a serious shortage of staff at the local court, so Se Maung was assigned to work in the town as a judge handling cases worth under 1,000 Burmese kyat. In 1953 he passed the selection examination for both the Burma Civil Service Senior Branch and the Burma Judicial Service Senior Branch; he chose to enter the former.

Se Maung began his career in the BCS in 1954, training in Sittwe District in Rakhine State. But he was quite unsatisfied with the assignment to that state, a remote place for Bahmans like him, and a posting

---

[10] John S. Furnivall, *The Governance of Modern Burma*, 2nd ed., extended (New York: Institute of Pacific Relations, 1960), p. 67.

[11] High-level generalist bureaucrats were criticized even in the colonial government in the 1930s, particularly in the bureaus where expertise was required such as in finance and justice. John S. Furnivall, *The Governance of Modern Burma*, 2nd ed., extended (New York: Institute of Pacific Relations, 1960), p. 64.

[12] U Se Maung, *kyàno ì pyidùwandânbàwà-tàyâyêkandà hnìn ou'chou'yê kandà-* [My life as a public servant in legal affairs and administration] (Yangon: Anonymous, 2001).

that once had meant a demotion. He protested all the way up to the secretary of home affairs, saying there was no reason for him to be assigned to Rakhine State right after entering the ministry.[13] The secretary persuaded him that the assignment was a practice still held over from the colonial days, and that the state needed a young administrative official to improve conditions there now that Burma was independent. On finishing his training, Se Maung worked in Rakhine State for three years as an assistant township officer in Minbya township, a revenue agent in Sittwe township, then the assistant township officer of that township. In 1958 he was transferred to Mandalay Division to head the treasury office in Mingyan township, then was assigned the position of assistant township officer of that township. This period coincided with the time of Ne Win's caretaker government, and one of Se Maung's jobs was complying with a government directive to collect up rifles that the citizenry in his jurisdiction had used to protect themselves against attacks by anti-government rebels.[14] Then in 1959 he was posted to Rangoon city hall for ten months to supervise the construction of Pazundaung market, after which he was appointed an assistant secretary in the Ministry of Home Affairs. There he was charged with an array of duties that included planning village development, parliamentary affairs, and supervising the issuing of passports.

Following his stint at the ministry, Se Maung was again posted to regional offices. He passed a promotion exam in 1964 after which he served as deputy district officer in Pakok District, Magway Division, for six months. This was now the time of Ne Win's revolution, and a district security and administration committee was set up in the district. The deputy district officer was made a member of the committee so that the Home Affairs Ministry and the security and administration committee could coordinate their work. Following this assignment, he was appointed district officer of Myeik in Tanintharyi Division in 1965. This region was well known as a transit point for smuggling goods from Thailand, and his term as district officer in Myeik lasted four and a half years instead of the usual two. In 1968 he transferred to Loikaw in Kayah State to work as a deputy secretary for the Kayah State Council. With administrative reforms in 1972, administrative officers holding legal degrees were

[13] Ibid., p. 228.
[14] Ibid., pp. 339–40.

moved into the Ministry of Justice, and Se Maung returned to Rangoon to work at the ministry where he remaining until his retirement.

Se Maung graduated from university after the war, but his autobiography shows that the ICS (BCS) framework established in the colonial period continued to function after independence. The path of promotion remained intact, alternating between postings in local administrative offices and appointments as administrative officers in central ministries or agencies as an official moved upward toward occupying higher-level positions in the bureaucracy. Se Maung also experienced the growing influence of the tatmadaw as it gradually penetrated into the "steel frame" of the civil service. In this sense, he was among the last generation of BCS bureaucrats to inherit the tradition and professionalism of the original ICS.

Although the administrative framework of the colonial period remained in place after independence, few former bureaucrats went into politics in Burma, unlike in Thailand where many assumed cabinet posts during the same period. This was largely because the politicians of the time were nationalists who gained political power in the struggle against the Japanese empire and in the negotiations with Britain for Burma's independence. They were young people who had come out of the nationalist movement and had risen rapidly to social prominence during the fluid political conditions under Japanese military rule.[15] Their political support was based in political parties, labor unions, and farmers' organizations, and they gained their seats in the Union Parliament by popular vote under the newly-introduced system of parliamentary democracy. Moreover, Burmese nationalism was attracted to socialist ideology and critical of the bureaucracy which most nationalists saw as bourgeois and a product of imperialist rule; bureaucrats were generally unpopular among politicians.[16] Over time, however, this attitude changed as politicians gradually recognized the importance of bureaucrats in governing the state; this was especially true of politicians who had experience as

[15] Likely there was also a generation gap between these young wartime nationalists and the prewar nationalist politicians. The latter group after the war, which including the well-known Ba Maw, formed only a conservative minority wielding limited political clout.

[16] For Lenin's view of the state and the general understanding that communists had of bureaucracy, see Vladimir I. Lenin, *The State and Revolution* (London: Penguin, 1992).

cabinet ministers.[17] In sum, the BCS bureaucracy in the 1950s and high-ranking bureaucrats who supported it succeeded to a considerable degree in defending their institution in the new and less conducive environment of parliamentary democracy.

Building a New Administration

In October 1958, when the tatmadaw intervened for the first time in politics and formed a caretaker government, Ne Win stated clearly that his tenure as prime minister and that of his government would last only until the third general election had taken place and a new cabinet installed. His caretaker government made no attempt to reform the administrative bureaucracy, and Ne Win only temporarily transferred 56 field-grade officers to secretary-level posts for coordination among the ministries.[18] Then to the surprise of many, following the third general election in February 1960, Ne Win did as he stated he would; he turned power over to the Union Party, the election victor, and sent his troops back to the barracks. Thereafter, however, as related in chapter 3, parliamentary politics grew dysfunctional following a split in the ruling Anti-Fascist People's Freedom League and U Nu's move toward the left. Meanwhile in the General Staff Office, moderates were marginalized as hardliners gained influence. Together these developments led to Ne Win's second political intervention via his coup d'état of 2 March 1962. This was not a temporary takeover of power as before. It was to be permanent, and Ne Win himself would pursue a wholesale reorganization of the state.

"The Burmese Way to Socialism" and Local Government

Soon after the March coup, the new military regime issued a policy declaration, *The Burmese Way to Socialism* (*myanmà hsousheli' lânzin*), which stated the following about the administrative bureaucracy.

[17] Furnivall, *The Governance of Modern Burma*, p. 68.

[18] For the accomplishments of the tatmadaw during the time of the caretaker government (1958–60) including military personnel seconded to the ministries, see Burma, Ministry of Information, *Is Trust Vindicated?: A Chronicle of the Various Accomplishments of the Government Headed by General Ne Win During the Period of Tenure from November 1958 to February 6, 1960* (Rangoon: Director of Information, Government of the Union of Burma; Bailey & Swinfen, 1960).

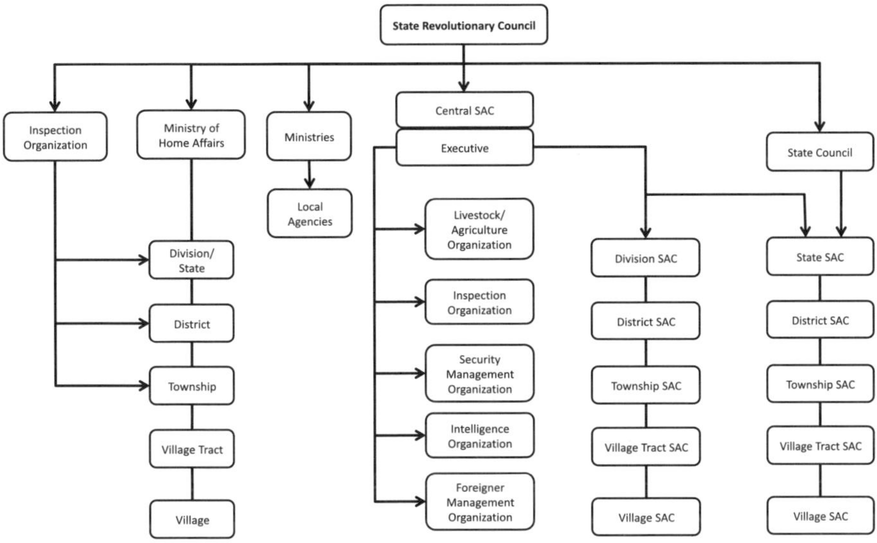

Source: Burma, anonymous. *naingando lounjounyêi hnìn ou'chou'hmù simankêin saou' "kà" [State Security and Administration Project Book, Vol. A]* (1962), Figure "kà"

Figure 5.1 Command Structure of the State Administration Planning

> On our road to socialism, the existing bureaucratic administration is a major stumbling block. To achieve our socialist aims with this effete machinery is impossible. Steps will have to be taken to remove this bureaucratic machinery and lay firm foundations for a socialist democratic one. (Article 15b)

This goal to "remove the bureaucratic machinery" was set forth in the "National Security and Administration Plan", which had two main objectives: building a system in which the directives of the Revolutionary Council (RC) would be carried out jointly by the administrative bureaucracy and the tatmadaw, and building a system that would continue to function as the administrative bureaucracy after stable security had been achieved. The reality of this plan, however, was intervention by the tatmadaw in the Ministry of Home Affairs. The tatmadaw sought to control local administration by setting up Security and Administration Committees (SAC). The organizational structure of this system is shown in Figure 5.1. SACs were installed at each administrative level: division/state, district, township, village tract, and in each village, and, along with handling home affairs administration, they were in charge of intelligence activities, agriculture, animal husbandry, and control of foreign nationals.

The headquarters of this new system was the Central SAC, which was composed of military and civilian personnel. The home affairs minister was chairman of the committee with the Colonel General Staff of the tatmadaw as deputy chairman. Others on the committee were the administrative officers, the secretaries of the main ministries (Home Affairs, Agriculture and Forestry, Defence, Finance and National Taxation, Justice, and National Planning), the administrative director of the border areas, the deputy commissioner of people's police, the police commissioner of Rangoon, the General Staff Officer (1) (Operation), and the secretary of the Home Affairs Ministry. However, the tatmadaw chain of command had priority over that of the Home Affairs Ministry when dealing with the regional SACs. Sixteen of these regional committees were set up at the state/division level based on the tatmadaw's five military regions (northwest, central, southwest, northeast, and east), and in many cases a military region commander was appointed committee chairman. At the district level, the battalion commander stationed in the district was made the committee chairman, and the district officer and the district police chief were among the committee members.

Each district SAC was responsible for selecting security and administration committee members at the township, ward, and village tract levels within the district, and tatmadaw officers holding the rank of captain served as chairmen of the township SACs. From its start Ne Win's coup regime and rule by the RC was intended to be a provisional government, and the SACs were likewise intended to continue only until the future shift to "civilian rule." Local civilian administration under the Ministry of Home Affairs, while continuing to coexist with the SACs through the 1960s, was undermined and gradually lost authority.

In 1974 the new constitution was promulgated. That same year local government administration was reorganized with the elimination of the district, which since colonial times had been the highest authority of local administration. In the new administrative structure, the state/division level dealt directly with the township administration which supervised the wards and village tracts. At each administrative level a people's council (*pyidù caunsi*) was set up (1974 Constitution Article 29). The official authority of these councils covered a broad range of 14 items, including (a) socio-economic activity and administration, (b) judicial administration, (c) regional security, defence and maintenance of law and order, and (d) ethnic group unity and conservation and promotion of traditional culture (Article 132). The members of the councils in each jurisdiction were elected by popular vote (Article 129), and elections were held every four years as with the People's Parliament at the national level (Article 131).[19] According to the People's Council Act of the Union of Socialist Burma that took effect on 28 January 1974, each people's council was to have a chairman group, an executive committee and a judicial committee (Article 12, Item 1), and an independent inspection committee was set up to oversee administrative activities (Article 26, Item 1). This framework of people's councils and inspection committees holding administrative authority in the divisions, states, and townships, with the Burma Socialist Programme Party (BSPP) local party committees and party branches at the township level providing leadership became the structure of the Ne Win regime at the local level following the shift to civilian rule.

This series of administrative reforms made the township people's councils composed of members chosen by election the main organization in charge of local government, and council members were responsible for the overall administration of their township. As a result, the status of the township officer in the civil bureaucracy of the Ministry of Home Affairs who had headed the township was in effect reduced to that of chief clerk. In his autobiography Se Maung reports that postings as township officers were where young civil service officials gained administrative experience, and one goal that these young bureaucrats aspired to was a tour of duty in a district, a posting that came with enormous authority. But this level of administration was abolished with Ne Win's reforms, which substantially diminished the authority of the civil bureaucracy and disrupted the path of promotion and transfer that civil servants had followed since colonial times, which once led from the local level up to the top administrative positions in the central government.

Abolishing the Secretariat Offices and Creating Deputy Ministers

In March 1969, Ne Win issued instructions to reform the secretariat offices in the central government ministries. In compliance, each ministry

[19] In the elections for the Fourth People's Parliament and People's Councils at each level in 1985, more than 17 million voters elected 475 members of the People's Parliament, 976 members of state/division People's Councils, 22,850 members of township People's Councils, and 16,742 members of ward and village tract People's Councils. But as will be discussed later, the elections were just a vote of confidence for candidates as only one candidate ran for each seat.

undertook a review of the reform plan,[20] and a Research Committee for a New Union of Burma Administrative System was organized to handle the overall coordination of the plan. The committee chairman was Brigadier General Sein Win, the construction minister, who concurrently served as a RC member, a BSPP Central Organizing Committee member, and a cabinet minister. Other members were Colonel Hla Han, who among other posts served as foreign affairs minister, education minister and health minister; Colonel Maung Lwin, who was minister of cooperatives and international trade minister; and Ba Nyein, a former senior member of the National United Front, the biggest opposition party during the period of parliamentary democracy. After discussions that extended over 32 meetings held from 12 June 1969 to 26 July 1971, the 27-volume report was submitted to the RC.

According to the report, Ne Win had issued instructions for reorganizing the central ministries at a joint meeting of the BSPP Central Organizing Committee and the Party Discipline Committee on 12 June 1969. The gist of the report was that the government administration that as then existed possessed no authority, and that power was in the hands of the top administrative officers (whom Ne Win referred to secretaries [*atwînwûn*]). These administrative officers not only reduced administrative efficiency, they formed a body that was originally created to defend British interests. Although reforms had been attempted since independence, nothing effective had ever been achieved, and now was the time to bring about real reform.[21]

Ne Win's reform plan singled out secretariat offices headed by the secretaries as targets for elimination from the new administrative bureaucracy. In his plan, all of the supposed complexity of the conventional administrative machinery was attributed to these offices and vice-ministers that were seen as a "product of colonial rule".

Figure 5.2 presents the diagram that was attached to the report showing the administrative structure of government from the time of colonization. The Burma Government Secretariat and the Burma Government Secretaries were diagrammed separately among the offices in the ministries to highlight their presence.

---

[20] "pyihtaunzù myanmanaingan ou'chou'yêi sani'thi' hpohtou'yêi saou'1 - pyihtaunzù myanmanaingan ou'chou'yê sani'thi' hpohtou' sìsi'yê ahpwè ì asîyinkhanza 1972.2.14 [Report on the Implementation of the New Administrative System oh the Union of Burma, vol. 1, 1972/2/14]" [NAD 3/(22) à-72 12213].

[21] Ibid., pp. 1–4.

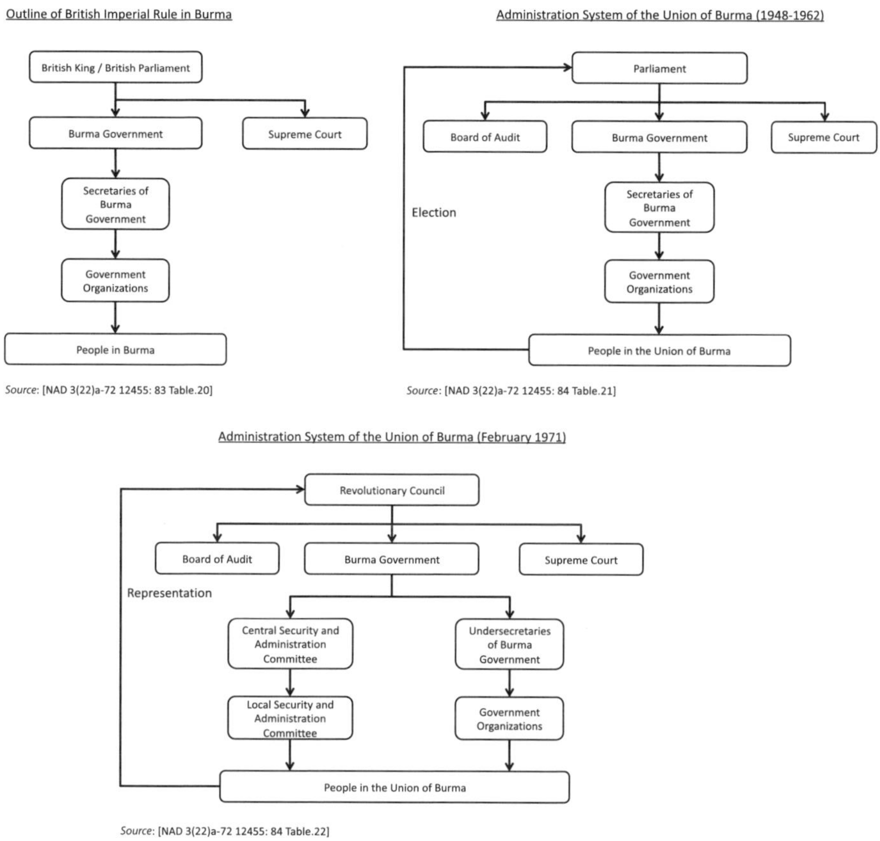

Figure 5.2 State Structure in the Report of Research Committee for New Administration System in the Union of Burma

Although this diagramming was done to criticize administrative control by generalist bureaucrats carried over from the ICS system, the reform plan only served to unilaterally reflect an exclusionary brand of nationalism that denied the heritage of the colonial period, rather than basing reforms on organizational rationalization and the needs of the time. However, the civil service bureaucracy had no way of resisting Ne Win's moves. This was evident from that fact that of the 31 people who attended the 32 meetings of the Research Committee for a New Union of Burma Administrative System (the average number of attendees per meeting being 5.5 people), 28 were active tatmadaw officers. Many of them were appointed to ministerial posts; however, their priority was to follow Ne Win's instructions to remove the secretaries. They were not

Table 5.2 Organizational Reformation of Ministries in 1972

Before Reform	*After Reform*	*Before Reform*	*After Reform*
Cabinet Office	Prime Minister Office	Education	Education
RC Chairman Office	RC Chairman Office	Health	Health
Foreign Affairs	Foreign Affairs	Labor	Labor
Defence	Defence	Agriculture & Forestry	Agriculture & Forestry
Law	Law	Land Nationalization	
Home Affairs	Home Affairs & Religion	Mine	Mine
Local Administration Democratization		Industry	Industry
Population Administration & National Registration		Public Works & Construction	Construction
Religion		Transportation & Communication	Transportation & Communication
Social Welfare	Social Welfare	Trade	Trade
Rehabilitation & Resettlement		Co-operative	Co-operative
Information	Information	Finance & Revenue	National Planning & Finance
Culture	Culture	National Planning	

focused on the interests of the ministries they now headed, nor on developing a more rational plan for reorganizing their ministries. Instead, the extended series of 32 meetings was directed at eliminating the secretaries, and planning for reorganizing the framework of each ministry was relegated to a later time, after the targeted officers had been removed.

After a year of review, the reform plan was set for implementation, and the shift to a new administrative system began in March 1972 following a decision by the RC. The first step was consolidating the 25 ministries into 20.[22] Then the minister's secretariat office was abolished in all 20 ministries. The function of these officers as assistants to the ministers was taken over by a newly-established ministers' office (*wangyîyôun*), and the duties of the secretaries as chief administrative officers were assigned to newly create deputy ministers, positions that had not existed in Burma until 1969. That year four deputy ministers were appointed but only as temporary postings which were then assigned to military region commanders who had finished their tours of duty, as discussed in Chapter 4. Deputy minister positions were set up in every ministry under the new administrative system to handle office work, and these positions were filled by election.

Eighteen deputy ministers had been appointed by the end of 1972. Table 5.3 shows their profile, suggesting that the government's entire bureaucratic arrangement changed for career civilian bureaucrats when Ne Win abolished the position of secretary in the ministries and in its stead created the post of deputy minister that was regularly filled by career tatmadaw officers. Among them, 13 of the deputy ministers whose career paths are known were from the tatmadaw. Seven of these officers had already been in senior positions such as director and deputy director in the General Staff Office or the Ministry of Defence, and as military region and deputy military region commanders. The remaining six people were officers who had been seconded to other ministries to experience working at the secretary level, or had been seconded to positions as presidents of people's state enterprises. While the background of some of the people shown in the table is not known, it is likely that none of them had been high-level career civil service officials. Only Chit Maung, the Deputy Minister of Finance and National Taxation, came from the civil service. However, he had never held a position in the BCS bureaucracy. He graduated from Rangoon University in 1950 and was made a deputy

[22] See Table 5.2 regarding the elimination and consolidation of ministries.

Table 5.3 Profiles of Deputy Ministers (December 1972)

Name	*Ministry*	*Profile*	*Military Officer*
Aung Hmi	Labor	n.a	n.a
Aung Pe	Industry	Commander of Eastern RM	✔
Aye Maung	Culture	Dy-Chairman of Peasants' Council	
Chit Khin	Home Affairs & Religion	Director of DDSI (MOD)	✔
Chit Maung	National Planning & Finance	Administrative Dy-Minister (Finance and Revenue)	
Hla Phone	Foreign Affairs	Commander of Yangon RM	✔
Hla Tin	Cabinet Council	n.a	n.a
Htin Kyaw	Construction	Army → Administrative Dy-Minister (Public Service & Construction)	✔
Maung Cho	Industry	Dy-Director of DDI, GM of Public Corporation (MOI)	✔
Mya Cho	Revolutionary Council	n.a	✔
Nyi Nyi	Education	Professor of Yangon University	
San Win	Trade	Army → GM of Trade Corporation (MOT)	✔
Tha Kyaw	Transportaton & Communication	Army → Administrative Dy-Minister (Transportation & Communication)	✔
Thein Aung	Health	Army → Administrative Dy-Minister (Health)	✔
Tin Oo	Defence	Commander of Central RM	✔
Htun Tin	Co-operative	Director of Directorate of Training & Planning (MOD)	✔
Ban Ku	Social Welfare	Dy-Commander of Southeast RM	✔
Ye Gaung	Agriculture & Forestry	Army → Administrative Dy-Minister (Agriculture and Forestry)	✔

Note: RM: Regional Military, DDSI: Department of Defence Services Intelligence, MOD: Ministry of Defence, DDI: Department of Defence Industry, GM: General Manager, MOI: Ministry of Industry, MOT: Ministry of Trade

Source: bahoukomiti winlâunmyâ î kôuyêi hma'tân acînjou' (1971?)

secretary under the caretaker government in 1958 after he had obtained a master's degree from Oxford University.

To summarize the two major changes in the administrative structure of the state, in local government administration, the district was abolished and people's councils were installed in divisions/states, townships, wards, and village tracts; in the ministries of the central government, the ministry secretary offices and their secretaries were eliminated with the introduction of the new administrative system in March 1972. They were replaced by deputy ministers appointed by the RC until 1974, after which they were elected from members of the People's Parliament. This last change was explained as the part of the practice of a socialist democracy (*hsousheli' dimokàresi*) and was presented as an example of the people's involvement in the administrative operation of government through elections. Consequently, under the new system the civil service bureaucracy inherited from the colonial period and its senior bureaucrats suffered a great loss of status and authority. The reality of Ne Win's new administrative system will be examined in the next section

Profiles of People's Council Members and Deputy Ministers

As was shown in Chapter 2, the Burmese state was constructed on the periphery of Britain's Indian Empire and gained its independence after having been a battlefield in the Pacific War. Thus, the ranks of its civil service were young and small in number, and the state was relatively weak in relation to the society. Moreover, many of the politicians were involved in the independence movement and were very left-leaning, which made them critical of civil bureaucrats whose roots were in colonial rule. And tatmadaw officers were political soldiers aspiring just like politicians to participate in the independence movement. Consequently, no coalition was formed between civilian bureaucrats and soldiers as was generally the case in developmental dictatorships. The result in Burma was the deep intervention of the military into the operations of the civil service.

The remainder of this section will examine the profiles of deputy ministers and senior members of people's councils at the division/state and township levels up until the Ne Win regime collapsed in 1988 in order to analyze how tatmadaw intervention into the civil bureaucracy was promoted.

According to a report by the Military Appointment General Office submitted to the 1969 Tatmadaw Convention, 5,070 officers were serving in the three branches of the tatmadaw (Army, Navy, and Air Force) as of

31 March 1968. Up to 909 officers (about 18 per cent) had been seconded to the BSPP and to ministries and other administrative bodies.[23] It is not known how many officers were seconded to what organizations, but letters of retirement issued in April 1973 in preparation for the shift to civilian rule the next year provide some clues that the BSPP was the major organization to which officers were seconded.[24] The letters of retirement were sent to 195 officers at the end of April that year, 162 of whom (83 per cent) were officers working for the BSPP.[25]

After the shift to "civilian" rule in 1974, the seconding of officers to the BSPP decreased in levels of the party below the Central Committee. Table 5.4 presents the numbers of seconded officers from the tatmadaw and the locations of their placements between 1972 and 1987 (excluding 1975 and 1976 due to the lack of information). Documentation in appointment letters confirms that 1,743 officers were seconded to ministries and related organizations. When estimates for the two years (1975 and 1976) not confirmed in the appointment letters are added in, about 2,000 officers were seconded from the tatmadaw between 1972 and 1987. Of the 1,743 confirmed transfers, 794 officers (45.6 per cent) were seconded to people's councils, making them by far the largest recipients of such officers.[26] This clearly shows that from 1974 the most frequent transfers from the tatmadaw were no longer to the BSPP, but to People's Councils. In comparison, far fewer were seconded to high-level positions in other organizations, e.g., 166 officers (9.2 per cent) were sent to the Ministry of Industry (mainly to a people's state enterprise under the ministry) and 155 officers (8.9 per cent) went to the Ministry of Home Affairs and Religion (mainly to the People's Police).

[23] "1968 ta'màdonilahkan si'yadûhhkàn atwînwan àsiyinhkanza [The 1968 Tatmadaw Conference Report of the Military Appointment General Office]", CD-883(10), DSMHRI, pp. 1–2.

[24] Revolutionary Council members including Ne Win and cabinet members were among those who retired.

[25] "si'yadûhkànamèinmyâ,htaunkôyâhkùni'selêihkù jannàwarilà hmà htaunkôyâhkùni' selêihkù zunlà àhtì" [Collected Military Appointment Letters–From January to June in 1974], DR-8378, DSMHRI.

[26] Appointment letters contained the following statement written above the name list of officers to be seconded: "The following officers are assigned to the military unit(s) below in order to be elected as candidates for the three organizations of the state/ division people's councils." ("si'yadûhkànamèinmyâ, htaunkôyâsi'seti'kù zulainlà hmà htaunkôyâsi'seti'kù dizinbalà àhtì"), DR-8389, 10/117/81/1981·9·4, DSMHRI.

Table 5.4 Transfers from the Military to Other Government Organization (1972–88)[1]

Government Organization	*Number of Transfer*	*Proportion*
People's Councils[2]	794	45.6 (%)
Ministry of Industry 1[3]	166	9.6
Ministry of Home Affairs & Religion	155	8.9
Security and Administration Committee	92	5.3
Ministry of Trade	79	4.6
Ministry of Transporation and Communication	77	4.4
Ministry of Industry 2	68	3.9
Ministry of Agriculture and Forestry	57	3.3
Ministry of Mine	44	2.5
Ministry of Livestock and Fishery	32	1.8
Ministry of National Planning and Finance	25	1.4
Ministry of Energy	22	1.3
Ministry of Construction	20	1.2
National Bureau of Intelligence	19	1.1
Ministry of Foreign Affairs	17	1.0
Ministry of Information	10	0.6
Office of State Council Chairman	9	0.5
Ministry of Social Welfare	8	0.5
Office of Prime Minister	7	0.4
Ministry of Health	7	0.4
Central Institute of Policial Science	6	0.3
Others	26	1.5
n.a	3	0.2
Total	1,743	100.0

Note: [1] This table does not include data of 1975 and 1976 because the DSMHRI lacks the documents of those years.

[2] People's Council include pople's council and inspection committees in all levels.

[3] Minister of Industry 1 includes officers who transfered to former Ministry of Industry.

Source: [DR-8380 DR-8381 DR-8382 DR-8383 DR-8384 DR-8385 DR-8386 DR-8387 DR-8388 DR-8389 DR-8390 DR-8391 DR-8392 DR-8502 DR-8503 DR-8504 DR-8506 DR-8514 DR-8515 DR-8566 DR-8600 DR-8601 DR-8602]

Elections for the People's Parliament and people's councils at each level were held in 1974, 1978, 1981, and 1985.[27] Voters could cast only a vote of confidence or no-confidence for the single candidate running for each seat, and votes were often manipulated to change no-confidence votes to ones of confidence. The resulting elections failed to engage the people politically; however they did succeed as a mechanism that periodically transferred military personnel into the government administration. This was particularly evident in the elections of 1981; the assigning of seconded officers was concentrated between October immediately after the election and January 1982. The same thing happened in November and December 1985 right after the elections that year. Transfers in 1985 were likely affected by the fallout of the purge stemming from the downfall two years earlier of Tin Oo, head of the National Intelligence Bureau, as well as by a generational change in the tatmadaw, and during that year 569 officers were seconded to government administrative posts and to people's councils.

Table 5.5 shows the ranks and positions of all the officers seconded to people's councils, the lowest rank and position at the bottom right, the highest at the upper left. The distribution of the table moves clearly from the lower right to the upper left indicating that the higher an officer's rank, the higher his position on the people's council. At the state/division level, people's councils, judicial committees and inspection committees contained many officers with the rank of lieutenant colonel, whether Army, Navy, or Air Force. At the township level, senior posts such as the chairmen of people's councils, of judicial committees, or of the inspection committees were held mainly by majors; and the positions of chief secretary and below went largely to officers at the rank of captain. The people's council and an officer's rank determined to a considerable degree how high his status was in the office to which he had been seconded. This indicates that military rank had a substantial influence on the selection of officers and the office to which they were seconded. It seems that matching officers' positions in people's council with their military status was done partly to avoid a reversal of standing between

[27] Originally the term of the Second People's Assembly was supposed to have been until 1982. However, the election for the Third People's Assembly was advanced by one year on the grounds that a new People's Assembly had to begin in November 1981 to coincide with the new four-year plan scheduled to start on 1 April 1982.

Table 5.5 Transfers from the Military to People's Council (1977–87)

	Rank	*Colonel*			*Lieutenant Colonel*			*Major*			*Captain*			*1st Lieutenant*			*2nd Lieutenant*				
	Position in People's Council	*A*	*N*	*AF*	*A*	*N*	*AF*	*A*	*N*	*AF*	*A*	*N*	*AF*	*A*	*N*	*AF*	*A*	*N*	*AF*	*n.a*	*total*
Division/State	Chairman of PC	2			5		1														8
	SG of PC				10			4		2											16
	ECM of PC				20			1			1										22
	Chairman of JC				9																9
	Member of JC				8			1													9
	Chairman of IC	3			4			1													8
	Member of IC				7			1													8
Township	Chairman of PC				32	3	4	189	3	13	77	1	1							2	325
	Chairman of JC						1	54	2	12	27	1	1							1	99
	Chairman of IC							32		6	22	1	1							1	63
	SG of PC							5			40	1	1								47
	Member of PC							2			75	1	1								79
	Member of IC										48	1					2				51
	Member of JC				1						35							1			37
	Unknown Position of PC							1			1						11				13
	Total	5	0	0	96	3	6	291	5	33	326	6	5	0	0	0	13	1	0	4	794

Note: PC: People's Council, SG: Secretary General, ECM: Executive Committee Member, JC: Judges' Committee, IC: Inspection Committee

Source: See Table 5.3

officers in rank and position at the office of transfer[28] and partly to prevent officers who were scheduled to retire at the office of transfer from feeling dissatisfied. Although the table does not show when officers were seconded, the rank at which they were seconded out of the tatmadaw gradually trended upward over the course of the 1970s and 1980s. This gradual rise seems to have reflected the parallel expansion of manpower in the tatmadaw.

Under Ne Win's control, the seconding of tatmadaw officers to senior positions on people's councils through elections was unofficially institutionalized. The framework of local government based on the ICS district officer that had spanned the whole of Burma during the nineteenth and first half of the twentieth century was now broken up into township units which broke down the framework organizationally, and its human resources were replaced by people's councils headed largely by officers seconded from the tatmadaw.

The situation was similar for central ministries. The secretaries of the civil service were removed and newly created deputy ministers became the top administrative officials. This opened the administrative bureaucracy to the recruitment of senior staff from the outside through "elections." As a result, a great number of military officers flowed into each ministry as deputy ministers. Table 5.6 shows this change. The table classifies personnel who became deputy ministers between 1974 and 1988 by career background. The following two points are evident.

One, there was a consistently high number of tatmadaw officers who became deputy ministers. Among 92 deputy ministers appointed during the 14 years, the careers of 78 are known, and, of these, 59 were tatmadaw officers. The table classifies these officers into seven groups according to their career background, but they can be roughly classified into three types: former operations officers, officers previously seconded to administrative positions, and officers previously seconded to the BSPP. Former operations officers could be appointed deputy ministers directly from positions of director in the Ministry of Defence or the General Staff Office or from their posting as military region commanders or deputy commanders. The second type, those who had previously been

[28] This was a situation where an officer of lower rank, who was seconded to an organization and then promoted to higher posts in the organization, ends up in a higher post than an officer who was seconded later to the same organization but who had ranked higher than the earlier officer when the two had been in the tatmadaw.

Table 5.6 Profiles of Deputy Ministers (1974–88)

	Profile	
Military Officer	General Staff Office, (Dy) Commander of MR	18
	Military → Public Corporation	11
	Military → Administrative Dy-Minister and DG of Ministries	9
	Military → Party Central Cadre	10
	Military → Party Local Cadre	6
	Military → Chairman of SAC	4
	Military → Ambassador	1
	Total	59
Civilian	DG of Ministry and GM of Public Corporation	6
	University Professor	7
	Party Cadre	4
	Medical Doctor	1
	Others	1
	Total	19
	n.a.	14
	Total	92

Note: MR: Military Region, DG: Director General, SAC: Security and Administration Committee, GM: General Manager

Source: See Table 5.3

seconded to administrative posts, were usually officers who, after having been seconded from the tatmadaw to be presidents of state enterprises or secretaries (prior to 1972) or top positions in the central government, were elected as deputy ministers in the ministry they had been seconded to. The third type, those previously seconded to the BSPP, were officers who had been seconded from the tatmadaw to the BSPP to work as top officials, such as director general in the party headquarters or chairmen of local party committees, after which they were elected as deputy ministers.

The second point evident from the table is that 19 civilian deputy ministers were elected, a large number compared with the number of civilian ministers during the same 14 years. However, only six of these 19 people had careers coming up through the ministries in the 1950s or 1960s and they had worked as ministry director generals or as presidents of people's state enterprise before becoming deputy ministers. Seven

Table 5.7 Education of Deputy Ministers (1974–88)

Education	*Number*	*Military Officers*
8th grade	5	5 (100%)
9th grade	4	4 (100%)
10th grade	34	32 (94%)
Liberal Arts Graduate	7	7 (100%)
TC Graduate	1	1 (100%)
Diplomat	2	2 (100%)
B.A	7	3 (43%)
B.Sc	7	4 (57%)
B.M	3	0 (0%)
Ph.D (Foreign)	6	0 (0%)
MBBS	2	1 (50%)
n.a	14	0 (0%)
Total	92	59 (64%)

Note: TC: Teachers college

Source: by the author based on *pyihtaunzu hsousheli'thammada myanmanainngando patamaacein pyidu thou yweichetinhmyau'hchin hkanyatho pyidu hlwu'to kozahlemya i koyeihma'tan akyinjou'* (1974), (1978), and (1981)

people were elected as deputy ministers directly from being college professors or after they worked at the director general level, but none of them went through a promotion process similar to that of the ICS/BCS where officials moved back and forth between postings to district offices and then to ministry secretariats in the central government.

From Table 5.7, which shows the educational background of deputy ministers, one can see that a few people among the civilians had obtained a master's degree in the country or a Ph.D. abroad and could be called technocrats. However, by far the greatest number of deputy ministers were tenth-grade graduates of Burmese high schools, and most of them were active or retired military officers. They had not even graduated from a military academy, which is the standard for a modern military. Burma's military academy, the Defence Services Academy, was not established until 1955, and many who became officers prior to that time had received only nine months of training at the Officers Training School. Clearly the less educated military officers who made up the majority of deputy ministers had a far greater presence in the government administration than did the few highly educated civilian technocrats.

The above examination into the careers of deputy ministers and top officials of the people's councils shows that a network of military officers from the tatmadaw spread through the BSPP and the government administration, creating a new framework that made possible stable military rule. The opening move to this outcome had been Ne Win's series of administrative reforms implemented in the early 1970s.

Conclusion

This chapter looked at the Burmese government administrative structure and the civil bureaucrats that served in it from its colonial beginnings and examined how this administrative structure was transformed during the Ne Win regime. In this transformation nearly the entire human and institutional heritage from the colonial ICS/BCS was largely lost. The decisive blows were the administrative reforms in 1972 intended to undermine colonial legacy and the 1974 Constitution meant to institutionalize a BSPP-led regime. The outcome, however, was not the party-led regime called for in the constitution, but the institutionalizing of a system that seconded military officers into positions of leadership in the administrative bureaucracy paving the way for greater military intervention into state and politics.

This wholesale reorganization of administrative structure and the accompanying distribution of government positions to tatmadaw officers had an enormous impact on the Ne Win regime and on Burma's political system. It allowed the tatmadaw to penetrate into the government administrative bureaucracy; it smoothed over contending personnel issues in the tatmadaw by securing positions outside of the tatmadaw that officers could be seconded to, which helped maintain military cohesion; and it checked the expansion of any influence by forces outside the tatmadaw, including the civil service. But the outcome was a government administrative system that stagnated institutionally and in human resources, a major factor for the country's retarded political and economic development compared with neighboring East and Southeast Asian countries. This was because the administrative bureaucracy lost the ability to develop rational policies and the capacity to implement programs for economic development.

Conversely, however, military intervention and the penetration of the tatmadaw into the administration of the government brought an end to Burma's political instability and intensifying conflict among the ruling political elite at the same time that it secured Ne Win's own political leadership. But the state's capacity to govern deteriorated along with the economic conditions of the country. In response Ne Win sought all the more to strengthen his support base by providing benefits to the tatmadaw. This vicious cycle of deteriorating national conditions leading to more benefits for the tatmadaw establishment is one of the structural factors characterizing the stagnation of Burmese politics.

But we need to seek beyond the factors within Ne Win's regime alone to understand the reasons for Burma's continued stagnation and the prolongation of its military regime. When the political leadership confronts a serious challenge from the society, we need to examine the configuration of forces among the elites which has a decisive effect on the outcome of the confrontation, something that will be clearly evident when examining the outbreak of the anti-government movement in Burma in 1988, the military coup that followed, and the military's ability to maintain its regime thereafter. The next chapter shifts the focus from the administrative structure and the civilian bureaucracy to the kinds of people who made up the political elite of the Ne Win regime.

CHAPTER 6

"Winner-Take-All:" An Analysis of Burma's Political Elite

An element of "winner-take-all" exists in the political culture of Burma and refers to the following events. In the Constituent Assembly election in 1947, the first substantive election in the history of Burma, the Anti-Fascist People's Freedom League (AFPFL) scored an overwhelming victory, gaining 248 of the 255 seats. Then, in 1962, Ne Win's regime took over the state and virtually removed all the influential politicians from power and banned all activities by existing political parties. Thereafter, in the general election of 1990, the first such election since 1960, the National League for Democracy obtained 392 of the 485 seats, although 2,209 candidates from 93 parties and 87 independent candidates ran in the election. Pointing to this repeated overwhelming win by one political actor at a time of regime transition, some observers argue that leaders are inclined to favor neither compromise nor cooperation and suggest that Burmese politics contains an element of "winner-take-all."[1]

Although based essentially on observation, the "winner-take-all" argument does point out an important characteristic of Burmese politics. Here "winner-take-all" is defined as a wholesale reshuffle of people in

[1] See, for example, Mary Callahan, "On Time Warps and Warped Time: Lessons from Burma's 'Democratic Era'", in *Burma: Prospects for a Democratic Future*, ed. Robert I. Rotberg (Washington, D.C.: Brookings Institution Press, 1998), p. 64, where Callahan states, "In any of the colonial, parliamentary, socialist or post-1988 military rule periods, a fight over ideas, visions and policies was always that of winner-take-all." Also Christina Fink wrote, "The mentality of 'winner-take-all' was still so normative that many examples of political violence and abuse of power prevented the development of democratic culture." See Christina Fink, *Living Silence: Burma under Military Rule* (Dhaka: University Press, 2001), p. 26.

important political posts during regime transition. Through an analysis of the profiles of the political elite in the Ne Win regime, this chapter will provide evidence of the existence of "winner-take-all" in a regime transition. Fortunately, I have been able to build up a database using official documents of the Burma Socialist Programme Party (BSPP) and the People's Parliament (PP) that profiles this elite between 1971 and 1987.[2] Who made up the political elite during the Ne Win regime? What careers did they have before obtaining important posts? And, how was the political elite transformed by the end of the 1980s? This chapter will examine these questions. It will also take up the following two significant points.

First, the chapter will show the uniqueness of Ne Win's revolution. It has been difficult to compare the Ne Win regime to other countries' military dictatorships because in Burma the military commanders created the socialist state. Normally, "generals' revolutions are rebellions of the status quo."[3] General-grade military officers are not prone to destabilize the existing order because they are already in positions of power. Although fitting the minimum definition of a revolution: a sudden and violent upset of existing political order,[4] Ne Win's revolution clearly differed from those in communist countries such as Vietnam, Laos, and China. This chapter will shed light on one aspect of the Ne Win regime's uniqueness, focusing on the changes it wrought on the human resources of the political elite.

Second, it will provide an understanding of state-society relations in Burma.[5] So far these relations have often been depicted in the media simply as "oppressor against victim." But no matter how oppressive the state may be, it is always tied to its own society in the sense that the same people who oppress others have also been born and raised in Burma, work for the state, and as members of the coercive apparatus are able to suppress others who belong to the same nation-state. Thus,

---

[2] The author acquired some of these documents from used bookshops and others from private collections in Burma. They were not available in archives or libraries.

[3] Janowitz Morris, *The Military in the Political Development of New Nations: an Essay in Comparative Analysis* (Chicago: University of Chicago Press, 1964), p. 65.

[4] Carl Joachim Friedrich, "An Introductory Note on Revolution," in *Revolution*, ed. Carl J. Friedrich (New York: Atherton, 1937), p. 5.

[5] See Joel S. Migdal, *Strong Societies and Weak States: State-Society Relations and State Capabilities in the Third World* (Princeton, N.J.: Princeton University Press, 1988).

society determines the nature of the state at the structural level, even if democracy has not emerged as an institution for political representation. Little attention has been paid to state-society relations in Burma. By examining attributes like age, ethnic group, religion, level of education and the career of elite agents of the state, it will be possible to shed light on the societal aspect of the state in Burma, contributing to a deeper understanding of it.

The remainder of this chapter will first define the political elite based on its official status. Then, we will examine the social profiles of this elite (age, ethnic group, religion, level of education and career), which will show that the closer people were to the center of power, the younger and less educated they were, and the more likely they were to be Bahman and Buddhist. Next, we will analyze the careers of the political elite, which will reveal that very few politicians of the 1950s were included in the Ne Win regime, a clear demonstration of "winner-take-all" in Burma's political culture. In the final section, the chapter will analyze the characteristics of the new party bureaucrats and how high their careers could advance in the BSPP.

The Political Elite

Who were the political elites of the Ne Win regime? The definition of political elite varies from scholar to scholar. Some define it by official status and others by substantial political influence.[6] Particularly in an undemocratic country official status may not necessarily correspond to substantial political influence. For instance, in the case of a national assembly, it may be wrong to regard all members of the assembly as part of the political elite because a parliament is often just a rubber-stamp legislature, in which case a few prominent leaders and their inner circle are influential. Even so, it is useful to define the political elite based on an official representative institution. That is because there has to have been some reasons that a person was elected as a representative, even when that person has little substantial political influence in the political process. For instance, if the person is an ethnic minority, religious minority, or gender minority, he or she may be required to participate in the political process as a symbol of national unity, may be called on to implement affirmative action programs, or may have to conciliate a specific

---

[6] Alan Zuckerman, "'Political Elite': Lessons from Mosca and Pareto," *The Journal of Politics* 39, 2 (1977).

political force. Whatever the matter, it must contain an element of politics. On this basis, I will define this elite as determined by the extent that its members can participate in the formal political decision-making process. In the case of this research, these participants include representatives in PP and as members of the BSPP's CC. To know how this participation worked, we need to understand the official organizational structure of the Socialist Republic of the Union of Burma as based on the 1974 Constitution. Then we can give a substantive definition of the political elite during Ne Win's rule.

The 1974 Constitution

Ne Win abolished the 1947 Constitution after his coup in 1962. Thereafter Burma was without a constitution, and it was not until his speech at the Fourth Party Seminar in November 1969 that Ne Win mentioned the need to draft a new one. On 29 November 1969 he convened 33 former politicians, including U Nu, Ba Swe, and Thakin Chit Maung, and organized the Internal Unity Advisory Board (*pyidwîn nyinyu'yêi àkyanpêi aphwè*). The purpose of this group was to provide advice on issues concerning national unity, politics, the economy, society, ethnic groups, and the drafting of a new constitution. The board submitted its conclusions in a final report to Ne Win on 31 May 1969. In the report, 18 members, including Ba Swe, advocated a new constitution based on amending the 1947 Constitution. Three other members, including Kyaw Nyein, added additional opinions to the majority opinion. Eleven others, including Thakin Lwin, maintained that a new constitution should be drafted as the basis for a socialist democracy. The one remaining member was U Nu, who requested that he be returned to power as prime minister before the drafting of a new constitution, arguing that his dismissal by Ne Win had been illegal. Then once returned as prime minister, he could convene the union parliament to elect Ne Win as president who in turn could convene a constituent assembly. Had the majority opinion been adopted, a constitution based on the amendment of the 1947 Constitution would have been adopted. However, Ne Win rejected this proposal claiming that the 1947 Constitution "does not protect the interests of the workers and farmers."[7]

[7] For a narration of events concerning the advisory board, see U Mya Han, Dr. Daw Khin Hla Han, U Kyaw Gyeing, U Than Lwin, and U Sein Myint, *myanmà nàinnganyêi sàni' pyâun kalà 1962–1974, pàtàmà* [Time of change in Burma's political regime 1962–1974] (Yangon: te'kàtomyâpounhnei'tai', 1993), pp. 72–5.

The work of drafting a new constitution formally began at the First BSPP Party Congress convened in June 1971. Then on 29 September of that year, a 97-member Constitution Drafting Commission (CDC) was organized chaired by Brigadier General San Yu.[8] This commission began drafting the new constitution based on the following six principles (*àcheikhanmu chau'che'*) that were announced at the First BSPP Party Congress.

(1) The goal of the state is the realization of a socialist regime.
(2) The state will construct a socialist economic system and will establish laws that firmly defend this economic system.
(3) The structure of the state is to be based on a regime of socialist democracy.
(4) Our pledge is to maintain the equality and indivisibility of the ethnic groups in the land, and for rich and poor to coexist in unity.
(5) The socialist regime and the state will faithfully fulfil their many responsibilities in order to enable worker citizens to enjoy their democratic and individual rights under a socialist regime.
(6) We will take the appropriate and necessary measures that contribute to the construction of a state under a regime of socialistic democracy.[9]

At its first meeting the commission set up nine committees, and it was further decided to organize a total of 15 regional sub-commissions in each division/state to hear people's opinions. According to a commission report, the BSPP, People's Peasants' Council, People's Workers' Councils, and the tatmadaw submitted opinion briefs, and public hearings were held by the sub-commissions. More than 105,000 people were reported to have participated in the series of meetings, and 3,458 representatives submitted their opinions to the regional sub-commissions.[10] The state-owned newspapers carried detailed reports on the progress of drafting the constitution. Although great deal of activity and coverage went into drawing up the Constitution, most likely the people's opinions were not reflected in the drafting process.

---

[8] Albert D. Moscotti, *Burma's Constitution and Elections of 1974: A Source Book* (Singapore: Institute of Southeast Asian Studies, 1977), pp. 7–8.

[9] U Thein Hlaing and Dr. Daw Khin Hla Han, eds., *myanmà nàinnganyêi sàni' pyâun kalà 1962–1974, tàtìyàtwê* [Time of change in Burma's political regime 1962–1974, vol. 3] (Yangon: te'kàtomyâpounhnei'tai', 1993), p. 80.

[10] Ibid., pp. 88–9.

In March 1972 the fourth meeting of the CDC discussed the first draft of the Constitution before submitting it to the fourth meeting of the BSPP CC. After receiving CC approval, this first draft was published on 30 April, and the second round of constitutional drafting began following the same stage-managed procedures. Nothing more clearly illustrates the leadership's attention to this staging than San Yu's speech at a public hearing on 24 November 1972, in which he said,

> The drawing up of the New State Constitution is not the work of a party or an organization or a group of people alone but that of all the people of the whole country. The Constitution that was drawn up after the gaining of independence was the work of a group of people in the Constituent Assembly, and the socialist system fervently desired by the people faded. The weaknesses and loopholes in the Constitution weakened the unity of the nationals of the Union of Burma. The birth rights of man were also undermined. To prevent the repetition of such a situation, arrangements were made to enable the widespread participation of the people in the drafting of the New State Constitution.[11]

The draft was amended a second and third time. Meanwhile preparations began for a referendum on the draft of the new constitution. A Referendum Commission was appointed on 16 August 1973, and the referendum on the third draft of the Constitution, approved at the Second BSPP Party Conference, began on 15 December. When it was over, more than 13 million votes, equivalent to 90.19 per cent of the total, had approved the new Constitution.

There are four important points to note about the new Constitution. First, the political structure prescribed in the Constitution was a party-state modelled on a socialist country. The guidance (*khaunhsaunhmu*) of the state by the BSPP was stipulated in Article 11. This guidance by the party was conducted by party organizations set up in the administrative machinery, the tatmadaw and the PP, or by party members appointed as senior officials to these organizations.

The second important point was that the People's Parliament (*pyidù hlu'to*) and the People's Councils (*pyidù kaunsi*) (PC) at each administrative level were expected to reflect the will of the people in the legislative process. According to the official view of the Revolutionary Council (RC),

[11] Moscotti, *Burma's Constitution and Elections of 1974*, p. 14.

the enactment of the 1974 Constitution was meant to return state power to the people, power that had been ceded to the RC after the 2 March 1962 coup; and the people here meant the PP and the PCs at each level. Therefore, the 1974 Constitution had established a four-year term unicameral PP as the highest state organ and the sole legislative body (Articles 41 and 44), wherein Affairs Committees were set up to review bills (Article 54), ensuring that the PP was the principal place for political decision making, all features that are common to constitutions of socialist countries in general. Regarding the tatmadaw, it was mentioned only in the provisions on court-martials in Article 99, and in Article 171 dealing with military training and conscription. Nothing at all was stipulated about its political role.

Third, the Constitution gave the President enormous powers through the Council of State (CS) (*naingando kaunsi*), an organization based on Article 64 of the Constitution. The membership of the CS was selected from among the members of the PP, 14 of whom were division/state representatives. The chairman and secretary general were chosen from among the CS members by a vote of CS membership (Article 65), and only the CS Chairman could be the President of the Union of Burma (Article 66). Because it was made up of CS members selected from the PP, the CS itself was responsible to the PP (Article 70); however, the Constitution conferred on the CS a great number of powers, including the authority to interpret the Constitution [Article 73(b)]; the right to promulgate laws [Article 73(c)]; the right to submit lists of candidates for membership to the Council of Ministers, the Council of People's Judges, the Council of People's Attorneys, the Council of People's Inspectors [Article 73(d)], and the Affairs Committee [Article 73(e)]; the right to make decisions concerning the establishment of diplomatic relations [Article 73(f)]; and the right to appoint and dismiss deputy ministers (Article 73(j)); and heads of bodies of public services (Article 73(l)). These in effect were powers of the President, the position held by Ne Win, which meant that his dictatorship was institutionally guaranteed.

Finally, the Constitution lacked the ideological terminology common to the constitutions of socialist states, which tend to advocate national ideals that clearly show the legitimacy of the state. For example, the 1975 Constitution of the People's Republic of China declares in the fourth paragraph of the Preamble that, "We must adhere to the basic line and policies of the Communist Party of China for the entire historical period of socialism and persist in continued revolution under the dictatorship of the proletariat, so that our great motherland will always advance along the road indicated by Marxism-Leninism-Mao Tsetung Thought."[12] North Korea's 1972 Constitution, Chapter 4, states that, "The Democratic People's Republic of Korea is guided in its activity by the Juche idea of the Korean Workers Party, which is a creative application of Marxism-Leninism to our country's reality."[13] Both of these constitutions present the ideological positions of the socialist regimes in the countries by combining Marxism-Leninism and the political ideas of their leaders.

Burma's 1974 Constitution was different. The phrase "Marxism-Leninism" never appeared. There was not even a statement pertaining to *The System of Correlation between Man and his Environment*. The Constitution only commented in the fifth paragraph of the Preamble that the BSPP had "drafted the Constitution of the Socialist Republic of the Union of Burma, in accordance with the wishes of the people, after extensive and thorough discussions with them, for the purpose of building a peaceful and prosperous socialist society to which the working people of the national races have long aspired." It seems, therefore, that the ideological foundation of the Constitution was not actually based on a particular political thought but rather on more general concepts like "the wishes of the people" and "the working people of the national races."[14] In this respect, Burma's 1974 Constitution was much less ideological than the constitutions of socialist countries that advocated relatively sophisticated ideas of Marxism-Leninism, Maoism, and the concept of Juche.

The Political Elite

Table 6.1 shows the composition of the political elite in the Ne Win regime after 1974. This section will focus on the members of three organizations: the PP, BSPP CC, and the tatmadaw officer corps. The PP and BSPP CC members were selected through elections. Table 6.2 shows the election dates and the number of candidates. As the figures indicate,

[12] The 1975 Constitution of the People's Republic of China, Preamble.

[13] The 1972 Constitution of the Democratic People's Republic of Korea, Article 4.

[14] The Constitution also avoided terms such as "working class" and "democratic centralism" which evoke Marxist-Leninism. Instead it used less ideological phrases such as "workers" and "socialist democracy." This less ideological terminology limited the scope of political participation, apparently as a rejection of communism and the communist party that although advocating socialism, was conducting an armed struggle against the government.

Table 6.1 Political Elite in the Ne Win Regime

Authority	*People's Parliament*	*BSPP*	*tatmadaw*
↑	President		
	Council of State Member	Chairman	CGS
	Cabinet Member	CEC Member	V-CGS (A, N, AF)
	Chairman and Secretary General of Affairs Committee	Chairman and Secretary General of Affairs Committee	Commander of BSO Commander of MR
	Parliament Member	CC Member/ Candidate Member	High-Ranking Officer

Note: CEC: Central Executive Committee, CC: Central Committee, CGS: Chief of General Staff of tatmadaw, V-CGS (A, N, AF): Vice-Chief of General Staff (Army, Navy, Air Force), BSO: Bureau of Special Operations, MR: Military Region

Source: by the author

Table 6.2 Elections for BSPP Central Committee and People's Parliament

Central Committee	*Election Date*	*Party Conference*	*Members (Candidate Mem)*	*Candidates*
1st CC	07/07/1971	1st Party Conference	150 (50)	300
2nd CC	10/17/1973	2nd Party Conference	150 (50)	300
3rd CC	02/26/1977	3rd Party Conference	180 (59)	360
4th CC	11/16/1977	Emergency Party Conference	250	
5th CC	08/06/1981	4th Party Conference	260	
6th CC	08/06/1985	5th Party Conference	280	
People's Parliament	*Election Date*	*PP Election*	*Seats*	
1st PP	01/27/1974	1st Election	451	
2nd PP	01/01/1978	2nd Election	464	
3rd PP	10/04/1981	3rd Election	475	
4th PP	10/06/1985	4th Election	489	

Source: by the author

and for the purposes of the study, the political elite of the CC included CC members, candidate members, and candidates who ran for election in the first through third CCs but were not elected. In the tatmadaw officer corps, the political elite included only senior military officers such as directors and above in the Ministry of Defence, deputy commanders and above (lieutenant colonels or colonels) of light infantry divisions, and general staff officers (colonels and above). Some 700 to 800 people fit these qualifications indicating that the political elite was not large, primarily because many of these people served concurrently in a number of positions.

An examination of the relationship among the three organizations will show how the members of the elite interacted. Looking first at the relationship between the BSPP CC and the officer corps, a conference of BSPP party members in the tatmadaw was held before every BSPP party congress from which around 40 senior military officers were chosen as tatmadaw candidates for the CC. After an officer was elected to the CC, he did not relinquish his tatmadaw post but concurrently served as a member of the military and the CC. The relationship of the officer corps to the PP was not close like that with the CC. There were no particular slots set aside for military officers in the PP. The only exception was the stipulation of the People's Parliament Act, Article 24(a), which required representation of the Ministry of Defence on the PP's Defence and Security Committee. The relationship between the PP and the CC was not stipulated in the Constitution except for the provision in Article 11 stating that the former was to provide guidance for the latter. But no organization existed that reflected the BSPP's will in the decisions of the PP, unlike in China where a "party group" exists in the National People's Congress.

The qualifications to be a candidate for the PP were stipulated in "The Act of 1974 on Phased Elections for the First People's Parliament and People's Councils" under Chapter 5, "Qualifications for People's Representatives." A candidate had to: (a) be born to parents of Burmese nationality [Article 11(a)], (b) be 28 years old [Article 11(d)], (c) reside in the township of candidacy [Article 12(a)(i)], and (d) be on the list of names that went through a meeting to select candidates to be on the ballots for election to the People's Parliament [Article 12 (c)(ii)]. But Article 19 of Chapter 7, "Submission of the Candidate Name List for People's Representatives," had a further stipulation. "To be considered for candidacy as a people's representative to the People's Parliament or a

People's Council at any [administrative] level, and for the party to provide guidance to the organized social classes and the voters in the constituencies, the BSPP must convene a meeting to select and handle the submission of the name list of candidates for people's representatives."

This stipulation allowed the BSPP to intervene when compiling the list of candidates, enabling the party to control the selection of all candidates and therefore of everyone who became a member of the PP. In PP elections one candidate ran in each constituency making the election essentially a vote of confidence, and voters had to be Burmese nationals 18 years old or older who voted by secret ballot. The end result was that one could not retain membership in the BSPP without following the party's decisions, and if not a party member, one could not become a member of the PP. This was the only formal limitation allowing the BSPP to control the process of selecting representatives to the PP.

The data for this analysis came from information on 1,389 PP members from the first three sessions of the People's Parliament (elected between 1974 and 1981);[15] 1,889 CC members and Party Discipline Committee members from the first to sixth sessions (elected in 1971, 1973, two 1977 elections, 1981, and 1985); 469 people from the Third Party Congress representing the Chin State and the Irrawaddy, Sagaing, and Mandalay divisions; and 319 people from regional party committees who were candidates for the BSPP CC.[16]

This data will be used in the next section to analyze the social profiles of the political elite, looking first at their age groups, ethnic background, and religion, then at their education to see what differences, if any, existed among the elite of the tatmadaw, BSPP, and the PP. The second section will test the "winner-take-all" hypothesis using data on the careers of the political elite. The analysis will show a discontinuity in the political elite between that of the Ne Win regime and the elite of the democratic period. The final section will examine the emergence of civilian BSPP bureaucrats and the limits placed on their promotion in the party.

---

[15] The members of the Fourth PP elected in 1985 were not part of this analysis because data was lacking and insufficient.

[16] Gender is not treated here because women constitute less than 5% of the membership in all three organizations.

Social Profiles

Age, Ethnicity and Religion

This section will examine the differences of PP and CC members and the officer corps in age, ethnicity, and religion. The PP in Burma, as in other socialist countries, functioned as a rubber stamp legislature. Once the party had approved a bill, it was all but guaranteed to be passed in PP. But the Ne Win regime needed the PP because it was the symbol of a government that ruled according to the "wishes of the people" (*pyidù hsandà*). The leaders had to display legitimacy through the due process of legislation by an assembly even if that process was virtually fictitious and did not necessarily reflect the real "wishes of the people." National unity was also embodied in the assembly through the inclusiveness of its membership.[17] Given the ritual character of PP and the gap between the de facto and de jure relationship among PP, CC, and the officer corps, we can surmise that the following three things were true of the PP under the Ne Win regime.

First, the turnover rate in the assembly was higher than that of the CC because the relative powerlessness of PP meant it was easy for the leadership to replace incumbents who could do little to protest such action. Second, since the PP's function was a ritual to legitimize the BSPP's guidance, older people were appointed as members because they were generally most respected in Burmese society, and the leadership took advantage of their social prestige. Therefore we can expect that the average age of PP members was higher than for members of the CC. Third, the ethnic and religious distribution within the PP membership was closer to the country's officially announced figures than it was in the CC. As the organization displaying the unity of the nation, the PP had to reflect the official distribution of ethnic groups. Otherwise it would have been difficult to show the ethnic and religious harmony of the Burmese nation and the people's wishes derived therefrom.

The turnover rate in PP membership can be ascertained from the proportion of new members in the second and third PP elections. In the second election that took place in 1978, 276 of the PP's 464 members were new, accounting for 59.5 per cent of the total, meaning that more

[17] Often in socialist countries the symbol of the people's unity comes in the form of leader worship, but Ne Win is said to have disliked personality cults, so no such cult developed to legitimize the government in Burma.

Table 6.3 New Members of the BSPP Central Committee

CC (Year)	*New Members*	*Total Members*	*Proportion of New Members*
First (1971)	200	200	100 (%)
Second (1973)	15	200	7.5
Third (1977)	67	239	28.0
Fourth (1977)	56	250	22.4
Fifth (1981)	60	260	23.1
Sixth (1985)	95	280	33.9
Total	493	1,429	34.5

Source: by the author

than half of the members were replaced. The number of new members in the third election in 1981 decreased to 160 of 464 for a turnover of 34.5 per cent, a considerable fall but still a high rate. With no data available for the Fourth PP, a trend cannot be established, but from the available data shown in Table 6.3, it can be seen that the turnover rate for PP members was higher than it was for members and candidate members of the CC. Only 15 new members and candidate members were elected to the second CC, two years after the first CC election, a turnover rate of only 7.5 per cent. Although that was an extreme case, all of the other CC elections had a turnover rate between 20 per cent and 30 per cent, except for the sixth CC which had a turnover rate of 33.9 per cent. These numbers suggest that the replacement of members in the PP was more common than the CC.

Figures 6.1 and 6.2 show the composition of the PP and CC, respectively, by age following each election. Figure 6.1 shows that after the 1974 election about 40 per cent of the PP members were in their 50s or older. This group increased in the next two elections, and in 1981, after the third assembly election, nearly 60 per cent of the members were in their 50s or older. From Figure 6.2 it can be seen that the CC members in the beginning were noticeable younger, 80 per cent of whom were in their 40s in the first CC elected in 1971. An important reason for this was the existence of tatmadaw officers. In the first CC, 119 of the 150 members were from the tatmadaw. Thereafter, in each succeeding election, members in their 50s and older steadily increased until they made up 70 per cent of the CC after the election in 1985. This was because active senior officers were getting older, and also because retired officers on the committee were increasing in number. Meanwhile, the average age

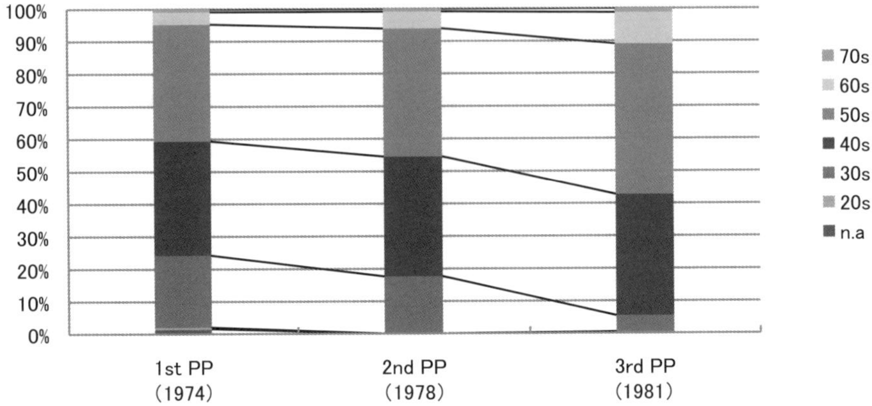

Source: by the author based on *pyihtaunzu hsousheli'thammada myanmanainngando patamaacein pyidu thou yweichetinhmyau'hchin hkanyatho pyidu hlwu'to kozahlemya i koyeihma'tan akyinjou'* (1974), (1978), and (1981)

Figure 6.1 Age Composition of PP Members

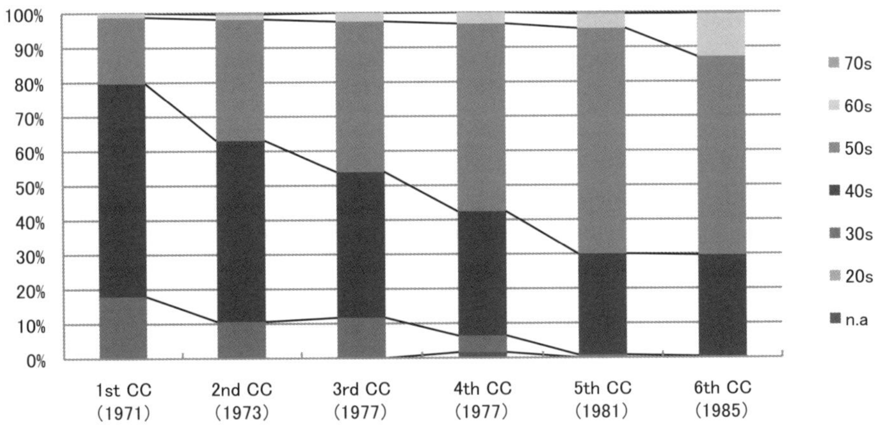

Source: by the author based on *bahoukomiti winlaunmya i kouyei hma'tan acinjou'* (1971?), (1973), (1977), (1981), and (1985); *ayeipoacein patinyilahkan bahoukomiti winlaunmya i kouyei hma'tan acinjou'* (1977)

Figure 6.2 Age Composition of CC Members

Table 6.4 Ethnic Composition of the PP Membership

Ethnicity	*First PP 1974*		*SecondPP 1978*		*Third PP 1981*	
Bahman	301	66.9%	314	67.7%	315	66.3%
Yakhain	24	5.3%	26	5.6%	25	5.3%
Shan	21	4.7%	23	5.0%	19	4.0%
Karen	18	4.0%	15	3.2%	18	3.8%
Chin	11	2.4%	18	3.9%	20	4.2%
Pao	4	0.9%	3	0.6%	4	0.8%
Paraung	2	0.4%	3	0.6%	3	0.6%
Kachin	10	2.2%	7	1.5%	11	2.3%
Kayah	5	1.1%	6	1.3%	3	0.6%
Shah/Burman	6	1.3%	6	1.3%	6	1.3%
Other	41	9.1%	43	9.3%	51	10.7%
Unknown	7	1.6%	0	0.0%	0	0.0%
Total	450	100%	464	100%	475	100%

Source: See Figure 6.1

of PP members, although also getting older, did not increase as quickly, most likely because of the higher turnover rate.

Looking at ethnic and religious composition, Tables 6.4 and 6.5 show the distribution pattern of ethnic groups among members of the PP and CC, respectively. From Table 6.4 it can be seen that the proportion of Bahmans in the PP was consistently about 67 per cent through the first three PPs, roughly in line with their ratio of the total population (67.9 per cent) in the 1973 population census.[18] The tables also indicate that the Shan and Karen peoples were slightly under-represented in the PP, as they respectively accounted for 8.9 per cent and 6.6 per cent of total population, but the representation of each was 5 per cent or less in the PP. In general, however, the representation of minority ethnic groups in PP was largely proportional to the size of the population, and there were no major changes in that proportion in the PP except for an increase of Chin parliament members from 11 (2.4 per cent) in 1974 to 20 (4.2 per cent) in 1981.[19]

[18] In Burma, the differences of ethnic composition between "all ages" and "over 21 years old" are 1% or less.

[19] The Chins make up 2.2% of the total population.

Table 6.5 Ethnicity of the Candidates for the Central Committee

Ethnicity	*First CC 1971*		*Second CC 1973*		*Third CC 1977*		*Fourth CC 1977*		*Fifth CC 1981*		*Sixth CC 1985*	
Bahman	267	80.9%	248	75.2%	265	73.6%	185	74.0%	186	71.5%	198	70.7%
Rakhine	15	4.5%	17	5.2%	18	5.0%	10	4.0%	10	3.8%	11	3.9%
Shan	6	1.8%	7	2.1%	9	2.5%	6	2.4%	7	2.7%	9	3.2%
Karen	7	2.1%	9	2.7%	11	3.1%	9	3.6%	12	4.6%	8	2.9%
Chin	6	1.8%	7	2.1%	9	2.5%	11	4.4%	12	4.6%	13	4.6%
Pao	3	0.9%	3	0.9%	5	1.4%	3	1.2%	3	1.2%	1	0.4%
Paraung	3	0.9%	2	0.6%	2	0.6%	1	0.4%	1	0.4%	2	0.7%
Kachin	2	0.6%	6	1.8%	7	1.9%	6	2.4%	6	2.3%	9	3.2%
Kayah	2	0.6%	3	0.9%	2	0.6%	2	0.8%	2	0.8%	3	1.1%
Shan/Burma	3	0.9%	5	1.5%	3	0.8%	1	0.4%	1	0.4%	1	0.4%
Other	16	4.8%	23	7.0%	29	8.1%	16	6.4%	20	7.7%	25	8.9%
Total	330	100%	330	100%	360	100%	250	100%	260	100%	280	100%

Source: See Figure 6.2

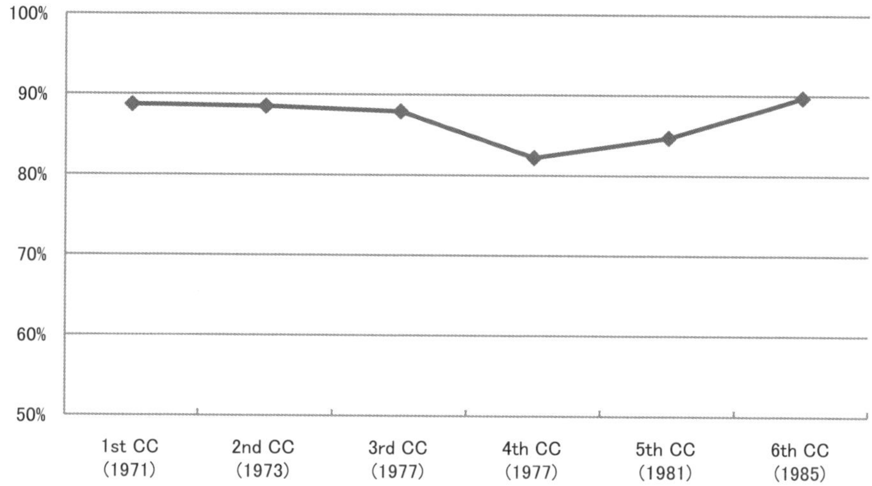

Source: See Figure 6.2

Figure 6.3 Percentage of High Ranking Officers on the CC who were Bahman

Looking at Table 6.5, which shows the ethnic composition of the CC, the ratio of Bahmans gradually decreased from 80.9 per cent in 1971 to 70.7 per cent in 1985, but their representation remained higher than that in the PP. This high percentage was a reflection of the ethnic composition of the officer corps. As seen in Figure 6.3, which shows the ethnicity of senior tatmadaw officers, the proportion of Bahman, although showing a slight decrease at the time of the fourth CC election in 1977, never dropped below 80 per cent, and it returned to around 90 per cent by 1985 with the sixth CC election. While the civilian members of the CC gradually became more multi-ethnic, the members from the military were consistently Bahmans, reflecting their overwhelming majority in the officer corps. Thus, when looking at the political elite as a whole and the importance of the tatmadaw in it, the closer one drew to the centre of power, the greater the number of Bahman.

The composition of religion is less well documented because information on the religions of PP members was recorded only for the Second and the Third PP. The available evidence shows that unlike the focus on ethnicity, the state leadership paid less attention to the religious composition of the assembly. Among the Second PP members, 89.7 per cent

(416 of the 464) were Buddhists, which changed only slightly, 89.3 per cent (424 of 475) in the Third PP (see Table 6.6). This predominance of Buddhists was followed by Christians (Baptists, Roman Catholics, and other Christians) who made up 9.6 per cent of the Second PP (Baptists 1.9 per cent, Roman Catholics 0.4 per cent, other Christians 7.3 per cent) and 10 per cent of the Third PP (0.6 per cent, 0.6 per cent, 8.8 per cent respectively). According to the 1973 census, the huge Buddhist representation in the PP was proportional to the country's Buddhist population. The census recorded a total population of 28.08 million, of which 24.97 million, or 89 per cent, were Buddhist. The census also showed that there were 1.29 million Christians accounting for 4.6 per cent of the total population, which meant that they were over-represented in the PP; 1.08 million, or 3.8 per cent, were Muslim; and 0.12 million, or 0.4 per cent, were Hindu.[20] Due to this study's lack of data for the First and Fourth PPs (and for all the CCs), it is not possible to confirm that the proportion of Christians represented in the PP, about 10 per cent, was larger than the proportion of Christians who resided in Burma. But the available data does confirm that Muslims were very much under-represented. There were many Muslims in urban areas like Rangoon and Mandalay, and, in some townships of Rakhine State Muslim residents were the majority. Nevertheless, in the Second PP there was only one Muslim representative who had been elected from Rakhine State.[21] None was elected to the Third PP.

[20] Although the accuracy of the official statistics is questionable, they are the best figures available at present.

[21] This chapter does not analyze the territorial connections of the political elite. Perhaps surprisingly, the relationship between politics and territorial connections is not a common topic in Burma politics unlike in other countries. Mainly for this reason there is no academic research on politics and territorial connections, and even among ordinary people when discussing politics, they usually do not talk about the territorial connections of politicians. It was difficult, for example, for this author to find out the hometowns of the political elite during the Ne Win regime because the career summary documents maintained on these people lacked a line for recording hometown. To find out this information, the author had to look through the descriptions of their careers. Many candidates for the BSPP CC and PP members did not put down their hometown, and only the birthplace or address(es) until high school of 291 of the 876 CC members, about one-third of the total, can be known for sure. Of the 904 PP members (excluding those of the Fourth PP), such information is known for 359 people. So the data is insufficient for an in-depth analysis of the elite and their territorial connections, unlike with age or ethnic group. However, there is enough

Table 6.6 Religious Affiliations of the People's Parliament Members

Devision/State	*Kachin*		*Kayah*		*Karen*		*Chin*		*Sagain*		*Tanintharyi*		*Pegu*		*Magway*	
Religion	*Second (1978)*	*Third (1981)*	*Second (1978)*	*Third (1981)*	*Second (1978)*	*Third (1981)*	*Second (1978)*	*Third (1981)*	*Second (1978)*	*Third (1981)*	*Second (1978)*	*Third (1981)*	*Second (1978)*	*Third (1981)*	*Second (1978)*	*Third (1981)*
Buddhist	9	6	3	4	10	10	6	5	45	49	12	12	44	47	38	39
Christian	7	11	1		4	4	5	8	4	3	1	1	2	4	1	
Baptist	3	2	2	1			2		1				1			
Roman Catholic			2	3												
Islam																
Nat (Animism)	1	1								1						
Unknown																
Total	20	20	8	8	14	14	13	13	50	53	13	13	47	51	39	39

Devision/State	*Mandalay*		*Rakhine*		*Yangon*		*Shan*		*Irrawaddy*		*Mon*		*Total*			
Religion	*Second (1978)*	*Third (1981)*	*Second (1978)*	*Third (1981)*	*Second (1978)*	*Third (1981)*	*Second (1978)*	*Third (1981)*	*Second (1978)*	*Third (1981)*	*Second (1978)*	*Third (1981)*	*Second (1978)*		*Third (1981)*	
Buddhist	53	53	23	25	52	55	53	52	49	48	19	19	416	89.7%	424	89.3%
Christian					2	1	6	7	1	2		1	34	7.3%	42	8.8%
Baptist													9	1.9%	3	0.6%
Roman Catholic													2	0.4%	3	0.6%
Islam			1										1	0.2%	0	0.0%
Nat (Animism)													1	0.2%	2	0.4%
Unknown			1					1					1	0.2%	1	0.2%
Total	53	53	25	25	54	56	59	60	50	50	19	20	464	100.0%	475	100.0%

Source: by the author based on *pyihtaunzu hsousheli'thammada myanmanainngando patamaacein pyidu thou yweichetinhmyau'hchin hkanyatho pyidu hlwu'to kozahlemya i koyeihma'tan akyinjou'* (1978) and (1981)

Education

Briefly outlining modern education in Burma, in 1931 when the last census of the colonial period was compiled, the number of students attending elementary, junior high and high schools (excluding colleges and monasteries) was around 720,000, equal to only about 5 per cent of Burma's then total population of 14.67 million. The number rose to 1.27 million students nationwide in 1955, and then to 1.89 million in 1960, indicating an almost threefold increase in the number of students over the 30 years.[22] By 1987, near the end of the Ne Win regime, the number of students in elementary, junior high, and high schools had increased to 5.05 million, 1.09 million, and 0.24 million, respectively, for a total of 6.38 million students equal to about 17 per cent of the population at the time.[23] The number of university students in that year stood at 85,000, more than a fourfold increase when compared with the approximately 20,000 university and college students in 1962. In sum, people with higher levels of education had gradually increased in Burma despite the severe social and economic dislocation caused by the Pacific War and the country's unstable security conditions after independence. The question here is how the level of education of the political elite changed compared with the overall rise in the education of the general population.

---

data to establish a trend. The data provide a firmer understanding of ethnic group distribution based on hometown. While the composition of the PP is roughly the same as that of the total population as recorded in the 1973 census at the state/division level, that of the CC indicates that the ratio of members from Pegu and Irrawaddy divisions is larger than that of the total population. This can be more clearly seen for military officers. As already pointed out in this study, the tatmadaw officer corps consisted chiefly of Bahman, and this is supported by the fact that their hometowns were concentrated in Bahman areas of the country. Unfortunately, it still is difficult to obtain data that can answer questions such as whether they were from cities or villages, or what their parents' economic status was.

[22] Teruko Saito and Lee King Kinong, *Statistics on the Burmese Economy: The 19th and 20th Centuries* (Singapore: Institute of Southeast Asian Studies, 1999): p. 238.

[23] simankêin hnìn bandayêi wangyîhtanà [Ministry of National Planning and Finance], *pyihtaunzù myanma naingando ì bandayêi, sîpwâyêi, luhmuyêi àcheiàneimyâ tinpyàche' 1990–91* [Financial, economic and social conditions in the Union of Burma 1990–91] (1990), p. 193.

Following Ne Win's coup d'état in 1962, officers of the tatmadaw came to form a large part of the political elite. Therefore, we would expect that among the Bahman of this elite, the level of education declined. This was because of there being more Bahman tatmadaw officers the closer one came to the centre of power, most of whom before the establishment of the four-year military Defence Services Academy (DSA) in 1955 had only graduated from the six-month course of the Officers Training School (OTS); in many cases they had not even finished high school. Therefore it would be expected that the CC with its proportionally greater number of tatmadaw officers had lower academic qualifications than the members of the PP.

To examine the level of education attained among the elite, it is convenient for the purpose of this study to divide this attainment into five categories. While many of the details describing the categories are not specifically part of the discussion in this section, they are needed to understand the tables and figures.

The first category is those that attended elementary school up to high school but did not graduated from high school. Burma has a 10-year system from elementary school through high school, which is commonly divided into first through tenth grades. In the documents on CC and PP members when describing the level of education attained, a person is said to be a "fourth-grade graduate" or an "eighth-grade graduate," meaning he completed four years or eight years of school. For the purpose of this study, a fourth-grade graduate is an elementary school graduate and an eighth-grade graduate is a junior high school graduate.[24] It will also be useful to break this category of education down into the sub-categories of "elementary school graduate," "junior high school graduate," "junior high school dropout" and "high school dropout." The second category is "high school graduate," a person who has graduated from the 10th year of schooling. The third category, known as *ùbàza* in Burmese, is for people whose education ended after completing the first two years of university. Because the data used here were based on documents written by the CC and PP members themselves, the descriptions are not necessarily consistent. In some cases, *ùbàza* is written together

[24] Some soldiers received a basic education in the tatmadaw, and they will also be classified according to the grade they completed. In addition, the final educational attainment alone will be written for people with teaching qualifications.

Table 6.7 Educational Background of the People's Parliament Members

	First PP (1974)		*Second PP (1978)*		*Third PP (1981)*	
Education	*Members*	*Proportion*	*Members*	*Proportion*	*Members*	*Proportion*
Under High-School	124	27.6%	106	22.8%	100	21.1%
Elementary	53	11.8%	28	6.0%	32	6.7%
Junior High	71	15.8%	78	16.8%	68	14.3%
High School	160	35.6%	150	32.3%	155	32.6%
Ubaza	34	7.6%	64	13.8%	69	14.5%
Bachelor's	89	19.8%	106	22.8%	106	22.3%
B. of Arts	58	12.9%	72	15.5%	75	15.8%
B. of Science	17	3.8%	17	3.7%	20	4.2%
B. of Medical	14	3.1%	17	3.7%	11	2.3%
Higher than Bachelor	26	5.8%	32	6.9%	39	8.2%
B(A)+B. of Law	9	2.0%	8	1.7%	12	2.5%
B(Sc)+B. of Law	1	0.2%	0	0.0%	3	0.6%
MA+B. of Law	1	0.2%	0	0.0%	0	0.0%
Gounghtu	2	0.4%	6	1.3%	3	0.6%
MA	0	0.0%	5	1.1%	6	1.3%
MA(Sc)	5	1.1%	1	0.2%	1	0.2%
MA(Sc) foreign	0	0.0%	3	0.6%	3	0.6%
Ph.D.	2	0.4%	1	0.2%	1	0.2%
MA foreign	0	0.0%	0	0.0%	0	0.0%
Ph.D. foreign	4	0.9%	6	1.3%	5	1.1%
Lawyer	2	0.4%	2	0.4%	5	1.1%
Other	10	2.2%	6	1.3%	4	0.8%
Unknown	7	1.6%	1	0.2%	2	0.4%
Total	450	100.0%	465	100.0%	475	100.0%

Source: See Figure 6.1

with either "liberal arts" (*wei'za*) or "sciences" (*tei'pan*), while in other cases only *ùbàza* is written. For the purpose of this analysis these are integrated into *ùbàza*, as shown in Tables 6.7 and 6.8. Stopping after *ùbàza* marked only the partial completion of college, but it was a socially recognized high educational achievement as there were very few university graduates in Burma at that time; and it will be used in this analysis as one index of high educational attainment. The fourth category is university graduate. For this analysis this category is subdivided into liberal arts, sciences, and Bachelor of Medicine (MBBS). The documents also show Bachelor of Commerce and Bachelor of Education degrees, but

Table 6.8 Educational Background of the BSPP Central Committee

	First CC (1971)		*Second CC (1973)*		*Third CC (1977)*		*Fourth CC (1977)*		*Fifth CC (1981)*		*Sixth CC (1985)*	
Education Proportion	*Members*	*Proportion*	*Members*	*Proportion*	*Members*	*Proportion*	*Members*	*Proportion*	*Members*	*Proportion*	*Members*	
Under High-School	98	29.7%	92	27.9%	83	23.1%	64	25.6%	62	23.8%	60	21.4%
Elementary	35	10.6%	31	9.4%	23	6.4%	15	6.0%	13	5.0%	15	5.4%
Junior High	63	19.1%	61	18.5%	60	16.7%	49	19.6%	49	18.8%	45	16.1%
High School	136	41.2%	132	40.0%	144	40.0%	85	34.0%	85	32.7%	87	31.1%
Ubaza	39	11.8%	40	12.1%	57	15.8%	46	18.4%	54	20.8%	51	18.2%
Bachelor	40	12.1%	44	13.3%	57	15.8%	38	15.2%	48	18.5%	70	25.0%
Art	20	6.1%	24	7.3%	40	11.1%	23	9.2%	35	13.5%	54	19.3%
Science	13	3.9%	14	4.2%	12	3.3%	9	3.6%	9	3.5%	10	3.6%
Medical	7	2.1%	6	1.8%	3	0.8%	6	2.4%	4	1.5%	4	1.4%
Unknown	0	0.0%	0	0.0%	2	0.6%	0	0.0%		0.0%	2	0.7%
Higher than Bachelor	11	3.3%	15	4.5%	15	4.2%	11	4.4%	10	3.8%	11	3.9%
B(A)+BL	5	1.5%	7	2.1%	6	1.7%	5	2.0%	4	1.5%	5	1.8%
B(Sc)+BL	1	0.3%	1	0.3%	1	0.3%	0	0.0%	1	0.4%	1	0.4%
Gounghtu	1	0.3%	1	0.3%	2	0.6%	1	0.4%	1	0.4%	0	0.0%
MA	0	0.0%	2	0.6%	1	0.3%	1	0.4%	1	0.4%	1	0.4%
Ph.D	2	0.6%	2	0.6%	2	0.6%	2	0.8%	1	0.4%	1	0.4%
MA(Sc) Foreign	0	0.0%	0	0.0%	0	0.0%	0	0.0%	0	0.0%	0	0.0%
Ph.D Foreign	2	0.6%	2	0.6%	3	0.8%	2	0.8%	2	0.8%	2	0.7%
Lawyer	0	0.0%	0	0.0%	0	0.0%	0	0.0%	0	0.0%	1	0.4%
Others	4	1.2%	5	1.5%	4	1.1%	3	1.2%	1	0.4%	1	0.4%
Unknown	2	0.6%	2	0.6%	0	0.0%	3	1.2%	0	0.0%	0	0.0%
Total	330	100.0%	330	100.0%	360	100.0%	250	100.0%	260	100.0%	280	100.0%

Source: See Figure 6.2

here these are included under liberal arts. The fifth category is post-baccalaureate graduate and includes everyone who acquired a master's or doctoral degree whether from a domestic or foreign university. It also includes *gounhtû*, which can be obtained in one year following a bachelor's degree, and Bachelor of Law (B.L.), which can be obtained after completing a two-year program following a bachelor's degree.

Table 6.7 shows the level of education attained by PP members (excluding the Fourth PP), while Table 6.8 shows that of the CC members. The most common characteristic of both groups is the significant number who fell into the first two categories of education, indicating a relatively low level of education for the groups. For CC members and candidate members, those with only a first-category level of education remained consistently in the 20th percentile: 29.7 per cent (first CC), 27.9 per cent (second CC), 23.1 per cent (third CC), 25.6 per cent (fourth CC), 24.8 per cent (fifth CC), and 21.4 per cent (sixth CC). If members in the second category are included, a relatively higher but still not high level of education, the ratio of less educated members on each CC rose to 70.9 per cent, 67.9 per cent, 63.1 per cent, 59.6 per cent, 56.5 per cent, and 52.5 per cent, respectively. Although it declined over time, the ratio of CC members with a high school education or less never went below half. Data on the Third PP elected in 1981 shows that 53.7 per cent of the members had a first-category level of education. No data is available on the members of the Fourth PP elected in 1985, but extrapolating from the data above on the CC members, the decrease between the fifth CC elected in 1981 and the sixth in 1985 was only 4 per cent. Assuming a similar decrease between the Third and Fourth PPs, the latter would still have had very close to half of its membership with only a first- and second-category level of education.

A comparison with Indonesia will show how low the level of educational attainment was for Burma's parliamentary members. In 1971, during the early years of Suharto's New Order regime in Indonesia (1965–97), the proportion of Golkar Assembly members who had less than a high school education made up 30.1 per cent of the assembly, or 32.6 per cent when not including those who graduated from military academies, showing clearly a higher level of education than seen even a decade later in Burma's PP.[25] Moreover, higher education progressed

[25] Golkar was formed by the Indonesian government in 1971 as the government-supported political party that included economic and professional groups, leading to majority rule in the parliament.

among Indonesia's assembly members during the succeeding decade, the ratio of those with less than a high school education decreasing to 17.8 per cent by 1982, almost half of what it had been eleven years earlier. Meanwhile members who were university graduates increased to 65.4 per cent, in stark contrast with Burma where the sixth CC elected in 1985 could claim only a little over a quarter of its members were university graduates. Although no data is available for the Fourth PP, also elected in 1985, without doubt university graduates made up a small minority of its membership.

However, even though it proceeded at a snail's pace, the educational level of members showed a gradual upward trend in both the PP and CC. But there was some difference between the two. From Table 6.8 it can be seen that 70.9 per cent of the first CC members and candidate members had a high school education or less. Ten years later, in the fifth CC elected in 1981, members in this category had fallen to 56.5 per cent, a 14.4 point decrease. It fell another 4 points to 52.5 per cent in the sixth CC elected in 1985. Despite this declining trend, by the end of the Ne Win era in 1988, over half of the CC still had a high school education or less, a comparatively low level of educational attainment for such a large number of people in the leadership of a nation-state.[26]

The main reason for the large proportion of CC members with a low level of completed education was the large numbers of active and retired tatmadaw officers on the committee. A set number of committee seats were allocated to tatmadaw officers who were on the tatmadaw party committees and who sat on the CC as representatives of the tatmadaw There was no such allocation of seats to tatmadaw officers in the PP, and a large number of the assembly's more than 450 members were civilians.

An upturn can be seen overall in the level of education in both the PP and CC, though not greatly. This was mainly due to the growing number of members holding domestic bachelor's degrees. Combining these degree holders with PP members who had completed the university *ùbàza* level and with those who had some university study, the ratio of members with high educational attainment (*ùbàza* and higher) rose from 24.9 per cent to 38.5 per cent between the First and Third PPs, and it

[26] As pointed out earlier, the high ratio of CC members who had less than a high school education was affected by the number of active-service officers. For example, of the 144 such officers who were candidates for election to the first BSPP CC, 102 of them (71%) had not graduated from high school.

rose from 27.4 per cent to 36.6 per cent between the first and fifth CCs. These better-educated members were young civilian BSPP executives, and the reason behind this increase was likely the recruiting policy the BSPP began from 1962. The party started to actively recruit young people with a higher educational background to train as executives based on the idea that they would eagerly embrace the party ideology and be enthusiastic to participate in political activities.

A former local party executive named TS from Magway is one such example of a young civilian BSPP executive. He graduated from the Rangoon Arts and Sciences University in 1960 and worked in his hometown as a deputy school inspector. In 1965, an army captain who had just been posted as TS's boss assigned him to attend a basic course on political science at the Central Institute of Political Science (CIPS). TS recalled that although he was not particularly interested in politics, the socialist ideal of a society without exploitation resonated deeply with him. In 1966 he was appointed the chief secretary of a party unit in Magway township where he started recruiting party members.[27] TS said that he paid specific attention to a person's age and educational background when looking for an executive candidate. According to him, it was generally recognized that the desirable candidate was a man in his twenties who had at least graduated from the 10th grade. TS himself was born at the end of the 1930s and was under 30 years old when he became a chief secretary.[28] In this study, people like TS will be referred to as the first generation of civilian party bureaucrats; they will be examined more closely later.

"Winner-Take-All" in Practice

Having examined the characteristics of the political elite under the Ne Win regime, we can turn now to the main theme of this chapter, that of "winner-take-all." As used here the concept does not mean that the winner, namely, the tatmadaw that seized control of the state in 1962, is able to monopolize every single one of the positions in the political elite. Rather it indicates the one-sided result in the competition for the leadership posts of the state as was examined in Chapter 4, which showed

---

[27] The head of the party unit was an active-service Army captain. (Interview with a former local party leader, 20 January 2005.)

[28] Interview with a former local party leader, 1 November 2004.

that the tatmadaw as the winner took possession of nearly all of the top positions of the state through its appointments of active and retired officers. This chapter expands the focus of the examination, looking at the extent that the "former winners" survived among the political elite as a whole after 1962, in other words, the degree to which they lost all.

The first step is to identify the former winners. This will be done using two criteria based on elements in the careers of the political elite. The first is their experience in social mobilization during the Japanese occupation. For the political elite in the 1950s, participation in the national liberation movement against the British and Japanese was widespread. Therefore examining whether the people in question had taken part in that movement can be an index for measuring the distribution of "winners." However, estimation by Dorothy Guyot indicates that during the Japanese occupation, upwards to 130,000 people from political, military, and social welfare organizations became involved in the mobilization movement.[29] The sheer number of participants is too large for this experience in itself to explain the historical disconnection that came about for the political elite after 1962. Therefore the second criterion is people's political experience during the period of parliament democracy (1948–61). Compared with the first criterion, far fewer people participated in politics during this period. The analysis will examine the careers among the political elite under the Ne Win regime to see how many of them were active in war time social mobilization, then involved in party politics from the time of independence to 1961.

The number of people elected to the first CC in 1971 who had been involved in wartime social mobilization and politics before 1961 will provide an index for how many pre-coup politicians survived after 1962. By 1971, 30 years had passed since the Japanese invasion and the massive damage that the war had inflicted on colonial Burma. Young people in their twenties at the time of the invasion had turned fifty by the early 1970s. As noted, the average age of the first CC members was 47.9 years old, so many had lived their mid-teens under Japanese occupation. This also indicates that few if any had been members of the colonial legislature, and that most of them had been student activists at most during the colonial period. Out of the combined 330 candidates for the first CC and the first Central Inspection Committee, 49 of them, or

---

[29] Dorothy Guyot, "The Political Impact of Japanese Occupation of Burma," PhD dissertation, Yale University, 1966, p. 275.

about one-fifth, had participated in student movements in high school or university; of these, 44 were active tatmadaw officers, indicating that few among the civilian candidates had participated in student movements before the war.

One of the biggest political changes under Japanese occupation was the social mobilization of youth by the Japanese military, as was discussed in Chapter 2. A number of Thakin Party leaders, who had been anti-establishment "radicals" until then, arrived in Burma together with the Japanese army in 1942, at the head of the Burma Independence Army (BIA), which they used to expand their power. Following the establishment of their military occupation, the Japanese set up organizations for mass mobilization to gain popular support from the native people. This provided opportunities for Burmese youth to awaken politically and take the initiative in the nation's struggle for independent. Those people who were mobilized into the military, political parties, and mass organizations played leading roles in politics thereafter.

Data on 904 PP members from the first three assemblies, and 814 CC members from all six CCs are available. Limiting the focus only to experience during the Japanese occupation, the data of 400 PP members and 401 CC members who were age 15 or older as of 1 January 1942 will be examined here. Based on the data, Tables 6.9 and 6.10 show how many PP and CC members experienced mobilization and in what organization during the Japanese occupation. From the data, the main organizations were the BIA, Burma Defence Army (BDA), the Officers Training School (OTS) of the BDA, Patriotic Burmese Forces (PBF), East Asia Youth League (EAYL), and the Anti-Fascist People's Freedom League (AFPFL). On the whole, the following analysis supports the argument that the senior political elite in Ne Win's regime had a shared experience of being mobilized by the Japanese army.

More than half of the members in both the PP and CC were mobilized by the Japanese military with the ratio of such members being about 13 percentage points higher for the CC. This mobilization was carried out in three ways: as a military officer (training in the OTS is included in this category), as a regular soldier, or as a member of a mass organization (EAYL and AFPFL). The tables clearly show that the greatest number of members in both the PP and CC were mobilized as military officers. Also many of the PP and CC members participated in the anti-Japan struggle either as officers or as soldiers: 38.5 per cent of PP members (officers: 18 per cent, soldiers: 20.5 per cent) and 51.6 per cent

Table 6.9 Experience of PP Members during the Japanese Occupation (who were 15 years old or older as of 1 January 1942)

	First PP	*Second PP*	*Third PP*	*Total*	
Officers	57	10	5	72	18.0%
BIA→OTS	28	4	1	33	8.3%
BDA+OTS	24	5	2	31	7.8%
EAYL→OTS	5	1	2	8	2.0%
Soldiers	58	17	7	82	20.5%
BIA→	33	7	4	44	11.0%
BDA→	21	4	3	28	7.0%
EAYL→BDA	1	3	0	4	1.0%
PBF→	1	2	0	3	0.8%
EAYL→PBF	2	1	0	3	0.8%
Mass Organizations	48	16	7	71	17.8%
EAYL	35	13	7	55	13.8%
BIA→EAYL	7	3	0	10	2.5%
AFPFL	6	0	0	6	1.5%
Other	95	44	31	170	36.0%
Unknown	5	0	0	5	1.3%
Total	263	87	50	400	100.0%

Source: See Figure 6.1

of CC members (officers: 16.7 per cent, soldiers: 34.9 per cent).[30] The majority of these people remained in military after the Pacific War.[31] People who were mobilized as part of a mass organization such as the EAYL and AFPFL accounted for 17.8 per cent of PP members and 18.7 per cent of CC members, nearly half of whom had joined the tatmadaw after the war.[32]

The next step is to explore the careers of these PP and CC members during the democracy period to find out how many "winners" of that

[30] There were also former soldiers of the colonial army who were members of the PP; four of them were in the First PP, two in the Second PP, and five in the Third PP. Three of them belonged to the tatmadaw after the war, however, all three had retired by 1960.

[31] Among the 112 candidates for the first CC who belonged to the BIA, BDA, or PBF, only 17 of them did not become military men.

[32] Of the 35 candidates for the first CC who were mobilized as part of a mass organization, 17 were officers when they were elected.

Table 6.10 Experience of CC, CC Candidate Members and Candidates during the Japanese Occupation (who were 15 years old or older as of 1 January 1942)

	1st CC (1971–73)	*2nd CC (1973–77)*	*3rd CC (1977)*	*4th CC (1977–81)*	*5th CC (1981–85)*	*6th CC (1985–88)*	*Total*	
Ex-Military Officer	48	5	8	0	6	0	67	16.7%
BIA→OTS	17	2	2	0	2	0	23	5.7%
BDA+OTS	28	2	4	0	3	0	37	9.2%
EAYL→OTS	3	1	2	0	1	0	7	1.7%
Ex-Military Soldier	75	26	21	13	3	2	140	34.9%
BIA→	41	11	9	2	2	1	66	16.4%
BDA→	30	14	12	8	1	0	65	16.2%
EAYL→BDA	2	0	0	2	0	1	5	1.2%
PBF→	1	1	0	0	0	0	2	0.5%
EAYL→PBF	1	0	0	1	0	0	2	0.5%
Mass Mobilization	34	13	16	6	2	1	72	18.0%
EAYL	25	12	14	6	2	1	60	14.9%
BIA→EAYL	5	0	2	0	0	0	7	1.7%
AFPFL	4	1	0	0	0	0	5	1.2%
Others	62	19	18	9	5	5	118	29.4%
Total	219	63	63	28	16	8	397	99.0%

Note: This table excludes the CC members, candidate members and candidates who were under 15 years old on 1 Jan. 1942.

Source: See Figure 6.2

Table 6.11 Profiles of Newly Elected Civilian Parliament Members (1948–62)

Occupation	*1st PP (1974)*	*2nd PP (1978)*	*3rd PP (1981)*	*Total*	
Student	51	52	29	132	24.7%
Teacher	55	48	38	141	26.4%
Public Officer	65	49	32	146	27.3%
Political Party	15	3	4	22	4.1%
Insurgent	4	1	2	7	1.3%
Business, Lawyer, Doctor, Company Employee	10	5	4	19	3.6%
Peasant	18	7	2	27	5.0%
Insufficient Information	5	5	3	13	2.4%
Other	13	7	2	22	4.1%
Unknown	6	0	0	6	1.1%
Total	242	177	116	535	100.0%

Source: See Figure 6.1

period, i.e., the "former winners" (ruling party politicians), were included in the Ne Win regime. The tatmadaw officers have been excluded from the data because they were never politicians during the democratic period.

Tables 6.11 and 6.12 show the democracy-period careers of the civilian CC members and PP members, candidate members plus candidate, respectively. Three points are of particular interest. First, in both the CC and the PP, people who had been teachers, public officials, and students composed approximate three-quarters of the total, the ratio of each being about 25 per cent. As most teachers in public schools and universities were public officials at that time, this means that more than half of the civilian political elite was comprised of former public officials. Only a few had been senior bureaucrats; the majority had been junior officials in the central government or local governments. Only the first CC was an exception where former political party members exceed students and public officials, whereas nearly 75 per cent of the First PP members were teachers, public officials, and students. It is probable that teachers and public officials were selected as candidates for the PP because they had social prestige especially in local areas and because they had to obey if their superiors assigned them to be candidates. A former PP member told this author that when she was working in a public high school, the principal unexpectedly assigned her to run as a candidate in a PP election.

Table 6.12 Profiles of Newly Elected Civilian CC Member (1948–62)

Occupation	*1st CC (1971)*	*2nd CC (1973)*	*3rd CC (1977.2)*	*4th CC (1977.11)*	*5th CC (1981)*	*6th CC (1985)*	*Total*	
Teacher	30	13	30	2	4	12	91	26.2%
Public Officer	19	13	30	1	7	13	83	23.9%
Student	13	8	29	1	9	26	86	24.8%
Political Party	22	3	2	0	0	0	27	7.8%
Insurgent	9	2	1	0	0	0	12	3.5%
Business, Lawyer, Doctor, Company Employee	5	3	4	0	1	1	14	4.0%
Peasant	1	1	0	0	0	0	2	0.6%
Other	11	1	5	0	0	1	18	5.2%
Insufficient Information	5	1	4	3	0	0	13	3.7%
Unknown	0	0	0	1	0	0	1	0.3%
Total	115	45	105	8	21	53	347	100.0%

Source: See Figure 6.2

The second point, the greatest number of former political party members was concentrated in the First CC and the First PP. After that their numbers were very few. Looking at the composition of these former political party members who were on the first CC, out of a total of 106 civilian CC candidates, only seven were former members of the AFPFL, the previous ruling party. But although all seven had worked as local AFPFL leaders; none had ever been Union Parliament members. Fourteen other people were former members of the opposition coalition, the National United Front (NUF). They were slightly more in number and had held higher positions. Some examples were people like Ba Nyein, a civilian bureaucrat in the Ministry of National Planning and a Union Parliament member from the Burma Workers Party (BWP) where he had been a politburo member from 1950 to 1962; Nyo Hmaing, a member of the Central Executive Committee of the NUF; and Phoung Aung, a politburo member of the People's Volunteer Organization Party. Regarding the First PP, although there were more former ruling party (AFPFL) members than former opposition party members, many of those with experience in the ruling party had been local level executives, such as chief secretaries of party units. PP members who had been former Union Parliament members included one AFPFL and three NUF politicians.[33]

In sum, people in the Ne Win regime who had experienced party politics in the democratic period were extremely few. They comprised only 7.8 per cent of the total civilian candidates of the First CC and only 4.1 per cent of the total civilian members of the First PP, extremely low percentages. And their numbers declined further in subsequent CC and PP elections. Without doubt there was a considerable disconnect between the civilian political elite of the Ne Win regime and the previous political elite of the democratic period.

The third point is the other kinds of people became CC and PP members. Both groups included people who had rebelled against the government. For instance, the early CCs included some former Burma Communist Party (BCP) members, and the PP had former members of the Karen National Union (KNU) and Karen National Defence Organization (KNDO). Ne Win appointed some BCP members to cooperate

[33] Only one person who had been a representative to the Chamber of Nationalities was elected the PP. This was Sumlut Gaung Gam who had represented Kachin State. People with experience in party politics individually left their parties to apply to join the BSPP.

in building BSPP party organization. There were even some CC members who had just been released from jail after nearly ten years imprisonment. Tables 6.9 and 6.10 also show a small number of professionals (lawyers and doctors) and businessmen who represented the interests of the middle-class.

To return to the main question of this section: the extent that "former winners" survived among the political elite in the Ne Win regime, using the criterion of mobilization during the Japanese occupation, over half of the senior political elite in the 1970s were "former winners." However, most of these people were military officers and therefore outside of the other criterion of having been involved in party politics between 1948 and 1961. By this criterion the number of surviving "former winners" was small, and amongst the biggest "former winners," the politicians of the AFPFL, the former ruling party, the survivors were very few indeed. Almost none of the pre-1962 political elite survived among the winners who made up the new elite of the Ne Win regime, making the disconnect almost complete.

After 1962, two kinds of people appeared in the political elite. One was a new generation of military officers who had joined the tatmadaw after independence. Chapter 7 will discuss this group. The other was the first generation of civilian BSPP party executives mentioned in the previous section. These new officers, the first-generation civilian party executives, were products of Ne Win's revolution, and will be analyzed in the following section.

Civilian Party Executives

The first generation of civilian party executives were described as young people with at least a high school education who were recruited from local areas to receive training at the CIPS, and then returned to the local areas to start careers as party executives. Before proceeding, we will first confirm this description. Were they really young high-school graduates?

Table 6.13 shows the average age at the time of party entry of local party executives who were sent as representatives to the Third Party Congress from five regional party committees,[34] and the percentage of those representatives who were under 30 years old at the time of entering the

[34] There are total of 14 BSPP regional committees in the country. Only 5 have been used here because of the lack or insufficiency of data on the profiles of the local representatives from the other 9 committees.

Table 6.13 Average Age of Local Party Executives at the Time of Party Entry

Regional Party Committee	*Average Age*	*Proportion under 30 Yrs Old*
Rangoon Division	32.5	37.8% (54/134)
Irrawaddy Division	31.5	41.1% (46/112)
Mandalay Division	30.0	53.7% (73/136)
Sagain Division	28.7	66.3% (53/80)
Chin State	27.1	72.0% (18/24)

Source: by the author based on carrier summaries of party executives who attended the 3rd Party Conference as representatives of Rangoon Division, Irrawaddy Division, Mandalay Division, Sagain Division, Chin State

party. The average age at entry ranged from 32.5 years old for a Rangoon Division Party Committee representative to 27.1 years old for a Chin State Party Committee representative. It can be seen from the table that the more distant the location was from Rangoon, the younger the representatives were. Thus, 72 per cent of the representatives from Chin State, the most distant of five regions, and 66.3 per cent from Sagaing Division, the second most distant region, were under 30 years old when they entered the party.

One likely reason for younger representatives from more distant regions was the reduced availability of human resources. More distant regions had fewer qualified people to recruit. The party targeted mainly men and women (mostly men) in their 20s as candidates for executive positions in the party. The figures indicate that the party was by and large successful. Another reason for the difference could have been because a representative to a party congress did not necessarily have to be selected from his own native division/state. The party conference representatives for Rangoon and Irrawaddy divisions included some top state officials such as the general manager of the Land Transportation State Enterprise, the general manager of the Public Electric Power Corporation, the director general of the People's Police, and the principal of the Central School for Public Administration along with the party unit leaders.

Table 6.14 shows the educational background of representatives from the five regions to the Third Party Congress. It divides the local representatives into the two categories of "44 years old or younger" and "45 years old or older."[35] Although the comparison of the two groups cannot be free from bias because of the difference in sample numbers,

[35] The categorization is based on whether an executive had reached 31 years old by 1 January 1962, the year the military took over the state by coup.

Table 6.14 Third Party Congress Representatives Having a Bachelor's Degree

	Chin State Party Committee		*Irrawaddy Division Party Committee*		*Mandalay Division Party Committee*		*Sagaing Division Party Committee*		*Yangon Division Party Committee*	
44 years old or younger	6	31.6%	20	32.8%	37	40.2%	29	50.0%	24	40.7%
45 years old or older	2	31.3%	5	9.8%	7	15.9%	3	22.7%	38	45.2%

Source: See Table 6.13

there is a good possibility that younger party executives had a relatively higher level of education than older executives. For example, 10 per cent more of the local party committee executives for Mandalay and Sagaing had studied in or graduated from university compared to the members of the PP in the same period. The exception was the Regional Party Committee of Rangoon, which had the concentrated human resources of the capital and high-ranking party members. Only this committee showed a higher percentage of university graduates among the senior executive (45.2 per cent) than among younger ones.

These young party executives had applied to join the BSPP shortly after graduating from high school, completing *ùbàza*, or graduating from university; otherwise, after having been employed as a teacher or public official, they applied to join the party then attended the party's leadership training school either on their own initiative or on recommendation by workplace superiors. After completing their leadership training, in most cases they took up positions as local party unit leaders becoming members of executive committees and chief secretaries at the township level. From there they aimed for further promotion to the party CC. In the late 1970s, these first-generation civilian party executives were in their 40s and had gradually risen into the higher levels of the party. It can be concluded, therefore, that after 1962 the BSPP succeeded to a certain extent in recruiting the new young elite in Burmese society whose educational qualifications were rising. At the party congress in 1985, of 245 people whose careers can be identified among the local party unit executives elected as representatives to the congress,[36] only 19 represen-

[36] The positions of the local party unit executive included party unit chiefs, secretaries, chief clerks and the Party Organizing Committee chairman. The chief clerks holding the position of People's Council Chairman of a division or state were excluded.

tatives were active and retired military officers (active: 9, retired: 10). Most of the rest were civilian party executives.[37] The average length of their careers in the party was 21 years 2 months (maximum: 22 years 6 months, minimum: 12 years 10 months). Age-wise, 156 people were still in their 40s, followed by 60 people in their 50s. In education, as well, among the executives in their 40s, 75 people out of 156 had education above the secondary level, and 56 had bachelor's degrees or above. Only 13 people had not graduated from high school. Considering the contemporary conditions in rural Burma, these figures are fairly high. They imply that the BSPP had become able to train party executives on its own.[38] The captains and majors of the tatmadaw who had been the leaders of the local party units in the 1960s were now being replaced mostly by civilian party leaders, 23 years after the establishment of the BSPP.

These civilian party executives gradually rose up the party hierarchy. Figures 6.4 through 6.6 show how their rise occurred after 1971. First, the ratios of civilians, active military officers and retired military officer are shown for the newly appointed members and candidate members of the second-sixth CCs. Then the ratios are shown for the same three groups of members dividing them into those born in 1927 or before and those born in 1928 or later.

Figure 6.4 suggests that a relatively large number of civilians were included in the CC until the political crisis of 1977, but the percentages of civilian party executives and active officers reversed in the fourth CC elected in November 1977. The number of civilians increased again in the fifth and sixth CCs in the 1980s. Analyzing the composition by generation, Figure 6.5 describing the older generation shows that civilians remained below 20 per cent except for the second CC while active and retired officers accounted for 80 to 90 per cent of the total. In Figure 6.6 showing the younger generation, the ratio of civilians dropped in 1977 because of the political crisis but recovered to over 50 per cent again in the sixth CC. The retired-officer party executives categorized as the Higher Party Path group in Chapter 4 steadily decreased as civilians

[37] The data here and hereafter related to local civilian party executives were calculated from the following source. Burma, anonymous, *pinsàmà acein patinyilahkan bahoukomiti winlâunmyâ î kôuyêi hma'tân acînjou'*. [Profiles of the Fifth Party Congress Central Committee member candidates] (1985).

[38] As was noted in Chapter 4, with the decrease in the seconding of officers from the tatmadaw to the BSPP, middle-level officers flowed into the People's Councils.

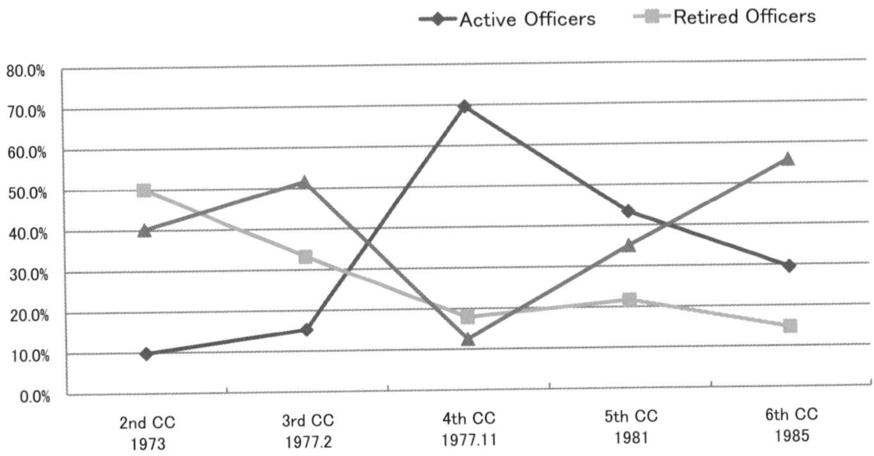

Source: See Figure 6.2

Figure 6.4 Percentage of Active Military Officers, Retired Military Officers and Civilians among Newly Elected CC Members

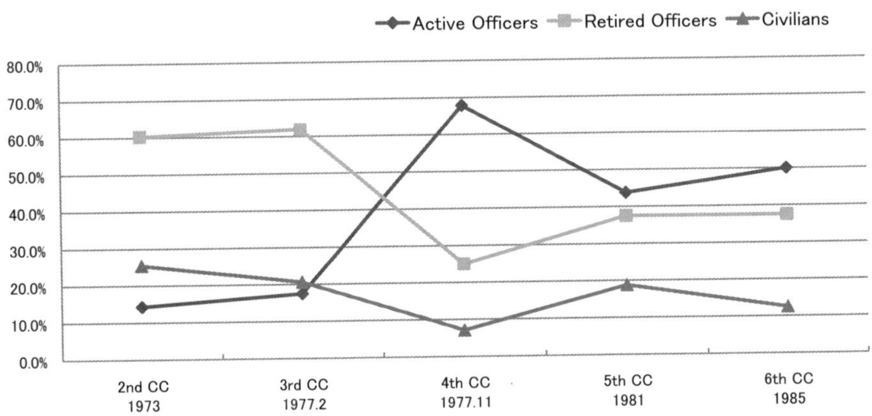

Note: "Older generation" refers the CC members who were 35 years old or older on 1 Jan 1962.
Source: See Figure 6.2

Figure 6.5 Percentage of Active Military Officer, Retired Military Officer and Civilians among the Older Generation of Newly Elected CC Members

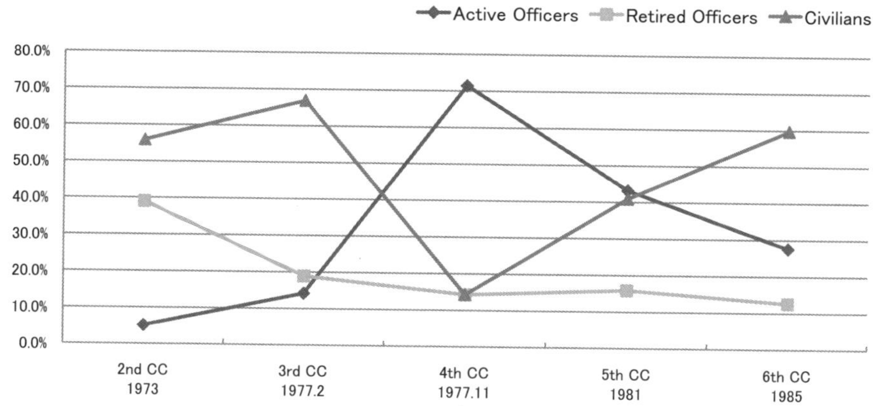

Note: "Younger generation" refers the CC members who were 34 years old or younger on 1 Jan 1962.
Source: See Figure 6.2

Figure 6.6 Percentage of Active Military Officers, Retired Military Officers and Civilians among the Younger Generation of Newly Elected CC Members

gradually replaced them. The proportion of active officers also decreased following the rise in their ratio in 1977 and the political crisis when a great many of them were sent to the CC to restore order in the party.

These figures alone do not demonstrate that the growing civilians in the CC really were the first generation of party executives referred to in this section. It is necessary to find out how many civilians recruited by the party as candidates for party executives and promoted within the party were actually among the CC members. It is also important to know what paths their careers took, and what the highest positions were that these civilian party leaders could hold.

First, regarding the number of civilian party executives who were CC members, of 75 civilians elected to the fifth CC in 1981, only eight people had no experience as a party unit leader.[39] Among them, only

[39] The positions of the eight people were Director General of the Prime Minister's Office, Deputy Minister of Finance and National Planning, Deputy Minister of Agriculture and Forestry, Secretary of the CC Affairs Committee, member of the State Council, professor at Rangoon University of Economics, and director of the Research Department of the Party Headquarters.

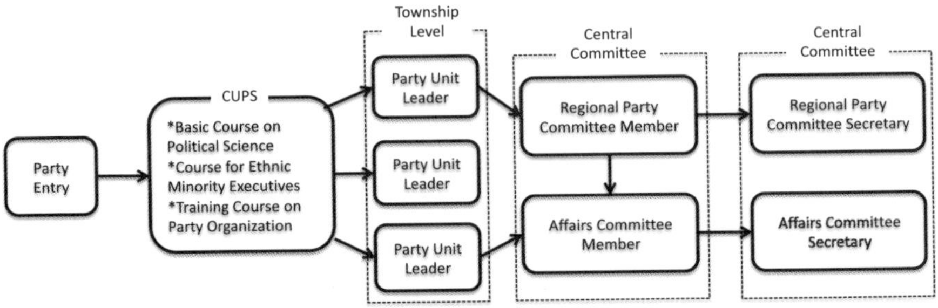

Figure 6.7 Career Paths of Civilian Party Executives

Dr. Chit, Secretary of the Affairs Committee for Cooperatives, Agriculture, Livestock and Forestry, who had taken a course at the CIPS; the rest were bureaucrats, college professors, or editors. All but one were born in the 1920s.

The other 67 people started their careers in a party unit at the township level. Although some original sources lack the relevant information, all of these people probably took the basic course on political science at the CIPS and had classes about party organizing activities. Some people spent many years at a particular party unit up to the time they became unit chairman, but more than a few moved several times to other party units. However, transfers across the borders between divisions and states were infrequent, with only six people having done so.[40] Spending one's career within the same division or state seems to have been common.[41]

Figure 6.7 shows the most common paths of promotion and the highest positions for civilian party executives. From this figure we can ascertain the highest posts attained in the careers of the civilian members

[40] This information on the members the fifth CC is based on Burma, anonymous, *pinsàmà acein patinyilahkan bahoukomiti winlâunmyâ î kôuyêi hma'tân acînjou'.* [Profiles of the Fifth Party Convention Central Committee member candidates] (1985).

[41] Many of these party unit executives had worked in less developed areas. Nine of the 67 people had worked as party unit chiefs in Shan State, eight in Magway Division, eight in Sagaing State, seven in Karen State, and five in Rangoon Division. Local party executives in less developed regions were more likely to get promoted to the central party organization.

on the sixth CC who were elected at the Fifth Party Congress in 1985. There were a total of 280 sixth CC members, which included 110 civilians. Among the civilians, only ten people had no experience as a party unit executive; instead they had come into the party from high positions in other government organizations. The remaining 100 were so-called genuine party bureaucrats. As already discussed, they had joined the party when young, and they had a relatively higher level of education.

Table 6.15 shows the posts of the civilian members on the sixth CC. The highest position was the Secretary of the Finance and National Planning Committee. The person holding that position in the Sixth CC was Han Shwe, a Bahman born in 1941, who had grown up in Pegu and obtained a bachelor's degree in liberal arts from Rangoon Arts and Sciences University in 1962. Immediately afterwards he had joined the BSPP and attended the CIPS. He was in the third class to take the basic course on political science so was among the party executives trained in the earliest stages of party building. His promotion was faster than others. This was because he skipped over being a regional party committee member, which party executives usually had to go through, to take a position as a member of the Finance and National Planning Committee at the Third Party Congress in 1977.[42] Below the Secretary of the Finance and National Planning Committee were the other affairs committees (as shown in the table) which civilian party executives could chair or be members of. How many of these affairs committees were chaired by civilian party executives? How many by tatmadaw officers? Had the former been increasing and the latter decreasing since previous CCs? These would help show if the BSPP was becoming a ruling party run by civilian bureaucrats as Ne Win seems to have intended.

What factors affected promotion? Though an interesting question, the answer is extremely unclear due to a lack of information. In interviews with party executives, some said promotion was affected by the results of one's organizing activities in the party unit; some said it was one's knowledge about policies; some said it was connections with people at the top, and some said it was just luck.

The highest position a civilian party executive could hope to rise to was the secretary of a CC affairs committee. Many of the civilians who

[42] Another high-ranking civilian party executive was Taik Soe, who was Deputy Minister of Information. His position in the party was as a part-time member of the Irrawaddy Division Regional Party Committee to the CC.

Table 6.15 Positions of Civilian Party Executives in the 5th CC

	Committee	*Position*	*Number*
	Finance & National Planning	Secretary	1
		Member	3
	International Relations & Foreign Affairs	Member	6
	Co-operative, Agricultural, Livestock Breeding and Forest	Member	5
Affairs Committee	Education, Health and Social Service	Member	3
	Mass & Class Organization	Member	4
	Political Education and Cultural	Member	2
	Commerce, Construction and Communication	Member	2
	Legan & Public Management	Member	1
Inspection Committee	Party Inspection Committee	Member	1
Discipline Committee	Party Inspection Committee	Member	4
	Yangon Divison	Member	4
	Rakhine State	Secretary	1
		Member	4
	Mon State	Secretary	1
		Member	3
	Mandalay Division	Secretary	1
		Member	7
	Magway Division	Secretary	1
		Member	6
	Pegu Division	Member	5
	Chin State	Secretary	1
		Member	2
Regional Party Committee	Tanintharhy Divison	Secretary	1
		Member	1
	Shan State	Member	10
	Sagaing Division	Secretary	1
		Member	2
	Karen State	Secretary	1
		Member	5
	Kayah State	Member	3
	Kachin State	Member	3
	Irrawaddy Division	Member	4
		Member (Part Time)	1

Source: by the author based on *bahoukomiti winlaunmya i kouyei hma'tan acinjou'* (1981)

took posts above this position had little or no experience working in the party, meaning there was almost no correlation between their careers as party executives and their high positions in the state. The limits of promotion for civilian party executives, the so-called genuine party bureaucrats, were not high if the BSPP really guided the state as stipulated in the 1974 Constitution. However, considering that Han Shwe was still his 40s in the 1980s, there might have been a possibility for his further promotion. Although active and retired military officers occupied the top party ranks, civilian party executives were increasing in the middle to lower levels of the party. So, if the sixth Party Congress had been held in 1989, a further breakthrough of civilian party executives might have taken place.

Conclusion

One of the aims of this chapter was to clarify the uniqueness of Ne Win's revolution in comparison with revolutions in communist countries. Although it is difficult to generalize the characteristics of communist countries due to the diversity of their revolutions and subsequent regimes, according to the classic study on political elites by Robert Putnam, activists and ideologues are replaced during post-revolution periods by managers of the bureaucratic machinery and subsequently by party bureaucrats with economic expertise. Thus over time as industrialization progresses practical capabilities gradually become more potent for promotion in the party.[43]

In Burma's case, Ne Win's revolution was a "revolution from above." It was not accompanied by any large-scale popular mobilization; only a few political activists and ideologues took part in the revolutionary phase.[44] As has been shown in this chapter, the power structure created after the revolution was one where the percentage of tatmadaw officers grew as one drew closer to the centre of power.

Ne Win's revolution was conducted by former young nationalists who had fought against the Japanese empire as soldiers and then against

---

[43] Robert R. Putnam, *The Comparative Study of Political Elites* (Englewood Cliffs, N.J.: Prentice-Hall, 1976), pp. 190–211.

[44] Refer to the following on "revolution from above:" Trimberger, Ellen Kay. *Revolution from Above: Military Bureaucrats and Development in Japan, Turkey, Egypt, and Peru* (N.J.: Transaction Books, 1978).

domestic insurgents as leaders of Burma's own national military. Surprisingly few civilians played important roles in the revolution. However, it has also been shown that people who could be called "party bureaucrats" gradually increased in Burma in the 1980s. There is no doubt that a career as a civilian party executive became increasingly more important in the operations of the BSPP.

But while the number of civilian party executives was growing in the party, the counter-insurgency generation of officers who had joined the tatmadaw after independence was becoming more influential in the tatmadaw. I would like to argue that this increase in civilian party executives and counter-insurgency generation officers in the power structure represented a gap between the 1974 Constitution and the real power structure. Moreover, this gap manifested the two aspects of Ne Win as an idealist and a realist. It was Ne Win as the radical idealist that created the BSPP and the civilian party executives, but Ne Win as the self-protecting realist that created the counter-insurgency generation officers as the main component of the political elite. The conflict between the ideal and self-protection within Ne Win arguably led to the conflict between the civilian party executives and the counter-insurgency generation officers. In the end Ne Win turned into a mediocre dictator clinging to his own self-protection, and because of this, the civilian party executives were consistently at a disadvantage with ultimate authority always in the hands of the tatmadaw.

Shortly after Ne Win's resignation as president of the BSPP in 1988 in the wake of a huge political crisis, a coup d'état took place that suspended all political activity, and the civilian party executives were removed from the centre of power. Thereafter although the BSPP was reorganized into the National Union Party (NUP) (*tâinyindâ sîlôun nyinyu'yêi pati*) for the 1990 multiparty elections, the party suffered a humiliating defeat, obtaining only ten of the 492 seats in an election won overwhelmingly by the National League for Democracy (NLD) under the leadership of Aung San Suu Kyi. During the ensuing years of military suppression, democracy stagnated in Burma, and the NUP, although continuing to exist, grew ineffectual as an organization. Its headquarters, still located slightly to the north of downtown Rangoon near the crossing of University Street and Gabaei Pagoda Street, is like a museum showcasing people who serve as a reminder of the "glory" of Ne Win's rule. These people are first-generation civilian party executives who still sit in the headquarters and hold positions in the party.

Twenty years after its defeat, the NUP put up 995 candidates for seats in the new national assembly and local assemblies in the 7 November 2010 elections. This was the second largest number after the 1,112 candidates of the Union Solidarity and Development Party (USDP) backed by the tatmadaw, and only these two parties were able to put up candidates nationwide. The results of the election, however, were another humiliating defeat for the NUP. The party obtained only 17 seats (3.4 per cent) in the national assembly and 46 seats (5.5 per cent) in local assemblies. Many of its candidates were civilian party executives, the same people, who had gained their training and political experience under the BSPP, and many of whom in 2010 were likely in their 50s or older. These help explain why the NUP suffered such a big defeat in the election. It was not just that the party and its political activities had stagnated since 1990. It was because the party, its leaders, and its candidates are of another age; they are people who were trained and have worked in the party since the days of Burmese way to socialism. In a real sense, the NUP is an incarnation of the BSPP and has not been able to connect with the Burma of today. Its capabilities as a political party have proven far inferior to those of the USDP and the nationally popular NLD. The failure of the NUP has proven the failure of the BSPP again. The enormous amounts of time and national treasure that Ne Win spent for 26 years on his political ideal has all gone for naught.

CHAPTER 7

Formation of a Garrison State: The Politics of Dictator–Military Relations

In Chapter 4, the Ne Win regime was referred to as a party-state manqué because although the revolutionary party of a party-state is usually a political group that guides a revolution, its counterpart in Burma, the Burma Socialist Programme Party (BSPP), was much less dominant and always under the influence of the tatmadaw. In effect, the political regime in Burma between 1974 and 1988 was an indirect military regime. This gave it the character of a "garrison state," a concept introduced by Harold Lasswell.[1] Inspired by the example of Manchuria established by the Japanese in March 1932, he explored the possibility that many future states would be led by "specialists on violence," i.e., soldiers, rather than "specialists on bargaining," i.e., businessman. "The function of management" in a garrison state is, he wrote, "the exercise of skill in supervising technical operations, in administrative organization, in personnel management, in public relations,"[2] skills which he saw as inherent in a military organization and applicable to the running of a government.

The accuracy of Lasswell's prediction is not of concern here. What is important is the positive relationship he identified between a military's personnel and organizational character and the management skills necessary for running the state. By and large, studies on civil-military relations fail to see this point and focus on the military's intervention for regime change. There is a great difference in required capability between seizing

[1] Harold Lasswell, "Sino-Japanese Crisis: The Garrison State versus the Civilian State," *China Quarterly* 11 (1937).

[2] Harold Lasswell, "The Garrison State," *American Journal of Sociology* 46, no. 4 (1941): 458.

power through a violent incident like a coup d'état and maintaining a grip on power through routine administrative work. Violence is necessary but not sufficient for the durability of a military regime; it is rather the military's strict organizational management that gives a government by the military the potential ability to carry out the decision-making process quickly and implement its decisions efficiently. However, this rarely happens because the expansion of the military's political role in authoritarian regimes often disrupts its own strict organizational management. Facing the risk of internal disputes caused by the conflict between its military and political role, the military has to choose one of two outcomes: factional political splits within the military which weaken the organizational management and the capability of the military, or a withdrawal from politics and government engagement in order to maintain cohesion.[3] Either way, a "garrison-state" cannot be realized.

Nevertheless, in Burma the tatmadaw has succeeded in keeping its cohesion despite intervening and running the government for five decades. How has this been possible? How did Ne Win control the tatmadaw successfully? What incentive structure prevented tatmadaw officers from dismissing the ruler and accelerating democratization as in the Philippines in 1986 and Indonesia in 1998? Previous works have paid less attention to these questions because they tend to take the strong consolidation of the Ne Win regime and the tatmadaw for granted.

This chapter explores the reform of the tatmadaw under Ne Win's rule and its political significance,[4] focusing on the way Ne Win took control of the tatmadaw and the limits of his control. The discussion will examine the period after Ne Win ceded his position as Chief of General

---

[3] Regarding politicization of the military, see the following studies; Alfred W. McCoy, *Closer than Brothers: Manhood at the Philippine Military Academy* (New Haven, Conn: Yale University Press, 1999), Chapter 7; Yasuhiro Takeda, *Minshuka no Hikaku Seijigaku — Higashi Ajia Shokoku no Taisei Hendo Katei* [The processes of regime transformation in East Asian countries] (Kyoto: Mineruva Shobo), pp. 165–8.

[4] There are few studies on Burmese civil-military relations after 1962. The following have examined aspects of these relations. John A. Wiant, "The Vanguard Army: The Tatmadaw and Politics in Revolutionary Burma," in *The Armed Forces in Contemporary Asian Societies*, ed. Edward A. Olson and Stephen Jurika Jr. (London and Boulder, Colo: Westview Press, 1986); John A. Wiant and David I. Steinberg, "Burmese military and National Development," in *Soldiers and Stability in Southeast Asia*, ed. Soedjati Djiwandono and Yong Mun Cheong (Singapore: Institute of Southeast Asian Studies, 1988); Andrew Selth, *Burma's Armed Forces: Power Without Glory* (Norwalk, CT: East Bridge, 2002).

Staff to his aide General San Yu in 1972. After that year, the tatmadaw was no longer under Ne Win's direct command, so he had to find a way to control it from outside. As argued in the theoretical approach of the "pact school" of democratization studies, democratization requires not only movements from the civil society but also political conflict and division between hardliners and moderates among ruling elites. As long as elites are able to sustain the consolidation among them, it is unlikely that social movements to democratize the government will bear fruit because of the severe crackdowns they incur as Burma witnessed in 1988 and 2007.[5] Therefore, the following questions need to be addressed to solve the riddle of Burma's non-democratic politics: How did Ne Win control the tatmadaw after 1972? To what extent did he succeed? What were the limits he was subject to?[6]

This chapter will first examine the benefit that the 1962 coup brought to the tatmadaw as an organization and show that Ne Win did not necessarily give the tatmadaw particularly preferential treatment as an organization. Nevertheless, Ne Win did not fail to gain the tatmadaw's support. Why was this? The chapter seeks to answer this question by analyzing two aspects of the military. One is BSPP-tatmadaw relations; the other is the informal institutionalization of rules managing military personnel. This leads to the conclusion that Ne Win's power base depended on the party's formal control over the tatmadaw and the development of informal control over military personnel by regularly reassigning tatmadaw officers to new posts and retiring them to positions in the civilian government sectors.

Coup d'état and the Military

Although a military coup is the takeover of a government by military officers, it does not necessarily lead to the favourable results for the entire military, even when the military leaders become the rulers of the state. Moreover, the quality and quantity of the coup's impact will differ for different parts of the military organization. The purpose of this section

---

[5] Gordon Tullock, *Autocracy* (Boston: Kuuwer Academic Pub, 1987), p. 20.

[6] It has been pointed out also in recent studies of political economy that it is not at all easy for a dictator to maintain power. See the distinguished review by Stephen Harber, "Authoritarian Government," in *The Oxford Handbook of Political Science*, ed. Barry R. Weingast and Donald A. Wittman (Oxford: Oxford University Press, 2006).

is to discuss the impact of the 2 March 1962 coup on the organization and activities, as well as on the corporate interests of the tatmadaw.

At the time of the coup, the three armed services of the tatmadaw totalled approximately 100 thousand officers and men. Official documentation recording the size of the tatmadaw in 1965 provided the following figures: 140,814 total personnel — 126,183 in the Army; 7,155 in the Navy; and 7,476 in the Air Force.[7] Because the Army was the paramount military branch accounting for 89.6 per cent of the tatmadaw's manpower, the Ministry of Defence (MOD) was effectively under the influence of the Army. The strategic focus of the tatmadaw also centered on the counter-insurgency operations of the Army.

The Army underwent a large-scale restructuring in 1961, one year before the coup, and changed the command structure from two regional commands and thirteen brigades to five regional commands (Southeastern, Southwestern, Central, Northwestern, and Eastern); the brigades were dissolved and reorganized. In 1972, further restructuring added four more regional commands: Rangoon, Northern, Northeastern and Western, and seven light infantry divisions were set up under the command of the General Staff Office (Army).[8] The number of infantry and light infantry battalions, the basic units of army operations, increased to 52 in 1962, 105 in 1972, 146 in 1982, and 168 in 1988. The number of Army personnel also increased to 122,228 (1964), 138,480 (1974), 163,700 (1981), 173,655 (1984) and 184,029 (1988), an increase of about 60,000 troops in 26 years.

To what extent were these incremental expansions of the Army related to the military's takeover of state power? It is generally accepted that under a military regime, the military receives preferential budgetary allocations to develop its organization and equipment. However, a look at the trend of the defence budget during the period does not support this view. Figure 7.1 presents the budgets of the government and the MOD, and shows that even though Ne Win took power in 1962, the

[7] "1966 khùhni' ta'màdaw nilahkan kagweyêhtanà ta'màdaw si'ûsîhsainya tinpyàche'myâ (khà) [1966 Tatmadaw Conference, the agenda of the Ministry of Defense Military Operations (b)]," CD-882(9), DSHMRI, p. 12.

[8] These were one division in 1966 (the 77th Light Infantry Division), two divisions in 1967 (the 88th and the 99th Light Infantry Divisions), one division in 1979 (the 44th Light Infantry Division), one division in 1980 (the 55th Light Infantry Division), and one division in 1984 (the 33rd Light Infantry Division).

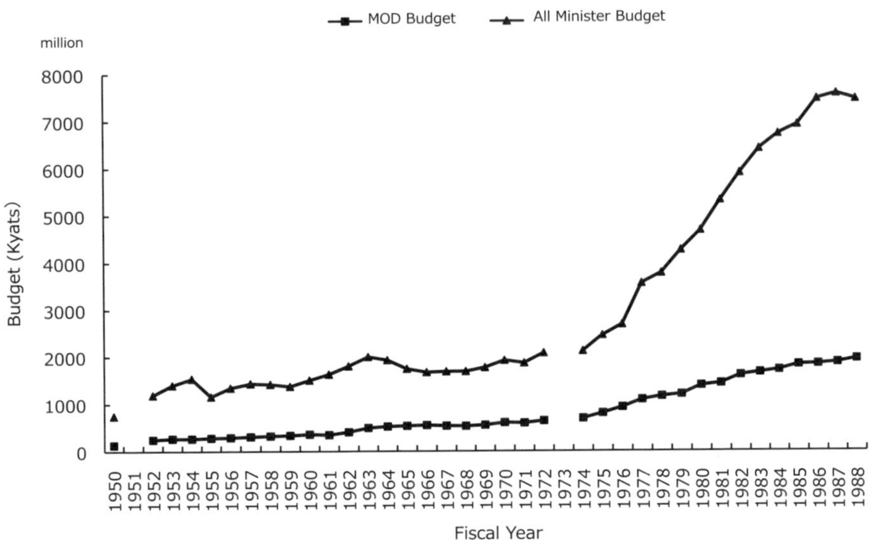

※The starting month of the fiscal year changed in 1974.

Source: *Myanmà naingan pyandân* (Myanmar Government Gazette).

Figure 7.1 Ministry of Defence Budget and Total Government Budget

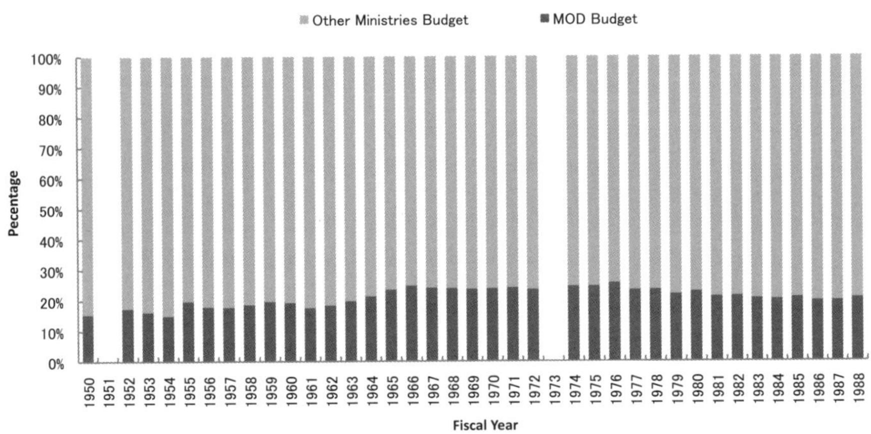

Source: *Myanmà naingan pyandân* (Myanmar Military Gazette).

Figure 7.2 Share of Defence Ministry Budget in Total Government Budget (1950–88)

budget size did not exceed one billion kyat until the middle of the 1970s, and even then it increased only slightly. When the total budget increased in the 1980s, mainly due to the acceptance of foreign aid, the growth in the MOD budget was less than that of the total budget, and moreover the share of the MOD budget in the total budget was decreasing (see Figure 7.2).

The same restraint can be seen in officers' salaries. They were revised on 1 October 1972 for the first time since independence [MOD, Adjutant General Office Order 1/544/ Military Affairs 2 (8)]. The changes in monthly salaries by rank were as follows: second lieutenant: from 250 to 320 kyat, lieutenant: from 350 to 410 kyat, captain: from 525 to 540 kyat, major: remained stable at 800 kyat, lieutenant colonel: remained stable at 1,100 kyat, colonel: remained stable at 1,300 kyat, brigadier general: remained stable at 1,400 kyat, major general: from 1,800 to 1,600 kyat, lieutenant general: from 2,500 to 1,800 kyat. As these numbers show, company-grade officer salaries were raised somewhat, those of field-grade officers and brigadier generals were left unchanged, and major generals and lieutenant generals had their salaries actually reduced. This may have been in recognition that many general-grade officers had other income from concurrently held positions as high-ranking BSPP executives or administrative executives in the government. And more than 20 per cent of the government budget was already being allocated to the MOD before the coup, meaning that compared with other ministries, the MOD had already been privileged in terms of budgetary allocation. Other than this already existing higher allocation, there is no evidence, at least in official documents, to show that Ne Win provided favorable budgetary treatment especially to the tatmadaw. In fact, the supply of personnel, training, weapons and equipment, facilities, and welfare were absolutely insufficient for the demands being put on the tatmadaw. The minutes of the annual Tatmadaw Conferences, which took place until 1969, vividly points out the difficulties that the military faced at the time, with problems including lack of weapons and ammunition, insufficient military training, shortage of communication equipment and transportation vehicles, flaws in the pension system, and salary arrears.[9] Moreover, Burma's endless counter-insurgency war imposed a massive burden on the tatmadaw. According to its estimates as of 1967, there

[9] "1962 khùhni' ta'màdaw nilahkan kagweyê ûsîgyou' (kyî) àsiyinkhanza [1962 Tatmadaw Conference, General Staff Office (Army) report]," CD-879(2), DSMHRI.

were 17,250 insurgents in the country, and 2,032 small to large battles took place annually.[10]

However, the MOD prioritized the realization of the "Burmese way to socialism" over demands for budget expansion, remaining steadfast against all requests for a budget increase. For instance, Colonel Kyi Maung, the general staff colonel, made the following statement at the 1969 Tatmadaw Conference: "Our state is in the midst of building a socialist economy and is a developing state. Therefore, we cannot afford to appropriate the national budget preferentially for only defence spending."[11]

As a result, waging counter-insurgency operations in jungles with insufficient equipment and frequent salary arrears produced between 2,000 and 5,000 deserters every year from the mid-1950s to the mid-1960s.[12] Table 7.1 shows the figures for annual troop recruitment and discharge from 1960 to 1965 along with those for the 18-month period from 1 April 1965 to 30 September 1966, and the 18-month period from 1 October 1966 to 31 March 1968. While an average of close to 18,000 recruits joined the military annually during the two 18-month periods, an average of about 16,000 soldiers left through desertion, resignation, discharge or death. This suggests a troop replacement rate of more than 10 per cent annually during the latter half of the 1960s, a rate that made it difficult to expand the tatmadaw as its leaders had expected.

Frontline units were chronically below troop strength.[13] It was not unusual for battalions that normally were supposed to have 750 men in

---

[10] "1968 khùhni' ta'màdaw nilahkan kagweyê ûsîgyou' (kyî) àsiyinkhanza (1-10-66 hmà 30-9-67 ye'nèàhtì) [1968 Tatmadaw Conference, General Staff Office (Army) report (1 October 1966–30 September 1967)]," CD-883(7), DSMHRI, 35, 43. See Table 5 for the numbers of insurgents in each regional command. However, the figure of only five *Mujahids* insurgents is an indication of the questionable accuracy of these statistics.

[11] "1969 khùhni' ta'màdaw nilahkan dùtìyàkagweyêi ûsîjou' (kyî) ì panama hnìn nìgôunjou' mèingûnmyâ [1969 Tatmadaw Conference, Vice-Chief of General Staff (Army)'s closing speech]," CD-884(2), DSMHRI, p. 11.

[12] Figures for the number of deserters each year during the latter half of the 1950s were 2,196 (1955), 2,320 (1956), 4,927 (1957), 4,377 (1958) and 4,132 (1959). These figures are based on "1965 khùhni' ta'màdaw nilahkan si'ûsî, si'yêi hnìn si'htau' hsainya tinpyà hswêinwêiche' myâ [1965 Tatmadaw Conference, discussion on operations, military affairs and logistics]," CD-874, DSMHRI, pp. 83–4.

[13] "1966 khùhni' ta'màdaw nilahkan dùtìyà kagweyê ûsîgyou' (kyî) ì mèingûn [1966 Tatmadaw Conference, Vice-Chief of General Staff (Army)'s closing speech]," CD-882(3), DSMHRI, p. 52.

Table 7.1 Number of Recruited and Discharged Soldiers (1960–68)

Fiscal Year	*Recruited Soldiers*	*Discharged Soldiers*					
		Total	*Deserted*	*Ordinary*	*Disciplinary*	*Death*	
						in Battle	*Other*
1960–61	4,183	9,352	3,563	4,150	1,094	296	249
1961–62	7,352	8,171	2,233	4,150	1,267	269	252
1962–63	11,977	11,899	2,034	8,468	815	258	324
1963–64	12,233	8,813	1,900	5,596	658	340	319
1964–65	11,951	9,852	3,872	4,290	907	431	352
1965–66	10,509	9,842	3,415	4,495	1,143	396	393
Total	58,205	57,929	17,017	31,149	5,884	1,990	1,889
1965/4/1–1966/9/30	17,384	15,761	6,233	6,693	1,665	611	559
1966/10/1–1968/3/31	18,420	16,501	4,768	8,424	2,139	627	543
Total	35,804	32,262	11,001	15,117	3,804	1,238	1,102

Source: Upper section (1960–1966) [DHMHRI CD-882(9): 32]; Lower section (1965–1968) [DHMHRI CD-883(9): 1]

five companies to be short by 100 to 150 men.[14] New recruits lacked sufficient training because the normal six months of basic training had been shortened to three. Insufficient training worsened operational capabilities which made it all the more dangerous and difficult for the units in the field. This inevitably resulted in a large number of casualties and desertions. In such a situation, counter-insurgency operations could not have been effective even if the tatmadaw had outnumbered the insurgents ten to one.

It is difficult to collect accurate data on tatmadaw troop strength and armaments in the 1970s and 1980s. Considering that there was no significant budget increase during that time, it is unlikely that the situation improved, which can be ascertained to a degree from Table 7.2.

[14] "1966 khùhni' ta'màdaw nilahkan kagweyêhtanà ta'màdaw si'ûsîhsainya tinpyàche' hnìn hswêinwêiche'myâ [1966 Tatmadaw Conference, Ministry of Defence, agenda and discussion on the military operations]," CD-882(4), DSMHRI, p. 25.

Table 7.2 Number of Dead, Wounded, Surrendered in Battle (1975–87)

			1975	*1976*	*1977*	*1978*	*1979*	*1980*	*1981*	*1982*	*1983*	*1984*	*1985*	*1986*	*1987*
Northern Military Region	Military	Dead		155	133	202	257	157	86	201	169	183	109	97	
		Wounded		281	252	435	431	333	181	510	415	390	302	25	
	Insurgent	Dead		162	168	51	110	301	99	323	304	217	309	307	376
		Captured		332	56	55	77	60	45	142	129	136	140	102	97
		Surrendered		58	44	89	55	70	78	310	436	400	161	91	157
Northeastern Military Region	Military	Dead	109	156	192	53	45	17	21	51	124	137	63	95	
		Wounded	189	460	392	79	144	38	45	96	337	266	165	689	
	Insurgent	Dead	57	163	124	59	283	93	109	316	317	405	308	617	204[1]
		Captured	54	71	4	59	191	70	58	98	95	135	97	172	56
		Surrendered	47	70	56	126	75	5	22	38	46	105	128	159	59
Eastern Military Region	Military	Dead	19	17			74	117	57	387	316	284	200	315	
		Wounded	27	65			139	273	78	958	915	736	428	736	
	Insurgent	Dead	35	57			175	221	75	858	1121	918	692	768	513
		Captured	65				70	33	48	243	297	154	88	102	89
		Surrendered	56				74	123	167	522	696	396	308	282	177
Southeastern Military Region	Military	Dead	134	170			167	136	60	206	235	661	304	306	
		Wounded	163	624			467	399	342	698	515	2286	1018	1045	
	Insurgent	Dead	174	255			201	162	141	292	374	369	519	554	313[2]
		Captured	271	158			46	64	25	148	119	69	108	93	84
		Surrendered	273	132			90	112	22	64	76	108	122	112	77
Yangon, Southwestern, Central MR (1977–79)	Military	Dead			52	10	36	2	34	31	40	67	168	99	73
		Wounded			266	15	136	8	141	131	145	328	585	303	201
Yangon, Southwestern, Western, Northwestern, Central MR (1980–1987)	Insurgent	Dead			50	52	118	21	171	79	100	118	348	122	64
		Captured			13	73	12	1	53	34	42	16	47	6	8
		Surrendered			21	358	6	37	106	22	15	15	56	10	8

Table 7.2 continued

			1975	*1976*	*1977*	*1978*	*1979*	*1980*	*1981*	*1982*	*1983*	*1984*	*1985*	*1986*	*1987*
Western Military Region	Military	Dead	11	25	20		4								
		Wounded	27	32	26		9								
	Insurgent	Dead	83	54	33		67								
		Captured	27	57	34		56								
		Surrendered	80	27	42		153								
Northwestern Military Region	Military	Dead	4		6	9	2								
		Wounded	61		34	18	4								
	Insurgent	Dead	17		59	9	32								
		Captured	21		39	99	53								
		Surrendered	29		116	28	58								
Central Military Region	Military	Dead	52	97											
		Wounded	321	359											
	Insurgent	Dead	107	147											
		Captured	152	75											
		Surrendered	179	29											

Note: Gray shaded cell means incomplete data.
[1] Number from 20 March 1987 to 20 March 1988
[2] Number from 21 March 1987 to 20 March 1988

Source: by the author based on [si'thàmâin pyàdai' hnìn ta'màdo mogûndai'hmûyôun 1998: 74–286]

The table shows the numbers of combat dead and wounded for both tatmadaw and insurgent forces from 1975 to 1987. In spite of some partial gaps in the data, looking only at the figures for combat deaths among the insurgents, after 1982 the number reached close to 2,000 combatants annually, so military operations seem to have been more effective compared to in the past. But, deaths of tatmadaw soldiers in 1984 largely exceeded the death tolls seen in the latter half of the 1970s. For example, more than 1,000 military personnel died in battle in 1984. The numbers indicate that battles were particularly fierce in the Northern, Northeastern, Eastern and Southeastern military regions. The number of tatmadaw combat deaths in these four commands from 1982 to 1986 averaged 888.6 men annually. This figure was about 2.5 times higher than the average number of deaths in battle in the latter half of the 1960s.

The status of military training during the period offers another example of the underdeveloped support for military operations. A "History of the Ministry of Defence, Directorate of Military Training," compiled in 1991, comments on military training. "[S]ome training directives pointed out the low quality of military training until around 1973, so efforts to improve training can again be seen." It also states:

> During the time of the fight against domestic insurgents, the training schools and units were never able to accomplish their original mission. It was not just because a large amount of their resources were spent on operational and production requirements and on activities for the people. It was also because training units were not provided with the sufficient numbers of well-qualified officers and non-commissioned officers who had the level of teaching skills needed to improve training. Even ammunition and weapons, the minimum equipment required for training, were not allocated because counter-insurgency operations always had priority on military affairs and logistical matériel, and little found its way to training units.[15]

Due to the failure of economic development and closed foreign relations during the Ne Win regime, the tatmadaw also lost opportunities to develop its human resources and equipment through international military cooperation or trade. For example, Figure 7.3 shows the trend

---

[15] "kagweyêi wangyîhtanà lèikyìnyêi hnyunkyâyêihmûyôun thamâinàkyîn 1991 khùhni' [History of the Ministry of Defense, Directorate of Military Training 1991]," DR-8452, DSMHRI, p. 486.

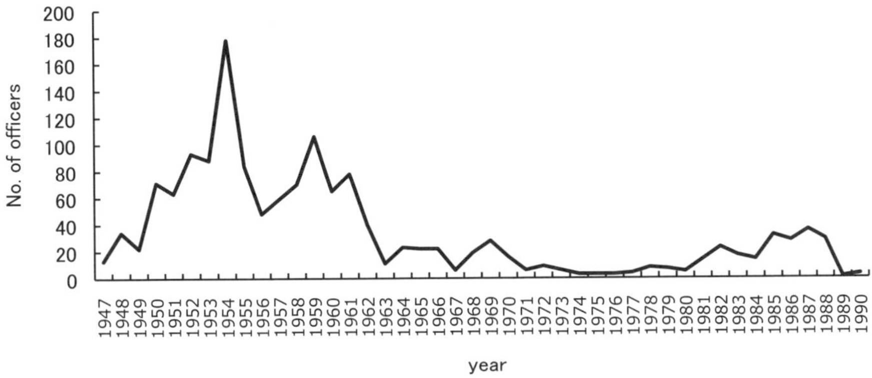

Source: [DSMHRI DR-8452: Appendix à1]

Figure 7.3 Number of the Tatmadaw Officers that Studied Abroad (1947–90)

in the number of officers who study abroad from independence to 1990. The decline after 1962 is clear, and the number dropped to single digits in the 1970s. Although recovering to double digits, at the peak in 1987 only 36 officers studied abroad, a figure only about one-third the 106 studying abroad in 1959.[16] Nothing more clearly illustrates the closed nature of the Ne Win regime than these figures. As a result, as weapons and equipment gradually aged and wore out, and officers could no longer draw on their exposure to an international perspective, important posts in the tatmadaw came to be occupied by officers whose experience was largely in counter-insurgency operations and who had moved up the ranks based primarily on their achievements in counter-insurgency warfare.

The data and these examples suggest that the development of the tatmadaw as a warfare organization was more limited under Ne Win's

[16] These figures are based on "kagweyêi wangyîhtanà lèikyìnyêi hnyunkyâyêihmûyôun thamâinàkyîn 1991 khùhni'" [History of the Ministry of Defence, Directorate of Military Training 1991]," DR-8452, DSMHRI, Table à1. Countries where tatmadaw officers were sent to study in the 1960s include Israel, India, Singapore, Japan, the United States, East Germany and the United Kingdom. The largest number went to the U.K., and even during the stagnant period of the 1970s there were officers studying there every year. The number of officers studying in East Germany and the United States increased in the 1980s.

rule than generally expected. More development might have been possible even under a civilian government.[17] This stagnation of the military after the coup suggests that Ne Win's focus was not primarily on military objectives. Therefore, the coup in 1962 did not necessarily lead to the pursuit of only military corporate interests, but that, in fact, the consequences of the coup were more complicated and diverse.

At least for Ne Win, the coup was the first step in a revolution to build a socialist state. For this reason, Alfred Stepan's argument of a "new professionalism", which asserts that military professionalism itself sometimes becomes connected with political intervention when the military perceives that political and economic problems are a security threat,[18] does not fit appropriately to the Burmese case, because Ne Win aimed at constructing a socialist state as a nationalist rather than as a professional military commander.

This does not mean, however, that the tatmadaw was not important for Ne Win's dictatorship. His goal of revolution was not shared by all of the officers, and many of them simply acted based on loyalty to their organization. The tatmadaw was Ne Win's actual power base, and he could not have maintained his rule without its support. If officers had abandoned him, Ne Win's revolution would have stalled immediately. At the same time, the tatmadaw was also the potential political threat to Ne Win. Despite this seeming danger, Ne Win did not give the tatmadaw any particularly preferential treatment. This fact implies that he used other ways to keep control over the tatmadaw. The next section will discuss this point.

---

[17] A case study by Gary Zuk and William, R. Thompson, "The Post-Coup Military Spending Question: A Pooled Cross-Sectional Time Series Analysis," *The American Political Science Review* 76, 1 (1982) found no positive correlation between coups and military budgets. After comparing the military budgets of 19 countries that had experienced a military government, 27 that had mixed regimes of military government and civilian government, and 23 civilian governments, it found no significant effect of a coup upon the military budget per capita. The only significant variable among several was GNP per capita. Although the study examined a period of only nine years and classified Iran, Iraq, Burma, and Indonesia as having the same form of military government, it shows that it is rare for a military to intervene in politics out of a motivation to benefit the military organization.

[18] See Alfred Stepan, *Rethinking Military Politics: Brazil and the Southern Cone* (Princeton, N.J.: Princeton University Press, 1988).

From National Army to People's Military

Military for the People, Military for the Party

Leaving the military underdeveloped has risks of creating opposition in "the military as an institution" against "the military as a government," and this intra-military struggle of officers engaged mainly in military affairs against those engaged mainly in politics can destabilize the political regime itself.[19] This destabilization never occurred during the two and a half decades of Ne Win's rule, in large part because of the patronage afforded to seconded tatmadaw officers in the BSPP, the civilian ministries, and the People's Parliament (discussed in Chapters 4 to 6). In tandem with this patronage, the internal reform of the military created and consolidated incentives for military officers to support Ne Win. Here I will focus on two factors behind this reform: the redefinition of the tatmadaw as a people's military and the establishment of promotion patterns in the officer coup.

Following the coup in 1962 and the commencement of *The Burmese Way to Socialism* (*The Way*), the position of the tatmadaw remained unclear. Article 15(3) of *The Way* stated, "The existing Defence Services (*ta'màdo*) will also be developed to become the national armed forces (*amyôdâ ta'màdo*) which will defend our socialist economy." Indeed, no consensus was reached in the tatmadaw on the specific details of the "national armed forces," and concerns were raised in the Tatmadaw Conference immediately after the coup. One objection was that the aim of defending "our socialist economy" was too narrow (Eastern Military Region representative's remark); another was that a more specific document needed to be published (Southeastern Military Region representative's remark).[20]

After that Tatmadaw Conference, the term "national army" was not used again. Instead, "people's military" (*pyidù ta'màdo*) emerged as the alternative. The people's military formed a counterpart to the "people's war doctrine" pronounced in 1964. The relationship between the people's

[19] Ibid., pp. 43–69.

[20] "1962 khùhni' ta'màdaw nilahkan kagweyê ûsîgyou' ì mèingûn myâ hnìn tâin si' htanàgyou' athìdî hmà hsêinwêiche' myâ [1962 Tatmadaw Conference, Chief of the General Staff's speech and discussion by Regional Command Headquarters]," CD-878(1), DSMHRI, pp. 134–98.

military and the people's war was clearly articulated in the following remark by Major Hla Thein, the Eastern Military Region representative, on the second day of the 1968 Tatmadaw Conference.

> A developing country like ours does not yet have enough people, material goods and money to be able to repel whatever enemies who may invade from anywhere, so we must be prepared for a people's war based on the people's military in which all the people participate. A people's war is one where all the people participate over the long term. At the same time, it is a war until we are victorious in our correct beliefs and until we basically achieve success on the five major fronts of politics, economy, society, people's management, and war.[21]

To fight enemies on each of the five fronts by mobilizing the entire population around the people's military was the main point of the new military doctrine of people's war. The idea itself was not the Burmese military's own. It was derived from a strategic concept advocated by Mao Tse-tung in the 1930s. He expounded a guerrilla war strategy, one that drew the enemy into the country where they would be "drowned in the sea of the people" rather than defending against them at the border.[22] The Burmese defence strategy has always been to target domestic insurgents rather than threats from outside, with the hypothetical enemy having always been the Burma Communist Party and ethnic minority insurgents.

People's Military ≠ Party's Military

Brigadier General San Yu, the Vice-Chief of General Staff (Army), said the following about the people's military in a speech at the 1966 Tatmadaw Conference. "The people's military is with the people's life. It must go though hardships with the people and share both happiness and misfortune. We have to realize a situation where it is no more possible to separate the people and military, than it is to draw a clear line on

[21] "1968 khùhni' ta'màdaw nilahkan tâinsi'htanàjou' àthîdî hmà hswêinwêi tinpyàche' myâ [1968 Tatmadaw Conference, agendas and discussions by Regional Command Headquarters]," CD-883(1), DSMHRI, p. 145.

[22] Kozo Kawashima, *Shakaishugi no Guntai* [The military in socialist countries] (Tokyo: Kodansha, 1990), p. 129.

water."[23] Clearly San Yu saw the people's military as involved intimately with the life of the people, but the question here is how the concept of the people's military was realized in practice. In communist party-states, such as the Soviet Union, China, and Vietnam, the conversion to a people's military meant that the military came under the communist party's absolute guidance because the communist party represented all the people. More specifically, such systems established the party's institutional control and education over soldiers. Control was achieved through the commissar system whereby a party committee was formed at each military unit level and a political officer sent from the party took part in the decision-making of the unit. "Correct" political education was attempted to achieve through the indoctrination of officers and soldiers with the party's ideology.

In Burma's case, the BSPP's control over the tatmadaw was set down in the "Organization Rules for the Burma Socialist Programme Party," adopted at the first Party Congress in 1971. Following this, party committees were established within the tatmadaw in accordance with the "Organization and Duties of Party Organizations within the tatmadaw" approved at the 89th meeting of the party's Central Organizing Committee. A tatmadaw Party Committee, composed of officers who were BSPP Central Committee members, was established in the MOD, and BSPP organizing committees headed by military officers were set up in the General Staff Office as well as in regional commands, divisions, military areas, garrisons, base commands, battalions, and companies. The role of the tatmadaw Party Committee was explained as follows: "Based on the BSPP's guidance, the tatmadaw Party Committee is to bring military officers and soldiers into more absolute acceptance of the party's leadership." Its duties were "... to follow the party's ideology and policies and to carry out their implementation, ... to build up the tatmadaw's might and its spirit to defend the state, ... to strengthen the solidarity of the military," and "... to form organizing committees along the chain of command within the tatmadaw to guide and organize its activities."[24]

[23] "1966 khùhni' ta'màdaw nilahkan dùtìyà kagweyê ûsîgyou' (kyî) ì mèingûn [1966 Tatmadaw Conference, Vice Chief of General Staff (Army)'s speech]," CD-882(3), DSMHRI, pp. 3–4.

[24] myanmà hsousheli' lânzinpati patisîyôunyêi bàhokomiti htanàjou' [Burma Socialist Programme Party Organizing Central Committee Headquarters] *ta'màdo àtwîn sì patiàphwèàsîmyâ ì phwèsîpoun hnìn lou'ngântawunmyâ* [Organization and duties of party organizations within the tatmadaw] (1971), p. 18.

This institutionalization of the party's control over the tatmadaw was based on the plan drafted by Thakin Tin Myat, a former communist and a committee member in the Workers Bureau in BSPP headquarters, and Bo Ye Htut, one of the "Thirty Comrades" and a committee member in the Public Relations Department in the party headquarters.[25] According to an interview I had with Thakin Tin Myat, Colonel Than Sein, who was the vice-secretary general of the Central Organizing Committee and the minister of transportation and telecommunications, was the first to propose the idea of organizing party committees in the tatmadaw at a meeting in 1966. It derived from his experience of appointing a political adviser for each regional commander in the Anti-Fascist Organization during the time of the Japanese occupation.[26]

Thakin Tin Myat and Bo Ye Htut, who were attending the meeting, opposed the proposal arguing that intervention by the party, could confuse the chain of command within the tatmadaw, that it should not be done at least while the BSPP was still under construction, and that it might conflict with the principle that the tatmadaw was the backbone (*kyoyôu*) of the party. Instead, they proposed that the party's involvement in the tatmadaw should be limited to installing education committees that would instruct soldiers politically on the party's ideology.[27] Ne Win eventually adopted their proposal. Party education committees were formed in the MOD, regional commands and each military unit. Instructors were sent from the Central Institute of Political Science to provide political education to military officers and soldiers. In 1971 the education committees were reorganized into party organizing committees; nevertheless, direct party intervention in the military continued to be avoided. The Tatmadaw Party Committee and party organizing committees consisted of military officers only from each unit. No commissar or similar

[25] Both fought against the Japanese as members of the Anti-Fascist People's Freedom League. Thakin Tin Myat was a Communist Party member. After taking part in underground activity with Thakin Soe in the late 1940s, he was arrested in Yangon in 1960 and left the Communist Party. Bo Ye Htut was one of the "Thirty Comrades." After independence he took command of the Third Burma Rifle Battalion but went underground after the failure of a coup conducted in collaboration with the Communist Party's anti-government movement. He surrendered in May 1963. Both Thakin Tin Myat and Thakin Soe were asked by Ne Win to join the Programme Party, and they worked at the party headquarters from the time of the BSPP's establishment.

[26] Interview with Thakin Tin Myat, 28 July 2005.

[27] Interview with Thakin Tin Myat, 28 July 2005.

political officer was ever created by the BSPP. The committees had an institutional arrangement, which could be termed "the tatmadaw's self-control through officer-led party committee." This system did not change until 1988; hence the BSPP's control over the military was rather limited during Ne Win's regime.

Two points need to be noted here. First, it is certain that the BSPP committee system as set up within the tatmadaw was a weak institution in terms of insuring the party's guidance of the tatmadaw, but in terms of political guidance, the 1977 Constitutions officially guaranteed the authority of the Council of State over the budget, over human resources, and over the military command (1974 Constitution, Chapter Five). However, because both the Council of State and the People's Parliament basically followed the BSPP Central Executive Committee's decisions, the authority of the Council of State in fact belonged to the BSPP president, Ne Win. Therefore, his political guidance over the tatmadaw was in effect guaranteed by the 1974 Constitution. Moreover, the responsibility for the drafting and adoption of defence policy belonged to the Defence and Security Committee of the People's Parliament and the party's Central Committee, both of which consisted of top active military officers and former (now retired) top officers. Consequently, one result of the reform to the people's military was that Ne Win and retired officers obtained formal ways to control the tatmadaw.

The second point concerns the military's "self-control." The existence of the regime's formal ideology and intelligence agencies, particularly the National Intelligence Bureau (NIB), curbed factionalism and political deviation within the tatmadaw. Tatmadaw members were expected to adhere ideologically to *The Way* under the guidance of the BSPP; in 1966, 4,195 officers, and 49,833 soldiers of the three services were registered as party members.[28] The NIB was organized in 1974 under the Directorate of Defence Services Intelligence. Although the prime minister was formally in charge of the bureau, it was headed by General Tin Oo, a military advisor to Ne Win as the president, so the NIB was substantially under Ne Win's command.[29] Following its establishment, soldiers' behavior was subject to constant NIB surveillance compelling them to follow formal rules. In fact, many officers received warnings from the Party Discipline Committee for violating one or more of the 18 items

[28] DSMHRC CD-882: 34.

[29] Selth, *Burma's Armed Forces*, p. 104.

contained in the Party Constitution, Article 47, "Party Member Rules of Conduct."

In summary, the reform of the tatmadaw into a people's military under the guidance of the party remained incomplete, which meant the party's guidance of the tatmadaw was only partial; and it would never obtain direct total control of the tatmadaw. There was no more than indirect control by the party chairman through organizations like the party's Central Executive Committee, People's Council, and the National Intelligence Bureau. Although this assured Ne Win's control over the tatmadaw, the mechanism largely relied on his personal dictatorship, not on institutional party leadership.

People's War

In Burma, no military doctrine was formulated until 1956. The failure of Operation "Victory Dragon" (*naga naing*) in 1953 against the Chinese Nationalist army triggered a movement toward a full-scale modernization of the tatmadaw, in the course of which discussions on military doctrine also began. At the Tatmadaw Conference in Meiktila in 1956, military doctrine was taken up for the first time as a major topic of the agenda. In 1958 Colonel Kyi Win submitted a report on military doctrine in which he emphasized that the tatmadaw had to adopt guerrilla rather than conventional warfare as a new strategy.[30]

At the 1964 Tatmadaw Conference, Brigadier General San Yu, Vice-Chief of General Staff (Army), repeated the need to review the existing doctrine and draw up a new one. The result was the adoption of the people's war doctrine. The next year a study tour led by Lieutenant Colonel Thura Htun Tin visited Switzerland, Yugoslavia, Czechoslovakia, and East Germany, and then submitted a report titled "Study on People's War."[31] The doctrine was put into effect with the formation of a people's militia led by the tatmadaw. From 1965 through 1966, the militia was organized experimentally where the White Flag Communist Party had

[30] Maung Aung Myoe, "Military Doctrine and Strategy in Myanmar: A Historical Perspective," SDSC Working Paper No. 339 (1999), p. 3.

[31] A survey on militia organizing was also conducted. A Staff Office report listed "internal anti-government insurgents," a "historical enemy with approximately equal power," and a "more powerful enemy" as enemies. "Historical enemy with approximately equal power" refers to Thailand and a "more powerful enemy" refers to China. See Maung Aung Myoe, "Military Doctrine and Strategy in Myanmar," pp. 6–7.

bases (Pinlebu and Banmauk in Kathar District and Phaungpyin in Mawlaik District) in the Northwestern Military Region. Thereafter the General Staff Office (Army) standardized the method for organizing the militia and made planning for a people's war one of the major items on the agenda of the 1968 Tatmadaw Conference.[32] It was estimated that from the total population, the country had a potential military force of 7.8 million men between the ages of 15 and 54, and 5 million women between the ages of 20 and 49. The conference participants also discussed the formation of militia units at the village level.[33] Thereafter, these units were organized in all military regions. By 1974 it was reported that these had been formed in 212 townships and 1,831 villages, with 67,736 people participating; they had received distribution of a total of 15,227 rifles.[34] If these statistics can be trusted, militia units nationwide had nearly 70,000 members that numerically made them a considerable fighting force. But they were armed with only a little over 15,000 guns indicating that as a force they were far too feeble to actually fight. So despite the new doctrine's emphasis on people's war, the militia could make little direct contribution to counter-insurgency operations. The low significance of the militia was also demonstrated by the fact that people's war was placed together with public relations under the control of the same bureau, the Directorate of People's War and Public Relations, within the General Staff Office (Army).

The reason for adopting the people's war doctrine at that time, despite the actual ineffectualness of the militia, lay in its relationship with the tatmadaw's strategy for counter-insurgency operations known as the "four cuts" (*phya'lêi phya'*).[35] This strategy focused on attacking the insurgents by cutting off the four resources of food, funding, information and recruits. It is said that the tatmadaw began adopting the strategy

---

[32] si'thàmâin pyàdai' hnìn ta'màdo mogûndai'hmûyôun [The Defence Services Military and Historical Research Institutes], *ta'madothamâin pinsàmàtwè* 1962–1974 [The Military History, Vol. 5, 1962–1974] (1997), pp. 139–59.

[33] "1968 khùhni' ta'màdaw nilahkan tâinsi'htanàjou' àthîdî hmà hswêinwêi tinpyàche' myâ [1968 Tatmadaw Conference, agenda and discussion from Regional Command Headquarters]," CD-883(1), DSMHRI, p. 210.

[34] pyihtaunzù myanmanaingan tawhlanyêi kaunsi. [Burmese Government Revolutionary Council], *tohlanyêi kaunsi ì lou'hsaunche' thàmâin àkyînjou'* [Concise history of the actions of the Revolutionary Council] (1982), p. 330.

[35] Maung Aung Myoe, "Military Doctrine and Strategy in Myanmar," p. 10.

from around the mid-1960s.[36] But in fact it is uncertain how extensively militia units were involved in military operations directed at the "four cuts." A former regional commander does not mention the militia in his memoir when writing about "four-cuts" operations in Pegu Yoma.[37]

Organizing residents in an operational area is essential in anti-guerrilla warfare. Some officers in the tatmadaw were already aware of this as early as the 1950s. A report by Colonel Kyi Win and the government's attempt to mobilize people through the National Solidarity Association during the caretaker government offer examples of this awareness.[38] However, the compulsory mobilization of residents living in the areas of operation was difficult to enforce before Ne Win's coup. The coup allowed the tatmadaw to intervene in home affairs and justice, even to the point of eliminating "suspicious" residents spatially and physically based on its own judgment for the sake of military operations. Moreover, the society was organized from above by organizations like the BSPP, the Workers Organization, the Farmers Organization, and party youth organizations which finally gave the tatmadaw the means to apply the "four-cuts" strategy against the insurgents' resources.

People's war in conjunction with the "four-cuts" strategy became the new military doctrine under the new political environment and social reorganization of the Ne Win regime. If the objective of Mao Tse-tung's people's war was the constant cultivation of the "sea of people" to defend the state against the external enemy, for the tatmadaw, the people's war was one of how to control the "sea of people" that was behind the support of the internal enemy. While Mao could basically rely on the "sea of people" he was cultivating, the "sea of people" the tatmadaw needed to mobilize, organize, and give weapons to could turn into the "enemy" at any moment. This made it extremely difficult to expand the militia amongst the people that the tatmadaw distrusted. Thus people's war, although now the new doctrine, did not fundamentally change the tatmadaw's mode of operation.

---

[36] Martin Smith, *Burma: Insurgency and the Politics of Ethnicity*, 2nd ed. (Dhaka: University Press, 1999), p. 259.

[37] Than Tin, *kothwè phyi'pa'myâ si'hsinyêipyî si'hsinyêi hmà* [From operation to operation: the events I experienced] (Yangon: auntankhun ponhnei'tai', 2004), pp. 492–525.

[38] "1968 khùhni' ta'màdaw nilahkan tâinsi'htanàjou' àthîdî hmà hswêinwêi tinpyàche'myâ [1968 CO's Conference, agenda and discussion from Regional Command Headquarters]," CD-883(1), DSMHRI, p. 245.

Images of the People's Military

The people's military was more important as an ideology than as an effective military force, and this affected the way it represented itself to the people. This section will examine a number of selected covers from issues of *People's Military Magazine* (*pyidù ta'màdo sazin*) to analyze the images that the people's military projected of itself.[39] This magazine was first published in 1964 immediately after the adoption of the people's military doctrine. The title suggested a close relationship between the doctrine and the magazine. Because the magazine was circulated within the tatmadaw, rather than sold into the general public, the military's desired depiction of the officers and ordinary soldiers of the people's military was expressed directly and stereotypically. The cover depictions fell into several categories; the self-image these depicted will be analyzed below.

One category was a self-image depicting a soldier working with a farmer. For example, Figure 7.4 is the cover of vol. 1 no. 3 (7 August 1964). On this cover, there is a farmer with a rifle hanging from his shoulder, and a soldier patting a water buffalo. This exchange of symbols (a soldier and a water buffalo/a farmer and a rifle) represented the fusion of a farmer and a soldier. There are several compositions of a soldier doing farmwork, such as a soldier sowing rice seed (Figure 7.5), a soldier driving a tractor (Figure 7.6), farmers and soldiers threshing rice together (Figure 7.7), and a farmer and a soldier having a meal together (Figure 7.8), all showing the unity between farmers and soldiers, thereby conveying the message that a farmer is a soldier, and a soldier is a farmer. With 70 per cent of Burma's population at the time living and working in villages, the depicting of soldiers working with farmers was a typical image of the people's military.[40]

Another category was the depiction of a soldier as responsible for national defense. The Independence Memorial and the national flag often represented the state, while a male farmer and a male worker represented the people. In Figure 7.9, modern factories and farmers harvesting rice in a paddy are shown under an army soldier holding a rifle with the

[39] The analysis below relies on the following study: Hiroyuki Tosa, *Gurobaru/Jenda Poritikkusu* (*Global/Gender Politics*) (Tokyo: Sekai Shisosha, 2000), pp. 15–24; however the depictions are examined from a different perspective in this section.

[40] There were some depictions showing farmers participating in military drills, and some centered on workers, but these were few in number.

Figure 7.4 A Military Man and a Farmer

Figure 7.5 A Military Man Engaged in Farm Work (1)

Figure 7.6 A Military Man Engaged in Farm Work (2)

Figure 7.7 Military Men Engaged in Farm Work

Figure 7.8 A Farmer and a Soldier Having a Meal Together

Figure 7.9 Image of the Ideal State

Figure 7.10 A Worker Shaking Hand with a Farmer

Figure 7.11 Representation of Ethnic Minorities (1)

Figure 7.12 Representation of Ethnic Minorities (2)

Figure 7.13 A Military Man and a Wreath (1)

Figure 7.14 A Military Man and a Wreath (2)

Figure 7.15 A Military Man as a Father

Figure 7.16 Images of General Aung San

national flag in the background. In the sky above the factories, the people rising up in the struggle against the Japanese empire are depicted so that a positive historical image of the tatmadaw and the ideal society are juxtaposed in one image. Figure 7.10 depicts a farmer and a worker shaking hands against the background of the Independence Memorial. A soldier with a gun can be seen in front of the memorial.

A third category depicted soldiers protecting ethnic minority people. Figures 7.11 and 7.12 show ethnic minority people and a soldier against a background of the national flag. It is clear that its purpose was to create an image of national unity, of soldiers coexisting with ethnic minorities. Furthermore, the depictions created stereotypical images of these people with ethnic costumes and musical instruments, making ethnicity something cultural rather than political. In most cases the people in ethnic costumes were women, which could be understood as intended to give ethnic minorities a feminine image of the peaceful and non-political in contrast to soldiers symbolizing masculinity. This femininity was not only a counterpart to the masculine soldier but was also intended to show an admiration of men (soldiers). Figures 7.13 and 7.14, respectively, depict a child and women offering flowers to soldiers. Every year on 27 March, Tatmadaw Memorial Day, a military parade took place in Yangon, and people put wreaths around soldiers' necks as they marched by.[41] The act of offering flowers to the ranks was intended to show admiration for the soldiers and the blood and sweat they expended every day in combat. In Figure 7.15, this image of femininity admiring soldiers is made to overlap with femininity as motherhood while the soldier, the image of masculinity, is depicted as the father.

A fourth category was idolization of Aung San. Ne Win was never depicted. Not one of the 150 issues of *People's Military Magazine* that this author collected had a cover with a picture of Ne Win. As pointed out in Chapter 3, Burma's state ideology never developed a cult of personality, something that Ne Win shunned. Instead, Aung San was idolized, and he appeared on covers of the magazine in a variety of motifs, some examples shown in Figure 7.16. Although a national hero since independence, Aung San's image as a symbol of the military did not begin appearing until around 1962 or 1963. During the 1950s, the magazine *Current Events* (*hki'yêi*),[42] which was directed at military personnel and

[41] There were pictures of fighting women, too.

[42] *Current Events* had many anti-communist propaganda articles, which reflected the extreme wariness of communist party sympathizers within the military in the 1950s.

circulated within the tatmadaw, never carried Aung San on its cover. But after Ne Win came to power, selective images of Aung San in military uniform began being used, and articles in *People's Military Magazine* often quoted from his speeches that centered on his support for socialism and harmony among all ethnic groups.[43]

As illustrated in these examples, the images that *People's Military Magazine* wanted to link to the people's military were the closeness between farmers and soldiers, the nonviolent relationship between ethnic minorities and soldiers, the complementary but unequal relationship between women and soldiers, and the idolization of General Aung San. One can easily see in the depictions the regime's appeal to the legitimacy of military rule, which can be seen through the historical representation of the tatmadaw as the army of national liberation that led the struggle for independence. "The Burmese Way to Socialism" is clearly seen as the path to realizing a better society for farmers and workers. One can also see the importance of passing on the significance of the independence struggle, which needed to be conveyed from the old to the new generation as the tatmadaw underwent a generational change, the topic we turn to next.

Generational Change in the tatmadaw

As examined earlier, the BSPP's control over the tatmadaw was limited. This was never a major problem while it was led by Ne Win's aides after he retired from the tatmadaw. But over time a new generation of officers began moving into leadership positions within the tatmadaw. This new generation did not share the experience of fighting against the Japanese with Ne Win and other first generation officers. Thus, the imagery and

[43] The dates of *People's Military Magazine* issues with his image on the cover are as follows: 7 Aug. 1964, vol. 1 no. 3 (Figure 7.4); 7 Nov. 1964, vol. 1 no. 9 (Figure 7.5); 7 Oct. 1964, vol. 1 no. 7 (Figure 7.6); 15 Aug. 1983, vol. 20 no. 8 (Figure 7.7); 15 Oct. 1965, vol. 2 no. 12 (Figure 7.8); 15 Mar. 1968, vol. 5 no. 3 (Figure 7.9); 15 Jan. 1968, vol. 5 no. 1 (Figure 7.10); 15 Feb. 1968, vol. 5 no. 2 (Figure 7.11); 15 Feb. 1976, vol. 13 no. 2 (Figure 7.12); 15 Aug. 1976, vol. 13 no. 8 (Figure 7.13); 15 July 1973, vol. 10 no. 7 (Figure 7.14); 15 Aug. 1976, vol.13 no. 10 (Figure 7.15); 15 Dec. 1971, vol. 8 no. 12 (Figure 7.16 upper left); 15 July 1971, vol. 8 no. 7 (Figure 7.16 upper center); 15 Jul. 1966, vol. 3 no. 9 (Figure 7.16 upper right), 15 July 1968, vol. 5 no. 7 (Figure 7.16 lower left); 15 June 1974, vol. 11 no. 6 (Figure 7.16 lower right).

depictions discussed above could be understood as an effort to convey the experience of the independence struggle to the new generation of soldiers, as well as to bring them closer to the farmers and workers, and to reinforce the stature of Aung San as the father of Burma's independence. However, it is not easy to convey the experience of one generation to the next only by imagery. Thus, generational change in the tatmadaw had the potential of undermining the legitimacy of socialism and Ne Win's leadership which were underpinned by historical memory. This section deals with this generational change focusing on Ne Win's control over the officer corps.

Organizational Structure

The General Staff Office, the Regional Commands and Officer Education

The tatmadaw has an Army, Navy, and Air Force, each headed by a Vice-Chief of General Staff, all under the Chief of General Staff of the tatmadaw. During most of the time between 1948 and 1962, civilian politicians filled the position of defence minister. The first was U Nu (14 September 1948 to 5 April 1945) followed by Ba Swe (16 March 1952 to 16 July 1958), then Bo Hmu Aung (16 July to 28 October 1958). Under Ne Win's caretaker government the tatmadaw was in control with Ne Win himself as defence minister. After the caretaker government stepped down and a civilian government again took control, U Nu was defence minister a second time (4 April 1960 to 2 March 1962). After 1962 until 1985, the Chief of General Staff of the tatmadaw also held the post of defence minister. Although the Chief of General Staff was formally in charge of the three armed services, he was in practice the commander in chief of the Army, far and away the largest of the armed services, with the Vice-Chief of General Staff (Army) in the number two position.

The MOD was not established until 1956. Prior to that date, the smaller War Office had headed the tatmadaw. Organizational reforms were carried out in 1963, 1969, 1971, 1973, 1974, 1979, and 1981. Through such reforms, the offices of the defence minister and the Chief of General Staff of the tatmadaw, as well as those of the general staff of each defence service were established within the MOD. Below these offices in the ministry were the Adjutant General Office, the Quartermaster General Office, Judge Advocate General Office and Inspector General Office. The Adjutant General Office was composed of the Directorate of Medical Services, the Directorate of Resettlement and the

Directorate of Ordnance Services, while the Quartermaster General Office was composed of the Directorate of Military Engineers, the Directorate of Supply and Transport, the Directorate of Procurement and the Directorate of Electrical and Mechanical Engineers.

According to the "History of the General Staff Office of the Army 1948–1984," the General Staff Office of the Army was re-organized in the mid-1950s into an office headed by the Vice Chief of General Staff-Army below which were the General Office of Duties, the General Office of Operations, the Directorate of Education and Psychological Warfare, the Directorate of Military Training, the Directorate of Armour and Artillery, the Directorate of Signals, the Directorate of Defence Services Intelligence and Provost Marshal's Office.[44] In 1969 the Directorate of Planning and the Directorate of Research were created.

Within the MOD, the Chief of General Staff of the tatmadaw and the Vice Chief of General Staff (Army) were the most important. The Adjutant General and the Quartermaster General were also highly important as they had authority over the management of all of the departments within the MOD and the General Staff Office (Army). Over time as military rule continued, the head of the Directorate of Defence Services Intelligence gained more influence; and the Colonel General Staff in charge of assisting the Vice Chief of General Staff (Army), a position for a relatively young promising officer, was also a position of importance. The six positions of Chief of General Staff of the tatmadaw, the Vice Chief of General Staff (Army), the Adjutant General, the Quartermaster General, the head of the Directorate of Defence Services Intelligence, and the Colonel General Staff roughly formed the power structure within the tatmadaw, and looking at these six positions makes it possible to roughly ascertain the political situation within the military over the course of the Ne Win regime.

The tatmadaw's main duty has always been counter-insurgency against communists and ethnic minority insurgents, and the bulk of

[44] "kagweyêi ûsîgyou' (kyî) thàmâin akyîn 1948–84 [History of the General Staff Office (Army) 1948–84]," DR-8482, DSMHRI, pp. 39–41. The number of officers in each bureau was as follows: the General Office of Duties: 24, the General Office of Operations: 14, the Directorate of Education and Psychological Warfare (N/A), the Directorate of Military Training: 15, the Directorate of Armor and Artillery: 14, the Directorate of Signals: 17, the Directorate of Defence Services Intelligence, p. 23 and the Provost Marshal's Office, p. 50.

military operations has been carried out by the Army. The basic combat unit is the infantry battalion composed of four companies with a total of about 800 officers and soldiers. Until 1961 the Army had followed the brigade system made up of 13 brigades each composed of several battalions that were stationed in the two military regions: Northern and Southern. The brigade system was abolished in 1961 replaced by the regional command system made up initially of the five military regions, which later were expanded to nine regions. From 1966 light infantry divisions composed of about ten battalions each started to be organized under the direct control of the General Staff Office (Army). This "battalion command" – "light infantry division command" – "military region command" organization formed the core of the tatmadaw's command structure, and the main tour of duty for officers spanned these three command organizations. Once an officer became a regional commander, he could also influence the local administration in the region, and former regional commanders occupied positions in the MOD and the General Staff Office (Army).

Looking at the training of officers, one of the characteristics of the tatmadaw was the delay in establishing a military academy. The Defence Services Academy (DSA) (*si' te'kàthoe*), a standard four-year military educational institution, opened in Bahtoo of Shan State in 1955.[45] Forty-five people were enrolled as officer cadets at the inauguration of the first class on 4 July 1955. Thereafter enrolment gradually increased, and the academy graduated about 200 officers every year in the latter half of the 1980s. An applicant had to be a high school graduate from 16 to 19 years old, and which of the three services a cadet would serve in was determined upon graduation.[46]

Prior to the establishment of the DSA, there were two main sources from which the tatmadaw had acquired officers. One was officers trained by the Japanese military during the Pacific War who had remained in the tatmadaw after independence. The Japanese army had set up an officer training school in Mingaladon, north of Rangoon, on 20 October

---

[45] The DSA was created after the model of West Point of the U.S. Army. It moved to Maymyo of Mandalay Region in 1957.

[46] Maung Aung Myoe, "Officer Education and Leadership Training in the Tatmadaw: A Survey" (Canberra: Strategic and Defence Studies Centre, Research School of Pacific and Asian Studies, Australian National University, 2000), p. 7.

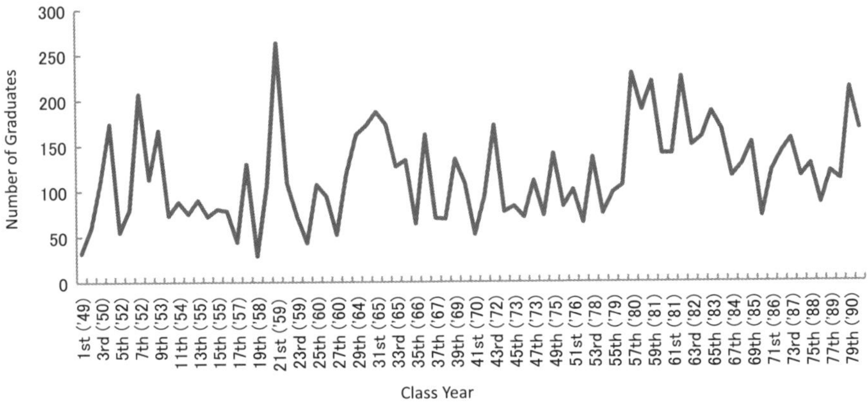

Source: [DSMHRI DR-8452: Appendix pà1]

Figure 7.17 Number of OTS Graduates (1949–80)

1942.[47] By March 1945, four classes totalling 937 cadets had graduated from the school; a fifth class of 179 cadets was in training.[48] Although many of these officers participated in the revolt against the Japanese and resigned from the army following the return of the British in 1945, some of them remained in the army after independence later to become officers when the tatmadaw was established.

The second source was the tatmadaw's Officers Training School (OTS) (*boe thindân kyâun*). The 120 cadets of the first class received their officer commissions in May 1949. Figure 7.17 shows the variation in the number of the OTS graduates from the first to the 80th class, the last receiving their commissions on 23 August 1990. In addition to educating young officer candidates much like at a military academy, the OTS also trained non-commissioned officers who could be promoted

[47] An officer candidate school is called "*boe thindân kyâun*" in Burmese, and the OTS discussed below was modeled after the officer candidate school set up during the time of Japanese military rule.

[48] "kagweyêi wangyîhtanà lèikyìnyêi hnyunkyâyêihmûyôun thamâinàkyîn 1991 khùhni' [History of the Ministry of Defence, Directorate of Military Training 1991]," DR-8452, DSMHRI, p. 9.

Table 7.3 Composition of Military Personnel in 1965

	Officers	*NCOs*	*Soldiers*	*New Soldiers*	*Civilians*	*Total*
Army	4,919	34,076	76,473	6,858	3,857	126,183
Navy	357	2,033	4,696		69	7,155
Air Force	383	2,370	3,939		784	7,476
Total	5,659	38,479	85,108	6,858	4,710	140,814

Source: [DSMHRI CDE-882(9): 12]

later to commissioned officers.[49] In some years multiple graduations took place, so the number of graduates in a year could vary widely. Furthermore, not discernible in the figure is that there were no graduates in 1962 and 1963, as officer training at the OTS was originally planned to end in 1961. The reason for its reopening was the rise in the number of seconded tatmadaw officers to other organizations after 1962, and the DSA alone was unable to train the needed number of officers, as will be discussed below.[50]

The Size of the Officer Corps and Generational Change

No accurate figures on the size of the officer corps in Burma have ever been formally announced. Even in the tatmadaw's official documents held in the military archives, the only figures that can be confirmed are those in a document submitted to the 1966 Tatmadaw Conference. Table 7.3 shows the size of the officer corps at that time. This data yields some interesting information.

First of all, it shows that the Army was vastly larger than the Navy and Air Force, the ratio being 17:1:1. The reason was the priority on

[49] The OTS opened in January 1949 and was originally in Maymyo, moving to Bahtoo in 1957. It was relocated to Hmawbi in 1964. It opened its doors to college graduates from the 29th class of 1964. See Maung Aung Myoe, "Building the Tatmadaw: The Organizational Development of the Armed Forces in Myanmar, 1948–98," Working Paper No. 327 (Strategic and Defence Studies Centre, Australian National University, 1998), p. 16.

[50] An institution for training low-ranking officers (*alou' thin boe*) was opened in 1971 that provided three years of training to 16- to 19-year-old high school graduates. This organization is not analyzed in this book because it was largely aimed at training officers of relatively lower rank.

counter-insurgency operations which cantered on army infantry battalions. The Army was so superior to the Navy and Air Force organizationally as well as politically that factional conflicts among Burma's armed services have never happened.

Second, the size of officer corps of the tatmadaw was relatively smaller with a ratio of officers to total military personnel of 1:25, compared to that of other militaries in contemporary developing countries such as 1:23 in Indonesia, 1:20 in Pakistan and Egypt, 1:17 in Turkey, 1:15 in Syria, 1:14 in Iran.[51] This shortage of officers affected counter-insurgency operations. For instance, at the 1963 Tatmadaw Conference, the Northwestern Military Region command reported on its shortage of staff, pointing out that of the 18 officers in charge of military affairs, five had to deal with legal affairs and three were needed in the Records Department, leaving only ten officers to handle the rest of the administrative work.[52] At the 1966 Tatmadaw Conference, the Eastern Military Region command reported a shortage of both officers and regular troops, one of its infantry battalions standing at only 675 men, 87 per cent of its required strength of 776 men.[53] The shortfall of officers had been exacerbated by the March 1962 coup. Despite the shortage, Ne Win decided to transfer officers to the BSPP and government ministries in order to consolidate his power.[54] A 1968 report recorded that as of 31 March 1968, out of a total of 5,077 officers, 883 had been seconded from the tatmadaw to other organizations on a full-time basis, accounting for about 17 per cent of the total officer corps.[55] To cope with the

[51] The figures are based on data taken from Morris Janowitz, *Military Institutions and Coercion in the Developing Nations* (Chicago: The University of Chicago Press, 1964), pp. 96–7.

[52] "1963 khùhni' ta'màdaw nilahkan kagweyê ûsîgyou' ì mèingûn myâ hnìn tâin si' htanàgyou' athîdî hmà si'ûsî, si'yêi hnìn si'htau' hsainya tinpyà hswêi nwêi che' myâ [1963 Tatmadaw Conference, Military Chief of Staff's speech and discussion from each regional command on operation, military affairs and logistics]," CD879, DSMHRI, p. 1.

[53] "1966 khùhni' ta'màdaw nilahkan dùtìyà kagweyê ûsîgyou' (kyî) ì mèingûn [1966 Tatmadaw Conference, Vice-Chief of Staff's speech]," CD-882(3), DSMHRI, p. 75.

[54] "1966 khùhni' ta'màdaw nilahkan dùtìyà kagweyê ûsîgyou' (kyî) ì mèingûn [1966 Tatmadaw Conference, Vice-Chief of General Staff (Army)'s speech]," CD-882(3), DSMHRI, pp. 65–6.

[55] "1968 ta'màdonilahkan si'yadûhhkàn atwînwan àsiyinhkanza [1968 Tatmadaw Conference, Office of Military Appointment general report]," CD-883(10), DSMHRI, p. 2.

Table 7.4 Age Composition of Officer Corps in 1965 (No. of Officers)

	Under 20	*21–30*	*31–40*	*41–45*	*Over 46*	*Total*
Army	5	1,393	2,220	857	440	4,915
Navy	0	202	112	37	17	368
Air Force	0	192	147	37	6	382
Total	5	1,787	2,479	931	463	5,665

Source: [DSMHRI CD-882(9): 12]

problem, discussions took place on reopening the OTS, which had closed in 1961.[56] It was reopened in 1964 with 162 cadets graduating in its 29th class.

Third, and most importantly, the data indicates that a generational change was occurring in the tatmadaw. Table 7.4 shows the composition of tatmadaw officers by age in 1965. There were more officers in the 31-to-40 age bracket than in other generations. Officers of this generation led combat operations against insurgents, and few of them had experience as officers during the Japanese occupation. They were over 30 years old in the mid 1960s, approaching the limit of their physical strength for command on the frontlines. This was one reason that rejuvenation of the tatmadaw was on the third day's agenda of the 1969 Tatmadaw Conference.[57] In his opening speech at the conference, Colonel Kyi Maung, General Staff Colonel (Army), stated the following.

> We must now review objectively the state of the tatmadaw. Looking at today's tatmadaw, we can see that there has been a general improvement in [combat] experience, but the forces are also suffering from

[56] "1963 khùhni' ta'màdaw nilahkan kagweyê ûsîgyou' ì mèingûn myâ hnìn tâin si' htanàgyou' athîdî hmà si'ûsî, si'yêi hnìn si'htau' hsainya tinpyà hswêi nwêi che' myâ [1963 Tatmadaw Conference, Chief of General Staff's speech and discussion from Regional Command Headquarters on operation, military affairs and logistics]," CD-879, DSMHRI, pp. 1–3.

[57] The "aging" of frontline officers had been mentioned by a representative of the East Regional Command back in 1966 on the first day of that year's Tatmadaw Conference, which had discussed the shortage of officers. "1966 khùhni' ta'màdaw nilahkan kagweyêhtanà ta'màdaw si'ûsîhsainya tinpyàche' hnìn hswêinwêiche'myâ [1966 Tatmadaw Conference, Ministry of Defence, agenda and discussion of military operations]," CD882(4), DSMHRI, pp. 62, 95.

> fatigue and aging. I believe you also know that a growing number of people, along with being soldiers, have become more burdened by responsibilities as household heads, have aged and weakened physically, have lost their health and need medical treatment. Because of this, the army is no longer able to achieve sufficiently [a balance in] the combat strength essential for frontline operations and the numbers [of officers] leaving the frontlines.[58]

The conference took up the issues of officer's age for leaving the frontlines, retirement age for each rank, and the correspondence between length of service and rank. The main subject of discussion was how to transfer frontline officers to the rear, and then how to divide them into those to be promoted and those who should retire. This discussion focused on officers in their mid-30s, the generation with the largest number in the officer corps.

The problem of maintaining a pyramid hierarchy in the military bureaucracy had not been seriously perceived until then because officers were generally young. However, by the end of the 1960s, military leaders faced the task of dealing with middle-ranking officers, and this became the turning point when the tatmadaw changed from a national liberation army to a modern bureaucracy. The 1969 Tatmadaw Conference was the first time the problem was openly discussed. Thereafter, the manner of maintaining stability in the hierarchy of the officer corps became an important task, both for the tatmadaw itself and for Ne Win's control of the tatmadaw.

Institutionalization of Career Paths

How did Ne Win keep organizational stability in the tatmadaw and succeed in securing his control? To answer this question, this section will focus on two points: limitation on the number of senior officers, and institutionalization of the career paths. The hypothesis that this chapter will examine is that these policies helped to create a hierarchically balanced bureaucracy and also allowed a systematic distribution of benefits among the members of the officer corps.

---

[58] "1969 khùhni' ta'màdaw nilahkan tâinsi'htanàjou' àthîdî hmà hswêinwêi tinpyàche' myâ [1969 Tatmadaw Conference, agendas and discussion from Regional Command Headquarters]," CD-884(1), DSMHRI, pp. 1–2.

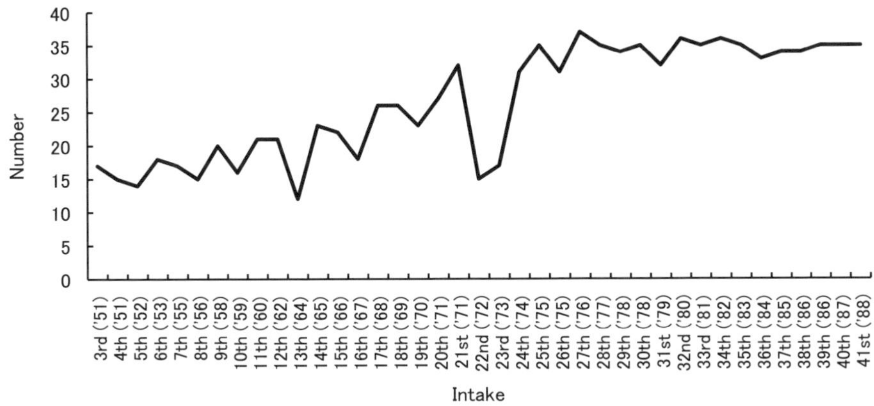

Source: [DSMHRI DR-8452: Appendix htà1]

Figure 7.18 Number of Command and General Staff College Graduates (1951–88)

Originally, the number of officers in ranks above lieutenant colonel was intentionally kept low in the tatmadaw.[59] There were approximately 70 colonels in 1969, and 15 generals.[60] Within the tatmadaw the perception prevailed that this limitation on the number of senior officers was essential for maintaining order in the tatmadaw. Even from the mid-1970s, when officers in the largest age group started being promoted to field-grade ranks, there was no rapid increase in the number of senior officers. Figure 7.18 shows the trend in the number of officers who completed the program at the Command and General Staff College. This college provided a nine-month program for majors and lieutenant colonels from the three services and the police, and many of those who completed the program were promoted to lieutenant colonel or colonel.[61]

[59] "1969 khùhni' ta'màdaw nilahkan tâinsi'htanàjou' àthîdî hmà hswêinwêi tinpyàche' myâ [1969 Tatmadaw Conference, agendas and discussion from Regional Command Headquarters]," CD-884(1), DSMHRI, p. 249.

[60] "1969 khùhni' ta'màdaw nilahkan tâinsi'htanàjou' àthîdî hmà hswêinwêi tinpyàche' myâ [1969 Tatmadaw Conference, agendas and discussion from Regional Command Headquarters]," CD-884(1), DSMHRI, p. 177.

[61] Maung Aung Myoe, "Officer Education and Leadership Training in the Tatmadaw," p. 13. This school was opened in Myamyo on 1 August 1948 as The Burma Army Staff College. It moved to Mingaladon in April 1952, then to Kalaw in April 1954, where its name was changed to the Command and General Staff College. The next year it moved to Bahtoo, and then returned to Kalaw in 1990.

Table 7.5 Number of Promotions

Oct 1, 1966 to Mar 31, 1968		*Oct 1, 1985 to Mar 31, 1987*	
Rank	*Number*	*Rank*	*Number*
2nd Lt → 1st Lt	1,011	Lt Col → Col	37
1st Lt → Cap	633	Col → B Gen	12
Cap → Maj	83	B Gen → Maj Gen	7
Maj → Lt Col	17	Mag Gen → Lt Gen	1
Lt Col → Col	6		

Source: Left side, [DSMHRI CD-883(10): 6]; Right side, [DSMHRI CD-882(9): 12]

This figure shows that the number of graduates annually was stable at between 30 to 35 officers after 1974.

Table 7.5 shows a comparison of the number of officers, by rank, who were promoted during an 18-month period in the second half of the 1960s and during a period of the same length in the middle of the 1980s. The available data for the two periods is different, so the comparison is not necessarily exact, but these figures do show that the number of officers promoted to lieutenant colonel in the earlier period and those promoted to colonel in the later one were nearly the same as the number of officers who completed the Command and General Staff College during each of those periods. Although the rank in the later period is one higher than in the period earlier, due to the gradual expansion of the officer corps, it can be inferred from the above correlation that the number of officers promoted to colonel or above was strictly controlled from the middle of the 1970s even under Ne Win's regime.

In general, refraining from excessive promotions is crucial for maintaining stability in the bureaucracy even in an environment where the military decides its own personnel policy. However, if promotions are too limited, resentment will develop among junior officers over the lack of opportunities for advancement.[62] At least two conditions are required to avoid this: one is the smooth retirement of aging officers; the other is the institutionalization, formally or informally, of career paths. In Burma the smooth retirement of officers was accomplished by moving people from the tatmadaw to the BSPP, to the People's Parliament and the People's Councils, and to the government ministries.

[62] One typical case is the 16 May 1961 military coup that occurred in South Korea.

This smooth retirement helped create the paths of promotion in the tatmadaw. Once the promotion paths became established, an officer was able to predict his own future and could anticipate both the negative and positive prospects. The negative prospect was the end of promotions. But a transfer out to an external organization into a position more or less commensurate with his military rank alleviated an officer's dissatisfaction. In the case of a disgruntled officer, a transfer out stripped him of the means (weapons, manpower, command position) to rebel or otherwise challenge his superiors. On the other hand, the positive prospect was continued promotion. Fixed promotion paths tend to make an officer's orientation and behavior more conservative, as a political change could likely harm his future prospects. Therefore, stable career paths that gave people predictability about their future was essential for maintaining the status quo of Burma's military rule.

These career paths for tatmadaw officers will be analyzed here. The analysis relies on data that the author gathered from the "Compiled Military Appointment Letters" for the years from 1977 to 1987 held in the Defence Services Museum and Historical Research Institute. Supposing there have been no omissions, it is possible to know the appointments, transfers and retirement of all officers during the relevant 11-year period. Considering the Burmese government's sensitivity about the outflow of internal information, this kind of data is extremely valuable.[63]

Three premises apply to the analysis. First, an officer's appointment as an infantry battalion commander is regarded as the starting point of competition for promotion in the Army. An officer's career began at the time of his graduation from the DSA or OTS when, in many cases, he was attached to an infantry battalion as a second lieutenant. After having some ten to fifteen years of experience in combat operations, and then being appointed an infantry battalion commander as a major or lieutenant colonel, competition for promotion started in earnest. Second, in this analysis, appointment as a commander of a military region is regarded as the terminal position in the competition for promotion. Above this position were those of Vice-Chief of General Staff (Army) and Chief of General Staff of the tatmadaw, but promotion to these two highest

[63] Nevertheless, this material is for no more than an 11-year period. A military career runs for nearly 40 years assuming a normal pattern from appointment until retirement, so information for an 11-year period alone may be far from sufficient. An analysis of personnel transfers over a longer period is desired in the years to come.

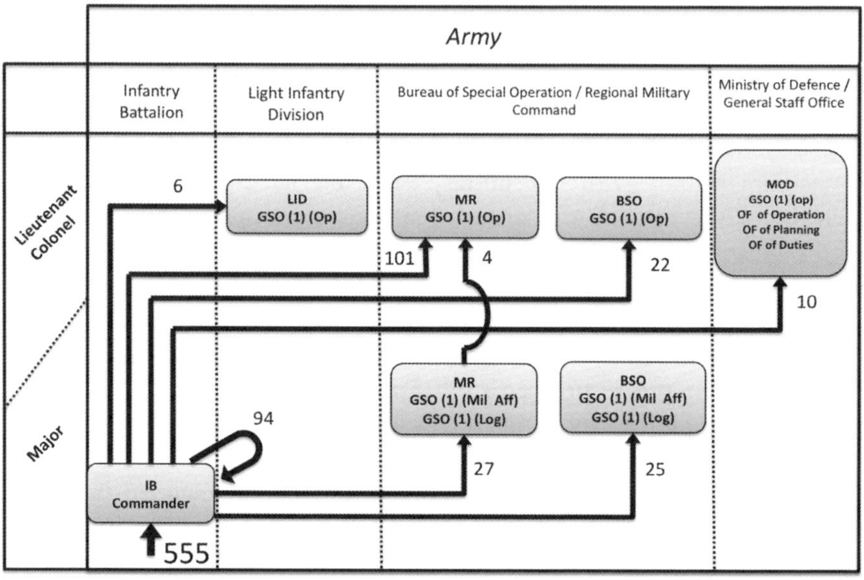

Source: [DSMHRI DR-8380][DSMHRI DR-8381][DSMHRI DR-8382][DSMHRI DR-8383][DSMHRI DR-8384][DSMHRI DR-8385][DSMHRI DR-8386][DSMHRI DR-8387][DSMHRI DR-8388][DSMHRI DR-8389][DSMHRI DR-8390][DSMHRI DR-8391][DSMHRI DR-8392][DSMHRI DR-8502][DSMHRI DR-8503][DSMHRI DR-8504][DSMHRI DR-8506][DSMHRI DR-8514][DSMHRI DR08515][DSMHRI DR-8566][DSMHRI DR8600][DSMHRI DR-8601][DSMHRI DR8602]

Figure 7.19 Promotion Path of Infantry Battalion Commanders (1977–87)

positions in the tatmadaw went only to senior officers who had experience as regional commanders. There was no other path of promotion into these two positions. Therefore, when examining the careers of the top military elite, it is important to understand the paths of promotion to becoming the commander of a military region. The third premise is that the course of an officer's career passed through four parts of the military system: the MOD/General Staff Office (Army), regional command, light infantry division command, infantry battalion command. Although there were exceptional cases in which an officer would move on to diplomatic missions abroad as a military attaché, or an officer would return to an important post in the tatmadaw after having been in the BSPP, these exceptions were too few to affect the third premise.

Figures 7.19 through 7.23 describe five possible promotion paths for officers between 1977 and 1987. Figure 7.19 describes the path for infantry battalion commanders, Figure 7.20 for General Staff Officer 1 (operations), Figure 7.21 for strategy directors of regional commands and for tactical directors of light infantry divisions, Figure 7.22 for deputy

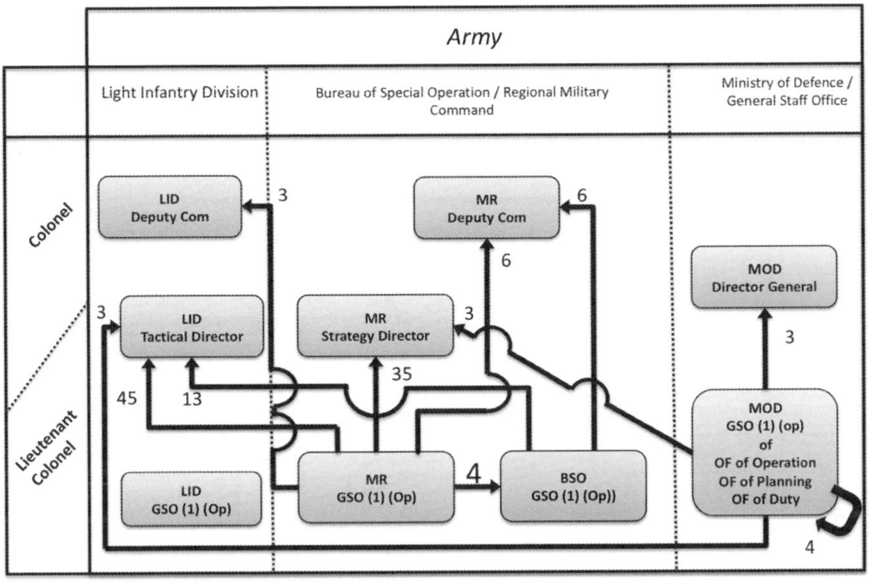

Source: See Figure 7.19

Figure 7.20 Promotion Path GSO1 (Operation) (1977–87)

commanders of military regions or light infantry divisions, Figure 7.23 for commanders of light infantry divisions. The numbers indicate how many promotions were awarded in the directions indicated by the arrows.

Looking first at Figure 7.19 describing the promotion paths for infantry battalion commanders, the figure shows the paths and the numbers promoted, including cases where an infantry battalion commander assumed the command of another infantry battalion. The most frequent promotion was to positions of GSO1 (operations) of regional commands, with 101 people promoted to that position. Although 27 commanders moved up to positions of GSO1 (administration) and GSO1 (logistics) in regional commands, and 25 moved up to the same positions in the Bureau of Special Operations (BSO); there were only four cases of promotions from GSO1 (administration) or GSO1 (logistics) in regional commands. This figure suggests that the first hurdle for battalion commanders was getting promoted to GSO1 (operations) of a light infantry division, a regional command, the BSO, or the three offices (operations, planning, and duties) of the MOD. Deviation from these paths made it almost impossible to rise to a higher position.

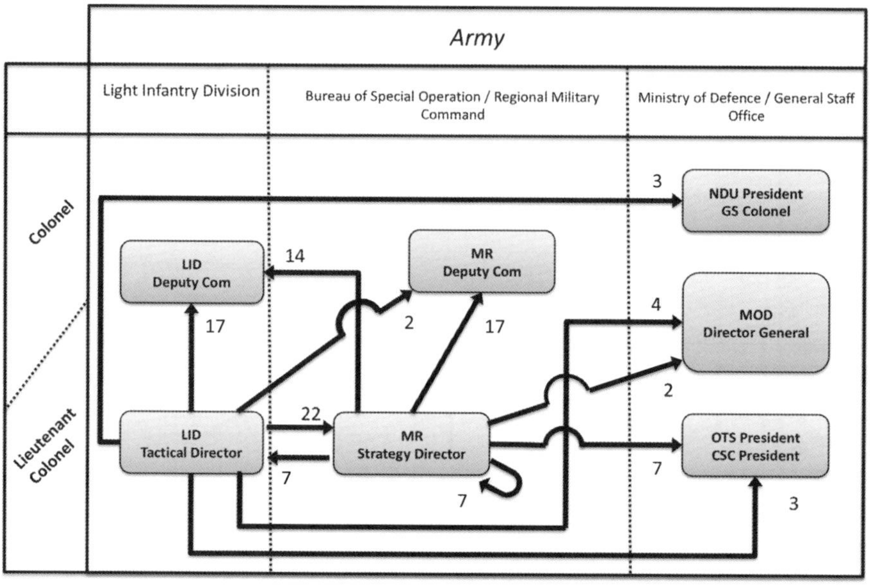

Source: See Figure 7.19

Figure 7.21 Promotion Path of MR Strategy Director and LID Tactics Director (1977–87)

Looking next at Figure 7.20 showing the promotion paths for GSO1 (operations) officers, it shows that there were no promotions from the GSO1 (operations) of light infantry divisions. It also shows that excluding promotions from the GSO1 (operations) of the BSO to tactical directors of infantry divisions, there were less than ten promotions from the GSO1 (operations) of infantry divisions. This suggests that promotion from commander of an infantry battalion to the GSO1 (operations) of a regional command was most advantageous for the next step in promotion. The figure shows two main paths of promotion from GSO1 (operations). One was to tactical director of a light infantry division; the other was to strategy director of a regional command. Although there were more strategy director posts, there were ten more promotions up the latter path, one reason being that the average tour of duty of a tactical director was shorter.

Figure 7.21, describing the promotion paths for strategy directors of regional commands and tactical directors of light infantry divisions, shows that there were a variety of promotion paths, but the cases of multiple paths are important. This is the case with tactical directors

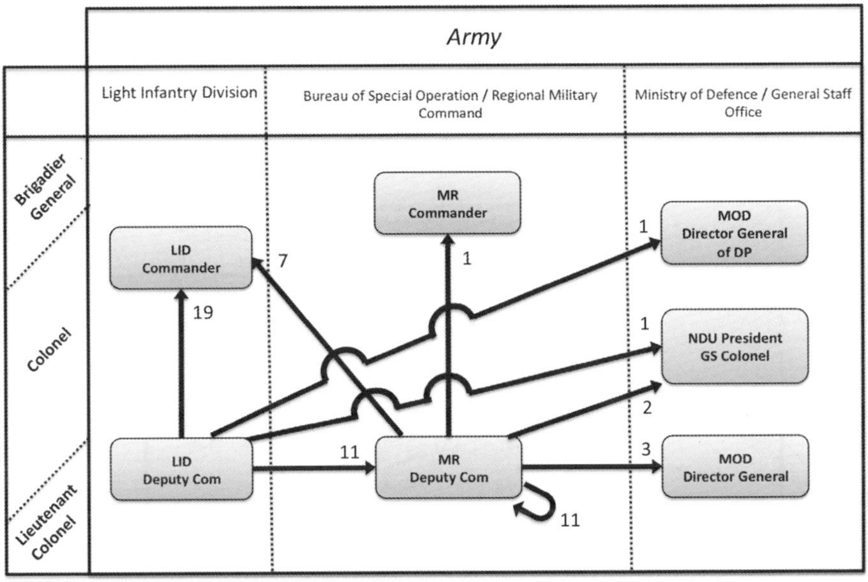

Source: See Figure 7.19

Figure 7.22 Promotion Path of RMC Dy-Commander and LID Dy-Commander (1977–87)

being promoted to strategy directors, tactical and strategy directors being promoted to deputy commanders of light infantry divisions, and strategy directors being promoted to deputy commanders of military regions. The most promotions were to deputy commander of a light infantry division. If at this point an officer moved up to become a director in the General Staff Office (Army) or became the principal of a military training school, he never got back on the promotion path to regional commander. It could be said that promotion to deputy commander of a light infantry division or of a military region was fairly advantageous. Even among those who moved over to the MOD and the Vice-Chief of General Staff (Army), the officer who became the head of the National Defence University or the General Staff Colonel still retained the possibility of promotion in the area of operations.

Figure 7.22 lays out the promotion paths for deputy commanders of light infantry divisions and military regions. It shows that a single officer only was promoted from deputy regional commander to regional commander. In this unique case, Myoe Nyunt, the deputy commander of the Rangoon Military Region assumed command of the same region on

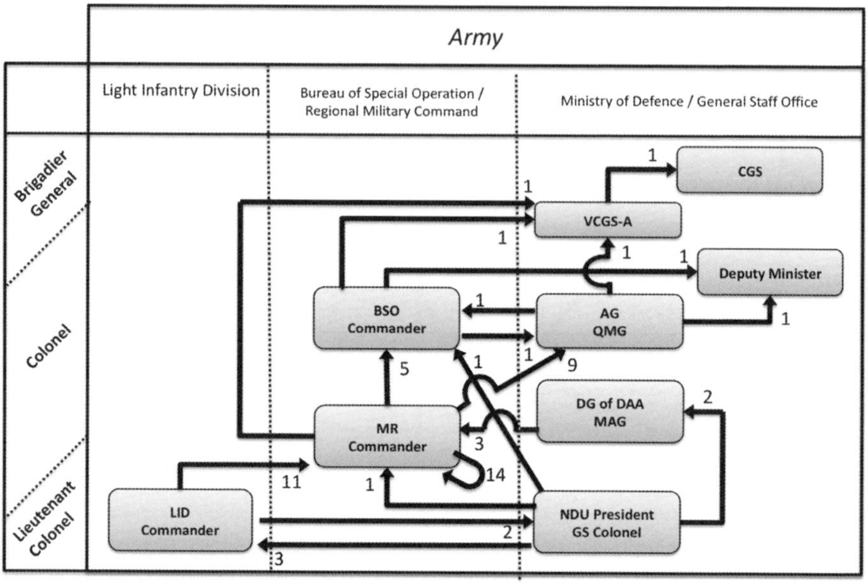

Source: See Figure 7.19

Figure 7.23 Promotion Path of LID Commanders and Others (1977–87)

4 November 1985. Usually it was necessary to serve as the commander of an light infantry division if an officer expected to become a regional commander, regardless of the paths his career had followed up to that time. Moreover, there were 12 more cases of deputy commanders of light infantry divisions being promoted to commanders of such divisions than were promoted from deputy commanders of military regions to commanders of light infantry divisions. This suggests that it was more likely for deputy regional commanders to have their promotions stopped than for deputy commanders of light infantry divisions.

Finally, Figure 7.23 describing the promotion paths to the position of regional commander and to posts thereafter, the largest number of officers, 11, became regional commanders from postings as commanders of light infantry divisions. Three people moved up from directors in the MOD, two in 1978, and one in 1979, but there were no such promotions in the 1980s. This suggests that promotion from commander of a light infantry division to regional commander became established in the 1980s. The single instance of the head of the National Defence University assuming the command of a military region was one in which the officer already had experience as a commander of a light infantry division. If an officer had not experienced being the commander of such a division, he could not expect promotion to higher positions, namely, commander of the BSO, the adjutant general and quartermaster general, deputy minister of the MOD, Vice-Chief of General Staff (Army), and Chief of General Staff of the tatmadaw. The only exceptional promotion was from head of the National Defence University to commander of the BSO. This occurred when the bureau was first organized and began functioning officially on 8 May 1978. No similar promotion occurred thereafter.

The implication from the evidence presented in Figure 7.23 is that by the late 1970s, the paths of promotion to the top echelon of the tatmadaw had become informally institutionalized with the conduit to these high-level posts passing through the position of light infantry division commander (there being not a single exception from 1980 until the end of the data in 1987). The promotion paths of lower-ranking officers described in Figures 7.19 to 7.23 indicate the paths that were advantageous for becoming a light infantry division commander, the most advantageous being promotion to deputy commander of such a division.

In order to confirm the above analysis, the author drew up Table 7.6 showing the positions held in the 1980s by officers who became regional commanders. Of 17 such commanders, 14 had been commanders of light infantry divisions. This suggests that those who had experience as a deputy commander of a light infantry division were more likely to be promoted to regional commander. Although about half of them had experienced working in the defence ministry and the General Staff Office, all of them also had been a deputy commander of a military region or a light infantry division, except for Pe Myain, who became commander of the Southeastern Military Region after having headed the National Defence University. This demonstrates again that experience as a field commander was crucially important for promotion.

The above analysis of career paths indicates that these became institutionalized over the course of the 1970s. In addition, two other factors contributed to transforming the tatmadaw into a modern bureaucracy in the Weberian sense. The first was the regular reshuffle of officers, and the other was promotion accompanied by spatial transfers. For example, of 16 regional commanders, only three (Phoung Myint, Aye Thaung and L. Kun Hpan) had served as the commander of a light infantry division that was in the military region he was assigned to command. These factors kept regional commanders from becoming warlord-type commanders rather than bureaucratic commanders.

Table 7.6 Military Region Commanders and the Positions They Previously Held (1980–87)

Present Positions		*Past Positions*			
Name	*Commander MR*	*Commander LID*	*Deputy Commander MR*	*Deputy Commander LID*	*Ministry of Defence*
Than Shwe	Southwestern	LID-88 (Magway)		LID-88	Assistant Director of Operations Bureau
Myint Aung	Southwestern	LID-44 (Thaton)	Northwestern	LID-88/55	Assistant Director of Operations Bureau
Mya Thein	Western	LID-44 (Thaton)	Southeastern		
Soe Myint	Western		Northeastern		Director of DPMPR
Tun Kyi	Northwestern	LID-88 (Magway)		LID-88	
Phone Myint	Central	LID-55 (Sagaing)		LID-66	
Aye Thaung	Central	LID-66 (Pyi)	Northeastern		
Pe Myain	Southeastern			LID-77	President of the National Defence College
Nyan Lin	Southeastern	LID-99 (Meikhtila)		LID-99	
Hla Maw	Eastern	LID-77 (Pegu)			CGS
Chit Swe	Northeastern	LID-77 (Pegu)	Eastern		Assistant Director of Operations Bureau
Sein Aung	Northeastern	LID-77 (Pegu)	Northwestern		CGS
Tun Shwe	Northeastern	LID-55 (Sagaing)		LID-55	
Maung Aye	Northeastern	LID-77 (Pegu)		LID-77	Director of DP
L. Kun Phan	Northern	LID-88 (Meikhtila)		LID-88	
Kyaw Ba	Northern	LID-99 (Sagaing)		LID-99	
Myo Nyunt	Yangon		Rangoon		

Note: LID: Light Infantry Division, CGS: Colonel General Staff

Source: Mya Win. *ta'madaw gaunzaun mya thamain akyinkyou' 1941 khuhni' hma 1990 pyihni' ahti.*; see Figure 7.19

Inner Circle and "Divide and Rule"

Ne Win placed his aides in the most important posts in the tatmadaw for longer durations. General San Yu, a Ne Win aide since the time of the Japanese occupation and his most trusted confidant, served as Vice-Chief of General Staff (Army) for nearly a decade from 1963 to 1972, and then as Chief of General Staff of the tatmadaw for two years before retiring in 1974. He was followed by Major General Tin Oo who took over as Chief of General Staff at the young age of 47. Tin Oo was a graduate of the third class in the officer training school during the Japanese occupation, and after the war he was appointed a second lieutenant in the newly organized tatmadaw. This made him more a part of the older generation than the new, but he was among the youngest of the older generation.[64] However, Tin Oo was dismissed and arrested in March 1976 only two years after his appointment as Chief of General Staff due to the reason which still remains unclear.

Tin Oo's successor was Major General Kyaw Htin, who had been Ne Win's subordinate in the Fourth Burma Rifles Battalion, which Ne Win was commanding at the time of independence. Kyaw Htin served for some 3,500 days (nearly 10 years) as Chief of General Staff of the tatmadaw, until 3 October 1985. Ne Win appointed Major General Aye Ko as Vice-Chief of General Staff (Army); he remained in that post for nearly 2,000 days (close to 5.5 years), until 1981.[65] Since he had also been an officer of the Fourth Burma Rifles, this led to a popular account that the tatmadaw was under control of the Fourth Burma Rifles Battalion network. During the same period, Major General Chit Hlaing

[64] In 1951 he became an infantry battalion commander and demonstrated success in combat against the Chinese Nationalist army. Thereafter his promotion was extremely rapid. In 1963, at only 36 years old, he was appointed a regional commander, and from 1964 he served for nearly seven and a half years as commander of the Central Military Region in Pegu Yoma, where the Burma Communist Party was particularly active. A highly successful commander in the war against the insurgents, Tin Oo's appointment to Chief of General Staff of the tatmadaw at such a young age could be construed as resulting from Ne Win's awareness of a generational change taking place in the tatmadaw.

[65] Both officers had served as Yangon Military Region commander in addition to being from the Fourth Burma Rifles. The main duty of the Yangon Regional Command has always been defense of the capital rather than suppression of anti-government insurgents. Thus the officers Ne Win put in charge of this command were people that he trusted.

Table 7.7 Length of Time as a MR/LID Commander (1970–88)*

Command Positions	*No. of Commanders*	*Length of Time (days)*
Northern MR	6 (6)	807.5
Northwestern MR	10 (9)	599.1
Eastern MR	5 (5)	1,129.8
Southeastern MR	6 (4)	1,259.8
Yangon MR	6 (4)	1,303.3
Southwestern MR	7 (6)	737.7
Western MR	5 (4)	1,007.0
Northwestern MR	5 (5)	1,193.4
Central MR	7 (6)	810.7
LID-33	1 (1)	372.0
LID-44	2 (2)	1,211.0
LID-55	3 (2)	1,211.0
LID-66	4 (3)	1,122.7
LID-77	10 (7)	776.3
LID-88	10 (7)	609.9
LID-99	10 (5)	858.2

Note: * This table does not include MR/LID commanders appointed from 18 Sep 1988 onward. The number in parentheses indicates the number of commanders whose length of time available in the data.

Source: See Table 7.6

served as Vice-Chief of General Staff (Navy) for 2,413 days (more than 6.5 years), and Major General Saw Pru, Vice-Chief of General Staff (Air Force), served for 2,202 days (nearly six years).

Under his regime Ne Win developed a combination of informally having his close aides hold top tatmadaw posts for long periods while reshuffling lower echelon officers at regular intervals. Table 7.7 shows the average number of days that commanders of military regions and light infantry divisions served in their posts. The longest posting among regional commanders was 1,303 days (over 3.5 years) in the Rangoon Military Region, while in most of the other regions replacements usually took place every two or three years. However, in the Northern Military Region in charge of Kachin State, the Northeastern Military Region charged with northern Shan State, the Southwestern Military Region responsible fro the Irrawaddy Delta, and the Central Military Region in charge of Pegu Yoma, commanders' tours of duty were two years or less. Those in assignments below commander of a region or a light infantry

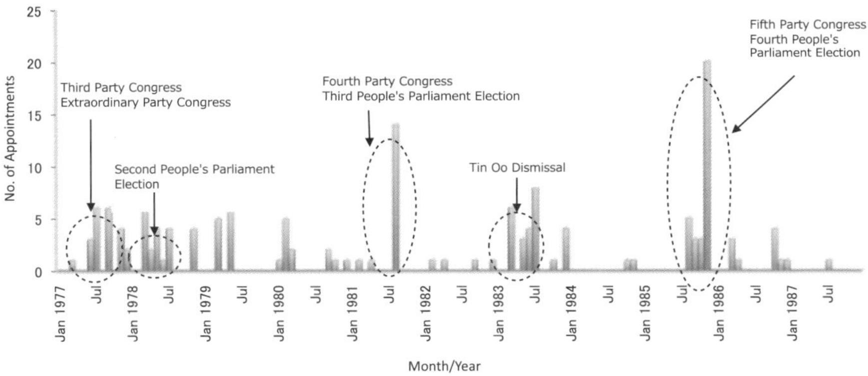

Source: See Figure 7.20

Figure 7.24 Number of Semi-annual Appointments to the Highest Tatmadaw Posts

division were reassigned even more often, so lower echelon officers were constantly being moved around the country.

Ne Win was able to achieve this combination of maintaining his closest aides in the highest tatmadaw posts for a long time while regularly reshuffling other senior officers largely because of the system of seconding these officers at the time of their retirement to sufficiently satisfying posts outside of the tatmadaw. These were senior positions in the BSPP, positions as cabinet ministers and deputy ministers, and as members of the Council of State, the Council of People's Judges, the Council of People's Attorneys, and the Council of People's Inspectors. Figure 7.24 shows the number of semi-annual appointments between 1977 and 1987 to the highest tatmadaw posts.[66] This clearly indicates that the waves of personnel reshuffles among military leaders overlapped with BSPP party congresses and People's Parliament elections, with the exception of the reshuffle in 1983, which followed the dismissal of Tin Oo and his clique. This means that the many retiring senior officers at the time of these reshuffles moved over to become party leaders at every BSPP party congress or moved into senior staff positions in ministries at every People's Parliament election (or into local People's Councils in elections held at the same time). Then the vacant positions they left in

[66] These included the Chief of General Staff of the tatmadaw, Vice-Chief of General Staff of the three armed services, directors in the Ministry of Defence, commander of the BSO, commanders of military regions, and commanders of light infantry divisions.

the tatmadaw was filled by the appointment of new officers to those positions. Of course, this is not to argue that elections under the Ne Win regime were held solely for the purpose of moving retiring officers out of the tatmadaw and into other state organizations. They were also held to give the regime's rule a semblance of legitimacy. Nevertheless, one of the functions of elections came to be facilitating the smooth reshuffle of personnel within as well as their exit from the tatmadaw. As each beat of the heart pumps blood through the whole body, each election regularly sent military officers off to different organizations of the state. This quasi-institutionalized system contributed greatly to the stability of the Ne Win regime in the first half of the 1980s after the turmoil of the late 1970s.

However, in the early 1980s, most officers of the first generation were already out of the tatmadaw, and the rise of a new generation and generational change in tatmadaw leadership were imminent. General Kyaw Htin, Chief of General Staff, was born in 1924 and General Aye Ko, Vice-Chief of General Staff (Army), in 1921. Both would reach the retirement age of 60 years old in the early 1980s. After the exit of his trusted aids from the top of the tatmadaw, how was Ne Win to control the tatmadaw? His answer was "divide and rule."

In general there are diverse mechanisms behind the formation of factions within a military. One of the most important is the unity formed among officers who were in the same class in the military academy.[67] Cadets in the same class bond together because of their shared experience of prolonged, arduous training during their days in the academy. During Ne Win's regime, Burma had two institutions for training officers, the OTS and the DSA. The training period at the OTS being less than a year was too short to foster strong unity among cadets in the same class. Added to this weakness was an informal rule that came into effect from the end of the 1970s of not having officers from the same graduating class occupy important posts at the same time. This is shown in Table 7.8. It is immediately clear that the distribution of graduates in the same class became more dispersed over time after 1977.

As of 1 April 1977, the top posts in the MOD and the General Staff Office (Army) were held by first generation officers, while officers in command of military regions or light infantry divisions were concentrated in particular OTS classes, such as five officers from the 6th class

[67] Yoshifumi Tamada, *Myths and Realities: The Democratization of Thai Politics* (Kyoto & Melbourne: Kyoto University Press and Trans Pacific Press, 2008), pp. 69–74.

Table 7.8 Number of Appointments in Army High Command by Cadet Cohort from BDA, OTS, and DSA

Day/Month/ Year	*1 April 1977*		*1 April 1978*		*1 April 1979*		*1 April 1980*		*1 April 1981*		*1 April 1982*		*1 April 1983*		*1 April 1984*		*1 April 1985*		*1 April 1986*		*1 April 1987*		*1 April 1988*	
Cadet Cohort	*FC**	*MOD*	*FC*	*MOD*	*FC*	*MOD*	*FC*	*MOD*	*FC*	*MOD*	*FC*	*MOD*	*FC*	*MOD*	*FC*	*MOD*	*FC*	*MOD*	*FC*	*MOD*	*FC*	*MOD*	*FC*	*MOD*
BDA	1	3	1	2		1	1	1	1	1	1	1	1	1		1		1						
OTS-3 (1950)	2		1		2		2		2		1		1			1		1						
OTS-4 (1951)			1		2		1	1	1	1	1	1	1		1		1							
OTS-5 (1952)																								
OTS-6 (1952)	5	1	3	3	4	2	4	1	4	1	1	2	1	2	1	1	1	1		1		1		1
OTS-7 (1952)	5	1	4		3	1	3	1	3	1	4		4		3	1	3	1		1		1		1
OTS-8 (1952)			1		1		1		1		1		1		1		1		1		1		1	
OTS-9 (1953)			1		2		4		4		4		4		4		4		1	2	1	2	1	2
OTS-10 (1953)						1		1		1	1		1		1		1		1		1		1	
OTS-11 (1954)		1	1	1	1	1	1	1	1	1	1	1		2										
OTS-12 (1954)															1		1		2		2		2	
OTS-13 (1955)											1		1		1		1		1		1		1	
OTS-14 (1956)																			1		1		1	
OTS-15 (1955)																								
OTS-16 (1957)																								
OTS-17 (1957)																								
OTS-18 (1958)																			2		2		2	
OTS-19 (1958)															1		1		1		1		1	
OTS-20 (1958)																	1							
DSA-1 (1959)											1	1	2		3		3		4		3		3	
OTS-21 (1959)																			2		2		2	
OTS-22 (1959)														1		1		1	1	1	1	1	1	1
OTS-23 (1959)																								
OTS-24 (1960)																								
DSA-2 (1960)																								
OTS-25 (1960)																1		1		1		1		1
OTS-26 (1960)																					1		1	
OTS-27 (1960)																			1		1		1	
Total	13	6	13	6	15	6	17	6	17	6	17	6	17	6	17	6	18	6	18	6	18	6	18	6

Notes: FC stands for field commanders that include commanders of military regions and light infantry divisions. MOD stands for Ministry of Defence that include posts of Chief of General Staff of the tatmadaw, Vice-Chief of General Staff of three services, Quartermaster General, Adjutant Genearl, Colonel General Staff, Director of Directorate of Military Intelligence

Source: See Figure 7.19, and *The Union of Burma Gazette*

and five from the 7th class. In 1978 and 1979 first generation officers decreased, with people from the 8th, 9th, 10th, and 11th OTS classes becoming regional commanders. The next significant change took place in April 1981 with the reshuffle of tatmadaw officers associated with the Fourth Party Congress and the election for the Third People's Parliament held that year when officers of the 1st DSA class began receiving appointments as regional commanders and to important positions in the General Staff Office. OTS graduates from the 15th, 16th and 17th classes were skipped over, and officers of the 19th class and later began to take up regional commands. On 1 April 1986, the last officers of the first generation finally disappeared from the tatmadaw. As of 1 January 1988, the 18 regional commander positions were distributed among officers from 12 different OTS classes, and the six important posts of the General Staff Office were held by officers from five different classes.

A generational change had taken place in these reshuffles transitioning from the first generation mobilized under the Japanese military to a new generation. The transition began when Lieutenant General Saw Maung became Vice-Chief of General Staff (Army) in July 1983, and was completed with the major personnel reshuffle that became effective on 4 November 1985, at which time Saw Maung took charge as Chief of General Staff of the tatmadaw. Excluding him, all of the other officers of the 6th OTS class and earlier were moved out of the tatmadaw. Other new generation officers who moved into top positions were Brigadier General Hpe Myaing (7th OTS class), promoted from Rangoon regional commander to Adjutant General, and Brigadier General Phoung Myint (9th OTS class), promoted from Central regional commander to quartermaster general. In that same year, officers in 16 of the 18 posts of regional commander and eight light infantry division commanders were reshuffled. As a result, commanding officers in the 4th, 6th, and 7th OTS classes were moved out to the BSPP and other positions in the government administration as younger officer from the 18th and 21st classes took over their posts. This was the first time in the history of the tatmadaw that such a sweeping personnel reshuffle had taken place, with the exception of the time when Maung Maung and 10 other top ranking officers dismissed in 1961.

Conclusion

The tatmadaw was the power base of and, at the same time, a threat to Ne Win's dictatorship. In order to maintain his power, he had to create an organizational structure that would facilitate his control over the tatmadaw yet prevent officers from becoming too dissatisfied. Ne Win adopted two basic policies for the purpose. The first was institutional control over the tatmadaw by the BSPP; the second was the development of informal personnel rules that led to "divide and rule." Using these two approaches plus providing retiring officers with positions in the BSPP and civilian ministries, Ne Win by and large succeeded in controlling the tatmadaw.

One step in the institutionalization of the BSPP's control was to reconceptualise the tatmadaw as a people's military, and this concept was coupled with a doctrine of people's war, whereby the tatmadaw's counter-insurgency struggle against the anti-government forces became a war demanding the participation of all the people. Both of these underpinned the self-image that the tatmadaw portrayed to the people, an image showing soldiers as protectors of all the peoples of Burma and involved in their daily livelihoods. The 1974 Constitution gave party control a statutory foundation. It gave the BSPP control over the tatmadaw high command and over its budget and personnel, and this in effect gave Ne Win as president of the BSPP institutional control over the tatmadaw. Party committees were formed within the tatmadaw made up of officers who were party members. Thereafter education committees were set up to instruct tatmadaw personnel in the party's ideology.

Along with this institutional control, Ne Win developed a system of promotion for military officers that over time became informally institutionalized. It had extremely restricted paths of promotion centered on operations officers, and the many officers who lost out in the competition for promotion were quickly moved out of the tatmadaw to positions in the BSPP, People's Parliament, and government administration. This system continually opened the way for younger officers to move up the ranks thereby alleviating the frustration that could arise from the lack of opportunity for advancement. This distribution of posts inside and outside the tatmadaw allowed Ne Win to maintain control of it. But not included in this system were a hand full of Ne Win's close aides from the period of Japanese military rule who held the most important posts in the tatmadaw.

As the 1970s progressed and the 1980s came, the tatmadaw underwent a generational change in leadership. A new generation of officers moved into high posts, a generation that had not experienced the time of Japanese rule and the struggle for independence. Not personally connected to this new generation and to deter the formation of factions among these younger offices that could evolve into a threat to his control, Ne Win developed a system of "divide and rule" whereby officers who graduated from different military academy classes were mixed among the commands. This was to prevent officers who had been together in the same class at the academy from becoming concentrated in a few places, a situation conducive to faction forming.

By means of these formally and informally institutionalized methods, and utilizing enhanced surveillance through his intelligence organizations, Ne Win maintained his regime and control over the tatmadaw. But his system for maintaining power greatly changed the relationship between the state and the tatmadaw, and his control was never perfect. The BSPP was not as autonomous an organization as the communist parties in socialist states. It was mostly the tatmadaw's party whose leadership was held by retired military officers on one hand, and relied on Ne Win's dictatorial leadership on the other. In such circumstances, it was extremely difficult for the party to control the military's routine activities, and were Ne Win's leadership to be called into question, the BSPP would promptly lose its ability to control the tatmadaw. This is what happened in 1988 when a huge popular protest movement broke out against Ne Win's rule.

CHAPTER 8

Conclusion: The End of Revolution

During the Ne Win regime's two-and-a-half-decade rule, the tatmadaw greatly expanded its political role. The author has argued that this expansion created the basic mechanisms for the tatmadaw to maintain its political influence over the state. Despite its strength, the Ne Win regime collapsed in 1988 and the renewed military rule led by the State Law and Order Restoration Council (SLORC) took control. Many people consider that Ne Win's "Burmese way to socialism" fell with him. It is true that the formal institutions that had supported Ne Win's rule, such as the 1974 Constitution, the Burma Socialist Programme Party (BSPP)'s guidance and the country's socialist economic system were abolished, but what makes the collapse of the regime difficult to understand is the fact that the tatmadaw rather than the citizenry put an end to it. We could simply discount the crisis as a failure of democratization; but that does not address the durability of the tatmadaw's political power because a failure of democratization does not explain sufficiently the differences between Ne Win's regime and that of the SLORC. Although ended, Ne Win's political project must have left some legacies to its successor.

This chapter will reconsider the political significance of the 1988 crisis, seeing it as an intra-regime transition. By doing so, the author will show that the large-scale anti-government movement that broke out in 1988 leading to the collapse of the regime and the coup d'état on 18 September of that year paved the way for a sweeping change of political leadership that was on the verge of stagnation, along with a separation of the BSPP from the state, thereby causing a generational change in the state leadership and an overhaul of the military regime.

This chapter will first examine this irony of history in that an anti-government movement calling for democracy contributed to the continuation of Burma's military regime. It will then return to and answer the research question posed in Chapter 1: Why has the military regime in Burma been able to maintain its political power for 50 years?

Reconsidering a Regime Collapse

The collapse of the Ne Win regime can be divided roughly into three phases. The first was a series of attempts at reform during which Ne Win admitted the mismanagement over the years and decided to change the regime's socialist policy. On 10 August 1987 at an urgently convened meeting with members of the BSPP Central Executive Committee (CEC) and Council of State (CS) leaders, Ne Win told the meeting that he had come to see that the leaders around him had not correctly reported the severity of the situation facing the country, and therefore he was announcing a reform policy that included amending the constitution.

The deteriorating economic conditions in the 1980s were behind these moves. Rice production had fallen after peaking in the early 1980s, and it was becoming more difficult to maintain compulsory procurements. Stronger government controls weakened farmer incentive, so production stagnated. Rice exports fell from 870 thousand tons in 1983 to 600 thousand tons in 1986.[1] Along with declining rice production, the performance of state enterprises deteriorated in the 1980s, causing bad loans to accumulate in the state-run banks. The investment funds provided by these banks had come from international aid that had expanded after the First Donors Conference for Burma in 1976, so their accumulating bad loans caused the Burmese government's foreign debt to swell and put pressure on the state's finances. On 1 September 1987 the government issued an official notice (No. 6/87), which finally abolished compulsory procurements. It also decided to liberalize trading in nine agricultural products including unprocessed rice.

Such easing of controls brought into question the very foundation of the economic system, but Ne Win attributed the cause of the past mismanagement to his aides' inaccurate reports, suggesting that his power base in the government was firm. In his opinion, the responsibility lay completely with his aides and other people surrounding him; it was as if his own responsibility, as the man who was supposed to have been chief executive, had simply vanished. On 5 September Ne Win suddenly

---

[1] Akio Takahashi, *Biruma Deruta no Beisakuson: "Shakaishugi" Taisei-ka no Noson Keizai* [Rice-growing villages in the Irrawaddy Delta: study of a socialist rural economy] (Tokyo: Ajia Keizai Shuppankai, 1992), p. 305.

announced the abolition of the 75-, 35-, and 25-kyat banknotes, in order to "punish" merchants who were gaining "undue" profits and also to cut funds circulating in the black market. While such demonetization had been executed before, in May 1964 and November 1985, this time the abolition was declared suddenly without a grace period during which to submit the relevant banknotes to a bank or exchange them for other bills.

In an interview with a person who had been a party CEC member at that time and with another who had been a member of the party's Finance and State Planning Committee, the author was told that the demonetization measure was determined with but a word from Ne Win.[2] Few people involved in economic policy making in Burma thought the abolition of large denomination notes would be effective for policy purposes, i.e., punishing the merchants; and while it could have some temporary effect toward correcting national income disparity and reducing rebel funding, it would also damage ordinary people. But everyone knew never to take issue with the president of the party. The order went out to begin demonetization immediately, and the disorder it caused instantly heightened the people's distrust of the government.

The second phase of the regime's collapse was expanding social and economic crises that Ne Win's decreed reforms did nothing to curtail. The abolition of compulsory procurements and the liberalization of trade in farm products led to abolition of the rationing system, which had supported the low and stable prices of basic consumption goods. Rapid inflation developed in urban areas along with speculation by wholesalers. People's discontent grew, and a fight among students in March 1988 at the Rangoon University of Technology erupted into a conflict between the students and the police as demonstrations expanded to Rangoon University. The government's hard-line crackdown against demonstrators resulted in a large number of casualties, the worst occurring in the Dada Phyu Incident,[3] and a spreading chain reaction of resistance ensued. A letter criticizing Ne Win, written by Aung Gyi, former Vice-Chief of General Staff (Army), began to circulate as demonstrations spread to

[2] Interview with a former party CEC member on 29 November 2004, and with a former party affairs committee member on 20 January 2005.

[3] The Dada Phyu Incident occurred when a crowd of student demonstrators was driven into Inya Lake near the Rangoon Arts and Sciences University by security forces on 16 March. Many of the students drowned or died from other causes.

other regions. On 22 July the government declared martial law in Prome in Pegu Division.

On 23 July, Ne Win convened an extraordinary party congress. In his opening speech he announced his resignation as chairman of the BSPP and proposed a referendum on the pros and cons of a multiparty system. This announcement took almost everyone in the BSPP by surprise. The congress voted down the holding of a referendum; then on the 26th it elected Vice Chairman Sein Lwin as the new chairman of the BSPP. The following day he was also appointed the new state president at an emergency congress of the People's Parliament. At that same meeting, Kyaw Htin, a deputy prime minister and minister of defence, was made the secretary-general of the Council of State, and Tun Tin, another deputy prime minister, was appointed as the new prime minister replacing Maung Maung Kha who had been in the post since 1977. These men were Ne Win aides, so although Ne Win's resignation itself was a big shock, the impact of the reshuffle was limited, and the people knew that the government had not actually changed. Particularly Sein Lwin, the newly-appointed party chairman, was known as the commander who in 1962 had ordered his troops to shoot students holding a protest rally at Rangoon University and then ordering the destruction of the university's student union office. The people knew that he took a consistently hard-line stance against movements for democracy and supported their suppression. But the anti-government movement continued to escalate energized by its success in forcing Ne Win's resignation, and Sein Lwin's appointment did not slacken the momentum.

The third phase of collapse was deepening socio-economic crisis coupled now with political crisis. Sein Lwin declared a state of martial law in Rangoon on 3 August in response to the expanding protest movement; however it showed no sign of abating as demonstrations of over ten thousand people took place day after day. The demonstrations spread to regional cities like Pegu and Mandalay, becoming a major movement involving Buddhist monks and citizens in addition to students. On 8 August 1988 more than one hundred thousand people joined a nationwide demonstration and a general strike. At first the deployed troops limited their response to warning shots, but as the movement became increasingly more violent, they aimed and shot directly at the crowds of demonstrators resulting in many casualties and arrests.[4] The indefinite

[4] According to figures announced by the government, from the 9 August through 11 August, 53 people were killed, 196 were injured, and 1,564 were arrested.

closure of all educational institutions declared the next day did not bring the situation under control. Sein Lwin resigned as president on the 12th after only two weeks in office, and on the 19th the People's Parliament and the BSPP congress elected Dr. Maung Maung, a civilian aide of Ne Win and one of the drafters of the 1974 Constitution, the new state president and party chairman.

Following Maung Maung's assumption of the presidency, shootings at crowds of demonstrators decreased and many political prisoners were released by amnesty. Consideration was given to social demands as shown by the announcement of a referendum, to be discussed, on introducing a multiparty system. However, the regime's reshuffling of its leadership did not quell the protests, and large-scale demonstrations continued every day in Rangoon forcing government organizations, railroads, banks and airports to remain closed. Mobs descended on the cooperative shops and looted their goods. These government shops existed throughout the country and distributed rationed goods to the people. Riots also broke out in the prisons in Insein, Sittwe and Magway, and prisoners attempted to escape. Within the protest movement itself people were tried as traitors before people's courts, and many died. But the organization of the movement gradually progressed, and leaders who were not student activists emerged, people such as Aung San Suu Kyi, Tin Oo (former Chief of General Staff of the tatmadaw) and U Nu. Nevertheless, none of these people had the power to control the unrest.

In Rangoon public officials could not get to work, and for a time government administration became dysfunctional. Conditions had reached the point where one-party rule by the BSPP was like a sinking ship, and it being suicidal to remain on a sinking ship, BSPP members across the country left the party in droves. Finally the tatmadaw also attempted to break away from the BSPP. President Maung Maung later made the following comment:

> The Regional commanders, the majority of them, had been given responsibility in their areas as chairmen of the party regional committees. Before that was done, a few undesirable clashes had taken place in some regions between the party and the army. Now that the single party system was winding up, Gen. Saw Maung proposed in the EC [CEC] held on the eve of the party congress that the regional commanders be relieved of party duties. The EC [CEC] had requested him to wait a little. Now, at the end of the party congress, I told Gen. Saw Maung that he and Gen. Than Shwe were released from their duties on the EC and they should feel free to send out signals to the

> regions to relieve the commanders and other officers from their party posts. I can always recall the faces of the two generals when I said that. They beamed with real joy. And off they went, like schoolboys running off as the bell rang to announce the end of the day.[5]

That observation is probably questionable, because Maung Maung was forced from the presidency by a coup on 18 September masterminded by Saw Maung and Than Shwe. Nevertheless, considering that Ne Win had resigned as chairman of the BSPP, plus the confused state of the political situation, it was quite possible that military leaders wanted to be free from the party's guidance.[6] Finally, at an extraordinary party congress on 10 September and an extraordinary People's Parliament meeting on the 11th, all tatmadaw personnel disaffiliated themselves from the party, and Article 11 of the Constitution, which stipulated one-party leadership by the BSPP, was abolished. The party lost the backing of the tatmadaw as well as its leadership over the state, leaving it with little real political influence. Meanwhile, the state had virtually ceased functioning amid the harsh national criticism, and the Ministry of Trade building was temporarily occupied by radical students on 17 September 1988. Meanwhile, since the 15th, tatmadaw and BSPP leaders had been huddled in a meeting, the details of which have never been revealed. But a person who had been one of the 17 members of the party's CEC at that time told this author in an interview that he had directed the Chief of General Staff of the tatmadaw, the Vice-Chief of General Staff (Army), and the regional commanders to carry out a coup.[7] This was corroborated to a considerable degree by another person who also had been a CEC member at that time and who acknowledged in an interview that some CEC members had directed the coup.[8] Although the testimonies of only two people, their credibility is supported by the following three points.

---

[5] Maung Maung, *The 1988 Uprising in Burma* (New Haven: Yale University Southeast Asia Studies, 1999), p. 191.

[6] Some military personnel had participated in demonstrations until then. On 21 August, instructors at the DSA appealed on state-run radio for the loyalty of all tatmadaw officers. On 7 September, a large-scale rally took place, which appealed for military personnel to support the anti-establishment movement. Then on 9 September, 200 air force soldiers in uniform participated in a demonstration in Mingaladon. See *Ajia Doko Nenpo 1989* (*Annual Report on Trends in Asia, 1989*), pp. 492–3.

[7] Interview with a former party CEC member on 20 January 2005.

[8] Interview with a former party CEC member on 4 February 2005.

First, the supreme decision-making body at that time in 1988 was still the party CEC, although the BSPP had been weakened by the tatmadaw's breakaway. In effect, the authority to direct the military leadership was still in the hands of the party CEC. Second, many of the CEC members were former superior officers of the then tatmadaw leaders, and very likely the latter, though the active-duty leaders of the tatmadaw, would have hesitated to suddenly defy their former superiors, even if the party now formally had little influence. Third, as was discussed in Chapter 7, Ne Win had kept the officer corps divided by employing his informal system of periodic reshuffles and transfers to prevent officers of the same Officer Training School (OTS) and Defence Services Academy (DSA) class from becoming concentrated in the top military leadership. Thus it was unlikely that Saw Maung and Than Shwe themselves had sufficient leadership stature to form a consensus on a coup in such a short period of time.

It has never been clarified whether Ne Win participated in the meeting of tatmadaw/BSPP leaders, or to what extent his intention was reflected in the 18 September coup. Robert Taylor wrote that a meeting was held in Ne Win's private residence on Ayedi Street in Rangoon, where he directed the tatmadaw to carry out the coup.[9] However, Taylor did not indicate any source for this information, so there is no clear basis for his assertion. And the information of the two former CEC members whom this author interviewed seems to undermine Taylor's assertion. Nevertheless, this study, likewise, cannot present conclusive evidence on the issue, so we are still unable to determine the extent of Ne Win's involvement in the 18 September coup. It is also unknown whether Dr. Maung Maung, the president, knew of the plan for the coup. He later wrote, "The coup was practically forced on the tatmadaw; circumstances made it a compelling duty."[10] So he probably agreed at the time that the coup was unavoidable. His later denunciations were directed at those citizens who became rioters rather than at the tatmadaw and its coup. It is also possible that the president as a civilian had no power to resist the intention of the military leadership and the CEC members, all of whom were retired officers.

If both Ne Win and Dr. Maung Maung were not deeply involved in planning the coup, in all likelihood it was carried out following a

---

[9] Robert Taylor, *The State in Myanmar* (London: Hurst & Company, 2009), p. 387.
[10] Maung Maung, *The 1988 Uprising in Burma*, p. 243.

Democratization Movement in 1988. (© AP/Aflo)

consensus among active-duty tatmadaw leaders in coordination with retired officers who were party CEC members. Even if Ne Win and Dr. Maung Maung were aware of the plan, without doubt there was coordination in the planning phase with retired officers on the CEC. At 4 p.m. on 18 September 1988, Saw Maung announced that the tatmadaw had taken control of all powers of the state. The SLORC, composed of 19 military leaders, was set up as the supreme ruling authority, and the Ne Win regime came to an end in a state of disorder.

Killing Fathers in 1988

There are several studies that describe the collapse of Ne Win's regime in detail.[11] They tend to emphasize the citizens' struggle to overthrow the military regime and establish a democratic government while highlighting

[11] See, for example, Hisao Tanabe, *Biruma Minshuka Undo 1988: Dokyumento* (The Democratization Movement in Burma in 1988: A Documentary) (Tokyo: Nashinokisha, 1989); Kenji Ino, "Myanma Minshuka Undo ni okeru Minshu Kodo no Syotokucho [The Characteristics of People's Behavior in Myanmar's Democratization Movement]," *Kita Kyushu Daigaku Hosei Ron Shu* 21, no. 1 (1993): 111–47.

the motivation and logic of the uprising. For example, in Bertil Lintner's *Outrage* — one of the best studies on the democratization movement of 1988 — detailed events are described one by one to reveal how a trivial fight among students developed into a national movement, and how the tatmadaw suppressed it.[12] Lintner interviewed people who escaped to the Thai border areas for fear of military suppression, and his description even uncovered the cooperative relationship between such people and the ethnic minority rebel groups based in the border areas. Although the studies like this one do not explicitly indicate why Burma was not democratized in 1988, they implicitly assume that the "failure" of democratization was caused by the anti-government movement's propensity to split and the tatmadaw's cruel suppression.

On the other hand, some studies have sought to use democratization theory to explain Burma's "failure" to democratize.[13] These studies juxtapose the Burmese case with other cases of democratization around the world through multilateral comparisons. Such a viewpoint is valuable because Burma is often seen as an unique case. However, such examinations use the Burmese case as a control experiment to reinforce an explanation of democratization; therefore, they are very often inherently preoccupied with the passive explanation that Burma's military rule continued due to the lack of factors for democratization. For instance, many of them attribute the failure of democratization to the absence of a cooperative relationship between the anti-government movements and moderates within the regime.

If this book successfully contributes to the series of studies focusing on democratization in Burma, it will be because it reveals a structural factor over a longer time span than previous studies, especially the weakness of political parties and the strength of unity of the tatmadaw. My argument is that political parties weakened in Burma partly because of

---

[12] Bertil Lintner, *Outrage: Burma's Struggle for Democracy* (Hong Kong: Review Publishing Co., 1989).

[13] See, for example, Gretchen Casper and Michelle M. Taylor, *Negotiating Democracy: Transitions from Authoritarian Rule* (Pittsburgh, Pa.: University of Pittsburgh Press, 1996); Vince Boudreau, *Resisting Dictatorship: Repression and Protest in Southeast Asia* (New York: Cambridge University Press, 2004); Kurt Shock, *Unarmed Insurrections: People Power Movements in Nondemocracies* (Minneapolis: University of Minnesota Press, 2005); Takeda, Yasuhiro, *Minshuka no Hikaku Seiji – Higashi Ajia Sokoku no Taisei Hendo Katei* [The comparative politics of democratization: the process of regime transformation in East Asian countries] (Kyoto: Mineruva Shobo, 2002).

the progressive depoliticization of the society after 1962 along with the one-party system of the BSPP; and also partly because the BSPP could not grow out of its condition of being "the tatmadaw's party," and politically it could not continue to exist without Ne Win's dictatorship. The reason for the strength of the tatmadaw's unity was because Ne Win's state reforms enabled the assignment of many state and party positions to members of a relatively small officer corps, as well as the fact that Ne Win actually controlled the tatmadaw.

The main concern here is not the problem of democratization itself but the question of why military regimes in Burma have become protracted. The years 1988 to 1990 become a transition period from the first to the second period of military rule. If 1988 is seen as the beginning of change within the system of long-term military rule, what significance did it have?

First, Ne Win stepped down from his position of supreme power. Although there is controversy over the extent of Ne Win's influence under the SLORC, the author is loathe to assume that after leaving his powerful public position, Ne Win would continue to exert great influence considering that the members of the party's CEC became "ordinary people" in 1988 after the 18 September coup.[14] There is no doubt that Ne Win was one of the founders of the tatmadaw and was respected by military men. Moreover, SLORC members, as military officers, were promoted under the Ne Win regime, meaning that Ne Win was their "benefactor" (*kyêizûshin*). When *Asia Week* asked in an interview, "But is Ne Win still in power behind the scenes?", General Saw Maung answered, "It's most difficult for us to explain these rumours and allegations.... When people see me visit Ne Win, they think I'm going for instruction or advice. But you see, he's like a parent to me."[15] Saw Maung was indicating that although it was true that he visited Ne Win, it was in the manner of an adult son visiting an aging parent, not for advice but out of respect and gratitude for all that the parent had done for the son. But the visits also indicated that Ne Win maintained contact with the SLORC; nevertheless, there is no doubt that without the institutional basis of his dictatorship centring on the BSPP, it was not possible for Ne Win to have enduring influence on political decisions.

---

[14] Interview with a former party CEC member on 4 February 2005.

[15] *Asia Week*, 27 January 1989.

The elderly Ne Win was apt to retreat to his private residence without attending even CEC meetings after he had resigned as president of the state in 1981, giving his aides more opportunity to exert control. After stepping down from his public position of party chairman in June 1988, his direct influence on the government was surely weakened considerably more. Ne Win appeared in public only a few times after the coup: when attending the tatmadaw Day dinner party on 27 March 1989, on his departure to Singapore for medical treatment on 4 January 1994, and while visiting Indonesia from 23 September 1997. He passed away on 5 December 2002. The front page of the state-run paper Myanmar Alin (*myanmà àlin*) of the following day carried the standard fare, including a note that Than Shwe, chairman of the State Peace and Development Council (SPDC),[16] had inspected a road construction project in Sagaing Division. The notice of the former dictator's death was to be found by readers in a corner of the obituary column on the last page. The article was very succinct and formal. It simply stated that Ne Win passed away at 7:30 a.m. on 5 December and was cremated at 1:30 p.m. on that day in accordance with his wishes. None of the SPDC members ever issued a statement on Ne Win's death.[17] From being a dictator whose whims could sway the state, Ne Win left this world with almost no acknowledgement of the very leadership whose members had enjoyed most the fruits of his failed revolution. Ne Win's name will gradually fade away from people's memory, but the "revolution" he attempted institutionally transformed the governance of Burma which the current regime has inherited. The state-wide mechanism for allocating benefits to the officer corps is the most important legacy Ne Win left, and the greatest obstacle to Burma's political and economic development.

The second significance of 1988 is that the coup realized a generational change among political leaders from the first to the second generation of officers. As seen in Chapter 7, the tatmadaw experienced a major generational change in 1985. This was due to the fact that Ne Win and other leaders strictly adhered to the retirement age of 60 years old. Such compliance with the retirement age dissipated feelings of stagnation among junior officers who were given the opportunity to advance. But

[16] The SPDC superseded the SLORC in 1997.

[17] Aye Zaw Win, the husband of Ne Win's daughter, and his three sons were arrested for attempting a coup in March 2002. It seems the SPDC's silence was related to this incident too.

the BSPP, where many retired tatmadaw leaders were "reemployed," had no stipulated retirement age. As mentioned in Chapter 4, the lack of turnover in the membership of the party's Central Committee came into question in the middle of the 1970s, exemplified by the stipulation that 55 per cent of candidates had to be new, a stipulation that had created instability in party politics and which was finally thrown out. With no real mechanism to bring in younger blood, the members of the CEC gradually aged, and by the time of the sixth CEC elected at the Fifth Party Congress in 1985, only one active-duty senior officer — the Chief of General Staff of the tatmadaw — could be found among its members (the Vice-Chief of General Staff (Army) later was made a member). The average age of members increased from 58.1 years old in the fifth CEC (elected in 1981) to 61.9 years old in the sixth CEC (elected in 1985). This aging meant the stagnation and lack of personnel change in the organization of the party leadership. When this static condition is placed alongside the dynamic condition of generational change within the tatmadaw, one can see that by 1985 the party and military leaderships had become reverse images of each other, between retired, first-generation and active-duty, second-generation tatmadaw leaders.

The first generation shared the experience of the struggle for independence and against the British and the Japanese empire, and they all held a similar leftist, socialistic political and economic orientation. In contrast, the new generation was the product of Burma's introversion and isolation. They had been given few opportunities to cultivate sensibilities (especially for international norms) despite their broad experience in combat against anti-government rebels. This becomes clear when considering how few of the officers studied abroad and the control of free speech within the country. It is not important whether the new generation believed in *The System of Correlation between Man and His Environment* or not. The problem is that they had few opportunities to be exposed to other ideas. In Indonesia, various training schools for military officers have functioned as importers of international trends as Jun Honna described;[18] however, Burmese military schools restricted overseas contact, as did other state organizations, so over the years the education of officers narrowed even declined.[19] The influence of the closed foreign policy

[18] See Jun Honna, *Military Politics and Democratization in Indonesia* (New York: Routledge Curzon, 2003), Chapter 4.

[19] Interview with a former party CEC member on 4 February 2005; DSMHRI DR-8452, p. 486.

during the Ne Win regime had a negative impact on the worldview of tatmadaw officers. Moreover, the new leaders were the generation of the counter-insurgency war. They were officers who had been fighting that war since the 1950s and had been promoted because of their achievements in battle as field operation officers, so they recognized fully the tatmadaw's difficult situation. Now, in 1988, in the midst of a difficult civil war and deteriorating economic and social conditions, the new tatmadaw leaders were eliminating the government's top decision-making organ, the CEC, a clear indication that they had become dissatisfied with the leaders of the state, including Ne Win.

When popular agitation destabilized Ne Win's rule leading to his departure from the BSPP, martial law was declared in Rangoon, and active-duty tatmadaw officers, having gradually acquired autonomy from the party, seized power in the 18 September coup. In an interview years later, a former party CEC member, who acknowledged that he had directed the coup, commented in hindsight that, "Our failure was that we didn't decide beforehand when they [SLORC] would leave office."[20] After the coup, there was no indication that party CEC members and former ministers — at least the ones the author interviewed — and SLORC members had any sort of joint involvement in state decision-making. It appears that as the party CEC lost power following the formal institutional changes that took place after the coup whereby the committee members became "ordinary people," the SLORC alone ran the government thereafter, meaning that the September coup had the character of a intra-tatmadaw coup, the unintentional end result being active-duty officers ousting retired officers, bringing about a generational change at the state level. The BSPP now was one of several political parties in a multiparty system; the People's Parliament was suspended; and the People's Councils were abolished. Naturally, many people who worked for these bodies lost their jobs, and people from ministries returned to the workplaces they had formerly belonged to. This restructuring provided legitimacy for the SLORC to abolish the former regime and build a new one. The irony of this reform and restructuring is that it was triggered by the popular democratization movement that brought down Ne Win.

The third significance of the changes in 1988 came when the new leadership under active-duty tatmadaw officers began to correct the

---

[20] Interview with a former CEC member on 4 February 2005.

previous regime's mismanagement in its own way, one example being the liberalization of the economy. The SLORC liberalized the import-export business in the month after the coup. It also abolished controls on the trade of agricultural products, except for those on cotton, jute and rice. The agricultural market became much freer, although the compulsory cultivation system remained. In 1989 the "State-owned Economic Enterprises Law" was amended, and the monopolies of state enterprises were limited to only 12 businesses. These SLORC reforms and policy changes underscored the realization that the previous controlled economic system had been a failure.

Much less apparent than the changes in economic policy was the expansion of the tatmadaw. Shortly after the coup, the SLORC drew up plans to increase the tatmadaw from about 200 thousand troops in 1988 to 270 thousand by the middle of 1992, with an ultimate goal of a force of 500 thousand troops;[21] as of 2007, the number stood at about 400 thousand. Imports of weapons also increased sharply during the ten years from 1988 to 1997, from some 20 million dollars to 280 million dollars in 1997.[22] As was discussed in Chapter 7, such military expansion does not necessarily occur after a military coup. This also seems to have been a reaction of the active-duty officers to the previous regime's less than satisfactory effort to provide the tatmadaw with sufficient resources for its counter-insurgency war.

The expanding tatmadaw led to expanded combat operations against the anti-government insurgents. At the same time, however, the SLORC pursued cease-fire negotiations led by its then first secretary, Khin Nyunt. A study by Zaw Oo and Win Min listed three main factors that encouraged the SLORC to begin cease-fire negotiations: the emergence of the 1988 anti-government movement as a new domestic threat, splits and weakening among the minority-group insurgents, and the need to undertake development in border areas associated with the transition to a market economy.[23] This strategy was a new approach, and the cease-fire

---

[21] Andrew Selth, *Transforming the Tatmadaw: the Burmese Armed Forces since 1988* (Canberra: Strategic and Defence Studies Centre, Research School of Pacific and Asian Studies, The Australian National University, 1996), p. 19.

[22] See Andrew Selth, *Burma's Armed Forces: Power without Glory* (Norwalk, CT: East Bridge, 2002), p. 138.

[23] Zaw Oo and Win Min, *Assessing Burma's Ceasefire Accords* (Washington: East-West Center, 2007), pp. 13–4.

negotiations ensured the insurgents of practical self-rule and the retention of their weapons in the controlled zones.

In this respect, the SLORC began its rule with a rejection of the policies implemented by the previous government, just as the Revolutionary Council had done back in 1962. The SLORC's next moves were also similar to those at the start of the Ne Win regime: implementing large-scale institutional reforms while dealing very conservatively with factors destabilizing to military politics, a notable example being reform of the state-owned corporations which did not proceed smoothly because these corporations provided job opportunities for active and retired tatmadaw officers. But the most outstanding example illustrating this conservatism was the slow change in politics. Compared with economic and military changes, it took until March 2011 to establish a new "civilian" government. This political stagnation has prevented economic assistance coming from overseas and hindered the inflow of foreign investment. Furthermore, the implementation of a market economy was allowed only to the extent that it did not destabilize the military regime. The regime also had the good fortune in the 2000s of expanding natural gas exports to Thailand, bringing Burma greatly increased revenue, which allowed the regime to consolidate its authoritarian rule based on the tatmadaw. Economic sanctions by Western countries only serve to increase the hardship in the lives of ordinary Burmese, so many people have questioned the effects and effectiveness of sanctions.[24]

The Central Argument Summarized: Failed Revolution Brought an Enduring Military Regime

The question that motivated this study is why the military regime in Burma has been unusually durable. When we look more closely at this riddle, we see that the durability has been a consequence of the military's

[24] See, for example, John H. Badgley, ed., *Reconciling Burma/Myanmar: Essays on U.S. Relations with Burma* [NBR Analysis 15(1)] (Seattle: The National Bureau of Asian Research, 2004); Morten B. Pederson, *Promoting Human Rights in Burma: A Critique of Western Sanctions Policy* (Lanham: Rowman & Littlefield Publishers, 2008); International Crisis Group, *Myanmar's Post-Election Landscape*, Asia Briefing No. 118 Jakarta/Brussels, 7 March 2011; Toshihiro Kudo, "Josho (Introduction)," in *Myanma Keizai no Jitsuzo: Naze Gunsei wa Ikinokoreta-noka* [The reality of the Myanmar economy: how could the military regime survive?], ed. Toshihiro Kudo (Chiba: Ajia Keizai Kenkyujo, 2008).

function in the state. In many cases, weak governance undermines the institutional stability of the military and causes political turmoil. Therefore, building a strong regime to overcome weak governance requires development of the civilian government sectors and economic growth. These conditions inevitably cause two changes in an authoritarian regime run by the military. One is a transformation to a personal dictatorship, and the other is a co-opting of important social forces into the regime. In both cases, a strong leader tends to keep a certain distance between the military and politics so that the government can improve its governance and obtain more support from the elite and the society as well. Then, in theory, when the state is in crisis, democratization happens with the military's departure from political intervention.

The Ne Win regime shared similar tendencies. As was shown in Chapter 4, Ne Win's rule was clearly enough of a dictatorship to protect his position through extra legal measures, and Chapter 6 showed that the BSPP was attempting to co-opt the social elites. When crisis came, however, the consequences were different from the outcome theorized. When the regime was hit by a serious crisis in 1988, the tatmadaw neither defended Ne Win nor sided with the democratization movement. Instead, it saw itself as the guardian of the state and the only actor capable of restoring order. This behavior of the tatmadaw in 1988 points us toward a more accurate line of inquiry.

Generally speaking, prolonged military rule conflicts with military cohesion. A most recent example is Egypt, where at the start of 2011 the loss of support from the military dealt a decisive blow to the dictatorship of a former general. Actions of the military were crucial in the collapse of the Marcos regime in the 1986 "Yellow Revolution" in the Philippines. Similarly in the 1998 collapse of Suharto's rule, triggered by the Asian economic crisis in 1977, the military ultimately withdrew its support of the leader, and the commander-in-chief of Indonesian National Armed Forces asked Suharto to step down. Also, as Yoshifumi Tamada points out, once the military loses its political cohesion, it is unlikely to carry out political intervention because of the lack of coordination among military leaders.[25] Conversely, once civilian leaders fail to effectively divide military cohesion, a coup can be triggered, as it was in

[25] Yoshifumi Tamada, *Myths and Realities: The Democratization of Thai Politics* (Kyoto & Melbourne: Kyoto University Press and Trans Pacific Press, 2008), Ch. 2.

Pakistan in 1999.[26] In Burma, the cohesion of the tatmadaw has never faced a decisive crisis, even when the Ne Win regime collapsed, and even though the military regime has continued for so long.

This cohesion is the key to solving the riddle of the enduring military regime in Burma. Through a historical analysis based on disaggregation of the regime's components and on original materials, I have argued throughout this book that Ne Win's revolution created a basic mechanism for maintaining the military's cohesion. However, this was not Ne Win's intended outcome. The strangeness of Burmese politics lies in a unique combination of general factors and timing rather than particularly unique factors.[27] For the consequences of Ne Win's revolution to have occurred, the revolution had to be a serious attempt at radical change rather than just a survival strategy by a dictator, and, at the same time, it had to be an unsuccessful attempt in the end, one that failed to establish a socialist state.

Ne Win aspired to revolution as the head of the military, a counter-revolutionary organization. Why did he do this? As Chapter 2 showed, a number of historical coincidences affected his political orientation. Counterfactual thinking would be helpful here. Supposing that the post-colonial army had become the successor of the colonial army, Ne Win would have never become the chief of general staff and his officers would never have become the nucleus of the revolution. He would have had two major difficulties in terms of age and institution. Ne Win was over 30 years old when he decided to be a soldier. That would have been too old to compete for the top officer position in a professional military. But his decision was made under unusual circumstances. He was one of the members who created the first national army, the Burma Independence Army (BIA), in December 1941. When the Japanese army and BIA invaded colonial Burma and undermined its colonial rule, Ne Win became a national hero as one of the "Thirty Comrades." This helped him overcome the handicap of his late career start. However, that did not guarantee his leadership in the post-colonial army because the tatmadaw was extremely fragile as an institution.

A major reason for the fragility was political and ethnic cleavages. In the early post-colonial years, officers who had come up through the

[26] Babar Sattar, "Pakistan: Return to Praetorianism," in *Coercion and Governance: The Declining Political Role of the Military in Asia*, ed. Muthiah Alagappa (Stanford: Stanford University Press, 2001), pp. 404–5.

[27] This approach is similar to historical institutionalism in political science.

colonial army, most of whom were from the ethnic minorities, took the initiative in the tatmadaw. The officers who had been trained by the Japanese army and had fought against Burma's colonial ruler, and who were mostly Bahman, were unhappy with the situation. Finally, ethnic conflicts between Bahman and Karen in the late 1940s deprived the former colonial army officers of leadership within the tatmadaw. Despite the resulting loss of many of the tatmadaw's best trained officers, their purging provided an opportunity for the tatmadaw to consolidate its officers under Ne Win, and it enabled politically motivated rather than professionally motivated officers to dominate the tatmadaw.

This consolidation of power under Ne Win did not directly lead to politicization of the tatmadaw or cause its intervention into politics. On the contrary, as Chapter 3 described, the tatmadaw leadership in the 1950s sought to avoid the military's involvement in politics, and was working to reform it into a more professional, more bureaucratic and non-political battle organization. An important finding of this book is that these circumstances in the tatmadaw at that time gave birth to the original idea that later was made the state ideology of the Ne Win regime. Chit Hlaing, who would draft the state ideology, wrote articles in the latter part of the 1950s on his idea for a Burmese type of socialism founded on an ideology he developed that he termed *namarupa wada*. His purpose at that time was not for justifying the tatmadaw's political role, but to create a norm for countering communism in the country and inside the tatmadaw and for respecting the significance of the 1947 Constitution. Thus the origin of the "Burmese way to socialism" needs to be understood in the context of the tatmadaw's anticommunism and constitutionalism in the 1950s. Chit Hlaing incorporated an abundance of Buddhist terminology in his ideology, not for a religious intent, but to provide a Burmese context that could overcome a dual dilemma. One was the issue of how to juxtapose religion (i.e., Buddhism), which is deeply rooted in the Burmese psyche, with the leftist, basically a religious socialist politico-economy that Burmese nationalist favoured. This problem had long troubled Burmese political discourse. The other difficulty concerned the anti-communism of the tatmadaw and Chit Hlaing's anti-communist propagandizing work. The tatmadaw leadership and Chit Hlaing himself favoured socialism but they were anti-communist. In his creation of *namarupa wada* with its Buddhist terminology, Chit Hlaing was able to put socialism into a Burmese context while simultaneously rejecting communism as dehumanizing. In this way his thesis upheld the anticommunism of the tatmadaw while at the same time supporting socialism and the political left that dominated the discourse on what constituted a legitimate Burmese state.

When Chit Hlaing wrote his *namarupa wada* articles, they were a part of his anti-communist propagandizing work for the tatmadaw and to bolster a constitutional basis for an apolitical military. He never intended nor ever expected his ideas to become the foundation for the state's ideology, and beyond his articles, he did little to further develop his ideas. However, their rise to political significance was a consequence of a power struggle within the tatmadaw leadership. By the early 1960s, that power had shifted from moderates to hardliners within the tatmadaw, which ultimately open the way for Ne Win's coup d'état in March 1962. Before that year was out, Ne Win had directed Chit Hlaing to draft an ideology for the BSPP. In response Chit Hlaing returned to his *namarupa wada* writings and turned them into an ideology for the party, which the new regime formally adopted in early 1963. In this way, a series of articles previously written to counter communism and support constitutionalism were suddenly turned into a document that justified extra-legal military intervention and new Burmese type of socialist state building. Such ad hoc formulation of ideology could never provide a foundation on which to actually build the institutions of a socialism suitable to Burma's social, political and economic context. The result, as Chapters 4 and 5 revealed, was a Ne Win regime whose formal institutional design was just an insufficient copy of existing socialist countries. Its essence was not the Burmese way at all. But the trajectory that Ne Win's revolution took as a result was highly unique in terms of political development. What factors helped create that unique political trajectory?

First, Ne Win's leadership to abolish the institutions of the parliamentary democracy period was highly effective, even if it did not lead to building new institutions as the 1974 Constitution described. At the beginning of his regime (possibly longer), Ne Win's source of power was the physical force of the tatmadaw and the people's support for his rule. He took advantage of these in order to restructure the alliance of the elites in politics, which led to excluding most of the civilian politicians and bureaucrats from the decision-making process. This was a replay of what in Chapter 6 was termed the "winner-take-all" outcome in Burmese politics in which the winner of the political contest gains an overwhelming victory leaving little or no opposition. However, abolishing the existing institutions is only a part of revolution; building new institutions is the other and surely more important part. Ne Win's revolution failed because after tearing down, he was unable to build anew.

Such failure would normally lead to questioning the responsibility of a political leader. But Ne Win survived. Indeed, he reinvented the state for his dictatorship. How did he do this? Ne Win had the tatmadaw intervene deeply in the state to consolidate his own power base. In the name of revolution, he shifted tatmadaw personnel into the administrative machinery of the state, and the civilian elite had no way of resisting such intervention. However, we should not confuse Ne Win's interest and the tatmadaw's corporate interest, because, as shown in Chapter 7, such political intervention obstructed the tatmadaw's primary duty of counter-insurgency operations, as it required shifting more officers to work in the civilian sectors of the government when the tatmadaw itself was suffering a perennial shortage of officers. While Ne Win's reliance on the tatmadaw arose from his aspiration for revolution, it meant he ran the risk of creating discontent within the tatmadaw. How did he control the tatmadaw in the process of the revolution? And how did the tatmadaw maintain its cohesion? The author argued that the critical factors were the weakness of Ne Win's leadership and the historical timing in the building of Burma's military institution.

Although Ne Win was a dictator in terms of his authority in the political decision-making process, he was never able to create a power base he trusted beyond the operational officers of the tatmadaw. As a result, he always relied on the officer corps which created an unusual imbalance between the tatmadaw and the civilian sectors in the state of Burma. This weakened him as a dictator. And despite his strong feelings about establishing a socialist state, he immediately expelled BSPP leaders as well as tatmadaw officers if they appeared threatening to him. He was not such a strong political leader that he could maintain his power for 26 years through charisma (*paràmi*) and influence (*ôza*) alone. He was largely supported by an institutional authority (*ana*) founded on the bureaucracy of the tatmadaw. When the tatmadaw withdrew its support, signalled by the 18 September coup and the creation of the SLORC, the institutional foundation of Ne Win's revolution collapsed, opening the way for the new government to abandoned the "Burmese way to socialism," along with its ideology and its party organization.

What needs to be emphasized here is the impact that Ne Win's reliance on the tatmadaw had on the its institution building. Chapter 7 revealed how few and young the tatmadaw officers were when the revolution allocated them to a great number of BSPP and ministerial positions. The tatmadaw's political intervention progressed in parallel with its maturation as a bureaucracy. Over time the informal seconding of officers to positions in the BSPP and government ministries became embedded in the career paths of tatmadaw officers. What is important here, however, was the way this embedding of positions was done, because allocating political posts to tatmadaw personnel can lead to the politicization of the tatmadaw, something that professional soldiers very much dislike.

Two things indicated that Ne Win was able to avoid the risk that assigning officers to positions outside of the tatmadaw would lead to politicization of the officer corps. First, the assignment of positions was implemented according to the hierarchy within the officer corps, meaning that an officer's promotion in the tatmadaw determined the limits of his promotion in the office he was seconded to. This prevented a conflict arising between the officers engaged in politics and those engaged in military affairs, because an active-duty or retired officer in the BSPP or government ministries would never have influence over an officer with a higher rank than his own in the tatmadaw. Were a reversal of positions to occur against this principle, it might have led to an unstable situation like the political crisis of 1977, as described in Chapter 4. This principle also contributed to controlling dissatisfaction among middle-ranking officers. But even in the cases of disaffected officers, once they were moved out of the military, they lost the means to mobilize other members of the officer corps. Moreover, officers in upper positions of the tatmadaw were retired and transferred out through regularly held party congresses and the People's Parliament elections. This enabled middle-ranking officers to expect their smooth promotions to those positions in the future.

The second indication was related to the behavioral norm of tatmadaw officers. Once an officer left the tatmadaw to take up an outside position, he almost never ever returned to it. This meant that the transfer was the end of promotion. This informal rule affected officer behavior in three ways. First, the perception that promising officers got promoted within the tatmadaw and a transfer out ruined one's success as a soldier took root in the minds of tatmadaw officers. Consequently, both the BSPP and the government administration were subordinate to the tatmadaw, reinforcing its paternalism. Second, officers instinctively behaved conservatively to ensure that they would stay on the path of promotion in the tatmadaw. This norm was further reinforced by the fixation on the narrow promotion path centered on field operation officers within the tatmadaw. Officers strived to maintain the existing order to minimize risk in the competition for promotion, and this tendency was more dominant among officers in higher posts. Finally, there was no legacy of accumulated administrative or political experience in the behavior of the officer corps. This was because improving one's competence as an administrative official or politician was not an incentive for most officers striving for promotion. In addition to staying on the path of promotion, the prolonged struggle against the anti-government insurgents affected the behavioral norm of the officer corps. Fighting, especially successfully, in counter-insurgency operations was vital for promotion. Moreover, the incentive structure determining officer behavior was accompanied by sanctions such as mutual surveillance among officers, spying on officers by the National Intelligence Bureau and unrelenting purges by Ne Win.

Through the interaction of all these factors, Ne Win succeeded in controlling the tatmadaw, and the tatmadaw maintained its cohesion even as Ne Win's revolution failed. In all likelihood his revolution would have inevitably failed because of the limitations of socialism and the one-party state as practiced in Burma. However, the important point here is not these limitation but the fact that the state in Burma had already undergone a major transformation before its leaders admitted the failure of the revolution and started to reform its political and economic system. The purpose of revolution had already died long before 1988. However, the means — the state centered on the military — survived. Over the long course of military rule in Burma, the informal institution of transferring officers out of the tatmadaw became self-perpetuating, and to this day it continues to retire and transfer officers to be ministers in the government, transfers that still disappoint upper-ranking tatmadaw officers, as exemplified by the two officers' stories on the opening pages of this book, because it means the end of promotion and signals their failure in the climb toward the top of the tatmadaw, an institution with more authority, more prestige and better benefits than the government institutions that administer the Burmese state. Thus a means that Ne Win had employed to maintain his power has now become a significant purpose of the state.

EPILOGUE

Post-1988 Politics

The tatmadaw (Myanmar Armed Forces), currently boasting a force of about 400,000 (Army: 375,000; Navy: 16,000; Air Force: 15,000), is an organization designed to defend national security and is the political backbone that has consistently supported the juntas since 1962. Since Independence, the tatmadaw's major duty has been counter-insurgency operations against communists and ethnic minority rebels. Its goal has been to establish a unified state free of armed struggle. The political role of the tatmadaw remained largely unchanged: to support Myanmar's authoritarian regime; and the system that Ne Win created is still working today.

Since 1988 Myanmar has experienced great changes in its politics, economy, society, and culture. Economic development has progressed through a transition to a market-oriented economy. Shops abound with goods compared with the past, and electric appliances such as televisions and air conditioners have become widespread. Automobiles and motorbikes are no longer rare even in the countryside, and Yangon and Mandalay boast luxury hotels. Exchanges with other countries have increased, and students and workers abroad now number several million. Controls on newspapers, television, periodicals, and other mass media were not relaxed until 2011; nonetheless, the media are much more diverse at present than in the socialist era. Urban residents can now easily access the Internet. The development of the media has provided greater means for gaining general information about Myanmar. However, information about civil-military relations still remains limited; to a considerable extent we are forced to rely on hearsay and guesswork for analysis. What we can do, though, is stand back and try to understand Myanmar's civil-military relations after 1988 from a broader perspective.

What has changed politically since 1988? To see the changes, we need to look back at the words that the military regime used to justify and legitimize its government. These were "revolution" and "the Burmese way to socialism," on which the Ne Win regime stood from 1962 to 1988. The goal was to set in place a revolution in the Burmese way, backed by the tatmadaw. But on 18 September 1988, Saw Maung, the Chief of General Staff of the tatmadaw, staged a coup, suspended the 1974 Constitution, and concentrated all state powers in the State Law and Order Restoration Council (SLORC). As the name of this organization implies, the legitimacy of this assumption of power was sought in the restoration of order, and in this light the military regime continued without interruption and without debate for another 20 years. During that time, the tatmadaw justified its rule by claiming to be both as a provisional government holding power until democratization and a non-partisan government that would benefit the entire nation.

It is clear, however, the junta's words to justify its rule did not persuade the people in effect, one main reason being the fact that 22 years is simply too long for a provisional government. Rather, it seems that the more the tatmadaw promised future democratization and service in the national interest, the more the words lost their meaning. Clearly, this was because the SLORC, backed as it was by the physical force of the military, could make any number of empty promises, leaving one with the impression that the function of the junta's formal pronouncements seems to have been to restrain any action that might have opposed the legitimacy of the regime.

A reliance on physical force against opposition and the emptiness of its words highlighted the weak legitimacy of the junta from 1988 to 2010. Moreover, neither Saw Maung, who led the coup d'état in 1988, nor Than Shwe, who took over as the leader of the state in 1992, possessed the charismatic qualities that might have made up for the regime's lack of legitimacy. Under the SLORC and its reincarnation, the State Peace and Development Council (SPDC), the tatmadaw lost all but a shadow of the respect it had previously earned as the army that had fought for the freedom of the nation. The legitimacy of the post-1988 military regime was seemingly more fragile than that of the Ne Win regime at the time of the latter's collapse. Yet the regime endured and did so until the tatmadaw guided transition to a "civilian" government in 2011. How was Than Shwe able to control the tatmadaw and the state for so long? How did the military change under his leadership? Moreover, what does the transition to the new regime in 2011 really mean?

Prescriptions for Restoration

The new military regime had a sanguinary beginning. The SLORC sought to appease the democratization movement by promising to hold a general election while at the same time cracking down violently on all those who still took to the streets. The number of deaths said to have exceeded 3,000. While the 1988 political crisis had a great impact on Burmese politics, the following two points are important for this study's focus on civil-military relations.

First, as was pointed out in Chapter 8, the political crisis of 1988 caused a generational change within the political regime. Although it is not clear to what extent Ne Win was involved in the coup plot, his influence was arguably limited after his resignation as BSPP chairman. The SLORC was composed of a new generation of officers who had taken leadership of the tatmadaw in 1985. But unlike the generational change that had taken place by design in the military leadership at that time, the change of generation in state leadership in 1988 occurred by chance because of a coup, so that the SLORC members suddenly came to be in control of the state.

The second point was the emergence of a new "threat:" the citizenry. Until that time the tatmadaw had never encountered a large-scale anti-government movement from Myanmar's citizens. Previously student movements had been the major force driving anti-government movements. Now Aung San Suu Kyi rose dramatically to become a popular leader after her decision to participate in the movement. Furthermore, the goal of the movement posed democratization, meaning a call for regime change. This was a genuine threat to the tatmadaw's political power. With insurgent groups still in control of the region east of the Salween River, it was possible that student anti-government activists who had fled Yangon to escape oppression would join them. It was also said that a U.S. naval warship had approached as close as 90 miles off the coast south of Yangon while the country was being swept by anti-government demonstrations.[1] The situation, as the tatmadaw saw it, presented a crisis of national security.

[1] This was later denied by the U.S. government. The decision to relocate the capital to Naypyidaw in 2005 is said to have been because of the "trauma" the government had felt at the time; but even today the veracity of this story is still unclear. See Andrew Selth, *Burma's Armed Forces: Power Without Glory* (Norwalk, CT: East Bridge, 2002), p. 40.

The SLORC drew up the following four prescriptions for managing the crisis and restoring order. First, Saw Maung emphasized that his government was different from the previous socialist one. But he also reiterated that saying it alone failed to resonate with people; their dissent arose from their discontent with the country's economic stagnation. Therefore, the SLORC abandoned the socialist economic system and moved quickly to liberalize the economy. In November 1988 foreign trade was opened up to private enterprise, and in the same month with enactment of the Union of Myanmar Foreign Investment Law it became possible for foreign investors to enter the country. In the following year the State-Owned Economic Enterprise Law was enacted which opened up the whole economy to private enterprise, except for 12 sectors, which remained the monopolies of state-owned enterprises.[2] This rapid succession of economic reforms was surprising for the Burmese government that had never been quick to make decisions. Part of the explanation could be that liberalization had begun in the agricultural sector at the end of the previous socialist regime, so in all likelihood economic policies for liberalizing other sectors had also been prepared while Ne Win was in power. Nevertheless, it was the SLORC that enacted them, and this had the effect of demonstrating that it was a new and different regime from the previous socialist one.

In contrast to its economic liberalization policies, the SLORC significantly tightened its control of politics. This might be called a militarization of politics wherein the clashing of opinions among parties and factions that is necessarily included in democratic politics was regarded as a threat to national security, combating this threat. This was the second prescription arising in the SLORC's handling of the situation. Part of this involved the junta linking Myanmar's internal political conditions to external threats by presenting democratization activities as unjustified intervention by the West. This tied in with what, since the coup, the military regime called "our three main national causes:" "no disintegration of the union," "no disintegration of national solidarity," and "consolidation of national sovereignty." The SLORC saw the political crisis in 1988 as exemplifying the need for these three national causes.

In addition to perceiving a new threat in the citizenry, the SLORC also exhibited a sense of paternalism, implying that only the tatmadaw

---

[2] Toshihiro Kudo, "Josho (Introduction)," in *Myanma Keizai no Jitsuzo: Naze Gunsei wa Ikinokoreta-noka* [The reality of the Myanmar economy: why could the military regime survive?], ed. Toshihiro Kudo (Chiba: Ajia Keizai Kenkyujo, 2008), pp. 10–4.

could serve the interests of the nation. According to this logic, political activities in disobedience of military guidance would lead to a state crisis.[3] Based on such reasoning, the SLORC ignored the results of the 1990 elections when the National League for Democracy (NLD) won by a wide margin. Thus the NLD's activities, which under the law were supposed to be allowed, were instead suppressed. The SLORC closed universities from 1996 through 2000 and relocated Yangon University and Mandalay University, which had been the centres of student movements, out to the suburbs. Student movements have now been almost completely destroyed as a result of these interventions.

Third, the tatmadaw proceeded with cease-fire negotiations by proposing political deals with the Burma Communist Party and ethnic insurgents. This began with cease-fire proposals to the Myanmar National Democratic Alliance (MNDA) [later the Myanmar National Democratic Alliance Army (MNDAA)], which had separated from the Burma Communist Party following an internal split in 1989, and to the United Wa State Army (UWSA), in return for allowing them to retain their weapons and to practice self-rule.[4] The tatmadaw acted strategically in promoting the exchange of weapons and development, and the SLORC encouraged the process by organizing the Central Committee for Development of Border Areas and National Races, which was headed by Saw Maung and included the heads of the Army, Navy and Air Force and the first and second secretaries of the SLORC.[5] An official announcement reported that cease-fire agreements had been concluded with 17 insurgent groups by the time a Border Guard Force (BGF) began being formed in 2009. General Khin Nyunt, the chief of military intelligence and the first secretary of the SLORC, led the cease-fire agreement negotiations. Border area development unofficially came to be the domain of the military intelligence office mainly through the Ministry for Progress of Border Areas and National Races and Development Affairs.

---

[3] See the following for a discussion of military paternalism. Kenji Ino, "Myanma kokugun no seiji kainyu no ronri: 'Kokumin Seiji' gainen wo chushin to shite [The logic of the Myanmar military's political intervention: focusing on the concept of 'national politics'']," *Tonan Ajia – Rekishi to Bunka* (Southeast Asia – History and Culture) 29 (2000): 29.

[4] Cease-fire negotiations were conducted before 1988 as well, but the Burmese government had called for armed groups to surrender their weapons and dissolve their organizations which was essentially demanding their surrender. See Win Min, "Looking Inside The Burmese Military," *Asian Survey* (2008): 7–11.

[5] 1989 Ordinance No. 23 issued in March 1989.

On the other hand, those military took the offensive against the insurgents that would not agree to a cease-fire. The fiercest battles after 1988 were those fought against the Karen National Liberation Army, the military wing of the Karen National Union (KNU). Although the tatmadaw gained the upper hand in the war, the KNU continued to resist, refusing to accept a cease-fire until 2012. In 1994 the tatmadaw and the Democratic Kayin Buddhist Army, which had split from the KNU, concluded a cease-fire agreement, and in 1995 the KNU bases of Wangka and Manaplaw fell to tatmadaw forces. After years of fighting the KNU's has been considerably weakened in part because the development of roads and other infrastructure has increased the efficiency of military operations in the border areas.

These operations were also enhanced by the tatmadaw's expansion and modernization — the fourth prescription. Although defence spending is usually the easiest index for understanding the expansion and modernization of the tatmadaw, Myanmar defense spending figures have never been published.[6] To understand the trends in the country's defense spending, we need to look at the changes in the budgets for all of the ministries as well as the budget for the Ministry of Defence (MOD). Figure E.1 shows the government budget, Defence Ministry Budget and share of the MOD's budget to the total government budget; and Figure E.2 shows the real values of the MOD budget and the ratio of the MOD budget going to capital expenditures. Three interesting points are worth noting.

First, while the MOD's budget was more than 30 per cent of the total budget through the 1990s, as the political and economic base of the regime became stable in the 2000s, the MOD budget declined to around the 20 per cent range due to the increase in the total budget. Although the MOD's budget has been given priority since 1988, the fiscal improvement that natural gas revenues have brought to the government has led to a decline in the MOD's relative share of the total budget. Nevertheless, all the findings need to be treated with some caution since the

---

[6] Estimates have been published by the Stockholm International Peace Research Institute, the International Institute for Strategic Studies in the United Kingdom and the Defence Intelligence Organisation of Australia. However, their respective definitions of defense spending are slightly different, and also, in the case of Myanmar, the amount changes depending on whether the official parity rate or market rate is being used for conversion to the dollar value. Therefore, it is not possible to accurately ascertain defense spending.

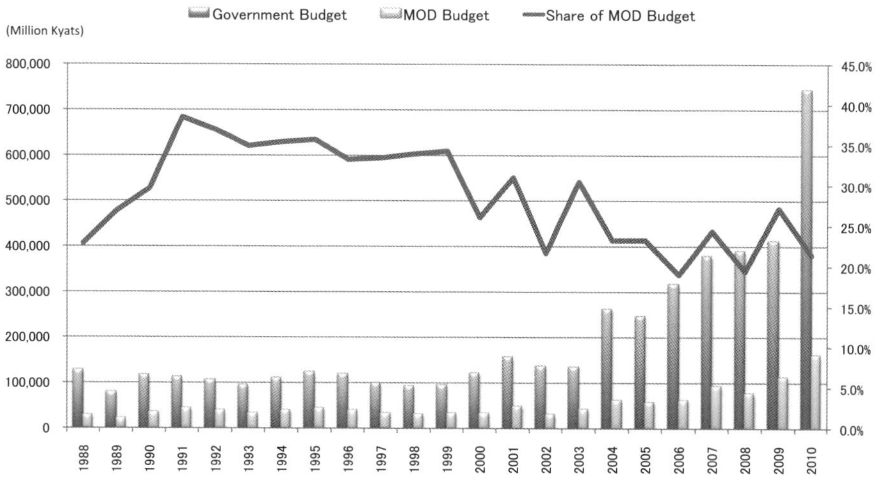

Source: Union of Myanmar Gazettes

Figure E.1 Government Budget, Defence Ministry Budget and Share of Defence Ministry Budget (FY1988 to FY2010)

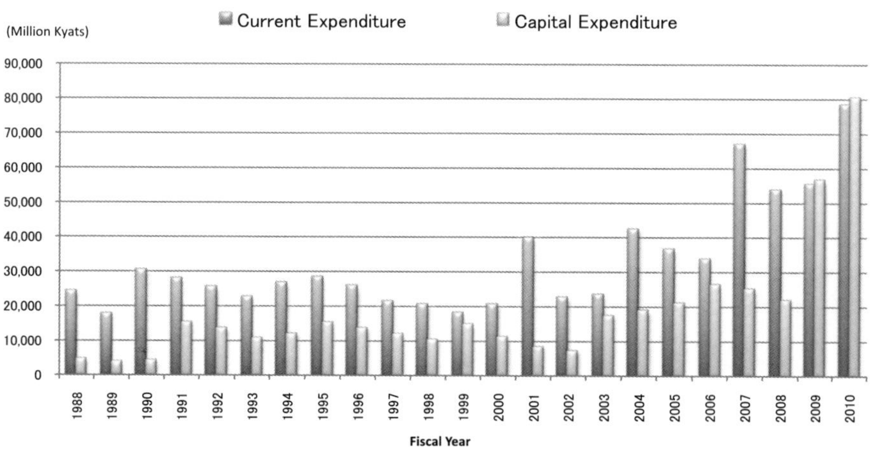

Source: Union of Myanmar Gazettes

Figure E.2 Defence Ministry Budget in Constant Price (FY1988 to FY2010)

decrease in the MOD budget does not necessarily mean that the defence budget itself has shrunk. The tatmadaw does obtain money from other sources.

Second, the MOD budget has fluctuated over the past two decades. It increased steadily in the early 1990s, partly because of the increased budget allocation to the MOD but also because of economic growth. The budget then stagnated in the late 1990s. It regained momentum from fiscal year 2004, and then underwent a marked increase from fiscal years 2007 to 2010.

Third, the growth of capital expenditures has been prominent. Its share of the MOD budget rose from the 10 per cent range in the 1980s to around 30 per cent range after 1991. The share remained high thereafter ranging from 20 per cent to 40 per cent, and then finally exceeded current expenditures in 2009 and 2010. A comparison of current expenditures and capital expenditures shows that the latter constituted the major part of the increase in defence spending up to 2003. Whereas the former increased little from 1988, the latter increased fourfold by 2003. It is extremely hard to ascertain accurately how capital expenditures were used, but some would have been spent on the construction of military facilities and the purchase of arms and ammunition, because normally capital expenditures on the acquisition of fixed assets can be written off over several years. This was closely connected to the modernization of the tatmadaw, which will be discussed below.

Military Expansion

This section reviews the organizational expansion and modernization of the tatmadaw. The size of the armed forces doubled from around 200,000 men in 1988 to 400,000 by 1999, which is close to the number that it is today; most of the expansion took place in the Army. This growth in manpower went hand in hand with organizational expansion. During the two decades from 1990, the number of Bureau of Special Operations (BSO) increased from two to six,[7] military region commands

[7] The six BSOs and the MRCs each currently controls are: BSO(1): Central, Northwest, North regional commands; BSO(2): Northeast, East, Delta regional commands; BSO(3): Southwest, South, West regional commands; BSO(4): Coastal, Southeast regional commands; BSO(5): Yangon Regional Command; BSO(6): Naypyidaw Regional Command.

(MRC) from nine to thirteen,[8] and light infantry divisions (LID) from eight to ten. New military operations commands (MOC), whose units are of regiment size, were established in Myeik and Loikaw in 1992, and then eleven more were added in May 1995 with more being organized from the end of the 1990s to the beginning of the 2000s; there are currently 21 MOCs. Meanwhile, as far as is currently known, the number of battalions, the tatmadaw's basic fighting unit, has increased from 168 to 605.

However, this increase, while clearly significant, did not meet the level for which the tatmadaw leaders originally had hoped: 500,000 active personnel by the turn of the century.[9] One of the reasons may have been the condition of the soldiers. As was learned, MOD current expenditures did not increase very much until 2003. However, the number of active military personnel doubled. This would suggest that even if current expenditures went mainly toward personnel expenses, the tatmadaw's treatment of its soldiers would have deteriorated over the course of time. Meanwhile, the soldiers were engaged in counter-insurgency operations of the sort described in the following quotation. This is from a book titled *Sen-yuu: Na mo naki yuusha-tachi* [Fellow soldiers: the brave men without names], written by Masaki Takabe, a former Japanese Self-Defence Force soldier who fought with the KNLA. In the quotation, "enemy soldiers" refers to the tatmadaw soldiers because Takabe was fighting against them as a member of the Karen National Liberation Army.

> The way the enemy bombardment with mortars and recoilless rifles was being concentrated between our defensive line and forward-most bunkers was normal. It was aimed at destroying the barbed wire, landmines and traps that had been laid there. Because of this, the enemy foot soldiers would halt their approach at some distance from our defensive line, and take the offensive after the bombardment was over. That was what they would normally do.
>
> But this time, we watched with our own eyes as the enemy soldiers advanced toward us through the storm of bombardment.... As always, this was no small number of artillery shells, and they were falling on our defensive line. A shell dropped and exploded at close range, right next to a foot soldier who had hit the deck. When the smoke and

[8] The following regional commands have been established since 1988: South Regional Command (1990), Delta Regional Command (1996), Coastal Regional Command (1996), and Naypyidaw Regional Command (2005).

[9] Andrew Selth, *Burma's Armed Forces*, p. 79.

> sand cleared, I could see that enemy soldiers nearby were no longer moving. This scene repeated itself again and again right in front of our eyes.
>
> "This can't be happening," I thought. "How could they be shelling us right over the heads of their own men?"[10]

Takabe's description clearly shows how the tatmadaw overwhelmed the enemy with sheer numbers. The increase in its soldiers enabled tatmadaw to adopt human-wave-like tactics in its operations. With its huge expansion of manpower after 1988, it almost seems as if the tatmadaw leadership was thinking that given the shortage of equipment, the most effective way to counter an enemy fighting a guerrilla war was by securing a great number of soldiers and relentlessly attacking.

This concentration on the Army's expansion began to change from the 2000s, after natural gas exports began giving the government financial leeway. Although not necessarily required for the current counter-insurgency, incremental upgrades to the Navy and Air Force have been progressing at considerable expense, a trend suggested by the tatmadaw's increased capital expenditures. In October 1989 Than Shwe, then Vice-Chief of General Staff (Army), visited China to conclude an arms deal worth USD 1.4 billion. Thereafter arms imports from China expanded, and consisted of tanks, armored vehicles, anti-aircraft weaponry, and other arms mainly to enhance the equipment of the Army.[11] In October 1996 Maung Aye visited China to conclude an agreement for military cooperation between Myanmar and China. Andrew Selth estimates that of the $1.38 billion in armaments supplied to Myanmar from 1987 through 1997, $1.16 billion, more than 80 per cent, came from China.[12] Indications are that this agreement included a new arms deal.[13] Weapons gradually grew in scale (e.g., surface-to-air and short-range ballistic missiles) in the 2000s, and in 2006 negotiations were held between Myanmar and Russia on the purchase of a Russian air defence

[10] Masaki Takabe, *Sen-yuu: Na mo naki yuusha-tachi* [Fellow soldiers: the brave men without names] (Tokyo: Namiki Shobo, 2008), pp. 33–4.

[11] For example, such weapons include in particular the T-69 (Type II) main battle tank, the 59D main battle tank, Type 63 light tank, Type 85 armored personnel carrier, and Type 90 armored personnel carrier. For this information, see Maung Aung Myoe, *Building the Tatmadaw: Myanmar Armed Forces since 1948* (Singapore: Institute of Southeast Asian Studies, 2009), p. 108.

[12] Selth, *Burma's Armed Forces*, Figure 14.

[13] Ibid., p. 137.

system.[14] Meanwhile, the Navy and Air Force, whose modernization had long been side-tracked because of fiscal restraints, began to get new equipment with twelve MIG-29/UBs purchased from Russia. It was also reported that the Air Force made another purchase of aircraft in 2009.[15]

In addition to Myanmar modernizing its military equipment, there has been constant speculation that the country has received support with nuclear technology from North Korea. In August 2009, the Sidney Morning Herald in Australia reported that the tatmadaw was constructing nuclear facilities, such as a plutonium extraction facility, with the support of North Korea, a report based on the testimony of a former Burmese military officer. Moreover, in August 2010, the Democratic Voice of Burma, an independent media organization based in Oslo, broadcasted a documentary and issued expert analysis on Myanmar's nuclear development plans. The conclusion of the analysis was that "it is likely that Myanmar is trying to attempt many of the nuclear program steps reported by previous sources. Unrealistic attempts, such as the Molecular Laser Isotope Separation project, unprofessional engineering drawings and the crude appearance of items in photos, suggest that success may be beyond Burma's reach."[16] Meanwhile, one expert points out that the military has been starting to shift its concern from domestic to external security.[17]

Although it is not known how far Myanmar's efforts to increase its military manpower and modernize its weaponry are based on a coherent grand strategy, these actions have steadily improved the capabilities of the tatmadaw. Compared with the situation in 1988, the influence of insurgents across Myanmar has been greatly diminished. There is no force capable of confronting the tatmadaw head-on in battle except for the UWSA, which controls the former Second Special Region (Wa State) and has about 20,000 soldiers.

Than Shwe's Leadership

General Than Shwe took command of the tatmadaw in 1992. He was not well known to people before his assumption of power. Nevertheless, he maintained his regime for nearly 20 years. How was he able to do this?

---

[14] Maung Aung Myoe, *Building the Tatmadaw*, p. 111.
[15] Ibid., p. 129.
[16] "Burma's Nuclear Ambitions," *Democratic Voice of Burma*, August 2010 <http://www.dvb.no/burmas-nuclear-ambitions/burmas-nuclear-ambitions-nuclear/expert-analysis/9297> [accessed 18 January 2011].
[17] Maung Aung Myoe, *Building the Tatmadaw*, p. 206.

Than Shwe was born in a village in Kyaukse Township, in present-day Mandalay Region, on 2 February 1933. He graduated from high school in 1951 following a break because of the Pacific War, then worked in a post office in Meiktilla in the same region for one year. In 1953 he entered the Officers Training School (OTS) as a cadet in the 9th class, received a commission as a second lieutenant and was assigned to the First Infantry Battalion. After participating in operations against the KNU and the BCP in Karen State, the southern Shan State and the region east of the Salween River, he was transferred to a psychological operations unit and worked for the Central Institute of Political Science, the training school for Burma Socialist Programme Party (BSPP) cadre. This took him away from the frontlines for four years. Then from 1966 he participated in operations in Karen State, the Irrawaddy delta and Pegu Yoma as a company commander in the 101st Light Infantry Battalion, which was part of the newly-established 77th Light Infantry Division. In 1970 at the age of 37 he assumed command of the 1st Infantry Battalion and fought in northern Shan State and in the region east of the Salween River.

He then returned to the general staff office in Yangon in 1975 to work in the Operations Bureau as a general staff officer (1) (operations) for about two years, after which he was appointed deputy commander of the 88th Light Infantry Division. He was promoted to division commander in 1980, and commanded counter-insurgency operations against the BCP in Shan State.[18] In 1983 he took command of the Southwest Military Region that controlled Irrawaddy Division, then assumed the post of Vice-Chief of General Staff (Army) in 1985, and joined in the coup in 1988. The reasons for Than Shwe's promotion to the number-two position in the tatmadaw were generally said to have been his achievements in military operations against the BCP in Shan State, and his obedience to his superiors. Then in 1992 when General Saw Maung, chairman of the SLORC and the Commander-in-Chief, fell ill and could no longer perform his duties, Than Shwe took over virtually becoming the head of state.[19]

---

[18] There are positives and negatives in his battle achievements during this period. See below for details. Benedict Rogers, *Than Shwe: Unmasking Burma's Tyrant* (Bangkok: Silkworm Books, 2010), pp. 97–100.

[19] This reason for Saw Maung's resignation is based on an official announcement (Ordinance 1992 No. 8), but what actually happened inside the regime is not clear.

Than Shwe's career suggests that he was a soldier to the core who reached the top via his battle experience and achievements in operations. Although in the 1980s he concurrently held a seat as a member of the BSPP's Central Committee, he had little political experience, a factor that helps explain the SLORC's (and later the SPDC's) seemingly parochial orientation in that it did not like negotiations or compromises, and associated political disputes with the disunity of the state. Immediately up on taking power, Than Shwe began giving priority to developing the tatmadaw. He never gained the support of the people, but this was not important to him or the tatmadaw. What carried weight with those inside the tatmadaw was Than Shwe's achievements in military operations along with the hefty number of medals he had accumulated as he steadily advanced through the ranks within the tatmadaw. Thus, the most important point for Than Shwe in his handling of the government was holding onto the support of the tatmadaw, rather than seeking to gain the support of the people. His 20-year dictatorship tells us that he was successful in maintaining this support. How did he succeed in doing this?

First of all, Than Shwe remained in control of the tatmadaw as the formal commander-in-chief by "violating" the formal rule on retirement. Neither he, nor Maung Aye, the Vice Commander-in-Chief, did not leave the tatmadaw even after they passed retirement age. While other officers in military operations left the tatmadaw in compliance with the retirement age, these two men along with aides like Thura Shwe Mann, then seen as a likely successor to Than Shwe, plus former Than Shwe aides Khin Nyunt and Tin Oo.

Officers leaving the tatmadaw moved to positions prepared for them in other government ministries and in state-owned enterprises. Those leaving posts as regional commanders usually took up positions at the level of minister or deputy minister. Middle-ranking officers had positions secured for them in accordance with their rank. Many of those at the level of minister served concurrently with their belonging, while middle-ranking officers retired after a certain period to become "civilian" officials. This method was handed down from Ne Win, without any changes. It facilitated the smooth operation of moving personnel out of the tatmadaw, thereby avoiding discontent in the officer corps over stagnant promotions while at the same time allowing Than Shwe himself to hold onto the position of the Commander-in-Chief for a long period of time. Moreover, the military's influence over the state could be retained by attaching officers to other ministries.

Than Shwe also expanded the officer corps.[20] For that, we simply have to look at the numbers of cadets attending the Defence Services Academy (DSA). There were 127 graduating cadets in the 30th class in 1989; thereafter in chronological order up to 1999 the numbers were: 120 (1990), 103 (1991), 83 (1992), 162 (1993), 130 (1994), 135 (1995), 229 (1996), 227 (1997), 207 (1998) and 237 (1999). This gradually rising trend turned sharply upward with 820 cadets for the Army alone in the DSA's 45th class in 2003. This number more then doubled to 1,922 in the 46th class of 2004.[21] There were 1,965 cadets in the 50th class of 2007; the 51st class in 2008 saw a decrease to 1,169 cadets for reasons that are unknown, but then the number jumped to 2,440 cadets in the 52nd class in 2009. It can be seen that ten times as many officer candidates are now being commissioned every year as compared with the end of the 1990s. With about 8,000 cadets at the DSA as of 2008,[22] officer training is expected to continue at this pace. When officer training facilities such as the Military Medical College (opened in 1993), the Military Institute of Technology (opened in 1994), and other officer training schools are included, the number of cadets commissioned in 2007, 2008 and 2009, as recorded in official gazettes, were 2,127, 1,585 and 2,948 respectively.

Such rapid expansion of the officer corps, basically a seniority-based bureaucratic body, needs to be supported financially. This requires the military to develop stable economic resources, because it can be assumed that new officers will serve for the next 30 to 40 years. The growth of Myanmar's natural gas revenues appears to be a major factor which made possible this increase in the 2000s. Another likely factor has been Myanmar's shift to a market-oriented economy which has offered the military

[20] The size of the officer corps has never been made public. A partial indicator, however, is the number of officers receiving commendation medals in 1995 in commemoration of 50 years since the establishment of the tatmadaw. These officers were those fulfilling the following four conditions: (1) they were in the military as of 27 March 1995, (2) they had served for 25 years or more as of that date, (3) they had fully performed their duties and (4) they had not committed a crime since the start of service. There were 1,174 officers (company grade or above) fulfilling these conditions (Army: 976, Navy: 105, Air Force: 93).

[21] In contrast, the numbers were small for the Navy and Air Force, with 50 and 68 cadets, respectively.

[22] *naungtakhit i aungsitthemya mweihpway myei* [The land where warriors of the next generation will be born] (Yangon: naingan goungye sapei taik, 2009), p. 110.

opportunities to build up a new structure of vested interests. One means for this is the military-owned corporate group. Below are two typical examples.

One example is the Union of Myanmar Economic Holding Limited (UMEHL), which was established in 1990. Its official purpose is to operate as a welfare program for active and retired tatmadaw soldiers. Its shares are held by the Directorate of Procurement of the MOD, active and retired soldiers (35,544 and 6,069 respectively) and units attached to the tatmadaw, and its authorized capital as of 2007 was 40 billion kyat.[23] Under the Adjutant General Office until 2002, the UMEHL is currently under the Directorate of Defence Industries and in 2007 had thirty-five 100 per cent-owned companies, nine subsidiary partnerships and seven affiliated partnerships. According to internal documents revealed by Aung Myoe, its profits were 12 billion kyat in fiscal year 2006.[24] Another corporate group owned by the tatmadaw is the Myanmar Economic Corporation established in 1997 under Ordinance No. 4 of that year. It is under the Quartermaster General Office of the MOD, and its fields of business encompass the production of iron and steel, cement, marble, sugar, methanol, roofing sheets, pharmaceuticals, wire, coal and beer, and are involved with trade, and others.[25] Besides such major ventures under the MOD, more than a few local army units have developed their own businesses.

Without doubt the tatmadaw has used its power to set up these corporate groups in order to expand its interests. This also indicates an insufficiency of income for officers and soldiers alike coming through the state budget. Although a little dated, a table showing the basic monthly salary for officers as of 2006 had the following: general: 800,000 kyat (about 640 USD), lieutenant general: 600,000 kyat (about 480 USD), major general: 400,000 kyat (about 320 USD), brigadier: 300,000 kyat (about 240 USD); for a private and lance corporal at the bottom of the salary scale, the numbers were 16,000 kyat (about 12.8 USD) and 22,000 kyat (about 17.6 USD) respectively.[26] These are clearly very low salaries. However, general-grade officers are a privileged social class in

---

[23] Maung Aung Myoe, *Building the Tatmadaw*, p. 176.

[24] Ibid., p. 178

[25] Ibid., pp. 181–4.

[26] The numbers in parentheses are calculated at the average rate in 2006 of 1 USD = 1,250 kyat. The data is from *Irrawaddy* (31 December 2009).

Thein Sein. (© Reuters/Aflo)

Aung San Suu Kyi. (© Reuters/Aflo)

Myanmar and are in fact very rich, meaning that generals get most of their income from sources that are off-budget, meaning those that are outside their official sources. The main off-budget sources are probably revenues from military corporations and "informal payments" from private companies in exchange for preferential treatment. An indication of this has been the emergence of entrepreneurs, notably the so-called tycoons like Tay Za of the Htoo group, Khin Shwe of the Zaygaba group and Zaw Zaw of the Max group, who actively seek to obtain concessions from the generals. The tatmadaw has thus used Myanmar's shift to a market-oriented economy to expand its economic interests.

In looking back on Than Shwe's leadership, he seized absolute power after 1992 by doubling as the head of the state and the Commander-in-Chief of the tatmadaw, and from his top post he maintained the smooth management and turnover of personnel in the officer corps by skilfully shuffling people in and out of posts. He controlled the tatmadaw by rebuilding its vested interests in response to Myanmar's transition to a market economy, thereby enabling his own position as dictator.

What is New?

In March 2011, at age 78, Than Shwe stepped down from his posts as Commander in Chief of the tatmadaw and the head of state to make way for "a transition to a new government." What does this transition mean for Myanmar? First of all, we should understand that the SPDC did not have to carry out the transition because of the regime's instability. The regime has incrementally increased its stability since 1988 and the establishment of the SLORC through a power structure centered on the tatmadaw and a financial foundation based on natural gas exports. Nevertheless, the SPDC has steadily proceeded with its "seven-step roadmap" issued in 2003, which included drafting a constitution, a referendum for approving the constitution and a general election.[27] In the meantime, Khin Nyunt, who as prime minister announced the roadmap

[27] The seven steps of the roadmap are as follows: (1) Reconvening of the National Convention that has been adjourned since 1996. (2) After the successful holding of the National Convention, step by step implementation of the process necessary for the emergence of a genuine and disciplined democratic system. (3) Drafting of a new constitution in accordance with basic principles and detailed basic principles laid down by the National Convention. (4) Adoption of the constitution through national

in his inaugural address, fell from power in November 2004, and a massive anti-government demonstration led by monks occurred in 2007. Despite such events, the roadmap was not withdrawn. This indicated Than Shwe's strong intention to proceed with the roadmap. So why did Than Shwe need the transition?

The main reason for the transition was clearly Than Shwe's age. He was already 70 years old in 2003 when the "seven-step roadmap" was issued. People age no matter how stable a regime; no dictator can live forever, even if wishing to do so. So what did Than Shwe prepare for the country and the tatmadaw after his retirement? In hindsight it would appear that he and the tatmadaw under his command carried out a slowly developing plan for the future, which included (1) ending the insurgencies that have plagued the nation since independence by incorporating anti-government armed groups into the tatmadaw, (2) bringing to an end the long years of provisional rule by enacting a new constitution and holding a general election, and (3) proceeding with a generational change in the leadership of the tatmadaw and of the state. Although this is all conjecture, since there has never been an acknowledgement of any such plan, developments since 2003 can be seen as heralding a transition period to a "post-Than Shwe" regime, which has thus begun to take place from 2011.

So far, what appears to have been Than Shwe's plan has moved steadily toward realization. When laying out the new post-SPDC political system, he was able to insert a political role for the tatmadaw into the new constitution, and was successful in fitting this into an official system. For instance, Article 6, "Basic Principles," Item 6 stipulates the tatmadaw's political participation as a principle of the new regime with the statement: "enabling the Defence Services to participate in the national political leadership of the State." Also, Article 17, Item 2 gives approval to the temporary transfer of tatmadaw officers to other ministries, and Articles 109 and 110 stipulate that a maximum of one-quarter of the members in both the House of Representatives and House of Nationalities are to be people designated by the Commander-in-Chief of the

referendum. (5) Holding of free and fair elections for Pyithu Hluttaws (Legislative bodies) according to the new constitution. (6) Convening of Hluttaws attended by Hluttaw members in accordance with the new constitution. (7) Building a modern, developed and democratic nation by the state leaders elected by the Hluttaw and the government and other central organs formed by the Hluttaw.

tatmadaw. Furthermore, Article 232, Item 2(c) states that the ministers of Defence, Home Affairs and Border Affairs are to be elected based on a list of candidates submitted by the Commander-in-Chief. In addition to these, a separate chapter on the "Defence Services" (Chapter 7) was created and put into the constitution.

The new Constitution took effect in May 2008 following approval in a referendum by the incredulously high 92.45 per cent of voters. The general election on 7 November 2010 was also held smoothly under extremely controlled conditions from the registration of political parties through to the announcement of voting results that declared a victory for the military-backed Union Solidarity and Development Party (USDP). Among the parliamentary members from the tatmadaw, several colonel-grade and many captain- and major-grade officers were designated for the People's Assembly, the House of Nationalities and each region/state assembly. Those influential officers previously excluded as military members of the parliament, and thus from acting as the conduit by which the tatmadaw leadership could reflect its will in parliament, were mainly middle-grade officers commissioned after 1988. From now on, however, the parliamentary seats designated by the Commander-in-Chief will also serve as temporary positions for captain- and major-grade officers commissioned 15 to 20 years earlier.[28] Although the democratization movement was expected to be more active following Aung San Suu Kyi's release from house arrest during the week following the general election,

[28] The members of each parliament are designated by the Commander-in-Chief. People's Assembly: Army 95 (colonel: 3, major: 50, captain: 42), Navy 6 (major: 6), Air Force 9 (major: 9). House of Nationalities: Army 54 (colonel: 2, major: 33, captain: 19), Navy 1 (major: 1), Air Force 1 (major: 1). Local assemblies: Kachin State Assembly: Army 13 (colonel: 1, major: 4, captain: 8). Kayah State Assembly: Army 5 (colonel: 1, major: 1, captain: 3). Kayin State Assembly: Army 6 (brigadier general: 1, colonel: 1, major: 1, captain: 3). Chin State Assembly: Army 6 (colonel: 1, major: 1, captain: 4). Sagaing Region Assembly: Army 25 (colonel: 1, major: 6, captain: 18). Tanintharyi Region Assembly: Army 7 (colonel: 1, major: 4, captain: 2). Pegu Region Assembly: Army 18 (colonel: 1, major: 6, captain: 11), Air Force 1 (major: 1). Magway Region Assembly: Army 17 (colonel: 1, major: 8, captain: 7), Air Force 1 (major: 1). Mandalay Region Assembly: Army 19 (colonel: 1, major: 12, captain: 6). Mon State Assembly: Army 6 (colonel: 1, major: 3, captain: 2). Yakain State Assembly: Army 10 (colonel: 1, major: 4, captain: 5), Navy 2 (major: 2). Yangon Region Assembly: Army 23 (colonel: 1, major: 16, captain: 6), Navy 6 (major: 6), Air Force 2 (major: 2). Shan State Assembly: Army 36 (colonel: 1, major: 9, captain: 26), Irrawaddy Region Assembly: Army 14 (colonel: 1, major: 2, captain: 11), Navy 2 (major: 2), Air Force 2 (major: 1, captain: 1).

thus far the military-led "democratization" process has progressed without confusion.

Regarding the generational change in the tatmadaw, a massive personnel reshuffle (37 positions alone involved regional commanders and above) was implemented on 27 August 2010, prior to the general election. Initially most people expected Lieutenant General Thura Shwe Mann, the joint chief of staff (Army, Navy, Air Force), to become the Commander-in-Chief of the tatmadaw; however, he retired from the military to run as a "civilian" candidate in the general election (and later was elected). It seems that this generational change was implemented more strictly because Thura Shwe Mann, born in 1947 and being 63 years old, had already passed retirement age. Speculation then varied regarding the next Commander-in-Chief and Vice Commander-in-Chief, some thinking that Than Shwe would stay in office, or that informal decisions had been made in favor of Lieutenant General Thura Myint Aung, a former Adjutant General, and Lieutenant General Ko Ko, a former commander of the BSO(3); however, at the presidential inauguration ceremony and the appointment of members of the Defence and Security Council, it was announced that Lieutenant General Min Aung Hlaing, who had become chief of the Joint Staff of the Three Armed Forces in August, was now the Commander-in-Chief. The Vice Commander-in-Chief position was taken by Major General Soe Win, a former chief of the BSO(6).

Lieutenant General Min Aung Hlaing graduated in 1978 in the 19th class of the DSA, and Major General Soe Win graduated in 1981 in the 22nd class (both ages estimated), so the Commander-in-Chief and his deputy are both 20 years younger than the men they replaced. Meanwhile, as mentioned previously, a major reshuffle of MR commanders and above had already taken place in August 2010, the positions going to officers who had graduated from the DSA up to the 24th class. Such a massive personnel reshuffling was not realized on an order from Than Shwe alone: high-ranking, influential commanders are not such an obedient group. They have been the most successful in the competition for promotion and have vested interests at stake, so decent alternative positions have been necessary to convince them to accept retirement. Therefore, cabinet posts or positions as the chief minister of a region or state have been prepared for these officers. Good examples are the officers who together with Lieutenant General Min Aung Hlaing were commanders of the six BSOs. Thar Aye, BSO (1) commander, became the chief minister of Sagaing Region; Ko Ko, who headed BSO (3), became Minister of Home Affairs; Khin Zaw, the BSO(4) commander, became the chief minister of Tanintharyi Region; Myint Swe of the BSO(5) became the chief minister of Yangon Region; and commander of BSO(6), Ohn Myint, became Minister of Co-operatives. It is evident that Than Shwe successfully executed a methodical generational change in the tatmadaw.

One aspect of Than Shwe's apparent plan that has not progressed smoothly has been the incorporation of insurgent groups into the tatmadaw. This was to be accomplished through the formation of the Border Guard Forces (BGF). The SPDC started to organize the BGF in April 2009 based on the 2008 Constitution, Article 338, which stipulates "All the armed forces in the Union shall be under the command of the Defence Services." The objective was to have the BGF under the command of tatmadaw officers, thereby bringing these forces under the tatmadaw chain of command, while the forces of the BGF were to be composed of insurgent groups that had reached cease-fire agreements with the tatmadaw. The negotiations were expected to run into difficulties, and did so when the MNDAA was incorporated into the BGF. On 27 August, only four months after negotiations had begun, a battle occurred between tatmadaw forces and the MNDAA side, which effectively controlled the First Special Region (Kokang). The death toll was 26 on the tatmadaw side and 8 on the MNDAA, with the MNDAA retreating across the border, turning over their weapons to the Chinese authorities and surrendering two days later. The tatmadaw won in this minor battle, and the MNDAA was incorporated into the BGF in December. Meanwhile the New Democratic Army — Kachin (NDA-K) and the Karenni People's Liberation Front — had been incorporated into the BGF in the previous month, but the UWSA, boasting the largest force (about 20,000 men), the Kachin Independence Organisation, the New Mon State Party and the KNU were still refusing to be incorporated. The odds favor the tatmadaw once this issue reaches the stage of armed conflict. However, negative effects such as the outflow of refugees can also be expected, and the tatmadaw would like to avoid any large-scale battle, something opposed by China and Thailand as well. The possibility of resolving the organizational issues of the BGF remains low in the short term.

Thus, although the war against insurgents could not be concluded prior to the advent of the "post-Than Shwe" period, the transition from a provisional government to a new regime itself proceeded smoothly. But while a representative government of sorts is being introduced, it is not democratization in the real sense of the word, nor can we expect it. The tatmadaw will retain its political influence from now on as the regime of Than Shwe has taken steps to imbed it formally into Myanmar's new political system, and so the confrontation with Aung San Suu Kyi and the democratization movement at large that she symbolizes is sure to continue.

Balancing and Charisma

The controlled transition did not mean that the "post-Than Shwe" period would be free of change as recent reforms clearly show. In fact, Than Shwe alluded to future report in a speech at the commencement of the 53rd class of the DSA on 10 December 2010. He talked about the results of economic development since 1988, spending more than half of his speech on this topic. Than Shwe listed examples since 1988 along with concrete figures, such as the acreage under rice cultivation, lengths of roads paved and number of bridges constructed during his rule, the numbers of new hospitals, clinics and schools, the amount of electricity generated; the number of industrial zones and the number of state-run factories, concluding his speech by stating that these were brought about by the conscientiousness (*sedàna*) of the tatmadaw.

Without doubt national defense and development policies have been used to justify the military's political involvement since 1988, but this speech was different from Than Shwe's abstract, sermonizing speeches of the past. The end of an era seemed to be present in that he spoke to the young officer cadets about the concrete results of development. The meaning in this may very well be that the USDP, even though a hastily formed pro-military political party, includes many business people, public officials and intellectuals. The year 2011 could be seen as the turning point when the security-oriented leadership of Than Shwe ended, and the new government changed direction toward the next era, namely, an era of developmentalism.

The government formed by President Thein Sein in March 2011 did not appear outwardly to have a reformers' cabinet. Thein Sein was the former prime minister and first secretary of the SPDC, and 26 of 30 new ministers were active or retired military officers, most of them former generals. Thus from a look at the list of those in power, it did not seem that real change would happen easily. With its constitution, a parliament and a check-and-balance mechanism in state power, the new government at least looked better than the previous junta for the near future. However, Thein Sein quickly proved such expectations wrong. Soon after his government formally took power, he set in motion a program of wide-ranging reforms.

The reforms have already enabled people to enjoy civil liberties, such as the right to organize labor unions, to take strike action in the work places, and to hold rallies and street demonstrations. Censorship of the print media has been gradually eased, resulting in the abolishment of nearly all formal media controls. As a result, today we can find Aung San Suu Kyi's portrait on the cover page of journals and even on state-owned newspapers. Such public displays not long ago were taboo and would have jeopardized one's safety. Economic reforms are also underway. The government started a managed float of the currency on 1 April 2012 to eliminate the negative effects caused by the gap between the greatly overvalued formal rate of the kyat and the market rate. On the same day, the government also adopted a market rate of 1 USD = 800 kyat for the calculation of its revenue. These steps were followed by the legislation of a new foreign investment law in November.

This top-down reform program is grappling with the ethnic-insurgency problem as well. The new leadership has given up, at least temporarily, trying to force the BGF scheme onto those insurgent groups that thus far have refused to be incorporated into the tatmadaw. Instead, the government has taken a softer approach, one aimed at attaining a long-term solution via a three-step process from concluding ceasefire agreements to building lasting peace accords. The process has begun well. Thus far Thein Sein has successfully generated what appears to be trust among those concerned in the new ceasefire negotiations. The UWSA has again accepted a ceasefire, and in January 2012 the government succeeded in concluding a ceasefire with the KNU, a historic event bringing to an end over 60 years of conflict between the two sides. Although some violent clashes have still occurred between the tatmadaw and Kachin Independent Army (KIA), we may soon be able to witness for the first time in Myanmar's post-independence history the cessation of combat between the tatmadaw and insurgent groups.

But the most striking move by the Thein Sein government has been its reconciliation with Aung San Suu Kyi. While Than Shwe never showed any sign of compromise or concession toward her and her party, Thein Sein quickly sought to build a more constructive relationship leading to his first meeting with Aung San Suu Kyi in the new capital of Nay Pyi Daw in August 2011. This was followed in October and again in January 2012 by the release of prisoners in an amnesty that included more than 500 so-called political prisoners. These moves eased Aung San Suu Kyi's cautious attitude toward Thein Sein, and she decided to have her NLD party legally registered and to participate in the April 2012 by-election, which resulted in its candidates winning in 43 of 45 parliamentary seats on the ballot.

Accompanying this national reconciliation was an improvement in Myanmar's international relations especially with Western countries. Re-engagement with the United States was crucial as it opened the way to Myanmar's reconnection with international society. In November 2011 Secretary of State Hillary Clinton paid a state visit, the first United States secretary of state to visit Myanmar in 56 years.[29] Clinton met with President Thein Sein in Nay Pyi Daw and then with Aung San Suu Kyi in Yangon, and this was followed by accelerated progress in 2012 toward the normalization of Myanmar-United States relations. Finally the United States announced the easing of economic sanctions on Myanmar, first in May and again in September. The second easing lifted the U.S. ban on the importing of goods from Myanmar, a diplomatic success offering the Myanmar government the opportunity to further its rapprochement with the U.S. This re-engagement of the United States with Myanmar gave the green light to other countries, notably Japan, which sent its foreign minister and then the minister of economy, trade and industry to Myanmar soon after Clinton's visit. Japan also decided to resume yen loans to Myanmar immediately while cancelling the country's $3.9 billion debt.

Myanmar's efforts to rebuild relations with the U.S. and its allies is also intended to rebalance its relations with China. Since the 1990s Myanmar has developed an overreliance on China which Thein Sein's government is seeking to reduce. On 30 September 2012, in the midst of the reengagement process with the U.S., Thein Sein announced the suspension of the Myitsone dam project in Kachin State, a major project started with China in 2006, because of its negative environmental and social impact.

How should we understand what is happening in Myanmar today? I would argue that Thein Sein is attempting two kinds of balancing: a China-United States balance in foreign policy and national security — developmentalism balancing in domestic policy. The previous military regime had put excessive weight on the relationship with China and

[29] The last visit was made by Secretary of State John Foster Dulles in 1955. In November 2012, U.S. President Barack Obama also visited Myanmar.

national security policy. While many people in the regime were aware that Myanmar's national interests were suffering from its unbalanced foreign and domestic policy orientation, Than Shwe did not (and likely could not) see Myanmar's reform as his responsibility, and other leaders around him had to follow his die-hard conservatism for their survival in power. With the transition to new leadership in March 2011, a chance to redress the policy imbalances emerged for the first time since 1988. The new leaders saw clearly that Myanmar's new government would have to acquire legitimacy with the United States and other Western countries, otherwise the sanctions these countries imposed on Myanmar would continue to be an obstacle to any reform effort.

This strategic thinking has led Thein Sein to undertake his series of domestic reforms and to seek reconciliation with the NLD. It appears that Aung San Suu Kyi also sees this moment as an opportunity and has decided to compromise to achieve a feasible solution given her age (she was born in 1945) and the organizational vulnerability of the NLD in the wake of the 15 years she spent under house arrest. During those many years she must have become aware of the realities of achieving her political goals. Given the seemingly favorable change in the political leadership, one can understand her decision to participate in the framework of the 2008 Constitution and to call for the easing of economic sanctions and for foreign capitals to invest in Myanmar, all of which she had once opposed.

This schematic understanding based on Thein Sein's dual balancing effort may suggest that he has successfully co-opted the opposition NLD into the new authoritarian regime, rather than a progressing toward democratization. Indeed, the USDP and the tatmadaw hold over 80 per cent of the seats in the Parliament while the NLD has less than seven per cent. In this respect Thein Sein's power is very secure, at least until the next general election. The easing of economic sanctions and pending investment boom will encourage the rapid growth of Myanmar's economy, as happened earlier in other Southeast Asian countries. If this growth improves the living standards of ordinary people, Thein Sein and the USDP's rule will become more stable, which could be a scenario similar to the developmental dictatorships that were once common in Southeast Asia.

However, this developmental dictatorship scenario based on Myanmar's objective political situation could very well play out differently because of the charismatic presence of Aung San Suu Kyi and her popularity in Myanmar and the world. Even though Thein Sein took the initiative in the current reforms, Aung San Suu Kyi's charisma appears to be co-opting some of his achievements. As a result, his leadership has so far not undermined her charisma. Meanwhile Thein Sein has helped Aung San Suu Kyi expand her political presence to a point where it is shaking the USDP's support base; in the last by-election USDP candidates lost in all four of Nay Pyi Daw's constituencies, where practically the only residents are government officers and their families. This result indicates that the USDP is no longer able to control the voting behavior of the electorate as it did in the previous general election.

It is difficult to imagine that the USDP will hold wide popular support by the time the next elections are held in 2015 or 2016, despite what might be its positive achievements, or that the NLD will develop as an institutionalized political party. Nevertheless, if the current political situation continues and the next elections are truly free and fair, then more than half of the seats in the parliament will most likely go to the opposition. Some political actors who prefer the status quo and gradual transition might not want to let that happen, and of course this expectation can affect the electoral strategies of both the USDP and NLD. But the present Myanmar has moved dramatically in a better direction bringing the country into a new political era. The direction that Myanmar takes will be determined by the interactions between its enduring military-centered power structure and the newly freed opposition under a charismatic leader.

BIBLIOGRAPHY

1. *Japanese*

Aoki Masahiko. *Hikaku Seido Bunseki ni Mukete* [Toward a comparative institutional analysis]. Tokyo: NTT Shuppan, 2001.

Akita Shigeru. "Teikoku to Guntai-Igirisu no Shokuminnchi Shihai to Indogun [Empire and the military — British colonial rule and the Indian Army]." In *Chiiki no Sekaishi II Shihai no Chiikishi* [Regional world history II: Regional histories of rule], ed. Takeshi Hamashita and Minoru Kawakita. Tokyo: Yamakawa Shuppansha, 2000, pp. 176–212.

Fujita Koichi., ed. *Myanma Iko Keizai no Hen'yo: Shijo to Tosei no Hazama de* [The transformation of Myanmar's transitional economy: Between market and control]. Chiba: Institute of Developing Economies, Japan External Trade Organization, 2005.

Fujiwara Kiichi. "Seifu-to to Zaiya-to: Tonan Ajia ni Okeru Seifu-to Taisei [The ruling party and the opposition party: The ruling party regime in Southeast Asia]." In *Koza Gendai Ajia, (3) Minshuka to Keizai Hatten* [Lectures on contemporary Asia, (3) Democratization and economic development], ed. Nobuyuki Ogiwara, pp. 229–69. Tokyo: Tokyo University Press, 1994.

———. "Minshuka Katei ni Okeru Gunbu: A. Stepan no Wakugumi to Firipin Kokugun [The military in the democratization process: The framework of A. Stepan and the Philippine military]." In *Nenpo Seijigaku* [Annual review of political science], pp. 141–58. Tokyo: Iwaanami Shoten, 1989.

Honda Takehiko. *Indo Shokuminchi Kanryo: Daieiteikoku no Cho Eriitotachi* [Indian colonial bureaucrats: Super-elites in the British Empire]. Tokyo: Kodansha Sensho Mechie, 2001.

Igarashi Seiichi. "Firipin to Biruma no Minshuka Hikaku Kosatsu: Togoteki Apurochi wo Tegakari to Shite [Comparative studies of democratization in the Philippines and Burma: A synthesized approach as a clue]." *Ajia Kenkyu* 48, no. 4 (2002): 52–72.

Igarashi Makoto. "Biruma ni Okeru Kokumin Togo to Minshushugi [National unity and democracy in Burma: The transformation process of the view on democracy in the military]." Master's thesis, Hitotsubashi University, Graduate School of Social Sciences, 2000.

Ikeda Kazuto. "Nihon Senryoki Biruma niokeru Myaunmya Jiken to Karen Shuwetuncha o Meguru Minzokuteki Keiken nitsuite [The Myaungmya

Incident and the Karen in Japanese-occupied Burma: Ethnic experience over Shwe Htun Kyar].” *Tonan Ajia: Rekishi to Bunka* 34 (2005): 40–79.

Izuoka Naoya. “Seigun Kankei wo Meguru Futatsu no Giron no Hihanteki Kento: Faina to Muzerisu [Two critical reviews of political-military relations].” *Hogaku* 51, no. 6 (1998): 1025–57.

———. “Kanryouteki Ken’ishugi, Fashizumu, Kokka Anzen Hosho Kokka: Nanbei Nanbu no Gunsei no Seikakuzuke wo Megutte (1) [Bureaucratic authoritarianism, fascism, and the national security state: On the characterization of military rules in southern South America (1)].” *Hogaku* 55, no. 4 (1991): 559–610.

———. “Kanryouteki Ken’ishugi, Fashizumu, Kokka Anzen Hosho Kokka: Nanbei Nanbu no Gunsei no Seikakuzuke wo Megutte (2) [Bureaucratic authoritarianism, fascism, and the national security state: On the characterization of military rules in southern South America (2)].” *Hogaku* 56, no. 4 (1992): 316–68.

Ishii Yoneo and Yumio Sakurai, eds. *Tonan Ajia Tairikubu* [Southeast Asia: The continental part]. Tokyo: Yamakawa Shuppansha, 1999.

Ito Toshikatsu. “Biruma Nomin no Ishiki Henka [Burmese farmers’ change in awareness].” In *Kawaru Tonan Ajia Shi Zo* [Changing Southeast Asian history’s image], ed. Ikehata Setsuho, pp. 285–306. Tokyo: Yamakawa Shuppansha, 2004.

Ino Kenji. “Myanma Minshuka Undo ni okeru Minshu Kodo no Syotokucho [The Characteristics of People’s Behavior in Myanmar’s Democratization Movement].” *Kita Kyushu Daigaku Hosei Ron Shu* 21, no. 1 (1993): 111–47.

———. “Myanma Kokugun no Seiji Kainyu no Ronri: ‘Kokumin Seiji’ Gainen o Chushin to Shite- [The Myanmar military’s logic of political intervention: Focusing on the concept of ‘national politics’].” *Tonan Ajia: Rekishi to Bunka* 29 (2000): 3–26.

Kamo Tomoki. *Gendai Chugoku Seiji to Jinmin Daihyo Taikai: Jindai no Kino Kaikaku to ‘Ryodo-Hiryodo’ Kankei no Henka* [Modern Chinese politics and the National People’s Congress: Functional reform of the People’s Congress and the change of ‘guider-guided’ Relations]. Tokyo: Keio Gijuku Daigaku Shuppankai, 2006.

Kawashima Kozo. *Shakaaishugi no Guntai* [The Socialistic Military]. Tokyo: Kodansha Gendai Shinsho, 1990.

Kida Junichi, ed. *Shakaishugikoku Kenposhu* [Collection of the Constitutions of Socialist States]. Tokyo: Chuo Daigaku Seikatsu Kyodo Kumiai Shuppankyoku, 1975.

Kiryu Minoru. “Biruma Shakaishugi to Sono Henyou Katei [Burmese socialism and its transformational process].” In *Biruma: Sono Syakai to Kachikan* [Burma: Society and social values], ed. Toru Ohno, Minoru Kiryu, and Teruko Satio, pp. 161–253. Tokyo: Gendai Ajia Shuppan-kai, 1975.

———. *Birumashiki Shakaishugi: Jiritsu Hatten heno Hitotsu no Jikken* [Burmese-style socialism: An experiment toward independence and development]. Tokyo: Kyoikusha, 1979.

Kimura Kan. *Kankoku niokeru "Keni Shugiteki" Taisei no Seiritsu: Ri Shoban Seiken no Hokai made* [The Establishment of an "Authoritarian" Regime in South Korea: The Collapse of the Rhee Syngman Regime]. Kyoto: Minerva Shobo, 2003.

———. *Minshuka no Kankoku Seiji: Boku Seiki to Yato Seijikatachi, 1961–1979* [Democratized South Korean Politics: Park Chung-hee and Opposition Politicians, 1961–1979]. Nagoya: Nagoya University Press, 2008.

Kudo Toshihiro. "Biruma [Myanma]: Birumashiki Shakaishugi: Kokumin Togo to Keizai Kaihatsu no Hazama de [Burma (Myanmar): Burmese style socialism: In the gap between national integration and economic development]." *Ajiken World Trend* 6, nos. 1 & 2 (2000): 26–30.

———. "Josho [Introduction]." In *Myanma Keizai no Jitsuzo: Naze Gunsei wa Ikinokoreta noka* [The reality of Myanmar's economy: How could the military regime survive?], ed. Toshihiro Kudo, pp. 3–24. Chiba: Ajia Keizai Kenkyujo, 2008.

Kumada Toru. "Myanma no Minshuka to Kokumin Togo Mondai ni okeru Gaisei Yoin: Beikoku Koshiki Kiroku ni Miru Shijitsu o Chushin to shite [Democratization in Myanmar and exogenous factors in integrating the people: Based on historical facts evidenced in the US official record]." *Ajia Kenkyu* 47, no. 3 (2001): 1–27.

Maung Tin. *Nomin Gaba: Biruma Jin no Senso Taiken* [Farmer Ngaba: The war experience of a Burmese]. Trans. Shizuo Katoda. Tokyo: The Daido Life Foundation, 1992.

Ministry of Foreign Affairs of Japan International Cooperation Bureau, ed. *Seifu Kaihatsu Enjo (ODA) Kunibetsu Deta Bukku* [Data book of the ODA by country]. Tokyo: Association for Promotion of International Cooperation, 2005.

Nakanishi Yoshihiro. "Kanryo-sei wo Hakaiseyo — Ne Win Taisei-ki Biruma ni Okeru Gyosei Kiko Kaikaku to Kokugun Shoko no Shukko [Destroy the bureaucracy: The administrative machinery reform in the Ne Win regime period and the transfer of military officers]." *Ajia afurika Chiiki Kenkkyu* 6, no. 2 (2007): 396–493.

Nishizawa Nobuyoshi. *Myanma no Keizai Kaikaku to Kaiho Seisaku: Gunsei 10-Nen no Sokatsu* [Economic reforms and liberation policy: Summary of the ten years under military rule] Tokyo: Keiseo Shobo, 2000.

Nemoto Kei. "1930 Nendai Biruma Nashonarizum ni Okeru Syakaishugi Juyou no Tokushitsu: Takin Too no Shiso Keisei wo Chushin ni [Properties of acceptance of socialism in the Burmese nationalism in 1930: Focusing on the thought formation of the Thakin Party]." *Tonan Ajia Kenky* 27, no. 4 (1990): 427–47.

———. *Aun San — Fuinsareta Dokuritsu Biruma no Yume* [Aung San: The locked-away dream of Burmese independence.) Tokyo: Iwanami Shoten, 1996.

———. "Biruma no Toshi Eriito to Nihon Senryoki: GCBA, Takinto, Shokuminchi Koto Bunkan wo Chushin ni [The urban elite in Burma and the Japanese occupation period: Focus on the GCBA, Thakin Party and colonial civil services]." In *Tonan Ajiashi no Naka no Nihon Senryo* [The Japanese occupation in the history of Southeast Asia.], ed. Aiko Kurashima, pp. 31–56. Tokyo: Waseda University Press, 1997.

———. "Biruma no Dokuritsu: Nihon Senryoki kara U Nu Jidai made [The Independence of Burma: From the Japanese Occupation to U Nu Era]." In *Iwanami Koza Tonan Ajia shi dai 8 kan: Kokumin Kokka Keisei no Jizai* [Iwanami course on the history of Southeast Asia, vol. 8, The era of nation-state building," ed. Kanichi Goto, pp. 173–202. Tokyo: Iwanami Shoten, 2002.

Ogiwara Nobuyuki. "Tonan Ajia no Seigun Kankei: Kindaika Katei ni Okeru Seigun Kankei [Political-military relations in Southeast Asia: Civil-military relations during the modernization process." In *Nenpo Seijigaku* [Annual review of political science], pp. 117–39. Tokyo: Iwaanami Shoten, 1989.

Ogushi Kazuo. *Gun to Kakumei: Peru Gunji Seiken no Kenkyu* [Military and revolution: A study of the Peruvian military regime]. Tokyo: Tokyo Daigaku Shuppan-kai, 1993.

Ohno Toru. "Biruma Kokugunshi (Sono 1) [History of the Burmese army (1)]." *Tonan Ajia Kenkyu* 8, no. 2 (1970a): 218–346.

———. "Biruma Kokugunshi (Sono 2) [History of the Burmese army (2)]." *Tonan Ajia Kenkyu* 8, no. 3 (1970b): 347–77.

———. "Biruma Kokugunshi (Sono 3) [History of the Burmese army (3)]." *Tonan Ajia Kenkyu* 8, no. 2 (1971): 534–65.

Okudaira Ryuji. "Kokumin Togo no Seiji Shiso: 'Birumateki Shakaishugiron' [Political ideas about national unity: An essay on 'Burmese socialism']." In *Koza Tonan Ajia-gaku Dai Rokkan Tonan Ajia no Shiso* [Lectures on Southeast Asian studies, vol. 6, The ideas of Southeast Asia], ed. Tsuchiya Kenji. Tokyo: Kobundo, 1990.

Saito Teruko. "Biruma no Momigome Kyoshutsu Seido to Noka Keizai: Chungare Mura no Jirei [The Burmese system of dedication of unprocessed rice and farmers' economy: The case of Chungale village]." *Ajia Keizai* 20, no. 6 (1979): 2–26.

———. "Biruma ni okeru Kome Yushutsu Keizai no Hatten [Development of the rice exporting economy in Burma]." In *Koza Tonan Ajiashi 6: Shokuminnchi Keizai no Hanei to Choraku* [Course history of Southeast Asia, vol. 6, Prosperity and the decline of colonial economy], ed. Teruko Saito. Tokyo: Iwanami Book Store, 2001.

———. "Nashonarizumu to Keizai Shiso: Biruma no Kokumin Keizai Koso o Megutte [Nationalism and economic ideas: On Burma's national economic plan]." In *Tonan Ajia ni Totte Nijusseiki towa Nani-ka: Nashonarizumu o Meguru Shiso Jokyo* [What is the 20th Century for Southeast Asia? The situation of nationalist ideas], ed. Kei Nemoto, pp. 39–59. Tokyo: Tokyo Gaikokugo Daigaku Ajia Afurika Gengo Bunka Kenkyujo, 2004.

Sakai Keiko. *Husein Iraku Seiken no Shihai Kozo* [The governance structure of Hussein's Iraqi administration.] Tokyo: Iwanami Shoten, 2003.

Sakuma Nobuyoshi. *Biruma [Myanmar] Gendai Seiji-shi Zoho-ban* [The modern political history of Burma (Myanmar), enlarged edition]. Tokyo: Keiso Shobo, 1993.

Shiokawa Nobuaki. *Genzonshita Shakaishugi Ribaiasan no Sugao* [Existed socialism: The true face of the leviathan] Tokyo: Keisou Shobou, 1999.

Shiraishi Takashi. *Shinban Indonesia* [Indonesia: A new edition]. Tokyo: NTT Press, 1996.

———. *Umi no Teikoku* [The empire in the sea]. Tokyo: Chuko Shinsho, 2000.

Suehiro Akira. "Tai no Gunbu to Minshuka Undo: 73 nen '10 Gatsu Seihen' kara 92 nen '5 Gatsu Ryuketsu Jiken' he [The Thai military and the democratization movement: From the 'October Revolution' of 1973 to the 'Bloody May Incident' of 1992]." *Shakai Kagaku Kenkyu* 44, no. 5 (1993): 48–95.

———. *Catch-Up Industrialization: The Trajectory and Prospects of Asian Economies.* Singapore: NUS Press, 2000.

Takahashi Akio. *Biruma Deruta no Beisaku Mura: 'Shakaishugi' Taiseika no Noson Keizai* [The economy of farm villages under the "socialist" regime in the Burmese delta]. Tokyo: Ajia Keizai Shuppankai, 1992.

———. "Biruma niakeru Nochi Hosei no Tenkai to Nomin no 'Shoyuken' [The development of agricultural land ownership legislation in Burma]." In *Tonan Ajia Noson Hatten no Shutai to Soshiki: Kindai Nihon tono Hikaku kara* [The subject and organization of the development of Southeast Asian villages: In comparison with modern Japan], ed. Hiroyoshi Kano, pp. 29–60. Tokyo: Asian Economic Research Institute, 1998.

———. "Myanma Konnan na Shijo Keizai heno Iko [Myanmar: Transition to difficult market economy]." In *Ajia Keizairon* [Theory of Asian economy], ed. Yonosuke Hara, pp. 295–323. Tokyo: NTT Press, 1999.

———. "Biruma: Gun ni Yoru 'Kaihatsu' no Teitai [Burma: The stagnation of "development" by the military]." In *Iwanami Koza Tonan Ajia-shi 9: "Kaihatsu" no Kidai to "Mosaku" no Jidai* [Iwanami Lectures, The History of Southeast Asia, 9: The Era of "Development" and "Searching"], ed. Akira Suehiro, pp. 205–30. Tokyo: Iwanami, 2002.

Takabe Masaki. *Sen-yuu: Na mo Naki Yuusha-tachi* [Fellow Soldiers: Brave Men without Names]. Tokyo: Namiki Shobo, 2008.

Takeshima Yoshinari. *Nihon Senryo to Biruma no Minzoku Undo: Takin Seiryoku no Seijiteki Josho* [Japanese occupation and the nationalist movement in Burma: The political rise of Thakin's forces]. Tokyo: Ryukei Shosha, 2003.

Takeda Yasuhiro. *Minshuka no Hikaku Seiji: Higashi-ajia Shokoku no Taisei Hendo Katei* [The comparative politics of democratization: The process of regime transformation in East Asian countries]. Tokyo: Mineruva Shobo, 2001.

Tsuchiya Kenji. *Karutini no Fukei* [The scenery of Kartini]. Tokyo: Mekon, 1991.

Tosa Hiroyuki. *Grobaru Jendah Poritikusu* [Global gender politics]. Tokyo: Sekai Shisosha, 2000.

Yano Toru. *Tai Biruma Gendai Seijishi Kenkyu* [A study of the contemporary political history of Thailand and Burma]. Kyoto: Center for Southeast Asian Studies, Kyoto University, 1968.

Yamamuro Shin'ichi, *Kimera* [Chimera]. Tokyo: Chukoshinsho, 1993.

2. *English*

Abinales, Patricio N. *Making Mindanao: Cotabato and Davao in the Formation of the Philippine Nation-State*. Quezon City: Ateneo de Manila University Press, 2000.

Acemoglu, Daron and James A. Robinson. *Economic Origins of Dictatorship and Democracy*. Cambridge: Cambridge University Press, 2006.

Adas, Michael. *The Burma Delta: Economic Development and Social Change on an Asian Rice Frontier, 1852–1941*. Madison: University of Wisconsin Press, 1974.

Adelman, Jonathan R. 1982. "Conclusion." In *Communist Armies in Politics*, ed. Jonathan R. Adelman, pp. 207–15. Boulder: Westview Press, 1982.

Alagappa, Muthiah, ed. *Coercion and Governance: The Declining Political Role of the Military in Asia*. Stanford: Stanford University Press, 2001.

——— ed., *Military Professionalism in Asia: Conceptual and Empirical Perspectives*. Honolulu: East-West Center, 2001.

Anderson, Benedict R. O'G. *Java in a Time of Revolution: Occupation and Resistance, 1944–1946*. Ithaca: Cornell University Press, 1972.

Anderson, Benedict. *Imagined Communities: Reflections on the Origin and Spread of Nationalism*. London; New York: Verso, 2006.

Anderson, Benedict. *The Spectre of Comparisons: Nationalism, Southeast Asia, and the World*. London: Verso, 1998.

Aung-Thwin, Maitrii. "Genealogy of a Rebellion Narrative: Law, Ethnology and Culture in Colonial Burma." *Journal of Southeast Asian Studies* 34, no. 3 (2003): 393–419.

Ba Maw. *Breakthrough in Burma: Memoirs of a Revolution, 1939–1946*. New Haven: Yale University Press, 1968.

Badgley, John H., ed. *Reconciling Burma/Myanmar: Essays on U.S. Relations with Burma*. NBR Analysis 15.1. Seattle: The National Bureau of Asian Research, 2004.

Badgley, John H. and Jon Wiant "The Ne Win BSPP Style of Bama Lo." In *The Future of Burma in Perspective: A Symposium*, ed. Josef Silverstein. Athens: Ohio University Center for International Studies, 1974.

Boudreau, Vince. *Resisting Dictatorship: Repression and Protest in Southeast Asia.* New York: Cambridge University Press, 2004.

Burma, Ministry of Information. *Is Trust Vindicated? A Chronicle of the Various Accomplishments of the Government Headed by General Ne Win during the Period of Tenure from November 1958 to February 6, 1960.* Rangoon: Director of Information, Government of the Union of Burma; Bailey & Swinfen, 1960.

Burma Socialist Programme Party. *The System of Correlation of Man and His Environment.* 1963.

———. *The Burmese Way to Socialism.* 1963.

———. "The Constitution of the Burma Socialist Programme Party." 1963.

Butwell, Richard. *U Nu of Burma.* Stanford: Stanford University Press, 1969.

Cady, John. F. *A History of Modern Burma.* Ithaca, N.Y.: Cornell University Press, 1958.

Callahan, Mary P. "On Time Warps and Warped Time: Lessons from Burma's 'Democratic Era'". In *Burma: Prospects for a Democratic Future*, ed. Robert I. Rotberg. Washington D.C: Brookings Institution Press, 1998.

———. "Cracks in the Edifice? Military-Society Relations in Burma since 1988." In *Burma-Myanmar: Strong Regime, Weak State?*, ed. Morten B. Pedersen, Emily Rudland, and Ronald J. May, pp. 22–51. Adelaide: Crawford House Publishing, 2000.

———. *Making Enemies: War and State Building in Burma.* Ithaca: Cornell University Press, 2003.

Capoccia, Giobanni and R. Daniel Kelemen, "The Study of Critical Junctures: Theory Narrative, and Counterfactuals in Historical Institutionalism." *World Politics* 59, no. 3 (2004): 341–69.

Casper, Gretchen and Michelle M. Taylor. *Negotiating Democracy: Transitions from Authoritarian Rule.* Pittsburgh: University of Pittsburgh Press, 1996.

Chandler, David P. *Brother Number One: A Political Biography of Pol Pot.* Boulder, CO: Westview Press, 1999.

Charney, Michael W. *A History of Modern Burma.* Cambridge: Cambridge University Press, 2009.

Collier, David, ed. *The New Authoritarianism in Latin America.* Princeton: Princeton University Press, 1979.

Colonel Chit Myaing. "In His Own Words." *Burma Debat*e 4, no. 3 (1996), <http://www.soros.org/burma/burmadebate/Bdjulaug97.html> (site is no longer available).

Commiso, Ellen Turkish. *Workers' Control under Plan and Market: Implications of Yugoslav Self-Management.* New Haven: Yale University Press, 1979.

Cottey, Andrew, Timothy Edmunds, and Anthony Forster, eds. *Democratic Control of the Military in Postcommunist Europe: Guarding the Guards.* Basingstoke: Palgrave, 2002.

Crouch, Harold. *The Army and Politics in Indonesia*. Ithaca: Cornell University Press, 1978.

Djilas, Milovan. *The New Class: An Analysis of the Communist System*. New York: F.A. Praeger, 1957.

Documentation and Research Department (DRD), Network for Democracy and Development (NDD), ed. *Civil & Military Administrative Echelon of State Peace and Development Council in Burma*. Mae Sot: DRD-NDD, 2007.

Dun, Smith *Memoirs of the Four-Foot Colonel*. Ithaca, NY: Southeast Asia Program, Department of Asian Studies, Cornell University, 1980.

Eztow, Natasha and Erica Frantz. *Dictators and Dictatorships: Understanding Authoritarian Regimes and Their Leaders*. New York: The Continuum International Publishing Group, 2011.

Feaver, Peter D. *Armed Servants: Agency, Oversight, and Civil-Military Relations*. Cambridge, MA: Harvard University Press, 2003.

Finer, Samuel E. *The Man on Horseback: The Role of the Military in Politics*. 2nd edition, extended. Boulder: Westview Press, 1988.

Fink, Christina. *Living Silence: Burma under Military Rule*. London: Zed Books, 2001.

Friedrich, Carl Joachim, "An Introductory Note on Revolution." In *Revolution*, ed. Carl J. Friedrich, pp. 3–9. New York: Atherton, 1937.

Fujita Koichi, Fumiharu Mieno, and Ikuko Okamoto. *The Economic Transition in Myanmar after 1988: Market Economy versus State Control*. Singapore: NUS Press, 2009.

Furnivall, John S. *The Fashioning of the Leviathan: The Beginnings of British Rule in Burma*. Canberra: Department of Anthropology, Research School of Pacific Studies, Australian National University, 1991.

———. *Education Progress in Southeast Asia*. New York: International Secretariat of the Institute of Pacific Relations, 1943.

———. *Colonial Policy and Practice: A Comparative Study of Burma and Netherlands India*. New York: New York University Press, 1956.

———. *A Study of the Social and Economic History of Burma (British Burma)*. Part III, *British Burma before the Opening of the Suez Canal 1861–62 to 1867–68*. Rangoon: The Economic and Social Board, Office of the Prime Minister, 1957.*

———. *A Study of the Social and Economic History of Burma (British Burma)*. Part IV, *British Burma from the Opening of the Suez Canal to the Annexation to Upper Burma, before the Opening of the Suez Canal 1868–69 to 1877–78*, Rangoon: The Economic and Social Board, Office of the Prime Minister, 1957.*

———. *A Study of the Social and Economic History of Burma (British Burma)*. Part V, *Burma under the Chief Commissioners, 1886–87 to 1896–97*. Rangoon: The Economic and Social Board, Office of the Prime Minister, 1957.*

———. *A Study of the Social and Economic History of Burma (British Burma).* Part VIa, *Burma under the Lieutenant-Governors, 1897–1898 to 1913–1914: The Pursuit of Efficiency*. Rangoon: The Economic and Social Board, Office of the Prime Minister, 1958.*

———. *A Study of the Social and Economic History of Burma (British Burma).* Part VIb, *Burma under the Lieutenant-Governors, 1913–1914 to 1923–1924: The Pursuit of Efficiency: The National Planning Commission*. Rangoon: The Economic and Social Board, Office of the Prime Minister, 1959.*

———. *A Study of the Social and Economic History of Burma (British Burma).* Part VII, *Dyarchy, 1923–1931: Boom, Depression and Recovery*. Rangoon: The Economic and Social Board, Office of the Prime Minister, 1960.*

———. *A Study of the Social and Economic History of Burma (British Burma).* Part VIII, *British Burma From the Rebellion of 1931 to the Japanese Invasion of 1941*. Rangoon: The Economic and Social Board, Office of the Prime Minister, 1960.*

———. *The Governance of Modern Burma*. 2nd edition, extended. New York: Institute of Pacific Relations, 1960.

Gandhi, Jennifer. *Political Institutions under Dictatorship*. Cambridge: Cambridge University Press, 2008.

Geddes, Barbara. "What Do We Know about Democratization After Twenty Years." *Annual Review of Political Science* 2 (1999): 115–44.

Geertz, Clifford. *Negara: The Theatre State in Nineteenth-Century Bali*. Princeton, NJ: Princeton University Press, 1980.

Guyot, Dorothy. "The Political Impact of Japanese Occupation of Burma." PhD dissertation, Yale University, 1966a.

———. "The Burma Independence Army: A Political Movement in Military Garb." In *Southeast Asia in World War II: Four Essays*, ed. Josef Silverstein. New Haven: Yale University, Southeast Asia Studies, 1966b.

Guyot, James F. "Bureaucratic Transformation in Burma." In *Asian Beaucratic Systems Emergent from the British Imperial Tradition*, ed. Ralph Braibanti, pp. 354–443. Durham, NC: Duke University Press, 1966.

Gyi Maung Maung. *Burmese Political Values: The Socio-Political Roots of Authoritarianism*. New York: Praeger, 1983.

Hlaing Kyaw Yin. "The Politics of State-Business Relations in Post-Colonial Burma." PhD dissertation, Cornell University, 2001.

* The seven volumes of reports and compilation of statistics are the reports submitted by Furnivall pursuant to a request from Ministry of National Planning of the Union of Burma. As they have 887 pages in total, they have not been published in book form. I would like to thank Professor Akiko Saito, who allowed me to view and copy those materials.

———. "Reconsidering the Failure of the Burma Socialist Programme Party Government to Eradicate Internal Economic Impediments." *South East Asia Research* 11, no. 1 (2003): 5–58.

Honna, Jun *Military Politics and Democratization in Indonesia*. New York: Routledge Curzon, 2003.

Horowitz, Donald L. *Coup Theories and Officers' Motives: Sri Lanka in Comparative Perspective*. Princeton, NJ: Princeton University Press, 1980.

Huntington, Samuel. *Political Order in Changing Societies*. New Haven: Yale University Press, 1968.

———. *The Soldier and the State: The Theory and Politics of Civil-Military Relations*. Harvard: Harvard University Press, 1985.

———. *The Third Wave: Democratization in the Late Twentieth Century*. Norman: University of Oklahoma Press, 1991.

Illeto, Reynaldo C. *Filipinos and Their Revolution: Event, Discourse, and Historiography*. Quezon City: Ateneo de Manila University Press, 1998.

Janowitz, Morris. *The Military in the Political Development of New Nations: An Essay in Comparative Analysis*. Chicago: University of Chicago Press, 1964.

Jenkins, David. *Suharto and His Generals: Indonesian Military Politics, 1975–1983*. Ithaca, NY: Cornell Modern Indonesia Project, Southeast Asia Program, Cornell University, 1984.

Kammen, Douglas and Siddharth Chandra. *A Tour of Duty: Changing Patterns of Military Politics in Indonesia in the 1990s*. Ithaca: Cornell Modern Indonesia Project, Southeast Asia Program, Cornell University, 1999.

Katzenstein, Peter J. and Rudra Sil. *Beyond Paradigms: Analytic Eclecticism in the Study of World Politics*. London: Palgrave Macmillan, 2010.

Kaufmann, Daniel, Aart Kraay and Massimo Mastruzzi. "Governance Matters IV: Governance Indicators for 1996–2004." World Bank Policy Research Working Paper 3630, 2005.

Kratoska, Paul H. *The Japanese Occupation of Malaya: A Social and Economic History*. London: Hurst, 1998.

Lasswell, Harold. "The Garrison State." *American Journal of Sociology* 46 (1941): 455–68.

———. "The Garrison State Hypothesis Today." In *Changing Patterns of Military Politics*, ed. S.P. Huntington. New York: The Free Press of Glencoe, 1962, pp. 51–70.

———. "Sino-Japanese Crisis: The Garrison State versus the Civilian State." *China Quarterly*, 11 (1937): 643–9.

Lenin, Vladimir I. *The State and Revolution*. London: Penguin, 1992.

Lintner, Bertil. *Outrage: Burma's Struggle for Democracy*. Hong Kong: Review Publishing Co., 1989.

———. *The Rise and Fall of the Communist Party of Burma (CPB)*. Ithaca, NY: Southeast Asia Program, Cornell University, 1990.

———. *Aung San Suu Kyi and Burma's Struggle for Democracy*. Chiang Mai: Silkworm Books, 2011.

Lissak, Moshe. *Military Roles in Modernization: Civil-Military Relations in Thailand and Burma*. Beverly Hills: Sage Publications, 1976.

Magaloni, Beatriz and Ruth Kricheli. "Political Order and One-Party Rule." *Annual Review of Political Science* 13 (2010): 123–43.

Maniruzzaman, Talukder. *Military Withdrawal from Politics: A Comparative Study*. Dhaka: University Press, 1988.

Mann, Michael. *The Sources of Social Power*. Vol. 2, *The Rise of Classes and Nation-States, 1760–1914*. Cambridge: Cambridge University Press, 1993.

Martinussen, John. Society, *State and Market: A Guide to Competing Theories of Development*. London & New Jersey: Zed Books Ltd, 1995.

Maung Maung. *Burma's Constitution*. The Hague: Martinus Nijhoff, 1959.

———. *Burma and General Ne Win*. New York: Asia Publishing House, 1969.

———. *The 1988 Uprising in Burma*. New Haven: Yale University Southeast Asia Studies, 1999.

McCoy, Alfred W. *Closer than Brothers: Manhood at the Philippine Military Academy*. New Haven: Yale University Press, 1999.

Michell, Brian R. *International Historical Statistics: Africa, Asia & Oceania, 1750–2005*. Basingsoke: Palgrave Macmillan, 2007.

Mietzner, Marcus. *The Politics of Military Reform in Post-Suharto Indonesia: Elite Conflict, Nationalism and Institutional Resistance*. Washington: East-West Center, 2006.

Migdal, Joel S. *Strong Societies and Weak States: State-Society Relations and State Capabilities in the Third World*. Princeton, NJ: Princeton University Press, 1988.

———. "Researching the State." In *Comparative Politics: Rationality, Culture, and Structure*, ed. Mark Irving Lichbach and Alan S. Zuckerman. Cambridge: Cambridge University Press, 2009, pp. 162–92.

Moscotti, Albert D. *Burma's Constitution and Elections of 1974: A Source Book*. Singapore: Institute of Southeast Asian Studies, 1977.

Mya Maung. *The Burma Road to Poverty*. New York: Praeger Publishers, 1991.

Mya Than and Nishizawa Nobuyoshi. "Agricultural Policy Reform and Agricultural Development in Myanmar." In *Myanmar Dilemma and Options: The Challenge of Economic Transition in the 1990s*, ed. Mya Than and J.L.H. Than. Singapore: Institute of Southeast Asian Studies, 1990.

Myint-U, Thant. *The Making of Modern Burma*. Cambridge: Cambridge University Press, 2001.

Myoe, Maung Aung. *Building the Tatmadaw: The Organizational Development of the Armed Forces in Myanmar, 1948–98*. Working Paper 327, Strategic and Defence Studies Centre, Australian National University, Canberra, 1998.

———. "Military Doctrine and Strategy in Myanmar: A Historical Perspective," Working Paper 339, Strategic and Defence Studies Centre, Australian National University, Canberra, 1999.

———. "Officer Education and Leadership Training in the Tatmadaw: A Survey." Working Paper 346, Strategic and Defence Studies Centre, Australian National University, Canberra, 2000.

———. *Building the Tatmadaw: Myanmar Armed Forces since 1948*. Singapore: Institute of Southeast Asian Studies, 2009.

Nemoto, Kei. "The Concepts of Dobama (Our Burma) and Thudo-bama (Their Burma) in Burmese Nationalism: 1930–1948." *The Journal of Burma Studies* 5 (2000): 1–16.

Nordlinger, Eric A. *Soldiers in Politics: Military Coups and Governments*. Englewood Cliffs, NJ: Prentice-Hall, 1977.

U Nu. *Saturday's Sun*. New Haven: Yale University Press, 1975.

O'Donnell, Guillermo A. *Modernization and Bureaucratic-Authoritarianism: Studies in South American Politics*. Berkeley: Institute of International Studies, University of California, 1979.

Pedersen, Morten B. *Promoting Human Rights in Burma: A Critique of Western Sanctions Policy*. Lanham, MD: Rowman & Littlefield Publishers, 2008.

Perlmutter, Amos. *The Military and Politics in Modern Times: On Professionals, Praetorians, and Revolutionary Soldiers*. New Haven: Yale University Press, 1977.

———. "The Comparative Analysis of Military Regimes." *World Politics* 33, no. 1 (1980): 96–120.

Pierson, Christopher. *The Modern State*. London: Routledge, 1996.

Pierson, Paul, *Politics in Time: History, Institutions, and Social Analysis*. Princeton: Princeton University Press, 2004.

Potter, David C. "Bureaucratic Change in India." In *Asian Bureaucratic Systems Emergent from the British Imperial Tradition*, ed. Ralph Braibanti, pp. 141–208. Durham, NC: Duke University Press, 1966.

Przeworsky, Adam, Michael E. Alvarez, Jose Antonio Cheibub, and Fernando Limongi. *Democracy and Development: Political Institutions and Well-Being in the World, 1950–1990*. New York: Cambridge University Press, 2000.

Putnam, Robert R. *The Comparative Study of Political Elites*. Englewood Cliffs, NJ: Prentice-Hall, 1976.

———. *Making Democracy Work: Civic Traditions in Modern Italy*. Princeton, NJ: Princeton University Press, 1993.

Pye, Lucian W. "The Army in Burmese Politics." In *The Role of The Military in Underdeveloped Countries*, ed. John J. Johnson, pp. 231–51. Princeton: Princeton University Press, 1962.

———. "Armies in the Process of Political Modernization." In *The Role of the Military in Underdeveloped Countries*, ed. John J. Johnson, pp. 68–89. Princeton, N.J.: Princeton University Press, 1962.

Revolutionary Council of the Union of Burma. *The Specific Characteristics of the Burma Socialist Programme Party*. Rangoon: the Central Committee of the BSPP, 1964.

Riggs, Fred W. *Thailand: The Modernization of a Bureaucratic Polity*. Honolulu: East-West Center Press, 1966.

Roeder, Philip G. *Where Nation-States Come From: Institutional Change in the Age of Nationalism*. Princeton & Oxford: Princeton University Press, 2007.

Rogers, Benedict. *Than Shwe: Unmasking Burma's Tyrant*. Chain Mai: Silkworm Books, 2010.

Rotberg, Robert I. *When States Fail: Causes and Consequences*. Princeton: Princeton University Press, 2004.

Rustow, Dankwart. A. "The Military in Middle Eastern Society and Politics." In *The Military in the Middle East*, ed. S.N. Fisher, pp. 3–20. Columbus: Ohio State University Press, 1963.

Saito Teruko and Lee King Kinong. *Statistics on the Burmese Economy: The 19th and 20th Centuries*. Singapore: Institute of Southeast Asian Studies, 1999.

Sattar, Babar. "Pakistan: Return to Praetorianism." In *Coercion and Governance: The Declining Political Role of the Military in Asia*, ed. Muthiah Alagappa, pp. 385–412. Stanford: Stanford University Press, 2001.

Scott, James C. *The Moral Economy of the Peasant: Rebellion and Subsistence in Southeast Asia*. New Haven: Yale University Press, 1976.

———. *Seeing Like a State: How Certain Schemes to Improve the Human Condition Have Failed*. New Haven: Yale University Press, 1998.

Sein Win. *The Split Story; An Account Of Recent Political Upheaval in Burma, with Emphasis on AFPFL*. Rangoon: The Guardian, 1959.

Selth, Andrew. *Transforming the Tatmadaw: the Burmese Armed Forces since 1988*. Canberra: Strategic and Defence Studies Centre, Research School of Pacific and Asian Studies, The Australian National University, 1996.

———. *Burma's Armed Forces: Power Without Glory*. Norwalk, CT: East Bridge, 2002.

Shiraishi, Takashi. "The Military in Thailand, Burma and Indonesia." In *Asian Political Institutionalization*, ed. Robert A. Scalapino, Seizaburo Sato, and Jusuf Wanandi, pp. 157–80. Berkeley, CA: Institute for East Asian Studies, 1986.

Shmitt, Carl. *Theory of the Partisan*. Translated by G.L. Ulmen. 2nd ed. New York: Telos Press, 2007.

Silverstein, Josef. *Burma: Military Rule and the Politics of Stagnation*. Ithaca, NY: Cornell University Press, 1977.

———. *Burmese Politics: The Dilemma of National Unity*. New Brunswick, NJ: Rutgers University Press, 1980.

Skidmore, Monique. *Karaoke Fascism: Burma and the Politics of Fear*. Philadelphia: University of Pennsylvania Press, 2004.

Slater, Dan. *Ordering Power: Contentious Politics and Authoritarian Leviathan in Southeast Asia*. Cambridge: Cambridge University Press, 2010.

Smith, Donald Eugene. *Religion and Politics in Burma*. Princeton: Princeton University Press, 1965.

Smith, Martin. *Burma: Insurgency and the Politics of Ethnicity*. 2nd ed. Dhaka: University Press, 1999.

Stepan, Alfred. *Rethinking Military Politics: Brazil and the Southern Cone*. Princeton: Princeton University Press, 1988.

Suehiro, Akira. *Catch-Up Industrialization: The Trajectory and Propsects of East Asian Economies*. Singapore: NUS Press, 2008.

Surachart Bamrungsuk. "Changing Patterns of Civil-Military Relations and Thailand's Regional Outlook." In *Civil-Military Relations: Building Democracy and Regional Security in Latin America, Southern Asia, and Central Europe*, ed. David R.Mares, pp. 187–205. Boulder: Westview Press, 1998.

Steinberg, David I. *Burma's Road Toward Development: Growth and Ideology under Military Rule*. Boulder: Westview Press, 1981.

———. *Burma: A Socialist Nation of Southeast Asia*. Boulder: Westview Press, 1982.

Stepan, Alfred. "The New Professionalism of Internal Warfare and Military Role Expansion." In *Authoritarian Brazil: Origins, Policies and Future*, ed. Alfred Stepan, pp. 47–65. New Haven: Yale University Press, 1973.

Stephen, Harber. "Authoritarian Government." In *The Oxford Handbook of Political Science*, ed. Barry R. Weingast and Donald A. Wittman. Oxford: Oxford University Press, 2006, pp. 693–707.

Tamada, Yoshifumi. *Myths and Realities: The Democratization of Thai Politics*. Kyoto & Meulbourne: Kyoto University Press and Trans Pacific Press, 2008.

Taylor, Robert. *Foreign and Domestic Consequences of the KMT Intervention in Burma*. Ithaca, NY: Southeast Asia Program, Department of Asian Studies, Cornell University, 1973.

———. "Burma." In *Military-Civilian Relations in South-East Asia*, ed. Zakaria Haji Ahmad and Harold Crouch, pp. 13–49. Oxford: Oxford University Press, 1985.

———. *The State in Burma*. Honolulu: University of Hawaii Press, 1987.

———. "Burma: Defence Expenditure and Threat Perception." In *Defence Spending in Southeast Asia*, ed. Chin Kin Wah, pp. 252–80. Singapore: Regional Strategic Studies Programme, Institute of Southeast Asian Studies, 1987.

———. *The State in Myanmar*. London: Hurst & Company, 2009.

Than, Tin Maung Maung. "Myanmar: Preoccupation with Regime Survival, National Unity and Stability." In *Asian Security Practice: Material and Ideational Influences*, ed. Muthiah Alagappa, pp. 390–416. Stanford: Stanford University Press, 1998.

Thawnghmung, Ardeth Maung. *Behind the Teak Curtain: Authoritarianism, Agricultural Policies and Political Legitimacy in Rural Burma/Myanmer*. London: K. Paul, 2004.

The World Bank. *A Decade of Measuring the Quality of Governance: Governance Matters 2007: Worldwide Governance Indicators, 1996–2006*. Washington: the World Bank, 2007.

Tinker, Hugh. *The Union of Burma: a Study of the First Years of Independence*. 2nd ed. London: Oxford University Press, 1959.

Tilly, Charles. "War Making and State Making as Organized Crime." In *Bringing the State Back In*, ed. Peter B. Evans, Dietrich Rueschemeyer, and Theda Skocpol, pp. 161–91. Cambridge: Cambridge University Press, 1985.

———. *Coercion, Capital, and European States, AD 990 –1990*. Cambridge: Basil Blackwell, 1990.

Tin Maung Maung Than. "Burma: The 'New Professionalism' of the Tatmadaw." In *Military Professionalsim in Asia: Conceptual and Empirical Perspectives*, ed. Muthiah Alagappa. Honolulu: East-West Center, 2002, pp. 163–78.

———. "Dreams and Nightmares: State Building and Ethnic Conflict in Myanmar (Burma)." In *Ethnic Conflicts in Southeast Asia*, ed. Kusuma Snitwongse and W. Scott Thompson, pp. 65–108. Singapore: Institute of Southeast Asian Studies, 2005.

Top, Saw Rock. "The Development and the Role of the Army in Burma (1941–1962)." PhD dissertation, Tokyo University, 1989.

Trinkunas, Harold Antanas. *Crafting Civilian Control of the Military in Venezuela: A Comparative Perspective*. Chapel Hill: University of North Carolina Press, 2005.

Trimberger, Ellen Kay. *Revolution from Above: Military Bureaucrats and Development in Japan, Turkey, Egypt, and Peru*. Piscatawy, NJ: Transaction Books, 1978.

Tullock, Gordon. *Autocracy*. Boston: Kuuwer Academic Pub, 1987.

U Thaung. *A Journal, a General and an Army in Burma*. Bangkok: White Lotus, 1995.

Van Doorn, J. "The Officer Corps: A Fusion of Profession and Organization." *European Journal of Sociology* 6 (1965): 262–82.

Walinsky, Louis J. *Economic Development in Burma, 1951–1960*. New York: Twentieth Century Fund, 1962.

Wiant, John A. "The Vanguard Army: The Tatmadaw and Politics in Revolutionary Burma." In *The Armed Forces in Contemporary Asian Societies*, ed. Edward A. Olson and Stephen Jurika Jr. London and Boulder, CO: Westview Press, 1986, pp. 241–67.

Wiant, John W. "Tradition in the Service of Revolution: The Political Symbolism of Taw-hlan-ye-khit." In *Military Rule in Burma Since 1962*, ed. F.K. Lehman, pp. 59–72. Tokyo: Maruzen Asia, 1981.

———. "Ideology and Organization in Revolutionary Burma." PhD dissertation, Cornell University, 1982.

Wiant, John W. and David I. Steinberg. "Burma: Military and National Development." In *Soldiers and Stability in Southeast Asia*, ed. Soedjati Djiwandono and Yong Mun Cheong, pp. 293–321. Singapore: Institute of Southeast Asian Studies, 1988.

Win Min. "Looking Inside The Burmese Military." *Asian Survey* 48, no. 6 (2008): 1018–37.

Wolters, O. W. *History, Culture, and Region in Southeast Asian Perspectives*. Ithaca, NY: Southeast Asia Program Publications, 1999.

Woo-Cumings, Meredith ed. *The Developmental State*. Ithaca: Cornell University Press, 1999.

Yawnghwe, Chao-Tzang. "The Politics of Authoritarianism: The State and Political Soldiers in Burma, Indonesia, and Thailand." PhD dissertation, The University of British Columbia, 1997.

Yergin, Daniel. *Shattered Peace: The Origins of the Cold War and the National Security State*. Boston: Houghton Mifflin, 1977.

Zaw Oo and Win Min. *Assessing Burma's Ceasefire Accords*. Washington, DC: East-West Center, 2007.

Zuckerman, Alan. "'Political Elite': Lessons from Mosca and Pareto." *The Journal of Politics* 39, no. 2 (1977): 324–44.

Zuk, Gary and William. R. Thompson. "The Post-Coup Military Spending Question: A Pooled Cross-Sectional Time Series Analysis." *The American Political Science Review* 76, no. 1 (1982): 60–74.

3. *Burmese*

Aung Gyi. *(màsàlà) bàhoe kawmiti thòe pê sa* [Letters to the (Programme Party) Central Committee], 1976.

Burma, anonymous. *naingando lounjounyêi hnìn ou'chou'hmù simankêin saou' "kà"* [State Security and Administration Project Book, vol. A], 1962.

______. *pyihtaunzù hsousheli'thammàdà myanmanainngando pàtàmàacein pyidù thòu ywêichetinhmyau'hchîn hkanyàthô pyidù hlwu'to kozâhlemyâ ì koyêihma'tân akyînjou' 1974* [Career summaries of candidates elected to the First People's Assembly of the Socialist Republic of the Union of Burma 1974].

______. *pyihtaunzù hsousheli'thammàdà myanmanainngando dùtìyàacein pyidù thòu ywêichetinhmyau'hchîn hkanyàthô pyidù hlwu'to kozâhlemyâ ì koyêihma'tân akyînjou' 1978* [Career summaries of candidates elected to the First People's Assembly of the Socialist Republic of the Union of Burma 1978].

______. *pyihtaunzù hsousheli'thammàdà myanmanainngando tàtìyàacein pyidù thòu ywêichetinhmyau'hchîn hkanyàthô pyidù hlwu'to kozâhlemyâ ì koyêihma'tân akyînjou' 1981* [Career summaries of candidates elected to the First People's Assembly of th Socialist Republic of the Union of Burma 1981].

______. *bahoukomiti winlâunmyâ î kôuyêi hma'tân acînjou'* [Career summaries of the Central Committee Member Candidates] [1971?].

______. *dùtìyàacein patinyilahkan bahoukomiti winlâunmyâ î kôuyêi hma'tân acînjou'* [Career summaries of the Central Committee Member Candidates for the Second Party Congress], 1973.

______. *tàtìyàacein patinyilahkan bahoukomiti winlâunmyâ î kôuyêi hma'tân acînjou'* [Career summaries of the Central Committee Member Candidates for the Third Party Congress], 1977.

———. *ayêipoacein patinyilahkan bahoukomiti winlâunmyâ î kôuyêi hma'tân acînjou'* [Career summaries of the Central Committee Member Candidates for the Emergency Party Congress], 1977.

———. *chînpyine dethápatikomiti tàtìyàacein patinyilahkan kouzâhlemyâ ì kôuyêi hma'tân acînjou'* [Career summaries of the representatives of the Chin State Local Party Committee for the Third Party Congress], 1977.

———. *d.ìrawàditâin dethápatikomiti tàtìyàacein patinyilahkan kouzâhlemyâ ì kôuyêi hma'tân acînjou'* [Career summaries of the representatives of the Irrawaddy Division Local Party Committee for the Third Party Congress], 1977.

———. *mandàlêitâin dethápatikomiti tàtìyàacein patinyilahkan kouzâhlemyâ ì kôuyêi hma'tân acînjou'* [Career summaries of the representatives of the Mandalay Division Local Party Committee for the Third Party Congress], 1977.

———. *yangountâin dethápatikomiti tàtìyàacein patinyilahkan kouzâhlemyâ ì kôuyêi hma'tân acînjou'* [Career summaries of the representatives of the Yangon Division Local Party Committee for the Third Party Congress], 1977.

———. *zagâintâin dethápatikomiti tàtìyàacein patinyilahkan kouzâhlemyâ ì kôuyêi hma'tân acînjou'* [Career summaries of the representatives of the Sagaing Division Local Party Committee for the Third Party Congress], 1977.

———. *sàdou'tà acein patinyilahkan bahoukomiti winlâunmyâ î kôuyêi hma'tân acînjou'* [Career summaries of the Central Committee Member Candidates for the Fourth Party Congress], 1981.

———. *pinsàmà acein patinyilahkan bahoukomiti winlâunmyâ î kôuyêi hma'tân acînjou'* [Career summaries of the Central Committee member candidates for the Fifth Party Congress (elected Central Committee candidates)], 1985.

———. *pinsàmà acein patinyilahkan bahoukomiti winlâunmyâ î kôuyêi hma'tân acînjou'*. [Career summaries of the Central Committee member candidates for the Fifth Party Congress (candidates from local party committees and the military party committee)], 1985.

Chit Hlaing. *myanmà hsousheli' lânzin hnin' lânzin pati ì twêkho myomyinpoun dabôtayâ pyi' polapoun akyîn khyou' hma' tân* [The way to Burmese Socialism and the summary of records for the ideological formation process of the Programme Party (housed by the Yangon University Historical Research Center)], 1992.

———. *lù thàbawà tayâ hnin' dimokàresi ì wehpan ta'thô tôte'yê dabôtayâ* [Human nature and the criticizable development principle of democracy], 1959

Ko Ko Maung. "pari twin thauntin hkè singà [Staying in Paris]." *myàwàdi* 3, no. 10 (1955).

———. "pari twin thauntin hkè singà [*Staying in Paris*]." *myàwàdi* 4, no. 2 (1955).

———. "pari twin thauntin hkè singà [*Staying in Paris*]." *myàwàdi* 4, no. 3 (1956).

———. "pari twin thauntin hkè singà [*Staying in Paris*]." *myàwàdi* 4, no. 10 (1956).

Shwe Moe. "shènau' ma ni thô [The Contradiction of Before and After]." *myàwàdi* 3, no. 6 (1955).

______. "kywunno thì thô u naun cho [The U Naung Cho That I Know]." *myàwàdi* 4, no. 9 (1956).

______. "o thakhin sô sô [Oh, Takhin Soe, Takhin Soe]." *myàwàdi* 5, no. 3 (1957).

______. "myanmanainngan hnin' dimokàresi hsousheli' wada [Burma and Democratic Socialism]." *myàwàdi* 5, no. 12 (1957).

______. "dimokàresi sousheli' sàni' hnin' namàrupa wada [Democratic Socialism and Namarupa wada]." *myàwàdi* 6, no. 1 (1957).

______. "namàrupà wada hnin' lu' lôkà hpyi'sin [Namarupa wada and the formation of human society]" *myàwàdi* 6, no. 2 (1957).

______. "namàrupà wada hnin' lu' lôkà hpyi'sin [Namarupa wada and the formation of human society]." *myàwàdi* 6, no. 3 (1958).

______. "namàrupà wada ì lù thàmâin [Namarupa wada and human history]." *myàwàdi* 6, no. 4 (1958).

kagwyêi wangyî htanà [Ministry of Defence]. *naingando wadà hnìn ta'màdo lou'ngânzin*. [National Ideology and the tatmadaw's activity], 1959.

Dr. Kyi, Daw Myint and Dr. Lin Naw In Gya. *1958–1962 myanmà nainganyê dùtìyàtwê* [Burmese politics 1958–1962, vol. 2]. Yangon: te'kàtomyâ pounhnei'tai' [Yangon: Yangon University Press], 1991.

Maung Maung, Bohmûgyî [Colonel Maung Maung]. *si'àcheikhandabomyâ* [The basis of the military doctrine]. si'pinnya àthîn [Military Knowledge Association], 1959.

Maung Soe. *hsousheli' wadà* [Socialism]. Yangon: htûnêi saou' phyànchiyêi htanà, 1939.

U Mya Han, Dr. Daw Khin Hla Han, U Kyaw Gyeing, U Than Lwin, and U Sein Myint. *myanmà nàinnganyêi sàni' pyâun kalà 1962–1974, pàtàmà* [Period of Change in the Burmese Political System 1962–1974]. Yangon: te'kàtomyâpounhnei'tai' [Yangon University Press], 1993.

Mya Win. *ta'madaw gâunzâun myâ thàmaîn akyînkyou' 1941 khùhni' hmà 1990 pyìhni' ahtì*. [The concise history of military leaders, from 1941 to 1990]. Yangon: pyankyàyê wankyîhtanà, 1991.

myanmà hsousheli' lânzin pati [Burma Socialist Programme Party]. *lu hnìn pa'wûnjin dòu ì innyàminnyà dabotayâ* [Principle of interaction between people and the environment], 1963.

myanmà hsousheli' lânzinpati patisîyôunyêi bàhokomiti htanàjou' [Burma Socialist Programme Party, Central Committee Headquarters]. *ta'màdo àtwîn sì patiàphwèàsîmyâ ì phwèsîpoun hnìn lou'ngântawunmyâ* [Formation and duty of the party organization within the military], 1971.

myanmà hsousheli' lânzinpati bàhokomiti htanàjou' [Burma Socialist Programme Party, Central Committee Headquarters]. *myanmà hsousheli' lânzinpati o'kàhtàgyî ì hki' pyâun tohlanyêi thàmâinwin mèingûn pâunjou' àhma' thi'*. [Burma Socialist Programme Party, chairman's historical speeches, vol. 1], 1985.

———. *myanmà hsousheli' lânzinpati o'kàhtàgyî ì hki' pyâun tohlanyêi thàmâinwin mèingûn pâunjou' àhma' hni'* [Burma Socialist Programme Party, chairman's historical speeches, vol. 2], 1985.

myanmà hsousheli' lânzinpati patisîyôunyêi bàhokomiti htanàjou' [Burma Socialist Programme Party, Party Organizing Central Committee Headquarters] *myanmà hsousheli' lânzinpati phwèsîpoun àchekhansîmyîn* [Burma Socialist Programme Party's organization rules], 1975.

myanmà hsousheli' lânzin pati bahoukomiti [Burma Socialist Programme Party Central Committee]. *tàtìyà acein patinyilahkan thò tinthwînthì bahoukomiti î nàinnganyêi àsiyinhkansa.* [The Central Committee political report submitted to the Third Party Congress], 1977.

myanmà hsousheli' lânzinpati bahoukomiti htanàjou' [Burma Socialist Programme Party, Organizing Central Committee Headquarters] *pinsàmà acein patinyilahkan thò tinthwînthì bahoukomiti î nàinnganyêi àsiyinhkansa* [The Central Committee political report submitted to the Fifth Party Congress], 1985.

myanmà hsousheli' lânzin pati ayêipo patinyilahkan [Burma Socialist Programme Party, Special Party Congress] *thàtînhlwa* (1988) [Information (1988)], 1988.

Myanmanainnganàsôeyà [Government of Burma] *thôunlàpa'zin àyasìsayîn* [List of senior officials in government]. Yangounmyò: myanmanainngando àsôeyà pounhnei'yêi kìrìya htanàwan, 1942.

myanmanainngan pyidêyêiwangyîhtanà àdwînwanjou'yôun [Burma, Ministry of Home Affairs, Office for the Secretary]. *myanmanaingan àyasìmyâ sayîn (tàhni' lêikyeinhtou') àhma'-thi', 1948 khùhtì* [List of senior officials in the Government of Burma, vol. 1, 1948]. myanmanainngando àsôeyà pounhnei'yêi kìrìya htanàwan, 1950.

———. *myanmanaingan àyasìmyâ sayîn,àhma'-lêi, 1951 khùhtì (tàhni' hna'kyeinhtou')* [List of the senior officials in the Government of Burma, vol. 4, up to 1951 (published semi-annually)]. myanmanainngando àsôeyà pounhnei'yêi kìrìya htanàwan, 1953.

———. *myanmanaingan àyasìmyâ sayîn,àhma'-ngâ (tàhni' hna'kyeinhtou'), 1953 khùhtì.* [List of the senior officials in the Government of Burma, vol. 5 (published semi-annually), up to 1953]. myanmanainngando àsôeyà pounhnei'yêi kìrìya htanàwan, 1954.

———. *myanmanaingan àyasìmyâ sayîn,àhma'-shi' (tàhni'thàkyeinhtou'), 1957 khùhtì.* [List of the senior officials in the Government of Burma, vol. 8 (published semi-annually), 1957]. myanmanainngando àsôeyà pounhnei'yêi kìrìya htanàwan, 1958.

———. *myanmanaingan àyasìmyâ sayîn,àhma'-hkôe (tàhni'thàkyeinhtou'), 1958 khùhtì.* [List of the Senior Officials in the Government of Burma, vol. 9 (published semi-annually) 1958]. myanmanainngando àsôeyà pounhnei'yêi kìrìya htanàwan, 1959.

———. *myanmanaingan àyasìmyâ sayîn,àhma'-ta'se (tàhni'thàkyeinhtou'), 1959 khùhtì.* [List of the Senior Officials in the Government of Burma, vol. 10 (published semi-annually) 1959]. myanmanainngando àsôeyà pounhnei'yêi kìrìya htanàwan, 1960.

———. *myanmanaingan àyasìmyâ sayîn,àhma'-sethi' (tàhni'thàkyeinhtou'), 1960 khùhtì.* [List of the Senior Officials in the Government of Burma, vol.11 (published semi-annually) 1960]. myanmanainngando àsôeyà pounhnei'yêi kìrìya htanàwan, 1961.

myanmanainngan pyidù kaunsi àhsìnhsìn hnìn àlou'àhmù hsaunàhpwè àhsìnhsìn dò ì tawan hnìn lou'paingwìn ùbàdei. [Duties and authorities of Burmese People's Councils at each level and executive organizations]. Yangon: pyidùhlu'to.

myanmanainngan tohlanyêi àsôeyà,pyidêyêiwangyîhtanà [Revolutionary Government of Burma, Ministry of Home Affirs]. *myanmanaingan tohlanyêi àsôeyà àyasìmyâ sayîn 1962* [List of the Senior Officials in the Government of Burma, 1962]. àsôeyà pounhnei'yêi kìrìya htanà, 1962.

naingan goungye sapei taik [National Pride Publication]. *naungtakhit i aungsitthemya mweihpway myei* [The Land Where Warriors of the Next Generation Will Be Born]. Yangon: naingan goungye sapei taik, 2009.

nainngando tohlanyêi kaunsi [State Revolutionary Council]. *myanmà hsousheli' lânzin* [The Burmese Way to Socialism], 1962.

nainngando kaunsi yôun [Office of State Council]. *myònepyidùkaunsi àlou' àhmùhsaunàhpwè ì tawan hnìn lou'painkhwìn hsainya hsaunywe' pounnîsàni' sazaun, 1982.9.22* [Institutions relating to duties and authorities of the Township People's Council Executive Organization, 1982.9.22].

Dr. Nyi Nyi. *myanmà nàinngan amyôuthâ môkwûn (1975): mye'hmau'kalà myanmà nàinngan hma'tân* [Burmese national memory 1975: A record of the contemporarry Burmese state], Yangon: pàgansaou', 1978.

pati sîyôunyê bahoukomiti [Party Organizing Central Committee]. *pàhtámà acein patinyilahkan pati bahoukomiti ou'katàgyî ì mèingônmyâ hhnìn pati sîyôunyê bahoukomiti î nàinnganyêi àsiyinhkansa* [First Party Congress, the Central Committee Chairman's speech and political report of the party organizing committee], 1971.

pyidaunsù myanmanainngando asôya kagweyê wangyîhtanà [Government of the Union of Burma Ministry of Defence]. *nainngando wadà hnìn ta'mado lou'ngânzin* [The national ideology and the role of the defence services], 1959.

pyihtaunzù myanmanaingan tawhlanyêi kaunsi [Burmese Government Revolutionary Council]. *myanmà hsousheli' lânzin pati ì wìthethàle'hkànamyâ* [The characterisics of Burma's Socialist Programme Party] Yangon: myanmà hsousheli' lânzin pati bàhoekawmàti htanàjou', 1964.

———. *tohlanyêi kaunsi ì lou'hsaunche' thàmâin àkyînjou'* [A concise history of the Revolutionary Council], 1982.

pyihtaunzù myanmanaingan tohlanyêi kaunsi ùbàdè myâ (tàtìyàtwê) (1973 khùhni' hmà 1974 khùhni'ahtì) [Laws of Union of the Burman Revolutionary Council (1973 to 1974)].

pyidêyêiwangyîhtanà [Ministry of Home Affairs]. *àhtweihtwei ou'chou'yêi ûsîhtanà lou'ngânmyâ hsainyathindânhma'sù* [The lecture note about activities of the Department of General Administration]. àhtweihtwei ou'chou'yêi ûsîhtanà, 1982.

U Se Maung. *kyàno ì pyidùwandânbàwà -tàyâyêkandà hnìn ou'chou'yê kandà-* [My Life as a public servant: Legal works and government]. Yangon: anonymous, 2001.

simankêin hnìn bandayêi wangyîhtanà [the Ministry of Planning and Finance]. *pyihtaunzù myanma naingando ì bandayêi, sîpwâyêi, luhmuyêi àcheiàneimyâ tinpyàche'* 1990–91 [Financial, economic and social situation in the Union of Burma 1990–91], 1993.

si'thàmâin pyàdai' hnìn ta'màdo mogûndai'hmûyôun [The Defence Services Museum and Historical Research Institute]. *ta'madothamâin sàtou'htàtwè 1948–1962* [The history of the military, vol. 4, 1948–1962], 1996.

———. *ta'madothamâin pinsàmàtwè* 1962–1974 [The history of the military, vol. 5, 1962–1974], 1997.

———. *ta'madothamâin hsàhtàmàtwè* 1974–1988 [The history of the military, vol. 6, 1974–1988], 1998.

Soe Min Htaik. *naungtakhit i aungsitthemya mweihpway myei* [The land where warriors of the next generation will be born]. Yangon: naingan goungye sapei taik, 2009.

U Thein Hlaing and Dr. Daw Khin Hla Han, eds. *myanmà nàinnganyêi sàni' pyâun kalà 1962–1974, tàtìyàtwê* [The phase of change in the Burmese politics 1962–1974, vol. 3]. Yangon: te'kàtomyâpounhnei'tai', 1993.

Than Tin. *kothwè phyi'pa'myâ si'hsinyêipyî si'hsinyêi hmà* [From operation to operation: The events I experienced]. Yangon: auntankhun ponhnei'tai', 2004.

4. *National Archives Department*

NAD 4/1(28) sà-1970 24447. hkàyain lounjounyêi hnìn ou'chou'hmùkomiti hpyapounhkàyain: hpyapounmyòe hkàyain atwîn hpwèsîhtâthô sîpwâyêi luhmùyêi hsainyaathîn ahpwèmyâ sayîn hnìn myònealai' hpwèsîhtâthô sîpwâyêi luhmùyêi hsainya athîn ahpwèmyâ sayîn [Security and Administration Committee, Phyapon District], 1972.1.6. National Archives Department, Yangon.

NAD 3/(22) à-72 12213. pyihtaunzù myanmanaingan ou'chou'yêi sani'thi' hpohtou'yêi saou'1 pyihtaunzù myanmanaingan ou'chou'yê sani'thi' hpohtou' sìsi'yê ahpwè ì asîyinkhanza 1972.2.14 [Report on the implementation of the new administrative system of the Union of Burma, vol. 1, 1972/2/14], 1972.

NAD 3/(22) à-72 (1971). pyihtaunzù myanmanaingan ou'chou'yêi sani'thi' hpohtou'yêi saou'2: ou'chou'yêisàni' thàmâin akyînjou' satânmyâ [Report on the implementation of the new administrative system of the Union of Burma, vol. 2].

NAD 3/(22) sà-1971 19814. pyihtaunzù myanmanaingan ou'chou'yêi sani'thi' hpohtou'yêi saou'3: tohlanyêikaunsi o'kàhtà ì hnyunkyâche' hnìn pyihtaunzù myanmanaingan ou'chou'yê sani'thi' hpohtou' sìsi'yê ahpwè ì asîawêi hma'tânmyâ 1971 jannawarilà [Report on the implementation of the new administrative system of the Union of Burma, vol. 3].

5. *Defence Services Museum and Historical Research Institute*

CD-173(6). 1961 khùhni' ta'màdaw nilahkan si'yêijou'yôun àsiyinkhanza (9-2-61).

CD-173(7). 1961 khùhni' ta'màdaw nilahkan si'htau'jou'yôun àsiyinhkanza.

CD-173(10). ta'màdaw nilahkan (1961) ta'màdaw luinâ (àyasi màhou'dumyâ).

CD-173(12). 1959 khùhni' àhma'(1)lèkyìnyêita' mingàladoun dwin kyînpàtho ta'màdaw nilahkan,kagweyêi ûsîjou' ì nilahkanphwìn mèingûn (14.9.59).

CD-173(17). 1959 khùhni' àhma'(1)lèkyìnyêita' mingàladoun dwin kyînpàtho ta'màdaw nilahkan,ta'màdaw hnìn pa'the'ywè pyiduludù ì htinmyinche'myâ ko sânsi'weiphanchîn hswêinwêibwê.

CD-173(19). 1959 khùhni' àhma'(1)lèkyìnyêita' mingàladoun dwin kyînpàtho ta'màdaw nilahkan,kyànkhainyêikei'sà hnìn pa'the'tho hswêinwêibwê.

CD-218. nangando kagweyêi polàsi. 1959.

CD-341(2). 1962 khùhni' ta'màdaw nilahkan kagweyê wangîhtanà kagweyê ûsîgyou' (kyî) àsiyinhkanza [1962 Tatmadaw Conference, Report of Ministry of Defence, General Staff Office (Army)].

CD-620(15). pyihtaunzù myanmanaingan tohlanyêi àsôeyà kagweyêhtanà kagweyê ûsîgyou' (kyî) [Union of Burma, Revolutionary Government, Ministry of Defence, General Staff Office (Army)]. saàhma'-8(kà)/yà/û3(kà), 1963/4/19.

CD-874. 1965 khùhni' ta'màdaw nilahkan si'ûsî,si'yêi hnìn si'htau' hsainya tinpyà hswêinwêiche' myâ [The 1965 Tatmadaw Conference, discussion on operations, military administration and logistics].

CD-878(1). 1962 khùhni' ta'màdaw nilahkan kagweyê ûsîgyou' ì mèingûn myâ hnìn tâin si' htanàgyou' athîdî hmà hsêinwêiche' myâ [The 1962 Tatmadaw Conference, Chief of General Staff's speech and discussion from the military region headquarters].

CD-879. 1963 khùhni' ta'màdaw nilahkan kagweyê ûsîgyou' ì mèingûn myâ hnìn tâin si' htanàgyou' athîdî hmà si'ûsî,si'yêi hnìn si'htau' hsainya tinpyà hswêi nwêi che' myâ [Chief of General Staff's speech and discussion from the military region headquarters on operation, military administration and logistics].

CD-879(2). 1962 khùhni' ta'màdaw nilahkan kagweyê ûsîgyou' (kyî) àsiyinkhanza [The 1962 Tatmadaw Conference, Report of the Chief of General Staff (Army)].

CD-880. 1964 khùhni' ta'màdaw nilahkan kagweyê ûsîgyou' (kyî) àsiyinkhanza [The 1964 Tatmadaw Conference, Report of General Staff Office (Army)].

CD-880(4). 1964 khùhni' ta'màdaw nilahkan si'htau'jou'yôun àsiyinkhanza [The 1964 Tatmadaw Conference, Report of Quartermaster General Office].

CD-880(6). 1964 khùhni' ta'màdaw nilahkan si'yadûkhàn àtwînwan ì àsiyinkhanza [The 1964 Tatmadaw Conference, Report of Military Appointment General Office].

CD-880(8). 1964 khùhni' ta'màdaw nilahkan si'yêijou'yôun àsiyinkhanza [The 1964 Tatmadaw Conference, Report of Adjutant General Office].

CD-881 1965 khùhni' ta'màdaw nilahkan tohlanyêi kaunsi o'kàhtà bojou'gyî ne wîn ì nilahkan hpwìn mèingûn (29-11-65) [The 1965 Tatmadaw Conference, Revolutionary Council Chairman General Ne Win's opening speech (29 November 1965)].

CD-881(5). 1965 khùhni' ta'màdaw nilahkan si'htau'jou'yôun àsiyinhkanza [The 1965 Tatmadaw Conference, Report of Quartermaster General's Office].

CD-881(6). 1965 khùhni' ta'màdaw nilahkan si'yêijou'yôun àsiyinkhanza [The 1965 Tatmadaw Conference, Report of the Adjutant General's Office].

CD-882(2). 1966. khùhni' ta'màdaw nilahkan kagweyê ûsîgyou' ì mèingûn [The 1966 Tatmadaw Conference, Report of Adjutant General's Office].

CD-882(3). 1966 khùhni' ta'màdaw nilahkan dùtìyà kagweyê ûsîgyou' (kyî) ì mèingûn [The 1966 Tatmadaw Conference, Vice-Chief of General Staff (Army)'s speech].

CD-882(4). 1966 khùhni' ta'màdaw nilahkan kagweyêhtanà ta'màdaw si'ûsîhsainya tinpyàche' hnìn hswêinwêiche'myâ [The 1966 Tatmadaw Conference, Ministry of Defence briefing and a discussion of the military operations].

CD-882(5). 1966 khùhni' ta'màdaw nilahkan kagweyêhtanà ta'màdaw si'yêihsainya tinpyàche' hnìn hswêinwêiche'myâ [The 1966 Tatmadaw Conference, Ministry of Defence briefing and a discussion of military affairs].

CD-882(6). 1966 khùhni' ta'màdaw nilahkan kagweyêhtanà pyidùta'màdawyêiya tinpyà che' hnìn hswêinwêiche'myâ [The 1966 Tatmadaw Conference, Ministry of Defence briefing and a discussion about the People's Military].

CD-882(9). 1966 khùhni' ta'màdaw nilahkan kagweyêhtanà ta'màdaw si'ûsîhsainya tinpyàche'myâ (khà) [The 1966 Tatmadaw Conference, Ministry of Defence briefing on military operations (a)].

CD-883(1). 1968 khùhni' ta'màdaw nilahkan tâinsi'htanàjou' àthìdì hmà hswêinwêi tinpyàche'myâ [The 1968 Tatmadaw Conference, briefing and discussion of Military Region Headquarters].

CD-883(7). 1968 khùhni' ta'màdaw nilahkan kagweyê ûsîgyou' (kyî) àsiyinkhanza (1-10-66 hmà 30-9-67 ye'nèàhtì) [The 1968 Tatmadaw Conference, report of the General Staff Office (Army) (1 October 1966 to 30 September 1967)].

CD-883(8). 1968 khùhni' ta'màdaw nilahkan kagweyê ûsîgyou' (kyî) àsiyinkhanza (1-10-67 hmà 30-9-68 ye'nèàhtì) [The 1968 Tatmadaw Conference report of General Staff Office (Army) (1 October 1967 to 30 September 1968)].

CD-883(9). 1968 khùhni' ta'màdaw nilahkan si'yêijou'yôun àsiyinkhanza [The 1968 Tatmadaw Conference, Report of the Adjutant General Office].

CD-883(10). 1968 ta'màdonilahkan si'yadûhhkàn atwînwan àsiyinhkanza [The 1968 Tatmadaw Conference, Military Appointment General Office].

CD-884(1). 1969 khùhni' ta'màdaw nilahkan tâinsi'htanàjou' àthîdî hmà hswêinwêi tinpyàche'myâ [The 1969 Tatmadaw Conference, briefing and discussion of Military Region Headquarters].

CD-884(2). 1969 khùhni' ta'màdaw nilahkan dùtìyàkagweyêi ûsîjou' (kyî) ì panama hnìn nìgôunjou' mèingûnmyâ [The 1969 Tatmadaw Conference, Vice-Chief of General Staff (Army), chairman's closing speech].

CD-884(4). 1969 khùhni' ta'màdaw nilahkan si'htau'jou'yôun àsiyinhkanza [The 1969 Tatmadaw Conference, Report of Quartermaster General Office].

CD-884(5). 1969 khùhni' ta'màdaw nilahkan kagweyêi wangyîhtanà kagweyê ûsîgyou' (kyî) àsiyinkhanza (1-4-68 hmà 31-3-69 ye'nèàhtì) [The 1969 Tatmadaw Conference, General Staff Office (Army) Report (1 April 1968 to 31 March 1969)].

DR-8373. si'yadûhkànamèinmyâ,htaunkôyâhkùni'sehnîhkù jannàwarilà hmà htaunkôyâhkùni'sehnîhkù èplilà àhtì [Compiled military appointment letters: January to April 1972].

DR-8374. si'yadûhkànamèinmyâ,htaunkôyâhkùni'sehnîhkù meilà hmà htaunkôyâhkùni'sehnîhkù zulainlà àhtì [Compiled military appointment letters: May to July 1972].

DR-8375. si'yadûhkànamèinmyâ,htaunkôyâhkùni'sehnîhkù ógou'là hmà htaunkôyâhkùni'sehnîhkù dizinbalà àhtì [Compiled military appointment letters: August to December 1972].

DR-8376. si'yadûhkànamèinmyâ,htaunkôyâhkùni'sethôunhkù jannàwarilà hmà htaunkôyâhkùni'sethôunhkù zunlà àhtì [Compiled military appointment letters: January to June 1973].

DR-8377. si'yadûhkànamèinmyâ,htaunkôyâhkùni'sethôunhkù zulainlà hmà htaunk ôyâhkùni'sethôunhkù dizinbalà àhtì [Compiled military appointment letters: July to December 1973].

DR-8378. si'yadûhkànamèinmyâ,htaunkôyâhkùni'selêihkù jannàwarilà hmà htaunkôyâhkùni'selêihkù zunlà àhtì [Compiled military appointment letters: January to June 1974].

DR-8379. si'yadûhkànamèinmyâ,htaunkôyâhkùni'selêihkù zulainlà hmà htaunkôyâhkùni'selêihkù dizinbalà àhtì [Compiled military appointment letters: July to December 1974].

DR-8380. si'yadûhkànamèinmyâ,htaunkôyâhkùni'sehkùni'hkù jannàwarilà hmà htaunkôyâhkùni'sehkùni'hkù zunlà àhtì [Compiled military appointment letters: January to June in 1977].

DR-8381. si'yadûhkànamèinmyâ,htaunkôyâhkùni'sehkùni'hkù zulainlà hmà htaunkôyâhkùni'sehkùni'hkù dizinbalà àhtì [Compiled military appointment letters: July to December 1977].

DR-8382. si'yadûhkànamèinmyâ,htaunkôyâhkùni'sehsi'hkù jannàwarilà hmà htaunkôyâhkùni'sehsi'hkù zunlà àhtì [Compiled military appointment letters: January to June 1978].

DR-8383. si'yadûhkànamèinmyâ,htaunkôyâhkùni'sehsi'hkù zulainlà hmà htaunkôyâhkùni'sehsi'hkù dizinbalà àhtì [Compiled military appointment letters: July to December 1978].

DR-8384. si'yadûhkànamèinmyâ,htaunkôyâhkùni'sekôkù jannàwarilà hmà htaunkôyâhkùni'sekôkù zunlà àhtì [Compiled military appointment letters: January to June 1979].

DR-8385. si'yadûhkànamèinmyâ,htaunkôyâhkùni'sekôkù zulainlà hmà htaunkôyâhkùni'sekôkù dizinbalà àhtì [Compiled military appointment letters: July to December 1979].

DR-8386. si'yadûhkànamèinmyâ,htaunkôyâsi'sekù jannàwarilà hmà htaunkôyâsi' sekù zunlà àhtì [Compiled military appointment letters: January to June 1980].

DR-8387. si'yadûhkànamèinmyâ,htaunkôyâsi'sekù zulainlà hmà htaunkôyâsi'sekù dizinbalà àhtì [Compiled military appointment letters: July to December 1980].

DR-8388. si'yadûhkànamèinmyâ,htaunkôyâsi'seti'kù jannàwarilà hmà htaunkôyâsi' seti'kù zunlà àhtì [Compiled military appointment letters: January to June 1980].

DR-8389. si'yadûhkànamèinmyâ,htaunkôyâsi'seti'kù zulainlà hmà htaunkôyâsi' seti'kù dizinbalà àhtì [Compiled military appointment letters: July to December 1981].

DR-8390. si'yadûhkànamèinmyâ,htaunkôyâsi'sehnîkù jannàwarilà hmà htaunkôyâsi'sehnîkù zunlà àhtì [Compiled military appointment letters: January to June 1981].

DR-8391. si'yadûhkànamèinmyâ,htaunkôyâsi'sehnîkù zulainlà hmà htaunkôyâsi' sehnîkù dizinbalà àhtì [Compiled military appointment letters: July to December 1982].

DR-8392. si'yadûhkànamèinmyâ,htaunkôyâsi'sethôunkù jannàwarilà hmà htaunkôyâsi'sethôunkù zunlà àhtì [Compiled military appointment letters: January to June 1983].

DR-8452. kagweyêi wangyîhtanà lèikyìnyêi hnyunkyâyêihmûyôun thamâinàkyîn 1991 khùhni' [History of the Ministry of Defence Training Agency (1991)].

DR-8460. kagweyêi wangyîhtanà si'yadûkhànjou' yôun thàmâin [History of the Ministry of Defence Personnel Bureau].

DR-8461. kagweyêi wangyîhtanà ta'màdaw si'hsêiyêi àyasìjou'yôun ì thàmâin [History of the Ministry of Defence Inspection Bureau].

DR-8482. kagweyêi ûsîgyou' (kyî) thàmâin akyîn 1948-84 [History of the General Staff Office (Army) 1948-84].

DR-8483. kagweyêi wangyîhtanà si'htau'jou'yôun àkyâunàya,kagweyêi wangyîhtan à,si'htau'jou'yôun thàmâin, 1985/7/15.

DR-9852. lèkyìnyêi hnyunkyâyêihmû yôun thàmâin àkyîn 1991 [History of Training Bureau (1991)].

DR-8502. si'yadûhkànamèinmyâ,htaunkôyâsi'sethôunkù zulainlà hmà htaunkôyâsi'sethôunkù dizinbalà àhtì [Compiled military appointment letters: July to December 1983].

DR-8503. si'yadûhkànamèinmyâ,htaunkôyâsi'selêikù jannàwarilà hmà htaunkôyâsi' selêikù zunlà àhtì [Compiled military appointment letters: January to June 1984].

DR-8504. si'yadûhkànamèinmyâ,htaunkôyâsi'selêikù zulainlà hmà htaunkôyâsi' selêikù dizinbalà àhtì [Compiled military appointment letters: July to December 1983].

DR-8506. si'yadûhkànamèinmyâ,htaunkôyâsi'sengâkù jannàwarilà hmà htaunkôyâsi'sengâkù zunlà àhtì [Compiled military appointment letters: January to June 1985].

DR-8514. si'yadûhkànamèinmyâ,htaunkôyâsi'sengâkù zulainlà hmà htaunkôyâsi' sengâkù se'tinbalà àhtì [Compiled military appointment letters: July to September 1985].

DR-8515. si'yadûhkànamèinmyâ,htaunkôyâsi'sengâkù au'toubalà hmà htaunkôyâsi'sengâkù dizinbalà àhtì [Compiled military appointment letters: October to December 1985].

DR-8566. si'yadûhkànamèinmyâ,htaunkôyâsi'sechau'kù jannàwarilà hmà htaunkôyâsi'sechau'kù zunlà àhtì [Compiled military appointment letters: January to June 1986].

DR-8600. si'yadûhkànamèinmyâ,htaunkôyâsi'sechau'kù zulainlà hmà htaunkôyâsi'sechau'kù dizinbalà àhtì [Compiled military appointment letters: July to December 1986].

DR-8601. si'yadûhkànamèinmyâ,htaunkôyâsi'sehkùni'kù jannàwarilà hmà htaunkôyâsi'sehkùni'kù zunlà àhtì [Compiled military appointment letters: January to June 1987].

DR-8601. si'yadûhkànamèinmyâ,htaunkôyâsi'sehkùni'kù zulainlàlà hmà htaunkôyâsi'sehkùni'kù dizinbalà àhtì [Compiled military appointment letters: July to December 1987].

6. *Periodicals and Newspaper*

Tonan Ajia Yoran; Southeast Asia Directory. Yearly version [Tonan Ajia Chosakai]

Ajia Doko Nenpo; *Asian Trends Annual Report*. Yearly version (Ajia Keizai Kenkyuujo; Institute of Developing Economies)

Sekai Shuho

Asian Survey

Asia Yearbook

Far Eastern Economic Review

Asian Week

Military Balance
Working People's Daily
pyihtaunzù myanmanaingando pyandân [Union of Burma Gazette]
cêimoun
pyidù ta'"màdo sazin
pati yêiya
hki' yêi
myàwàdi
myanmà àlin

INDEX

KYOTO CSEAS SERIES ON ASIAN STUDIES
Center for Southeast Asian Studies, Kyoto University

The Economic Transition in Myanmar after 1988: Market Economy versus State Control, edited by Koichi Fujita, Fumiharu Mieno and Ikuko Okamoto, 2009

Populism in Asia, edited by Kosuke Mizuno and Pasuk Phongpaichit, 2009

Traveling Nation-Makers: Transnational Flows and Movements in the Making of Modern Southeast Asia, edited by Caroline S. Hau and Kasian Tejapira, 2011

China and the Shaping of Indonesia, 1949–1965, by Hong Liu, 2011

Questioning Modernity in Indonesia and Malaysia, edited by Wendy Mee and Joel S. Kahn, 2012

Industrialization with a Weak State: Thailand's Development in Historical Perspective, by Somboon Siriprachai, edited by Kaoru Sugihara, Pasuk Phongpaichit, and Chris Baker, 2012

Popular Culture Co-productions and Collaborations in East and Southeast Asia, edited by Nissim Otmazgin and Eyal Ben-Ari, 2012